A HISTORY
OF TRANSPORTATION
IN CANADA

BY

G. P. de T. GLAZEBROOK
UNIVERSITY OF TORONTO

FOREWORD BY

H. A. INNIS

GREENWOOD PRESS, PUBLISHERS
NEW YORK

PREFACE

Students of Canadian history have long recognized that the problems and methods of transportation constitute an essential thread in the development of the country. The present volume represents an attempt to trace the story of transportation through the whole range of the history of Canada, describing the methods, and relating them to the more general theme of the rise of Canadian civilization. The confines of a single volume have necessarily limited the treatment of both aspects of the subject. This study is not intended to be an interpretation of Canadian history, but has grown, for the author at least, into a vantage point from which the march of Canadian history might be observed. As the examination of the subject developed, it seemed to become more and more apparent that the purely technical aspects of transportation had little meaning if divorced from the conditions in which they were used and the circumstances which led to their employment. All factors in Canadian history have a bearing on the development of transportation: physical geography, the extent and distribution of population, economics, politics, imperial and foreign relations. It is no less true that the changing modes of transportation have influenced the whole course of Canadian development. It has been necessary to set some limits to the subject covered in this book. Firstly, it is a history of inland transportation, and therefore shipping on the lower St. Lawrence and on the oceans can only be mentioned in its effect on the main theme. Secondly, the ancillary enterprises of the Canadian railway companies—hotels, steamships, lands, and industries—are not discussed.

My thanks are due to the scholars who have been good enough to help me through a complicated field with advice and criticism. Dr. J. T. Shotwell, general editor of the series on the relations of the United States and Canada, has given encouragement and assistance. The editor of the section in which this volume appears, Professor H. A. Innis, has helped me through every stage and over many obstacles. Such merits as the book has are due in large part to his patience and judgment. Professor W. T. Jackman, Colonel W. J. Wilgus, Professor J. L. McDougall, and Professor Samuel

McKee have all read the entire manuscript, and by their suggestions have saved me from many mistakes of omission and commission. To others who have read particular chapters I can only express my thanks in general terms. I am grateful to the Governor and Committee of the Hudson's Bay Company for the privilege of working in the company's archives, and to the company's archivist, Mr. R. G. Leveson Gower, for aiding me to find materials. The staff of the Library of the University of Toronto and of the Public Archives of Canada have been at all times most helpful. I am glad to acknowledge the assistance of Mr. G. W. Yates and Mr. Robert Dorman of the department of railways and canals, Mr. J. A. Wilson, controller of civil aviation, and Mr. G. S. Wrong of the bureau of statistics.

G. P. deT. G.

UNIVERSITY OF TORONTO,
    January, 1937.

INTRODUCTION TO STUDIES ON TRANSPORTATION CANADIAN-AMERICAN RELATIONS

THE present volume by Professor Glazebrook, and those by Mr. W. J. Wilgus, *The Railway Interrelations of the United States and Canada* (New Haven, 1937), Professor S. McKee, *History of Great Lakes Shipping*, and Professor W. W. McLaren, *A History of Tariffs*, cover the field of transportation in the Canadian-American Relations Series and constitute important additions to literature on the subject of transportation on the North American continent, and particularly the interrelations between the large political areas of Canada and the United States. An attempt is made in this introduction to stress the more significant interrelationships outlined in these volumes and to coordinate the general conclusions.

The study of transportation in tracing routes of travel, and in appraising the work of the engineer in overcoming obstacles and lessening distance, is an approach to its study as a fundamental part of the national economy. The integration of national life depends on problems of distribution and of marketing, and these largely determine the direction of international policy. Nowhere are these elemental truths more clearly seen than in the economy of northern North America. There is the oceanic relationship with the mother countries in Europe, and there are not only the two national economies of Canada, and the United States of America, but also varied local systems on each side of the border. An historical survey will show how deeply these elements have affected the political as well as the economic development of the communities that have wrested these areas from the wilderness and erected their similar but variant forms of social life.

Expansion of trade from Europe to North America assumed the existence of vessels of sufficient size to cross the Atlantic Ocean, and knowledge of prevailing winds and ocean currents at various seasons. Vessels from the ports of Europe carried on the fishing industry along the coast of Newfoundland and adjacent territory in the early part of the sixteenth century, and on the banks, the shores of Nova Scotia and in the Gulf of St. Lawrence and the Gulf of Maine later in the same century and in the seventeenth century. To England the fishing industry provided a supply of food for consumption by the crews of fishing vessels, and also for the home market, including ships in the navy and those going below the line, and for export to Spain and the Mediterranean. France, with a large Catholic population, was less concerned with export trade and with the dry fishing industry in the New World.

In the late sixteenth and the early seventeenth century, the fishing industry and the shipping of Europe, and particularly of England, responded to the effects of imports of specie into Spain from the New World. English settlements emerged in Newfoundland and New England, and French settlements in Nova Scotia and at Gaspé in the Gulf of St. Lawrence. The rise of settlements in New England and the growth of trade and shipping stimulated expansion of the continental colonies and of sugar production in the West Indies. Small vessels suited to the fishing industry and the coastal trade were built on a large scale. Improved methods in the manufacture and handling of vessels, increase in numbers of aggressive traders, and the growth of settlements facilitated the capture of New York from the Dutch in 1664, of Nova Scotia from the French in 1710 and of Cape Breton and Canada in 1763.

The importance of the home market in France facilitated the growth of the fur trade which followed contact with the Indians of the St. Lawrence. The short season, the high value and low bulk of furs, the centralizing influence of a large river and the use of canoes and boats which characterized the St. Lawrence and the Mississippi, accentuated the importance of the large ocean-going vessels. These large rivers drained the energies of France to the interior of the continent and tended to divide rather than unite the Empire. Moreover large vessels from the St. Lawrence which supported canoes to the interior were unable to compete with English vessels going direct to the mouths of the rivers flowing into Hudson Bay. Ship building[1] on the St. Lawrence was limited and shipping[2] was handicapped by closed seasons, long distances,

1. *Select Documents in Canadian Economic History* (1497–1783), ed. H. A. Innis, pp. 385 et seq.

2. Ships were unable to arrive in some cases early enough to forward supplies to the Upper Lakes in the same season. See *ibid.*, pp. 399 et seq.

limited facilities, and dependence on staple products, particularly in the fur trade with its heavy one-way upstream cargo.

With the collapse of the French Empire, vessels from England and the colonies swarmed up the St. Lawrence; and the route up the Hudson to Albany and Oswego, which had been developed during the French régime, became a basis for expansion to the territory vacated by the French. Anglo-American traders began to resort to Montreal. By using boats they succeeded in mastering Great Lakes navigation more effectively than the French, and made it a support to the Ottawa canoe route and a basis for re-establishment of the connections (confirmed by the Quebec Act), with the Ohio and the Mississippi. Restriction of access to the interior by the British government was resented by the coastal colonies even more than restriction by the French. This obstruction, combined with the increasing burdens of the English colonial system on external trade, led to the collapse of the British Empire following the withdrawal of opposition from the French. Sir Joshua Child's predictions were fulfilled: "New England", he had written[3], "is the most prejudicial to this kingdom because of all the American plantations, His Majesty has none so apt for building of shipping as New England, none comparably so qualified for the breeding of seamen not only by reason of the national industry of that people but principally by reason of their cod and mackerel fisheries, and in my poor opinion, there is nothing more prejudicial and in prospect more dangerous to any mother country than the increase of shipping in her colonies, plantations or provinces." The effectiveness of colonial shipping broke the chains of the British commercial system directly and indirectly. Control over raw materials for ship-building such as masts[4] contributed to the defeat of the British in the struggle for independence.

The second British Empire gradually retreated from the Mississippi to the St. Lawrence, driven back by the population which poured across the Alleghanies. In contrast to the fur trade, which involved taking heavy manufactured goods up the Mississippi, settlements around the headwaters sent heavy goods down the

3. Quoted in R. F. Grant, *Canadian Atlantic Fishery* (Toronto, 1934), xii–xiii.
4. See the interesting thesis advanced in R. G. Albion, *Forests and Sea Power.* (Cambridge, 1926.)

river. The failure of Americans to gain control over the St. Lawrence in the War of 1812 was offset by the increasing importance of the steamboat on the Mississippi. The Canadian fur trade withdrew northward, especially after the Jay Treaty, pushed on to the Saskatchewan and the Athabasca and eventually to the Pacific. Competition from Hudson Bay with the advantage of shorter distances and the use of boats on the rivers was followed, in 1821, by the disappearance of the fur trade from the St. Lawrence.

The effects of the disappearance of the fur trade were alleviated by the rise of the square timber trade. This was sharply restricted to the drainage basins whereas the fur trade overcame these boundaries by the canoe and the portage. British preferences during the Napoleonic wars and afterward fostered the timber trade on the long rivers of New Brunswick and on the tributaries of the St. Lawrence. Cheap English shipping after the war and abundance of white pine which could be floated long distances downstream meant bulky cargoes for Great Britain and provided cheap reciprocal transportation for settlers coming to Canada.

Competition for the traffic of the upper Mississippi valley from Montreal and from New Orleans led to the construction of the Erie Canal from New York to Buffalo on the Upper Lakes, with a branch to Oswego on Lake Ontario. To avoid the St. Lawrence rapids and to strengthen colonial policy and military control on the St. Lawrence, Great Britain constructed the Rideau Canal. Construction of the Welland Canal was intended to offset competition on the Upper Lakes. The Act of Union (of Upper and Lower Canada) provided a broader financial base for construction of canals on the upper St. Lawrence and for improvement of the Welland. Improvements on the St. Lawrence were offset, however, by a decline in the colonial system involving decreased preferences on wheat and timber and by the passing of bonding laws in the United States which facilitated shipments from New York to Upper Canada. The losses, real or imaginary, were in part responsible for the Annexationist Manifesto of 1849 and for attempts to secure reciprocity with the United States. The completion of the canals on the St. Lawrence was followed by a period of truce, from the competitive wars of transport rates and tariffs, brought about by the Reciprocity Treaty of 1854-1866. Controversies over the fishing industry in Nova Scotia were also given a respite.

The inability of the French and British empires to maintain a balance within their own boundaries has been made evident, especially after 1713, by smuggling in Cape Breton, in the West Indies and at Oswego on Lake Ontario, and it affected the readjustment of boundaries by the Treaty of Paris. The colonial system[5] of Great Britain was extended to territory captured from the French; but, unable to maintain a balance between the diverse interests of different regions, it broke down in turn. It was consequently adjusted to oppose the United States, especially in the Maritimes, the West Indies, and the St. Lawrence. After the War of 1812 and under the Convention of 1818 the United States was excluded from the British coastal fishery. Barred from these areas, more American shipping went to South America and to the Pacific Coast. American traders staked out a claim to the Oregon. The aggressiveness of the United States contributed to the breakdown of the British colonial system in the Trade Acts of the twenties, in the concession of admission to the West Indies trade in 1830, in the abolition of the Corn Laws in 1846, and of the Navigation Acts in 1849. Equilibrium was established by the ending of the colonial system; and the Reciprocity Treaty permitted relative freedom of trade between British North America and the United States, access of Americans to the St. Lawrence, and admission of American fishing vessels into Canadian waters, and of Canadian fish into the American market.

The truce was gradually broken down by continued improvements in transportation. An increase in the size of vessels on the Upper Lakes made it impossible for them to proceed to Lake Ontario by the Welland Canal. In 1853 New York was connected with Chicago by a railway along the south shore of Lake Erie, and in 1855 by the Great Western through southern Ontario. To offset the effects of this competition Canada supported an energetic programme of railway construction. All the year round open ports, such as Boston and Portland, competing with New York, joined with Montreal to build connecting lines to Montreal and in the

5. See D. G. Creighton, *The Commercial Empire of the St. Lawrence* (Toronto, 1937).

early fifties the Grand Trunk Railway was extended westward to
Toronto (1856) and Sarnia (1859) and eastward by the Victoria
Bridge to Rivière du Loup (1860). A tariff was imposed in 1858
to secure revenue to support the outlay on improvements of
transportation and to build up traffic.

The Civil War was evidence of disturbances to equilibrium
between the North and South, and its outcome established the
dominance of the North, and stimulated resistance from Canada.
The significance of the debt incurred for the construction of canals
and railways by the Canadian political structure which had been
built up on the Act of Union necessitated dependence on Great
Britain for capital support, and, in its turn, for a general policy of
development. The financial difficulties of the government and of
the Grand Trunk Railway, and an inability to compete with
American lines to the seaboard led imperial-minded capitalists
such as Sir Edward Watkin to propose an extension eastward to
Canadian Atlantic ports and westward to the Pacific. In 1863
control of the Hudson's Bay Company was acquired by his group
and plans were laid for construction of a railway through its
territory to British Columbia. The Reciprocity Treaty was abrogated in 1866, and Confederation, with the construction of the
Intercolonial between Canada and the Maritime provinces as a
sine qua non, became a reality in 1867. It was completed to Rivière
du Loup in 1876.

The discovery of gold in California in 1848 and in other regions
of the Pacific coast, including British Columbia in the late fifties
and the early sixties, was followed by migration of population
on a large scale. The construction of railways was begun from
the Mississippi, and the Union Pacific was completed in 1869.
Steamships were introduced along the Pacific Coast and crossed
the Pacific to Australia. With the Suez Canal completed in the
same year, Great Britain had alternative routes to the East,
although one was partly on American territory. The Northern
Pacific was planned to run from the American seaboard through
Canada to Sault Ste. Marie and the Pacific, under the direction
of Sir Hugh Allan in Montreal and Jay Cooke in Chicago. But the
stubborn resistance of Toronto interests, and of the Grand Trunk,
to American participation, and the crash of 1873, which precipi-

tated the Pacific Scandal, brought an end to the project[6]. The Northern Pacific was completed under American control from Duluth to Puget Sound in 1883. The Grand Trunk, with its lines from Sarnia and Detroit to the seaboard, became increasingly concerned with the possibilities of the expanding traffic of the Mississippi Valley and extended its lines to Chicago in 1880-1. In its increasing interest in traffic from the western states its hostility to alternative lines from western Canada to the Atlantic seaboard was enhanced. It refused to coöperate with either the Northern Pacific project via Sault Ste. Marie or with the Canadian government in its determination to build a line around the north shore of Lake Superior in Canadian territory. After the addition of British Columbia to Confederation under an agreement to build a railway to the Pacific, and the difficulties with the Grand Trunk, the Canadian government started to build the line. Finally an agreement was drawn up with the Canadian Pacific Railway Company, which was forced to depend on capital centres other than London and which consequently secured large-scale support in lands, cash, and a completed railway from the federal government. In 1885 a railway was constructed north of Lake Superior and across the prairies, close to the United States boundary, to Vancouver, providing an alternative all-British route to the Far East and a competitive Canadian line for important long-haul Pacific traffic.

The determination to build north of Lake Superior led to the resignation of J. J. Hill from the Canadian Pacific directorate and to the extension by him of the Great Northern to the coast, following a route between the boundary and the Northern Pacific (1893). As a result of competition for long haul traffic, the Canadian Pacific acquired the Duluth, South Shore and Atlantic to Duluth, and the Minneapolis, St. Paul and Sault Ste. Marie to the Twin Cities in 1890, and to the main line of the C.P.R. via Portal in 1893. It built, with government support, a line through the Crow's Nest Pass, obtained control of the Trail Smelter[7] and, with the

6. See H. A. Innis, *A History of the Canadian Pacific Railway* (London, 1923), pp. 79 et seq. Excellent maps on the transport routes should be consulted not only in this volume but also in those of Mr. Wilgus and Professor McKee.

7. See H. A. Innis, *Settlement and the Mining Frontier* (Toronto, 1936).

assistance of the tariff, largely excluded American competition. The Canadian tariff was designed, along with other measures (including the monopoly clause, excluding railways south of its main line in the prairies), to check competition from American railways and to compel the prairie and Pacific coast regions to purchase goods manufactured in eastern Canada rather than the eastern States. With the gold discoveries in the Yukon, and renewed severe competition[8] between the Canadian Pacific and American lines and between Seattle and Vancouver and Victoria, the tariff was used to throw trade toward Eastern Canadian manufacturers. Similarly a customs post on Herschell Island[9] checked the exploitation of the Canadian Western Arctic by American traders to the north of Alaska.

The extension of the Canadian Pacific to the more densely populated industrial areas of eastern Canada brought competition with the Grand Trunk, and led to its amalgamation with the Great Western Railway. The growth of remunerative traffic to western Canada after the turn of the century led the Grand Trunk to assume an aggressive policy with plans to extend its line from Chicago to Winnipeg. Again the tariff and the refusal of the Canadian government to support a line through American territory compelled it to rely on government support and to agree to coöperate in the construction of the National Transcontinental Railway from Quebec to Winnipeg in the west and to Moncton in the east, and to build, under a subsidiary, the Grand Trunk Pacific, a line from Winnipeg to Prince Rupert. The result was a transcontinental line from Moncton to Prince Rupert with no close connections to the parent system and ill adapted as a direct entry to western Canada.

The federal government secured a line suited to the development of northern Quebec and northern Ontario and intended as a means of exporting grain through Quebec or Maritime ports. After the Reciprocity Treaty, the construction of railways, and the introduction of steamships, wooden shipping in the Maritimes had declined sharply from its peak in 1874. The devastating effect on the

8. See H. A. Innis, *A History of the Canadian Pacific Railway* (London, 1923), pp. 206–207.

9. See H. H. Bodfish, *Chasing the Bowhead* (Cambridge, 1936).

economic life of the Maritimes of the shift from wood, wind, and water to coal and iron necessitated government support, with tariffs designed to increase the consumption of Cape Breton coal, railways across the Strait of Canso through Cape Breton to Sydney, bounties on iron and steel, and the extension of the National Transcontinental to Moncton. The Grand Trunk Pacific, and the National Transcontinental as a through transcontinental from Moncton to Quebec, Winnipeg and Prince Rupert via the Yellowhead Pass tapped the vast area in the clay belt and the prairies north of the southern location of the Canadian Pacific Railway.

The protests of settlers in western Canada against monopoly control of the Canadian Pacific Railway had been capitalized at an earlier date by the acquisition of a charter by Mackenzie and Mann for the construction of a line from Winnipeg to Hudson Bay. This line was extended as the Canadian Northern, with federal and provincial support, to tap the more promising traffic regions of the northern area; and it eventually reached Edmonton and Vancouver in the west, and Port Arthur, Toronto and Montreal in the east. Whereas the Canadian Pacific was concerned primarily with Montreal, and the Grand Trunk Pacific with Quebec and Maritime ports, the Canadian Northern provided the most direct line from western Canada to Toronto and offset the competitive position of Montreal and the effects of the Grand Trunk's strategic blockade of a direct entrance to Toronto by the Canadian Pacific. (The latter secured a direct line to Toronto in 1908 but Montreal was its headquarters and terminus.)

The inability of the federal government to provide grants of land as a result of previous grants to the Canadian Pacific Railway compelled the Grand Trunk Pacific and the Canadian Northern to depend on cash grants and on funds provided through the guaranteed bonds of the Dominion and the provinces. Government support, access to the London market, and the boom which characterized the period from 1900 to 1914 financed the enormous increase in Canadian railway mileage. The outbreak of the war and the closing of the London market brought serious problems to lines without established traffic areas. During the war and the post-war period the Grand Trunk, the Grand Trunk Pacific, the

National Transcontinental, the Canadian Northern and the Intercolonial were amalgamated under government control under the name of the Canadian National Railways. The diverse parts of the system were combined and strengthened to compete with the Canadian Pacific Railway and the American transcontinental lines. The Grand Trunk main line to Chicago became an effective competitor for seaboard traffic and an important contributor to earnings through its access to an intensive industrial, and densely populated, area. The linking of the Canadian Northern with the National Transcontinental at Long Lac provided effective competition to Winnipeg. The extension of branch lines from the Grand Trunk Pacific and the Canadian Northern brought marked increase in traffic in western Canada, and lower grades by the Yellowhead Pass to Vancouver were an advantage in the growth of traffic following the opening of the Panama Canal.

Increased competition in the dense traffic areas accentuated demands for efficient operation. Wheat from western Canada moved over the established routes, especially with improved Great Lakes shipping, to New York and Montreal, and efforts to stimulate shipments by alternative routes such as the National Transcontinental to Quebec and Maritime ports were largely unsuccessful. Consequently, demands for compensation arose from areas penalized by intensive competition and loss of traffic. The Maritime Freight Rates Act of 1927 introduced lower rates from the Maritimes. Areas with sharply fluctuating income, such as the prairies, secured lower rates in the renewal and extension of the Crow's Nest Pass rates agreement. The opening of the Panama Canal was followed by vigorous competition for traffic from the prairies to British Columbia ports and by the lowering of rates. Demands for increased earnings on the one hand, and for regional compensation on the other, were the basis for conflicting statements of efficient operation and of extravagance regarding the Canadian National Railways.

The significance of the St. Lawrence in the history of Canadian transportation is in striking contrast to the development of coastal transportation in the United States, accompanied by numerous approaches from the Atlantic to the interior. Control from Europe was effective on the St. Lawrence and ineffective in the United States. Cheap water transportation in the St. Lawrence economy accentuated dependence on exports of staples to Europe, the specialization of technique in relation to these commodities, and support from government intervention. The canoe was borrowed from the hunting Indians of the Canadian Shield and adapted to expansion in the northern half of North America. The square-timber trade involved the use of cribs on the Ottawa and of rafts on the St. Lawrence to Quebec and of cheaply built wooden ships to Great Britain. Seasonal navigation which was a handicap to the St. Lawrence, was an advantage to the United States. Wooden sailing vessels turned from the Quebec timber trade in summer to the cotton trade of the southern States in winter, just as the later steamship changes its terminus from Montreal and Quebec to American ports. Dependence on Europe in the French and British régimes necessitated government assistance in the form of posts at strategic points on the Great Lakes and of active hostilities against competition from the south and north. The restrictions which the fur trade put on settlers required active intervention by the French government to support such widely varying activities as the construction of roads in New France and the conducting of naval wars in Hudson Bay.

When the British assumed control, they maintained an effective colonial system on the lower and upper St. Lawrence and overcame the St. Lawrence rapids, first by the construction of the Rideau Canal and later by tangible support in the form of guarantees of funds for the construction of the St. Lawrence canals. Trunk roads were planned and built in Upper Canada under imperial direction and support. Following the gold rush in British Columbia roads were built under the supervision of the Royal Engineers to supplement the rivers. The need for funds on a large scale to overcome obstacles of a major character such as the St. Lawrence rapids and Niagara Falls hastened the demand for domestic control over taxation and expenditures which was the essence of responsible government. The Act of Union, the construction and deepening of canals, the support of the Grand Trunk Railway, Confederation, the construction of the Intercolonial, the National Policy, and the support of the Canadian Pacific, the Grand Trunk Pacific, the National Transcontinental, and the Canadian Northern were a result of the necessity of checking competition from the United States, and of overcoming the seasonal handicaps of the St. Lawrence, and the handicaps incidental to the pre-cambrian formation and the Rocky Mountains. To build canals and improve the St. Lawrence system, railways to the Maritimes and across the pre-cambrian formation north of Lake Superior to British Columbia from Montreal, from Quebec and Maritime ports, and from Toronto necessitated reorganization of the political structure, grants in land and cash, and the tariff, particularly the national policy and the imperial preferences.

Dependence on the Canadian political structure and on support from Great Britain to carry out these vast projects involved rigidity of finances without benefit of bankruptcy (the Grand Trunk arbitration award notwithstanding), and government ownership. Implications of control from Great Britain were evident in the payment of dividends on the Grand Trunk under conditions in which they were not warranted, in its consequent difficulties, and in the necessity of appealing to the government for support, of extending its line to Chicago, and of precluding it from participation in expansion to western Canada until after the turn of the century and in the face of the entrenched position of the Canadian Pacific. In the early sixties before it felt the pull of the western States, it attempted, to hasten construction to the Pacific by securing control of the Hudson's Bay Company, and in the seventies, after it felt the pull, to delay construction. The delay was accompanied by steady improvement of transportation west of the Mississippi; it was followed by the rush to completion of the Canadian Pacific in the early eighties and by its consolidation by the turn of the century. Payment of large dividends by the Canadian Pacific Railway after the turn of the century on the other hand hastened the construction of additional transcontinental lines. Difficulties of control from Great Britain intensified by the geographic background shown in the importance of rail and water competition[10] in Eastern Canada were evident in financial deficits in the operation of the canals, the Grand Trunk, including the Grand Trunk Pacific and the National Trans-

10. See D. A. MacGibbon, *Railway Rates and the Canadian Railway Commission* (Boston, 1917).

continental, and the Intercolonial. These difficulties were further enhanced by the occupation of strategic territory, geographical and political, by the Canadian Pacific.

Control from Great Britain was strengthened throughout by migration of technique from the United States[11]. Retardation, through control by Great Britain, was followed by acceleration, through support from the United States. Boats suited to the waterways of the United States were adopted by the North West Company on the Great Lakes and by forwarders from Montreal on the St. Lawrence and supported expanding trade in Upper Canada and in the northwest. Equipment displaced by new inventions in the United States migrated to less developed areas and to Canada. Steamboats on the Mississippi were moved to the Red River, the Saskatchewan, and eventually the Mackenzie, and Mississippi pilots and captains manned them as well as those on the Fraser and the Yukon. The Red River cart was displaced by the steamboat from St. Paul to Red River and in turn from Red River to the Saskatchewan and Edmonton. The railway displaced the steamboat on river after river. The Canadian Pacific was directed and built in western Canada by men trained in railway construction and operation in the prairies of the United States and later railway construction borrowed much from American experience. The acceleration of development in Canada through contributions from the United States accentuated dependence on British capital and the increase of public debt.

During the war and post-war period imports of capital funds have accompanied imports of American technique from the United States in response to the demands of government owner-ship in the Canadian National Railways and of the expansion of new forms of transportation. The automobile was first imported, and then built by American firms in Canadian territory for the domestic and the imperial market. Federal, provincial and munici-pal governments have been concerned with extensive road con-struction for domestic demands and tourist travel. To the rigidities of finance peculiar to control from London have been added those involved by New York. The rigidities of finance incidental to

11. See *The Dairy Industry in Canada*, ed. H. A. Innis (Toronto, 1937), pp. v–xxvi.

government activity in the ownership of railways and roads involved encroachment on the elasticity of finance characteristic of the Canadian Pacific Railway. The elasticity incidental to government support in its construction and operation has declined with government support in the construction and operation of the Canadian National Railways. The results have been evident in the appointment and recommendations of the Duff Commission and the legislation which followed it, and in the royal commission on Dominion-provincial relations.

Rigidities of finance have an important effect on traffic movements between Canada and the United States. The influence of competition and regulation by the Interstate Commerce Commission and the Board of Railway Commissioners respectively on railway rates in the United States and Canada are offset by varying tariffs between the two countries, by disturbances of exchange rates and by statutory transportation rates, all of which directly influence, and are directly influenced by, financial rigidities. Rigidity of finance in Canada in her relations with the United States and Great Britain enhances adverse exchange rates. The application by either country of higher tariffs, including dumping duties and the use of the cost-of-production principle, checks the influence of the flow of goods as an equilibrating measure and accentuates the importance of the tourist trade and of more intangible items in the balance of trade. They tend to injure railway traffic between Canada and the United States and to encourage automobile transport in Canada. The decline in the influence of the flow of goods on exchange rates is not offset and may be made greater by increasing flexibility in other items during a depression in a country largely dependent on exports to world markets. The significance to Canadian railways of a restricted flow of goods between Canada and the United States would be more serious to the basic Montreal-Chicago route of the Canadian National and less serious to its transcontinental portions, and to the Canadian Pacific Railway, in spite of its extensive United States connections.

The problem of debt not only involves exceedingly complex short-run problems of adjustment between Canada and the United States, but it restricts the powers of the governments of North

America in regard to long-run problems of development. It strengthens the powers of the provinces and weakens the treaty-making power of the Dominion. The St. Lawrence waterway is sacrificed on the altar of impotent constitutions. The position of the Senate as the grave-yard of American treaties is paralleled by the position of the provinces in Canada.

H. A. I.

CONTENTS

CONTENTS XXV

MAPS

PART I

CONTINENTAL STRATEGY

A HISTORY OF TRANSPORTATION IN CANADA

CHAPTER I

WATER TRANSPORT IN THE FRENCH RÉGIME

1. WATER TRANSPORT

IN the early history of Canada water-travel plays an important part. Those French navigators who braved the known and unknown dangers of the Atlantic to reach the unmapped shores of Canada were the forerunners of the countless captains who maintained the lines of communication between the colony and its European owners. The awkward ships of the sixteenth and seventeenth centuries could, with care, be sailed up the great St. Lawrence to the port and fortress of Quebec; they could with more ease visit the many harbours of Acadia; run past the French West Indies to the mouth of the Mississippi; or make dashing trips into Hudson Bay, with its twin dangers of encompassing ice and English guns. Without the courage and ability of her seamen, France could neither have gained nor maintained her American empire. But the ships that came from France could do no more than carry men and goods between the mother country and the colony. Behind the ocean ports lay the whole body of this New France.

They came to the fishing grounds of the new world where settlements were established along the Atlantic coast of Acadia and in the sheltered and fertile valleys of the Bay of Fundy. When Acadia became the English colony of Nova Scotia in 1713 many of the French inhabitants drove their cattle across the narrow isthmus of Chignecto to be sent to the new establishments at Louisburg, in Cape Breton, and in Prince Edward Island. With settlement in Cape Breton, small fishing boats were employed and schooners were purchased in New England. On the Gaspé peninsula and at other points boats were imported in sections from France and put together on the shore by carpenters brought

1

for the purpose.[1] In some cases boats were brought complete from France, or made in the settlements on the Bay of Fundy and in the fishing areas.

The population of the Maritime Provinces under French rule was never large.[2] The first census of Acadia, in 1671, gives a total of 441, of whom 363 lived in Port Royal. The next figures are for 1686, and show 885 people in all, of whom 592 were in Port Royal and 127 in Beaubassin or Chignecto. In 1714, or just after Acadia ceased to be French, the population was 1,179. For Ile St. Jean (Prince Edward Island) the first census shows 330 people in 1728, of whom 138 lived at Hâvre St. Pierre. By 1767, just after it was ceded to England, the island had only 519 people, of whom more than half were French. Ile Royale (Cape Breton Island) had a considerably larger population, but it was almost entirely concentrated at Louisburg, either as garrison or in the fisheries.

As the ships from France proceeded up the St. Lawrence toward Tadoussac and Quebec, small boats were used to sound the channel and mark out the route.[3] From Quebec larger boats of various types continued on to Montreal. Inland travel—essential to the colony—was, first and always, largely dependent on the many waterways that nature seemed to have offered as compensation for the forest-covered land. Strange as the St. Lawrence and the great fresh-water lakes must have seemed to the Europeans, no less strange were the craft which they found in use on them, and which they quickly adopted for their own purposes. The characteristic one in Canada was the canoe, which, in its various forms, was the sole craft known to and used by the aboriginal Indians. The canoe *par excellence*, and the one which was used almost exclusively by the French, was that made of the bark of the birch tree. This was an Algonquin type of canoe and was made with astonishing skill by the various tribes of the Algonquin family with the crude instruments at their command. Of paper-like thin-

1. N. Denys, *The description and natural history of the coasts of North America*, Ed. W. F. Ganong (Toronto, 1908), p. 295.

2. *Census of Canada, 1870–1871*, vol. iv. The figures for this period are nearly all doubtful.

3. H. A. Innis, *Select documents in Canadian economic history, 1497–1783* (Toronto, 1929), p. 318.

ness, the birch canoe might nevertheless last for some time under careful treatment. It combined speed and carrying capacity with extreme lightness, so that it could be carried—"portaged"— past unnavigable sections with comparative ease; and yet it was strong enough to stand the rapids down which it was steered. The French were amazed to find a vessel that could carry a heavy load so efficiently. "Si Dieu me fait la grâce de retourner en France," wrote Gallinée in 1669, "je tascheray d'y faire porter un de ces canots pour le faire voir a ceux qui n'en auroient point veu . . . il n'y a point de voiture ny meilleure ny plus prompte que celle du canot . . . je n'ay rien trouvé icy de plus beau ny de plus commode; et sans cela, il seroit impossible de naviguer au dessus de Montréal ny dans aucune des rivières de ce pays. . . ."[4]

Fortunately, many of the French who travelled in Canada were accustomed to write at length of what they saw and did for the benefit of Europeans curious to know of this new land. Since the canoe was both important and novel, there are in print many contemporary descriptions of it. Denys, for example, writing of Acadia at the latter part of the seventeenth century, gives a good detailed account of the method of making canoes:

. . . they sought the largest Birch trees they could find. They removed the bark of the length of the canoe, which was of three to four fathoms and a half [in length: that is, from eighteen to twenty-seven feet]. The breadth was about two feet in the middle, and always diminished towards the two ends, falling away to nothing. The depth was such that for a man seated it came up to his armpits. The lining inside for strengthening it was of slats, of the length of the canoe and some four inches broad, lessening towards the ends in order that they might match together. On the inside the canoe was lined with them completely, as well as all along it from one end to the other. These slats were made of cedar, which is light, and which they split in as great length as they wished, and also as thin as they pleased. They also made from the same wood half-circles to form ribs, and gave them their forms in the fire.

For sewing the canoe, they took roots of Fir of the thickness of the little finger, and even smaller; they were very long. They split these roots into three or four parts, that is the largest ones. These split more easily than the Osiers used in making baskets. They made these into packages, which

4. P. Margry, *Découvertes et établissements des Français* (Paris, 1879-1888), i, 119.

they placed in the water for fear lest they might dry up. There were also necessary two sticks of the length of the canoe, entirely round, and of the thickness of a large cane, and four other shorter sticks of Beech. All these things being ready, they took thin bark and bent and fixed it in the form the canoe should have; then they placed the two long pieces all along and sewed them to the rim inside with these roots.

To sew they pierced the bark with a punch of pointed bone and passed through the hole an end of the wicker, drawing and tightening the stick as closely as they could against the bark, and always enwrapping the stick with the wicker so that they were in contact with one another. The sticks being well sewed on all along they placed also the smaller pieces of beech crosswise, one in the middle, entering at its two ends into holes made in the pieces with which the Canoe is rimmed, and three others in front of it, distant a half fathom from one another, which lessened in length with the shape of the canoe. Three others also were placed backward at the same distances. All these pieces entered also at their ends into holes which were made in the pieces sewed all along the canoe, to which they were so firmly attached on both sides that the canoe could neither enlarge nor narrow.

Then are placed in position those big slats with which they lined all the interior of the canoe from top to bottom, and they were all made to touch one another. To hold them in place, they put over them those half-circles, the ends of which were brought to join on both sides below those pieces which were sewn all around on the top. They drove these in with force, and they lined all the canoe with them from one end to the other. This made the canoe stiff to such a degree that it did not yield at any point.

There were seams in it, for in order to narrow it at the two ends, they split the bark from above downwards; they then overlapped the two edges one over the other, and sewed them. But to prevent the seams from admitting water, the women and girls chewed the gum of the Fir every day until it became a salve which they applied by aid of fire all along the seams, and this tightened them better than pitch. All this being done, the canoe was finished, and it was so light that a single man could carry it on his head.[5]

From this and other descriptions may be gleaned a sufficiently accurate idea of the making and navigation of a birch-bark canoe; and, indeed, the birch canoes still made by the Ojibway Indians are in all essentials the same as those of the seventeenth century. The exact shapes and method of making varied from place to place —for example, the height of bow and stern and the shape of the

5. Denys, op. cit., p. 420.

sections of bark—but in general the effect was the same. Lahontan states that canoes varied from ten to twenty-eight feet long, and carried from two to fourteen persons.[6] West of the lakes small birch canoes of a somewhat different type were found. The *Relation* of 1669 speaks of the "little canoes" of the Sioux[7]; and again in a *Relation* a few years later these Indians were said to use small bark canoes holding at most three.[8] According to this account, the Sioux paddled first on one side and then on the other—a clumsy method of steering, but apparently they got along fast enough.

While the French learnt to handle the unfamiliar canoes with no less skill than the Indians, they seldom tried to construct them. "There are few French", wrote Charlevoix, "who can make a canoe even so much as tolerably well."[9] In some tribes the work of making all or part of the canoes was left to the women, while in others the men did the whole process. Lahontan gives the price of a canoe as eighty crowns. Gallinée says a canoe costs "neuf ou dix escus de hardes" if bought direct from an Indian, but much more if bought from another Frenchman. His own, he says, cost eighty livres.[10] The canoe was normally paddled from a kneeling position, but an expert could stand up and pole in rapids. It seems clear that sails were not used by the Indians, either because they did not understand the principle or because they had no material with which to make them. Sails, however, were introduced by the French. According to LeJeune's *Relation* of 1636, the missionaries were laughed at for their weakness when they held up sheets to save paddling.[11] Lahontan, writing nearly fifty years later, says that canoes commonly carry small sails, but only in a light wind. By the beginning of the eighteenth century Charlevoix declared that "all these canoes, the smallest not excepted, carry sail."[12] On the whole the bark canoe was not well suited to sailing,

6. Baron de Lahontan, *New voyages to North America* (Chicago, 1905), i, 62.

7. R. G. Thwaites (ed.), *The Jesuit Relations and allied documents* (Cleveland, 1896–1901), liv, 193.

8. *Ibid.*, lxvi, 299.

9. P. F. X. Charlevoix, *Journal of a voyage to North America* (Chicago, 1923), i, 278.

10. Margry, *op. cit.*, i, 118.

11. *Jesuit Relations*, ix, 277.

12. Charlevoix, *loc. cit.*

and it is probable that sails were used only when running before a moderate breeze. All but the larger canoes could be carried on a man's back over the longest portages, leaving the cargo for the rest of the crew. The birch canoe was easily and frequently damaged. Anything but a slight graze on a rock spelt disaster in rapids. On the other hand, small accidents at less critical moments, or decay from age were not necessarily serious, for repairs were easily carried out. Bark, gum and fibre for this purpose were always either carried, or available near by in the woods. A birch-bark canoe is an amazingly seaworthy craft, but it was not customary to run unnecessary risks while traversing the large lakes where large waves might be met. That this was not due to any general timidity is proved by the hazardous nature of the rapids that were run; rather it was to avoid straining the canoe or losing the cargo. During heavy weather on the lakes the crew of a canoe usually waited on the shore. For travelling amongst broken ice, "peaux de veau crues" (apparently blown-up skins) were hung on the bow to protect it from being crushed.

The canoe made of birch bark had geographical limits which were defined partly by the character of the rivers, and partly by the presence of birch and the resinous trees which were used for seams. The canoe birch was plentiful in the St. Lawrence valley, but gave out in the Iroquois country, and was not found much south of the Great Lakes or west of the Rockies. The northern limit was roughly the tree line.

Outside this "birch area" were found other types of canoes. The bark of different trees was used in the same way as the birch, but with less satisfactory results. The Iroquois made their canoes of the bark of elm trees, which made a heavier yet less durable craft, and seems to have been generally recognized as inferior. On an occasion when Lahontan found himself pursued by a party of Iroquois over the Niagara portage, he felt safe once he and his party were launched on Lake Erie, "for the *Iroquese* canows are so dull and large, that they cannot sail [i.e., travel] near so quick as those made of Birch-bark. The former are made of Elm-bark, which is very heavy, and their form is very aukard; for they are so long and broad that thirty Men row in them two abreast, whether sitting or standing, and the sides are so low, that they dare not venture 'em upon the lakes, tho' the wind be very slack."[13] There are many other testimonies to the same effect. LeJeune pointed out as early as 1637 that the Iroquois canoes were heavier than the Algonquin ones.[14] Gallinée said that the Iroquois canoes were made of various kinds of bark, were heavy and badly constructed, and would last only a month.[15] The writer of the *Narrative of the most remarkable Occurrences in Canada, 1690, 1691*, describing an attempted expedition against Canada, says that ". . . sixteen hundred English joined the Indians with the intention of coming to attack Montreal . . . but they were always unwilling to go on board the elm canoes which the Iroquois had made for them, for fear, as they said, of being drowned."[16] Charlevoix, writing some thirty years later, speaks of canoes "of the bark of elm, wider, and of very coarse workmanship, but commonly the longest. I know no nation but the Iroquois, which have any of this sort."[17]

The Eskimos in the far north beyond the tree line used a kind of canoe known as a kayak, which was also said to have been used on Labrador and the north shore of the Gulf of St. Lawrence. These were ingenious vessels, which were made of seal skins. The single paddler knelt in a small well in the middle, and fastened skins about his waist, so that no water could enter the canoe. Although the French probably never had occasion to use kayaks, Lescarbot speaks of them with respect, and a Jesuit writer of 1659 finds that their "structure and speed are indeed astonishing."[18]

Another form of canoe, which was more primitive, but more widely used, was the dug-out, or "pirogue" as the French called it. This type of canoe was that commonly used on the Mississippi, which was outside the birch area and where there were no portages.[19]

13. Lahontan, *op. cit.*, i, 138.
14. *Jesuit Relations*, xii, 181.
15. Margry, *op. cit.*, i, 118.
16. E. B. O'Callaghan (ed.), *Documents relating to the colonial history of the State of New York* (Albany, 1856–1887), ix, 513.
17. Charlevoix, *op. cit.*, i, 377.
18. *Jesuit Relations*, xlv, 65.
19. An extract from Marquette's account of his first voyage on the Mississippi suggests that Algonquin canoes were not known there: 'We embark in the sight of all the people, who admire our little Canoes, for they have never seen any like them.'

It was common, too, amongst the Iroquois, who made it of pine; and there was a highly decorative type found on the Pacific coast. A description of dug-out canoes is given in the *Relation* for 1673, referring to Marquette's expedition to the Mississippi.

> The most vigorous trees that one sees there are a species of cotton-tree, of extraordinary girth and height. The savages therefore use these trees for making canoes—all of one piece, fifty feet in length and three in width, in which thirty men with all their baggage can embark. They make them of much more graceful shape than we do ours. They have so great a number of them that in a single village one sees as many as 280 together.[20]

A later *Relation*, of 1712, speaks of a pirogue of forty feet, which seems to have been the average size.

All the craft so far mentioned were of Indian invention and manufacture, and simply adopted by the French. There were, however, in addition, some craft introduced by the French into Canada. In general they brought in boats, as distinct from canoes. The French boats were built of wood and were meant to be rowed or sailed, or both. They were much heavier than canoes, and the smallest could with difficulty be taken over portages; thus their use was primarily in waters where there were no rapids, for example, on the St. Lawrence below Lachine, and on the lakes. The word "bateau" appears frequently in contemporary accounts of travel, and it is certain that this general word covered rowing and sailing boats of widely differing kinds: anything, apparently, from a small rowboat to a sloop. Presumably a number of boats were once brought complete to all parts of New France. The small boats used by the early explorers were simply those ordinarily carried by the ships. After the early years, however, boats of many types and sizes were made locally. What was commonly called a bateau, that is, an open boat for rowing or sailing, and of varied size, could apparently be constructed without difficulty. In 1685 Denonville ordered a hundred bateaux to be built within quite a short time.[21]

In the total absence of canals, only canoes could be used for

(Edna Kenton, *The Jesuit Relations and allied documents* [Toronto, 1925], p. 356). Marquette's experience, however, showed that birch canoes could be used on the Mississippi.

20. *Jesuit Relations*, lviii, 97.

21. O'Callaghan, *op. cit.*, ix, 284.

long-distance travel, but, while canoes retained the monopoly of passing rapids with comparative ease, the common method of water-travel below Montreal was in boats. Some examples may be taken from that excellent observer, Peter Kalm, which show the character and speed of the boats.[22] In his travels in 1749 Kalm went in a bateau from La Prairie to Montreal, and remarks that, "The river is very rapid, but not very deep near Prairie, so that the yachts cannot go higher than Montreal, except in spring with the high water, when they can come up to Prairie, but no further." On August 2 Kalm left Montreal early in the morning in a bateau with sails. At three o'clock they reached the Richelieu, at which point, he remarks, there is a large island, passed by the "yachts" on the south-east side, but by boats on the north-east side. At eleven in the morning of August 3 they reached Three Rivers. At dawn they set off again, and they arrived at Quebec at 4 p.m. on the fifth on what was a comparatively leisurely journey. Later in the month Kalm went in a similar boat to Baie St. Paul. In September he was taken in one of the "King's boats" from Quebec to Montreal. There were seven men besides himself. They left Quebec in the evening of September 11 and arrived at Montreal at 4 p.m. on the fifteenth. He notes that near Montreal the current was in some places so strong that the boat had to be towed from the shore.

Even above Montreal on the boisterous upper St. Lawrence the French were not content to rely exclusively upon canoes. There was no difficulty in constructing small boats for rowing or sailing on the lakes at such places as Fort Frontenac, at the east end of Lake Ontario. More ambitiously, the French tried two other extensions of their water-travel: to go in bateaux up the river to Fort Frontenac, and to build larger sailboats above the rapids. In 1671 Courcelles set out for Lake Ontario in a "bateau plat du port" weighing two to three tons, and accompanied by canoes.[23] On reaching the first rapid the canoes were pulled up, but great difficulty was experienced with the bateau. The tow-rope broke three or four times, but finally the boat was somehow dragged through. At the second rapid they had to lever a big rock out of

22. Peter Kalm, *Travels into North America* (London, 1772), ii, 223 et seq.
23. Margry, *op. cit.*, i, 182.

the way to get the boat past, and so it went at every rapid. After ten days Lake Ontario was reached, but only after most strenuous labours. The same method was tried again two years later when Frontenac began his policy of strengthening the colony against the Iroquois by a show of force on Lake Ontario, and decided to use two boats similar to that of Courcelles. These were built for the purpose, designed to carry sixteen men, with provisions. By using these boats Frontenac wished to show that "les saults et les rapides dont la rivière est pleine en beaucoup d'endroits, n'estoient pas des barrières assez fortes pour empescher les François . . ."[24] When the boats were ready, the expedition, consisting of the boats and a number of canoes, set out. It proved to be no easy matter to get the boats up the rapids, and took more than fifty men, who were often up to their shoulders in water, to pull them. The work required was reported as extremely hard, as may well be gathered. The men cut their feet and legs on the rocks, while struggling to pull the heavy boats through the rapids. While Frontenac had demonstrated the possibility of a through journey from Montreal to Lake Ontario, it was evidently a quite unsatisfactory means of regular transportation.

It is evident that sailing boats were also used on the lower lakes, but they do not appear to have been numerous. La Salle, the ambitious ship-builder of the French régime, hoped to use them in the pursuit of his plan of extending French influence to the mouth of the Mississippi. He had four small boats built, but the exact size, and the rigging of these, and of his most ambitious venture, the *Griffon*, are not known. The *Griffon*, of about sixty tons, was built on the shores of Lake Erie, for use on that and the western connecting waters. She had a short career, being lost with all hands and a valuable cargo of furs on Lake Michigan not long after launching. It was probably this disaster that cooled the ardour of the ship-builders. The carriage of furs, which were the only articles of commerce coming from the west, could be more cheaply accomplished in canoes by the Ottawa than in ships by the lakes. To lose a valuable ship and cargo was a disaster, but canoes, if caught in the lakes in a storm, represented at worst only a small loss. Hennepin speaks of seeing three barques "all deck'd and

24. *Ibid.*, i, 197.

mounted," and later of embarking in "a Brigantine of about ten
Tuns"—the latter being one of La Salle's boats. In a letter to the
minister in 1736, Beauharnois and Hocquart state that two sloops
are being navigated on Lake Ontario;[25] while in an earlier despatch
to France it is stated that "sloops . . . experience no difficulty in
navigating the Lake. They make the trip from Fort Frontenac
to Niagara and return in less than 14 days."[26] Kalm writes of
sailing on a "yacht" on Lake Champlain, which, he says, was the
first to be built there. In 1752 Franquet refers to a barque of
forty-five tons on that lake.[27]

2. The Fur Trade and Expansion

With the birch canoe as means and the fur trade as chief object,
the French penetrated beyond the St. Lawrence valley far into
the interior of the continent. The trade in furs began as a
by-product of the fisheries, but soon was seen to be of great value
in itself, and came to be the chief commercial interest of Canada.
For more than a century Canada was governed by companies
acting under royal charters, by the terms of which they agreed
to bear the expenses of the colony—including the cost of bringing
out settlers—in consideration of a monopoly of trade. Changes
then came both in trade and government. As early as 1635 a
warning was given in the Jesuit *Relation* that indiscriminate
slaughter of beaver would lead to their extermination in the
country around Three Rivers.[28] In spite of such warnings, the
increasing demand for furs did lead to the disappearance of the
beaver near the settled areas, and necessitated constant search
for new supplies. After 1663 the chartered companies were given
up as hopeless for governmental purposes, and the colony was
organized as a royal province with institutions in general similar
to those in the mother country. The increase of population which
followed hastened the process already under way by which the
traders were forced to go ever further afield.

25. O'Callaghan, *op. cit.*, ix, 1050.
26. *Ibid.*, ix, 976.
27. L. Franquet, "Voyages et mémoires sur le Canada" (*Annuaire de
l'Institut Canadien de Québec, 1889*).
28. H. A. Innis, *The fur trade in Canada* (New Haven, 1930), p. 25.

To obtain furs from the interior the French first relied on the Indians, not only for the acquisition of the furs, but also for their transport to the colony. The Hurons in the region of the Ottawa River, no longer able to find beaver in their own country, adopted the rôles of purchasing and transport agents for the French. Having secured articles of European manufacture on credit, they bartered these for furs from the Indians to the west, and annually brought stocks of furs down the Ottawa for sale at the great fairs in Montreal. The Hurons, however, were not long left unmolested in the peaceful pursuit of this profitable occupation. First the Dutch and then the English fur traders of the Atlantic coast had an arrangement with the Iroquois that was similar to that of the French with the Hurons. The Iroquois, having early exhausted the supply of fur-bearing animals in their own country, bought furs from the western tribes and sold them in New York or other colonies. Albany, on the Hudson, was the most important market for furs. The two tribes—Hurons and Iroquois—found themselves rivals for the western supply, which was not unlimited, and in any case rivalry was disadvantageous as it raised the cost of furs. The Iroquois, then, proceeded with a relentless logic and a high degree of ferocity to solve the problem by virtually destroying the Huron tribes, and leaving nothing but scattered and terrified fugitives. They first closed the Great Lakes route to French trade, and finally made even the Ottawa River unsafe for the allies of the French. To complete the process, they carried the war to the very gates of Montreal. In 1653 there was said to have been not a single beaver skin sold there.[29] The people of New France were unable to humble the Iroquois with their own scanty forces, but in 1664 the Carignan-Salières regiment was sent from France to save the colony; and by 1667 the Iroquois were forced to sue for peace. The channels of trade were once more opened, but the problem of competition remained.

When the fur-bearing animals became scarce in the region around the eastern lakes the main trapping ground shifted to the territory west of Lake Michigan. The English and French were competing for a limited supply of furs. The English prices were better: for example, in 1689 a gun could be bought in Albany for

29. E. Salone, *La colonisation de la Nouvelle-France* (Paris, 1906), 128.

two beaver skins, while in Montreal it cost five; and a blanket cost
one beaver in Albany and two in Montreal.[30] The Indians were
naturally inclined to gravitate towards New York, and even French
traders were again and again found taking furs to the English.
The problem before the French government was, therefore, to
defeat their twin rivals, the English and Iroquois. The most
sweeping solution that was suggested was to get rid of the English
colonies. In 1681 the intendant, Duchesneau, suggested buying
"Manatte and Orange," which, as he pointed out, were also of
value in themselves.[31] In 1689 de Callières advocated the capture
of New York by force, and the king agreed.[32] This heroic course
was long under consideration, but never proved feasible. While
the French expeditions against the Iroquois eventually made the
settlement immune from attack, they were not successful in
controlling the Iroquois as fur traders.

The only remaining solution of the problem was to establish
fortified posts as near as possible to the sources of furs in order to
build up an influence over the local tribes, and to bring the trading
goods nearer to them. The problem, as will be shown in the following section, arose not only out of the competition from New York,
but also out of that from Hudson Bay. Trapping was still left to
the Indians, but the French were no longer able to wait for the
furs at depots on the St. Lawrence, and had themselves to provide
for the transportation both of goods into the interior—the *pays
d'en haut*—and of furs back to Montreal. Their purpose being to
intercept the Indian sellers of furs, the French naturally placed
their posts at strategic points on the waterways, over which all
such freight had to move. To some extent this process was carried
on in the area north of the lower St. Lawrence. Maison des Dorvals,
for example, was established at Lake Mistassini, just beyond the
watershed far above Lake St. John, and Fort Abitibi was built on
the lake of that name in 1686. The principal drive, however, was
toward the western Great Lakes and the country beyond. Two
waterways were available. The Ottawa River route, discovered by
Champlain, had the advantage of lying beyond the range of

30. O'Callaghan, *op. cit.*, ix, 408.
31. *Ibid.*, 165.
32. *Ibid.*, 405, 422.

English penetration, but it could only be used by canoes, and even with these was laborious because of the large number of portages. The Ottawa and Mattawa rivers were followed to Lake Nipissing, whence the French River ran into the Georgian Bay. A number of small posts were erected along this route for local trading, but its chief importance was as a means of access to the upper lakes. On the southern or St. Lawrence route to the west larger posts were needed not only for trading, but also as a means of protecting the waterway against the English. Thus Cataraqui was built in 1673 at the junction of the St. Lawrence and Lake Ontario, Niagara in 1678 to guard the portage into Lake Erie, and Detroit in 1701 at the narrows between Lakes Erie and Huron. In 1679 Fort Michilimackinac was built on St. Mary's River, between Lakes Huron and Superior; while to protect a more southerly district another post was established on Green Bay (1670). Traders going by the southern route had to make portages on the upper St. Lawrence, had an uninterrupted passage along Lake Ontario (except when it was too rough), made a long portage at Niagara, and thence could proceed along Lake Erie and into Lake Huron. It was a longer way than by the Ottawa and close to the English rivals. It was partly to reduce the cost that La Salle experimented with sailing vessels, but the attempt was not very successful. The government had difficulty, too, in keeping the eastbound parties from calling at Oswego where prices were higher, and issued orders that canoes must keep to the north shore of Lake Ontario.

As they gradually penetrated beyond the Great Lakes the French continued to place forts along the waterways. The west was then occupied only by Indians, and was open to the explorers of both nations; and those of New France covered an enormous area. One of their most ambitious designs was to hold the line of the Mississippi, and to that end they placed a succession of forts as far as New Orleans. Manifest destiny, as they read it, gave them, if not the whole continent, at least all but the strip between the Alleghanies and the Atlantic; and the entrance to the interior was to be by way of the St. Lawrence. Here, however, we are primarily concerned with the French system of transportation between the upper lakes and what is now the Canadian west. Their principal route began at Fort Kaministiquia on Lake Superior (where Fort William now stands). Jacques de Noyon, who discovered the route in 1688, later wrote a description of it,[33] which shows that it led by the Kaministiquia River to Rainy Lake, and by Rainy River to Lake of the Woods. Particularly in the early part of the trip there were long portages. An alternative way of reaching Rainy Lake was by the Pigeon River, which empties into Lake Superior at the present international boundary. This, too, involved a number of small lakes and rivers, as well as portages. Although this "Grand Portage" was for a time the main route of the North West Company, it was, apparently, not extensively used in the French period. From the Lake of the Woods La Vérendrye and his sons passed over Rat Portage, down the Winnipeg River to its mouth in Lake Winnipeg, and on to the Red River, at which point they founded Fort Maurepas in 1733. Lake Winnipeg was the hub of the waterway system of the west. The Red River led from there to the Mississippi and the south; the Assiniboine and the Saskatchewan to the west; and the Nelson and Hayes rivers to Hudson Bay.

Led on by a love of adventure, the fur trade, missionary zeal, and the search for the western sea, the French steadily worked their way along the rivers and lakes of the western prairie. The discovery of the northern and western limits of the continent was to be left to a later age, but much of the western land was revealed before the French colony was overthrown. The struggle to control the western part of the continent resulted in a diversion of energy from the colony on the St. Lawrence that was regarded with some alarm by the most responsible officials. Efforts to control the exit by means of a licensing system were ineffective, since the majority of those engaged in trading were illegal traders known as *coureurs de bois*, without licenses, and all attempts to restrain them were in vain. As early as 1679 the intendant Duchesneau wrote to the minister:

I must not conceal from you that it [the disobedience of the *coureurs de bois*] has at length reached such a point that every body boldly contravenes the King's interdiction; that there is no longer any concealment, and that

33. E. Voorhis, *Historic forts and trading posts of the French régime and of the English fur-trading companies* (mimeographed, Ottawa, 1930), p. 8.

even parties are collected with astonishing insolence to go and trade in the Indian country.

I have done all in my power to prevent this misfortune, which may be productive of the ruin of the Colony. I have enacted ordinances against the *Coureurs de bois;* against the merchants who furnish them with goods; against the gentlemen and others who harbour them, and even against those who have any knowledge of them and will not inform the justices nearest the spot. All that has been in vain, inasmuch as several of the most considerable families in this country are interested therein, so that the Governor lets them go on, and even shares in their profits.[34]

There was no means of policing the woods, and when an intendant could write that "there is not a family of any condition and quality soever that has not children, brothers, uncles and nephews" as *coureurs de bois*, it will be seen that the trouble was widespread indeed. The only effective means of stopping illegal trading was to make impossible the sale in Montreal of furs that were brought by *coureurs de bois;* and such an action would have defeated the purpose of the government, for the *coureurs de bois* would have taken their furs to Oswego; New France would lose her trade, and possibly her best soldiers as well.

The further west the fur traders spread their net, the greater the labour that was involved. It has been estimated that, at the end of the seventeenth century, there were some 1,000 to 1,500 Frenchmen—with and without licenses—at the forts or in the woods.[33] Apart from the sporadic attempts to make use of sailing vessels, all transportation was by canoe; and west of the Great Lakes this was the only craft that could be used. Canoes of moderate size seem to have been the rule, for the normal crew was five or six men. The cost of carriage rose steadily as the distance from Montreal to the point at which the furs were secured increased, and, since price was an important factor in competition between the French and the English, as the line of communication from Montreal was stretched further and further along the waterways, the problem became more and more acute of maintaining the St. Lawrence route as the chief outlet for the north-west.

34. O'Callaghan, *op. cit.*, ix, 131.

35. W. B. Munro, "The coureurs de bois" (*Proceedings of the Massachusetts Historical Society*, vol. lvii).

3. COMPETITION IN THE CANADIAN WEST

In Canadian history "the west" is a term which is applied to different areas at different periods. For purposes of a study of transportation in the period before the English conquest of Canada, it may be defined as the area beginning between the Great Lakes and James Bay and extending westward like a fan to Hudson Bay, the Arctic, and the Pacific. A glance at the topography of this great region will make clearer the problems of transport. Beginning at its eastern boundary we find a wooded land, based on the pre-cambrian shield, which was, for the most part, unsuited for agriculture but rich in fur-bearing animals. The height of land, formed by the Laurentian Mountains, is not far from Lake Superior, and from that height rivers run to James Bay on the north and the Great Lakes on the south. The watershed then curves to the south around the end of Lake Superior, leaving the central and southern parts of the prairies within the Hudson Bay drainage basin. On its southern boundary this basin reaches down well into the present state of Minnesota, and extends westward to the Rocky Mountains. From a point near the present city of Edmonton the height of land bends to the east, and passes to the eastward of Lake Athabasca and Great Slave Lake up beyond the northern reaches of Hudson Bay. Taking Edmonton again as a marker, with the height of land on the east and the Rockies on the west, we have the region between these three points as the Arctic drainage basin, centering on the Athabasca River, Great Slave Lake and the Mackenzie River. The fourth drainage basin, that of the Pacific, was undiscovered until the end of the eighteenth century.

In order to find new sources of furs the French traders crossed the watershed both northward from the Ottawa and the Great Lakes, and westward in the direction of Lake Winnipeg. Wherever they went they found adequate waterways, but were inevitably lengthening their line of communication with Montreal. In the eighteenth century the tireless French explorers made their way along the great Saskatchewan River almost to the foothills of the Rockies. Nearer to Hudson Bay they advanced along the rivers of the pre-cambrian shield, finding an ideal fur country in that forested area. Once beyond Kaministiquia and the height of land, they were within the Hudson Bay drainage basin, in a generally level country, and with portages but no further watersheds over which they had laboriously to carry canoes and goods.

From their base at Montreal the French traders could paddle their bark canoes, loaded with food for the voyage, and with kettles, knives, guns, trinkets and brandy to use in the trade, right across the southern prairie, or up into land beside the bay. It was, however, a long and expensive journey; and the further they went the more expensive it became. Two of the most adventurous of the French traders were Groseilliers and Radisson, who made a number of expeditions toward the "sea of the north" in order to tap fresh sources of furs. According to their own statement, they reached the shores of James Bay in 1662. Their objectives were, apparently, both to find a new outlet to the Atlantic and to exploit a hitherto untouched area and bring the furs to Montreal. When, in 1663, the two adventurers arrived back in Quebec with some hundreds of Indians and a great cargo of furs, they were heavily fined for illegal trading. Looking for a more profitable undertaking, they sought support in France without success. It is possible that the attitude of the French government was due to the distance of Hudson Bay from the St. Lawrence and the fear of over-expansion. In England, however, they succeeded in enlisting the interest of Prince Rupert and some merchants, with the result that Groseilliers guided a ship in 1668 into the bay to which, half a century earlier, Henry Hudson had given his life and his name. "Mr. Gooseberry," as he was solemnly called by his English employers, showed great skill and energy in initiating trade with the Indians of the Bay; and when the *Nonsuch* returned to England she carried a valuable cargo of furs.

The success of the voyage prompted the original group to apply for a royal charter, which would allow them to stake a claim to this gold mine. In May 1670 the desired charter was granted to "The Governor and Company of Adventurers of England, trading into Hudson's Bay." The terms were generous to a degree, for the king granted to the new company,

the sole Trade and Commerce of all those Seas, Streights, Bays, Rivers, Lakes, Creeks, and Sounds, in whatsoever Latitude they shall be, that lie within the Entrance of the Streights commonly called *Hudson's Streights*, together with all the Lands and Territories upon the Countries, Coasts, and Confines of the Seas, Bays, Lakes, Rivers, Creeks, and Sounds aforesaid, that are not already actually possessed by the subjects of any other Christian Prince or State, with all the Fishing . . . and all Mines Royal, as well discovered as not discovered . . . ; and that the Land be from henceforth reckoned and reputed as one of our Plantations or Colonies in *America*, called *Rupert's Land*.

And farther, We do by these Presents, for Us, Our Heirs and Successors, make, create, and constitute the said Governor and Company . . . the true and absolute Lords and Proprietors of the same Territories, Limits, and Places aforesaid . . . to be holden of us in free and common Socage.

Long years of dispute and litigation were to follow this grand gesture, but for the present no one could guess at the extent of the territory that was involved, or that the Hudson Bay drainage basin, here so airily granted, extended to the Rockies. Meanwhile the Adventurers of England hastened to exploit their kingdom. The chief post on the bay was changed from the original one at Rupert's River on the east side, to the Albany River, higher up the coast of James Bay and on the west side. Further posts were established on Hudson Bay proper, at the mouths of the Nelson and Churchill rivers. The trade prospered, for in 1684 a dividend of fifty per cent was declared, followed by a like dividend four years later.

The plan of the company was to trade at their posts on the bay, and not to go inland as the French had long done; but in order to encourage the Indians to bring down furs they soon found it necessary to send representatives into the interior. In 1683 Henry Sargeant, at Charlton Island, was ordered "to choose from amongst our Servants such as are best qualified with Strength of Body and the Country Language, to travel and to penetrate into the Country, to draw down the *Indians* by fair and gentle Means to trade with us."[36] By 1685 Sargeant had not found anyone willing to undertake the task, and those who had been mentioned said they would resign rather than accept such a perilous task. It was not until Henry Kelsey began his explora-

36. *Report from the Committee appointed to inquire into the State and conditions of the countries adjoining to Hudson's Bay, and of the trade carried on there, 1749*, p. 274.

tions that the company found a man who was willing and able to make these long expeditions. In 1689 Kelsey made a reconnaissance near Churchill, but without much success. In 1690 he travelled inland from York Fort for six hundred miles, and in the following year was on the Saskatchewan River. In 1692 he was back at the fort with "a good Fleet of *Indians*."

There was good reason for the company to send envoys to the Indians, for their trade was falling off. The arrival of the English on Hudson Bay was at once viewed with alarm in Canada, for it threatened to cut off the trade at source. The harsh treatment of Groseilliers and Radisson had not prevented an appreciation of the value of their discoveries, and the French were not prepared to let go their growing position in the west without a struggle. The new posts on James Bay commanded a country the value of which was just being appreciated at Quebec; and if the French imagined—as they may well have done—that the newcomers would adopt the same methods as themselves, they might picture them as paddling up the rivers that flowed into the bay, and drawing the rich traffic away from the St. Lawrence. Indeed, they already felt at Lake St. John and Sault Ste. Marie the effects of English competition. The sea route into the interior of the continent enabled the English merchants to carry their goods at less expense than the French could by canoe from Montreal, and the Indians were as ready to trade with them as to barter their furs with Indian middlemen or the advanced French expeditions.

The French, therefore, began to take active steps, which were, indeed, the first round of a battle of routes that was to last for a century and a half. They found that the Assiniboines around Lake Winnipeg had taken their furs to the bay as early as 1673, and the tribes to the north of Lake Superior were within much easier distance of Forts Moose and Albany than of any French posts. The French then began an active policy of establishing posts in the interior, and working out the routes to the west which have already been described. In this competition they had a disadvantage as to distance, but on the other hand they knew the technique of dealing with the Indians, and had long been familiar with the birch canoe. In an even more direct method of competition they laid claim to Hudson Bay, and sent a number of expeditions

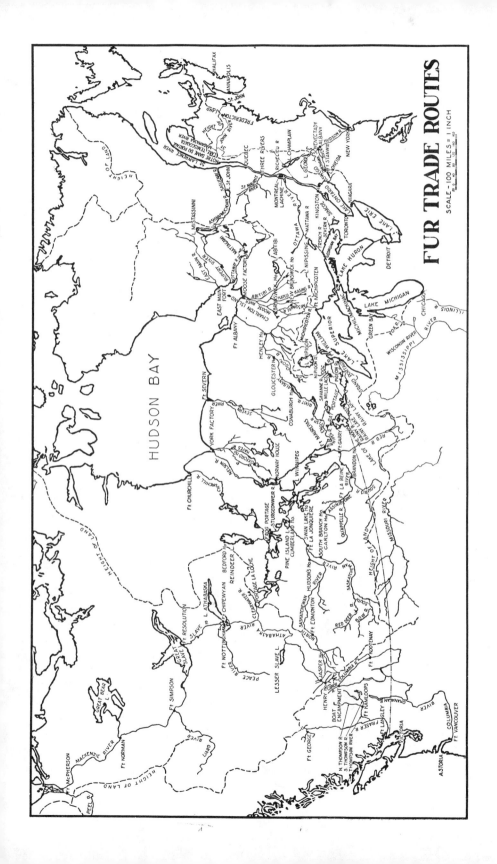

FUR TRADE ROUTES

SCALE–100 MILES = 1 INCH

to capture the English forts. In this they had a partial success, so that the company was for years engaged in an armed struggle as well as in commercial rivalry, with some of their posts in the hands of the French for varying periods. The prolonged battle ended for a time in 1713, when France abandoned her claims to Hudson Bay in the Treaty of Utrecht.

The success of the French traders, both before and after 1713, in keeping the Indians away from the English posts was a source of constant worry to the company. Those posts which felt the strain most were the southern ones, Albany and Moose. Their hope lay in the higher prices they offered to the Indians. In 1716 the factor in charge at Albany gave a characteristic account of his troubles in a letter to London.

It is certain The french Begun their neue settlement up the River last summer and had Build 2 Houses, In the Center of those Indians, that hath used this place Ever since Itt was settled By The English, Your Honors may be Assured of the Same, for severall Indians came to trade, that traded with the ffrench this spring, and was Cloathed in ffrench Cloath and Blankets with Gunns and other Trading Goods. They all in Generall told me that the french Trades hard with them, and that I give twice the valew for Beaver and all other furrs, Catts Excepted . . . where the ffrench has made this new settlement Is not Above 7 Days Paddling up the River. . . .[37]

In the following year a pointed reference was made to the difference in method between the company and the French traders. In that summer forty canoes of Indians were reported as coming to Albany, bringing with them prime beaver; but they brought no marten. "What Martins the french trades," the writer adds, "Is with a Nation of Indians that is Distant from hence near 800 miles; the french haveing Collonies In the center of their Countrey for which reason it will be a hard matter to Draw them to this place."[38] Still no steps were taken to establish inland posts, and the reports of French intercepting the Indians, and persuading or warning them not to go to the bay, continue. In 1741 the first inland post,

37. Archives of the Hudson's Bay Company. Inward letters, Albany, July 16, 1716. This and subsequent letters are published by permission of the Governor and Committee of the Hudson's Bay Company.
38. *Ibid.*, August 20, 1717.

Henley House, was built 150 miles up the Albany River, and goods were carried to it from Albany in flat boats. It was built, according to a letter from Albany, "in order to prevent the French taking possession of that place, who would entirely intercept the Trade with the foreign Indians, and draw the Seaside Indians from us, by that means, we should not have been able, to procure a Trade of above one Thousand Skins."[39] The problem, however, was not yet solved, for in the next few years several bands of Indians who came to Albany either brought only what skins the French had refused, or else reported that their countrymen would not come to the bay when they could trade with the French without making a journey. In 1754 six canoes arrived at Albany with such remnants, and the factor reported that "by what I can learn by ye Indians, find that ye french Swarm all over the Country and Come within fifty miles of ye Sea to ye North of Albany river towards York Fort."[40]

Further light is thrown on the triangular relation of English, French, and Indians by evidence given to the parliamentary committee of 1749. Joseph Robson, in reply to questions as to the conduct of the trade, said

That the *Indians* bring down Beavers, and that he does not aprehended [*sic*] any of the Produce of the Country is sold by Factors to the *French;* but he Thinks, that the Beavers which are brought down to the Company, are refused by the *French*, from their being a heavy Commodity; for the Natives who come to trade with the Company, dispose of their small valuable Furs to the *French*, and bring down their heavy Goods to the Company, in Summer, when the Rivers are open, which they sell, and supply the *French* with *European* goods, purchased from the Company.[41]

Fort Albany, and its subsidiary Henley House, were thus subjected to constant interference by French traders. York Fort, further to the north, was too far away to be so early affected, but by the 'fifties the decrease in trade suggested that the French had penetrated into that district as well. In 1755 the chief factor wrote to London that the French are "actually upon all quarters

39. *Ibid.*, August 22, 1746.
40. *Ibid.*, June 6, 1754.
41. *Report from the Committee* . . ., p. 216.

of us, otherwise where could those Indians gett those french goods new that the sloops company see if their was not a french settlement near."[42] There was talk of establishing posts in the interior, but the factor was warned to be cautious until it was certain that the French were near. In the meanwhile Anthony Henday was sent in charge of a large expedition inland in 1754, and went as far as the Saskatchewan, travelling in canoes by way of the Hayes River, and brought back a good cargo of furs. Churchill further up the bay, was free from French competition.

Up to the end of the French régime the struggle for the control of the fur trade of the west involved two differences in method. The French, masters of the birch canoe and accustomed to live in the Indian country, adopted an aggressive policy of trading in the areas where the Indians trapped, and thus attempted to keep them away from Hudson Bay. Their goods were more expensive, but they were delivered at the Indians' villages. The English traders, on the other hand, clung to the other technique of giving better prices, but forcing the Indians to come to them. They had few men whom they could send into the interior, and it was long before they adopted the canoe as a regular method of transport. Apart from Henley House, they built no posts inland, and attempted to make up for this deficiency by sending expeditions to the further tribes to encourage them to come to the bay. They suffered severely from French competition, and the total number of furs received decreased. In 1690 the stock was trebled, but paid no dividend until 1718 (that is, during the period of active warfare). In the latter year the stock was again increased, to £103,950, and paid an annual dividend thereafter of from seven to ten per cent for the next fifty years.[43]

The second difference in method, and one related to the first, was the transportation system. As soon as the company's posts were established on the bay—and perhaps earlier—the French in Canada saw the significance of the new entrance to the continent, enabling, as it did, sea-going vessels to sail into the heart of the

42. Archives of the Hudson's Bay Company. Inward letters, York, September 2, 1755.

43. These figures are from transcripts in the Archives of the Hudson's Bay Company.

fur country. It presented to them a problem not unlike that caused by the English entry by New York and the Hudson River. They tried to secure control of the route themselves by force of arms, and came within sight of success. But failing in the end to achieve this object, they were forced back on the long canoe route to Montreal, and a higher transportation cost that made competition increasingly difficult. Given the inherent difficulties in the position, the French traders achieved startling results; for, failing to dislodge the company's servants from their stone forts, they cast a ring of posts about them that all but confined them to the shores of the bay.

This rivalry between French and English traders was but the first act of the great struggle between routes that ties the fur trade so closely to the history of transportation. The successors of the men of the French régime, the Scots and *voyageurs* of the second half of the century, carried on with unabated vigour, and perhaps increased violence, the battle for the control of the west by the St. Lawrence valley.

CHAPTER II

THE FUR TRADERS, 1763-1821

1. VARIATIONS ON A FRENCH THEME

THE Seven Years' War, last of the series of conflicts between France and England in North America, culminated in the capture of Quebec and Montreal, and led to the transfer of Canada from King Louis to King George. The effects of this political change on the development of the economy, and hence the transportation system, of the colony were at first not fundamental. The French political empire fell, but French civilization remained. The colony on the St. Lawrence retained its traditional characteristics, with the language, law, church, and customs of its mother country. A new element was added, however, which was to have an increasing influence on the economic aims of the colony. Close on the heels of the conquering British armies came a group of Scottish-American merchants from northern New York, claiming to be the rightful heirs to this new jewel in the British crown.

Their principal interest was in the fur trade. Long experience in competition with the traders of Montreal had convinced them that they could more profitably conduct the trade from the St. Lawrence than from the Hudson. Now the political barriers were down and they were free to work from the new base. They were regarded with distrust and suspicion by French inhabitants and English officials alike, and the political barometer soon registered the storm that arose from the conflicting interests of the two elements. The former felt that they were being dispossessed of a land rightfully theirs, and the newcomers chafed at the conservative outlook of the French which impeded the development of the colony. In the fur trade, however, men of both races worked together. The French were the canoemen, the *voyageurs*, and gave to the English-speaking employers a supply of trained and capable workers. Become Canadians by adoption, the newcomers zealously struggled against their late compatriots, rivals for western business, for the competition between Albany, Montreal, and Hudson Bay continued; and when the political boundary was again established after the American Revolution, that competition once more assumed the character of a national as well as a commercial struggle. For some years, therefore, the fur trade continues to be a main thread in the development of transportation. Its interest in this respect is, in the main, twofold: in the first place, it gave the prime stimulus to the organization of an effective system of transport in the Canadian west, and to the further discovery and mapping of that area; secondly, on it focused the triangular struggle of routes.

The personnel of the Canadian fur trade fell into two main divisions: those who carried trading goods to the Indian country and brought back skins in return, and those in Montreal who purchased goods for trading, financed the trade, and finally sold the skins. The deeds of the first are better known and more picturesque; but those who stayed in Montreal have a significant place in Canadian history, for it was they who built up the financial and commercial houses, which, after the collapse of the St. Lawrence fur trade, had already instituted a more general for-warding business to the newly-settled districts.

In every sense, therefore, the fur trade is a transitional as well as an overlapping factor. Although the pace was accelerated, the methods of the North West Company were, only slightly modified, the methods of the French traders of the earlier eighteenth century. The *coureur de bois* becomes the *voyageur;* he lives the same life, and is as willing to serve the incoming Scots as he was his French masters. It is transitional, too, in that it carries within it the scaffolding for the more general economy which took its place. When the smoke of the conflict between the Nor'Westers and the men of the bay had cleared away, there could be seen already at Montreal a group of merchants who had begun to use the St. Lawrence for other and less transient purposes.

In essence, the problems differed little from those of French days. The goods and the food for the employees had to be carried over an ever-increasing distance, just as the furs bought from the Indians had to be brought back from further and further west. From the north, south, and east, traders converged on the prairie country. Political developments drew a line between British and

American traders, and the competition was gradually narrowed down to lie between the traders from Montreal and those from the bay. In the end it was the cost of transportation which settled the dispute. Montreal perforce capitulated and the trade flowed only north. But it was not a final defeat for Montreal as the base for expansion westward, but only for expansion based on furs and canoes. Unwillingly, Montreal was obliged to *reculer pour mieux sauter.* The weakness of French expansion (which overlapped the conquest by sixty years) was that it was built on an inadequate system of transport. By accident the collapse of the Montreal fur trade did for Canada what the Alleghanies had done for the American colonies: forced the building of foundations in a limited area. When, a generation later, the people of the St. Lawrence valley once more sought to make the north-west Canadian, they had much greater population and wealth, and had in the railway a mode of transport which offered new hopes of success. Thus, though the Montreal fur traders discovered the west, the Montreal railway builders captured it.

2. THE HUDSON VS. THE ST. LAWRENCE

The cessation of hostilities in 1760 allowed the fur trade to be re-established. No longer did that trade take the form of rivalry between British and French interests, and for a time—before there was once more a political boundary between Canada and the Atlantic colonies—the merchants of both were free to seek their fortunes in the west. Many of those of New York, who had already seen the advantage of the St. Lawrence entry, now established themselves in Montreal; while others sought to make use of both the St. Lawrence and the Hudson rivers. During the years before the American Revolution there were no large concerns operating in the fur trade. A number of partnerships were formed, both in New York and Canada, and these carried on their business with a limited capital.

The route chiefly followed by the American traders was described by Peter Pond.[1] From New York the goods were shipped up the Hudson River to Albany, whence they were carried on waggons

1. "Journal of Peter Pond," in *Collections of the State Historical Society of Wisconsin*, vol. xviii.

for fourteen miles to Schenectady. From there bateaux were used up the Mohawk River to Fort Stanwix, and thence over a one-mile portage to Wood Creek, and so by Lake Oneida and the Oswego River to Lake Ontario. Boats or small sailing vessels carried the goods along Lake Ontario to the Niagara portage. Traders to the north-western country then made for Michilimackinac by way of Detroit and Lake Huron. Except beyond Michilimackinac the New York traders made no use of canoes, but developed a system of transport by boats. Transport from Montreal was divided into two stages: from Montreal to Lake Superior, and from there to the inland posts. To reach Lake Superior three routes were followed. The first was the historic highway discovered by the French—the Ottawa valley. After the goods had been taken past the first rapids above Montreal by means of carts, they were shipped in canoes at Lachine and started on their long voyage. The canoes left in "brigades" during May and followed the Ottawa River to its junction with the Mattawa River where they turned west towards Lake Nipissing. After crossing that lake they entered the French River, when for the first time they had the current with them. They then crossed the Georgian Bay and Lake Huron to Sault Ste. Marie, where portages took them to Lake Superior. Hugging fairly closely the north shore of the lake, they finally arrived at the Grand Portage on the west side of the lake early in July.

The chief objection to the Ottawa route was the number of portages and *décharges* that it entailed. A *décharge* was a modified portage. The cargo was carried overland and the canoe run light past rapids or in shallow water. The number varied according to the depth of the water and whether passengers or freight were carried. Alexander MacKenzie describes twenty-nine portages and seven *décharges* between Lachine and the Grand Portage.[2] Other figures are considerably higher. John Macdonell, for example, writing in 1793, says there were, between Lachine and Georgian Bay, thirty-six portages and about the same number of *décharges*.[3] But writing some years later, in 1821, Nicholas Garry

2. Quoted in E. Voorhis, *Historic forts and trading posts of the French régime and of the English fur-trading companies* (mimeographed, Ottawa, 1930), p. 10.

3. C. M. Gates, *Five fur traders of the Northwest* (Minneapolis, 1933), p. 87.

gives a detailed description of the route from Lachine to Fort
William, on which, he says, there were twenty-two portages
and twelve *décharges*.[4] The character of the Ottawa route meant
that only canoes could be used. These were of birch and generally
of the character described in the first chapter, but they tended to
increase in size. As far as Grand Portage the "Montreal canoe,"
or *canot du maître*, was used. Miss Nute describes this as thirty-
five to forty feet long,[5] but it is probable that somewhat smaller
ones were used in the early years of the trade. A *canot du maître*
as described would take a crew of about fourteen, and was capable
of carrying about four thousand pounds of freight, which was
made up of packs or kegs weighing approximately ninety pounds.
One, two, or even three of these parcels could be carried at a time
over a portage.

The crew were all French Canadians. They were not big men
(long legs were not suitable to a birch canoe), but were of great
strength and endurance. They took a remarkable pride in their
work, and the competitive spirit in which they raced their canoes,
or hurried over portages, must have been as refreshing to their
employers as it was alarming and exhausting to any passengers
who were new to this mode of travelling. Long days were the rule,
and *voyageurs* could paddle from twelve to fifteen or even eighteen
hours a day. They used light paddles and rapid strokes; one
traveller counted forty strokes a minute and another a stroke each
second. Whenever possible square sails were used, and these were
mounted on one mast, or on two set side by side. Birch canoes
could not be used in rough weather on the lakes, for it was
dangerous to the cargo and crew and—what was a more pressing
cause—liable to strain the frail craft. The experts of the crew
were the bowsman and the steersman. The former was the director
of operations in running rapids, while the steersman invariably
stood up in his place at the stern and steered with a long paddle,
not attempting to keep stroke with the others. All the food for
the crews on the Ottawa route had either to be taken from
Montreal, or sent from Detroit to Michilimackinac, where it
could be picked up. Biscuits and pork, that staple of North

4. "Diary of Nicholas Garry" (*Royal Society of Canada*, 1900, ii, 197).
5. G. L. Nute, *The Voyageur* (New York, 1931), p. 24.

America, were easily carried and apparently acceptable. Fish could sometimes be obtained *en route*, but not much time was left from the working day for quiet fishing. Trolling was sometimes possible, and nets were set at night.

In general it will be seen that transport by the Ottawa had not changed materially in route or methods since the days when it was one of the main highways of the French. And still on the river could be seen the cheerful *voyageur* with his energy, skill, and ready song. These journeys were his life, his canoe was his chief pride; and as he sang to it,

> Tu es mon compagnon de voyage!—
> Je veux mourir dans mon canot,

one cannot help wondering whether the *voyageur*, the chief link with the old régime, saw, like the followers of Pontiac, that the British invasion of the west was gradually to destroy him.

A second route to Lake Superior, which avoided the detour by Detroit and was an alternative to the Ottawa, was by way of the St. Lawrence and Lake Ontario to Toronto, and thence over the thirty-mile portage from near the mouth of the Humber River, up to the Holland River and Lake Simcoe. Crossing Lake Simcoe and Lake Couchiching, the canoes could take the Severn River to Georgian Bay and so on by Sault Ste. Marie to Lake Superior. Canoes were, of course, required west of Toronto, but—particularly after the first few years—boats were employed to carry the goods and furs along the St. Lawrence and Lake Ontario. There is reason to believe that little traffic passed by way of Toronto in the early years after the conquest, although the mouth of the Humber had been an important outlet for furs for many years of the French régime.

The third route is of particular importance in that it modified the transportation system of the fur trade. The French had attempted to use sailing vessels for heavy transportation on the Great Lakes, but had not met with success. It was left to the Albany traders to develop this method. Operating from Oswego on Lake Ontario, they went by way of the Niagara portage and Lake Erie to Detroit, and thence up Lake Huron to Michilimackinac. The advantages of such a route were immediately obvious to the

Montreal traders, for it enabled them to ship food and other heavy goods through the lakes and still retain the rapid canoe transport on the Ottawa for furs and light goods. The two routes thus became complementary. The first problem was a lack of boats. A sloop was built at Detroit for traders in 1769 and a second in 1770. A list of merchant vessels in 1775—intended, apparently, to cover Lakes Ontario, Erie, and Huron—shows three completed and two on the stocks, in all 310 tons, belonging to Alexander Grant; one sloop belonging to McTavish and McBeath of Detroit; and one to John Askin.[6] In the absence of sufficient tonnage, bateaux were pressed into service. In 1770 a Captain Grant advertised his willingness to carry traders' goods in "three handed Battoes," which were capable of carrying twelve barrels, and were probably small, open sailing boats. He pointed out that "by adopting this manner of conveyance to the several posts, the property of an Indian trader, and his credit . . . with his merchant, will become infinitely less liable to hazard than in that of proceeding single and defenceless in small open boats, which subjects them to be seized by the Savages, who thereby become possessed of ammunition and Cloathing, that may enable them to carry on a long series of hostilities against out posts and settlements. . . ."[7]

Increase in larger vessels was hindered by the war-regulations of 1777, under which only the king's vessels were allowed to navigate the lakes. There were many protests by the traders, who continually complained of vexatious delays and unreasonable charges, but the regulations were continued even after the war, partly for purposes of defence and partly from commercial rivalry. "The navigation of these lakes by the King's Vessels only", wrote the governor, "is an Object so nearly connected with the entire preservation of the Furr trade, that I have withstood several applications for building and navigating private Vessels and Boats upon the Lakes; the Rivers and Outlets from them to the American States are so numerous that no precautions which could be taken, in that case, would be effectual in preventing a great part of the Furrs from going directly into the American States. . . ."[8]

6. Canadian Archives, Q 11, p. 226.
7. *Quebec Gazette*, May 31, 1770.
8. Canadian Archives, Q, 25, p. 295. Haldimand to Sydney, March 16, 1785.

The traders were evidently not impressed by the urgency of this consideration, for they continued to protest, and gave force to their views by failing to pay the freight charges to the government. As a result, the regulations were modified in 1785 and abandoned in 1788. In that year three ordinances were passed: one prohibiting the export of furs to the United States, a second to facilitate the payment of the debts, and a third providing for the use of privately-owned vessels. Under the authority of this last ordinance goods might be carried in vessels under ninety tons burden, provided the vessels were built on British soil and the crew were British subjects. All vessels over ten tons were to carry registers and certain other documents. Superintendents of navigation were appointed to grant registers, manifests, and clearances, and generally to see that the new regulations were obeyed.

The number of merchant vessels built after the relaxation of the restrictions does not seem large in comparison with the vigour of the demands for permission to do so. The sloop *Beaver* was launched at Detroit in 1785, and the *Otter* at Sault Ste. Marie (on Lake Superior) in the same year. In the following year two schooners, of twenty-five and sixty-five tons, were built at Detroit; and in 1787 the schooner *Lady Dorchester*, of a hundred tons, was built near Kingston. From then until the end of 1792 the famous *Nancy* and another small schooner were launched on Lake Erie, and two small sloops and two schooners on Lake Ontario.[9] In 1794 the largest vessel yet to appear on the lakes, the *Governor Simcoe*, of 137 tons, was built on Lake Ontario by a group of fur-trading firms.

The point of junction of Lakes Huron, Michigan, and Superior marked the branching of the routes to the west, south-west, and north-west. From Lake Michigan two courses could be followed to the Mississippi: by the Chicago and Illinois Rivers or from La Baye (Green Bay) by the Fox and Wisconsin Rivers. Michilimackinac, on the strait between Lakes Michigan and Huron, was an important trading and distributing centre as well as on one of the main roads to the north-west. Trading canoes, after calling at this post, made their way by the St. Mary's River to Lake Superior and along the north shore of that lake to the Grand

9. C. A. Cuthbertson, *Freshwater* (Toronto, 1931), p. 282.

Portage, which was on the north-western side of Lake Superior, just south of the present international border. It was a nine-mile portage around rapids on the Pigeon River and involved heavy work. Grand Portage was the meeting place of the traders and the point at which the goods or furs were transferred from the *canots du maître* to the *canots du nord*. Here the *mangeurs de lard*, as the *voyageurs* who plied between Montreal and the Portage were called, deposited their bales and took on packages of furs for the return trip.[10] West of the Grand Portage only the smaller canoes were suitable. They were some twenty-five feet long and carried a crew of eight.[11]

From the Grand Portage a chain of lakes and rivers made a comparatively easy way downstream to the interior: by Pigeon River, Rainy Lake, Rainy River, Lake of the Woods, and Winnipeg River, to Lake Winnipeg. From Lake Winnipeg long rivers offered routes to the great western country. The Saskatchewan, with its two branches, gave access to an enormous tract of country. It was, however, principally after 1783 that trade was organized in this western area. In the meantime plenty of furs were found in the region north-west and west of Lake Winnipeg, and though the country around Detroit was becoming denuded, it was still an important post. Michilimackinac rivalled the Grand Portage in this period, and was often the starting point of western expeditions via Green Bay.

Although many of the colonial traders moved their headquarters to Montreal after the conquest, an active fur trade was still carried on from the Atlantic colonies, and in the years 1760–1775 this involved no international complications. The Quebec Act of 1774, however, gave over to Canadian administration the Ohio country, and in the following year the outbreak of hostilities added the element of political and military rivalry to the trade war that was already going on. The colonial trade was in the hands of several relatively small organizations, which had the great advantage of securing their goods from local establishments or from England, and had in New York an all-year port. Near the Mississippi their

10. After the opening of the Athabasca area some of the Montreal canoes went on to Rainy Lake.

11. Nute, *op. cit.*, p. 24.

trading activities were greatly hampered by the rival ones of the French and Spanish, but they were also concerned with the territory around the northern Great Lakes. To get to the St. Lawrence and the lakes they followed two principal routes: from Albany, by way of the Mohawk River and Oneida Lake to Oswego, or overland from Philadelphia by way of Fort Pitt. Detroit and Michilimackinac both knew these traders well. The traders from Albany and Montreal alike converged on Lake Ontario and went west from there by way of the Niagara portage.

The American Revolution had both temporary and lasting effects on the fur trade. No trade, of course, was possible in the actual war area, and furthermore communications between Albany and the upper lakes were cut. It was a gain for Montreal. Important traders, such as Simon McTavish and Phyn, Ellice and Company moved there from Albany; and those who had formerly obtained their goods from New York were now obliged to turn to Montreal alone. The obstacles which the revolution put in the way of the normal increase of the Canadian trade were more than offset by the hold secured on the trading area by British influence among the Indians at this period. One of the annoyances suffered by the Canadian traders was the order against the navigation of the lakes by private craft—a measure intended to prevent the smuggling of contraband to the enemy. Yet the British command of the lakes during the war was of great benefit to the traders.

The fact [writes Stevens] that the British were able to maintain commercial relations with the Indians of the Northwest accounts in large measure for their ascendancy in that region during the war and the years which followed. The British laid the foundations of their monopoly of the fur trade during the Revolution, a monopoly which they had no idea of giving up after hostilities had ceased and the country south of the Great Lakes had been yielded by treaty to the Americans.[12]

The Peace of Paris brought to an end the first British empire in North America and recognized an independent state south of the Great Lakes. The frontier established by the treaty, however, was not accepted as definitive by either Great Britain or the United States until another war laid the main issue at rest. The dispute

12. W. E. Stevens, *The Northwest fur trade* (Urbana, 1928), p. 67.

over the west drew its force chiefly from the competition for furs, the actual area in dispute being defined by the lines of water communication. Then, as in all periods of Canadian history, the St. Lawrence-Great Lakes system played a dominating part in economic development and in international relations.

The impetus given to the Canadian fur trade by the situation at the end of the war led to unified companies and greatly accelerated energy. During the difficult years of the war the Montreal traders began to organize larger combinations than had hitherto been known, and in 1783 this tendency blossomed into the North West Company, which became the dominating influence in the trade. Although known as a company, it was never chartered, probably never incorporated, and was "purely a partnership with transferable shares."[13] It was a federation of a number of smaller partnerships and answered most closely to the name given it by its members, "the concern." For a time a number of traders formed a rival organization, variously known as "The New North West Company," "Sir Alexander MacKenzie and Company," and—from the mark on its packs of furs—"The X Y Company"; but in 1804 the disadvantages of competition led the two companies to amalgamate.

A new and forceful figure appeared on the American stage. Soon after the creation of the United States, John Jacob Astor began to establish his series of fur-trading organizations, some of which, particularly at first, brought his activities well into Canadian territory. His method for this part of the business was to appoint agents at various points and arrange for them to ship furs to New York; but in addition he made annual trips to Montreal to buy furs. From about 1788 to 1810 he spent four months in the summer and autumn of every year on these buying expeditions. Up to 1796 the furs thus purchased had to be shipped to England.[14]

This complication was but one of many ways in which the question of the frontiers affected both Canadian and American traders, and it raises the whole question of the relations between the countries. By the Treaty of Paris in 1783 the boundary was laid down, but for many years it was a boundary on paper only.

13. G. C. Davidson, *The North West Company* (Berkeley, 1918), p. 13.
14. K. W. Porter, *John Jacob Astor* (Cambridge, Mass., 1931), i, 50.

The British government was not satisfied that the new confederation would hold together, an attitude which was given positive support by the secession movement in Vermont (which is interesting in itself, being based as it was on a desire to use the St. Lawrence outlet). In the meanwhile the preservation of the fur trade, chief source of commercial wealth in Canada, had to be considered. The British had one great advantage in the friendship of the Indians; for, two decades after the Pontiac war, the mantle of the Great Onontio had fallen on the British governor of Canada, and the Indians looked to the British for aid rather than to the land-hungry Americans. An unfortunate aspect of the treaty from the Canadian point of view was that it ceded to the United States western posts which had strategic value for the fur trade. The posts involved were: Dutchman's Point and Pointe-au-Fer on the Montreal-Albany route; Oswegatchie, Oswego, and Niagara, covering navigation from the upper St. Lawrence to Lake Erie; Fort Erie, near the eastern end of that lake; Detroit, on the straits between Lakes Erie and Huron; and Michilimackinac at the entrance to Lake Michigan. But for the time being the posts could still be held since, as Sydney explained to Haldimand in 1784, the treaty only called for evacuation "with all convenient speed," and could be delayed "at least until we are enabled to secure the fur traders in the Interior Country and withdraw their property."[15]

They were not finally given up until 1796, under the Jay Treaty. They were places to which the Indians had been accustomed to bring furs, but had originally been selected because of their command of the water communications, as will most readily be seen in the case of Detroit. In the negotiations for a peaceful settlement of the claims of both Britain and the United States, the effort to secure unfettered travel for the traders played a leading part. The final treaty contains the following:

It is agreed that it shall at all times be free to His Majesty's subjects, and to the citizens of the United States, and also to the Indians dwelling on either side of the said boundary line, freely to pass and repass by land or inland navigation, into the respective territories and countries of the two

15. S. F. Bemis, *Jay's treaty: a study in commerce* (New York, 1924), p. 10.

parties, on the continent of America, (the country within the limits of the Hudson's Bay Company only excepted), and to navigate all the lakes, rivers and waters thereof, and freely to carry on trade and commerce with each other. . . . No duty of entry shall ever be levied by either party on peltries brought by land or inland navigation into the said territories respectively. . . .

While for many years Detroit and Michilimackinac remained fur-trading posts, the area covered by the traders constantly widened. But no matter how far the posts were extended to the west and north, the lines of communication between Montreal and the Lake Superior junctions remained the same. The war-time regulation that only the king's vessels could navigate the Great Lakes was continued for five years after the peace, and was much resented by the merchants who claimed that it led to expense and inconvenience. A few merchant vessels existed in 1788 when the restrictions on navigation were withdrawn, and several more were built after that date.[16]

At the same time as commercial vessels were being developed on the lakes two of the principal portages were improved. Up to the American Revolution the Niagara portage was on the east side of the river, but soon after the treaty of 1783 the British government began to build a road on the west side. By 1789 a group of traders had inaugurated a service over the road. In the following year a contract was awarded to a syndicate consisting of the same men, who agreed to carry all government stores for 1/8 (New York currency) per 112 pounds, with an abatement of 2d. for road maintenance. It was understood that the syndicate was to employ settlers and their teams. The road, which ran from Chippawa to Queenston, remained crude for many years, but canoes, boats, and goods were regularly pulled over the eleven miles by horses or oxen. About 1800 a great feat was accomplished when a vessel of 75–100 tons was portaged.[17]

Another vital portage was that at Sault Ste. Marie, which lay on the only route to Lake Superior, whether the Ottawa or the Great Lakes were first followed. When the posts were given up

16. *See above*, page 32.

17. E. Green, "The Niagara portage road" (*Ontario Historical Society, Papers and Records*, vol. xxiii).

in 1796 it became imperative to find a route at Sault Ste. Marie which was in British territory. A survey was made, with Dorchester's sanction, in 1796 and a way found. In 1797 or 1798 the North West Company improved the portage by a road and canal. As they wrote in a petition, they had "actually cut a road forty-five feet wide across the carrying-place, and opened a canal, upwards of three thousand feet in length, with a lock which raises the water nine feet, and have also erected thereon a sawmill, storehouses and other necessary buildings for facilitating the navigation of said canal."[18] A later investigation of the scene revealed a lock forty feet long and eight feet, nine inches wide, made of two-inch plank. Remains of a wharf and what had apparently been a dam were also found.[19] Shortly afterwards the X Y Company built a parallel road, for in the period of bitter competition, the North West Company made every effort to keep its rival from making use of the facilities at the portage.

A similar problem arose in regard to the Grand Portage at the western end of Lake Superior, which fell just within American territory. At that time the Grand Portage route was the only satisfactory one known, and the traders were plunged into deep gloom at the thought of losing it to the United States. Some of them wrote to Simcoe in 1791 that, if the treaty of 1783 were carried out, it would destroy the fur trade.[20] A few months later Charles Stevenson wrote to George Hammond that the only other possible route was six weeks longer.[21] In the spring of 1792 the traders again wrote to Simcoe on the subject, arguing that, by some means—perhaps reciprocity—they must be able to use their old route.[22] Until the posts were actually given up it was possible to use the Grand Portage, but the cession of the posts was accompanied by the imposition of duties by the American government. Continued efforts were made to find a passage on British soil. The North West Company sent Umfreville to look for a new route

18. *Report of the Canadian Archives, 1888*, p. xxvi.

19. *Report of the Canadian Archives, 1890*, p. xxxviii.

20. E. A. Cruikshank (ed.), *The Correspondence of Lieut. Governor Sir John Graves Simcoe* (Toronto, 1923–31), i, 92.

21. *Ibid.*, i, 117.

22. *Ibid.*, i, 133.

by the Nipigon River, but it was judged to be impracticable. Some ten years later, in 1797, Roderick McKenzie heard from Indians near Rainy Lake that there was to the north "une route bonne pour les grands canots." The clue was promptly followed up, and the remains of the old French fort at Kaministiquia discovered, as well as the route which had, by some curious chance, been forgotten ever since the French régime.[23] In 1803, after preparations had been made, the headquarters of the North West Company were moved to Kaministiquia, which, in 1807, was renamed Fort William. In 1804 the X Y Company also moved to the mouth of the river.

From the beginning of the century, then, the Kaministiquia route became the only important Canadian one from Lake Superior to the north-west. The following were the details of the way: the Kaministiquia River was followed for fifty-two miles, then Little Dog Lake and Great Dog Lake for another twelve miles. Over this section there were thirteen portages and *décharges*. From there the Dog River was taken for thirty-three miles with two portages. A series of lakes and rivers was then followed, of which the chief were Savanne River, Thousand Lakes, Pickerel Lake, Sturgeon Lake—adding another 165 miles and nineteen portages and *décharges*. Further small lakes and rivers took the canoes to Rainy Lake, and so by way of Rainy River, Lake of the Woods, and Winnipeg River to Lake Winnipeg. In all the distance from Lake Superior to Lake Winnipeg was 657 miles, and there were 53 portages and 9 décharges. Most of the portages were less than a mile, but one—Prairie Portage, between Cold Water Lake and Height of Land Lake—was two miles, fifty chains. At that point the track rose to 885.55 feet above Lake Superior. Not an easy route certainly, and longer (by 55.48 miles) than the Pigeon River route.[24] On the other hand, it did avoid the long Grand Portage, which had always been a pet aversion of the *voyageurs*.

23. L. R. Masson, *Les bourgeois de la Compagnie du Nord-Ouest* (Quebec, 1890), i, 71–72.

24. H. Y. Hind, *Narrative of the Canadian Red River exploring expedition of 1857 and of the Assiniboine and Saskatchewan exploring expedition of 1858* (London, 1860), ii, 399 et seq.

Fort William was not, however, the terminus for the Athabasca and Upper Columbia brigades, which, having a longer journey to make, went no further east than Rainy Lake, where they met special brigades from Montreal.[25]

Little further need be said of the Ottawa route to Michili-mackinac, except that it retained its importance after 1783. No figures are available for the relative quantity of goods going by the lakes and the Ottawa, but Marbois says that it was preferred as shorter.[26] Weld, too, writing in 1798, says "the [North West] company principally carries on its trade by means of the Utawas or Grand River," and in another place: "Besides the furs and pelts, thus conveyed down to Montreal from the north-western parts of the continent, by means of the Utawas River, there are large quantities also brought there across the lakes, and down the River St. Lawrence."[27] A memorandum from Montreal fur traders to Simcoe, undated, but written in the early 'nineties, speaks of the Ottawa route as "most generally used from Lower Canada to the Western and Northwest country. . . ."[28] For the east-bound cargoes of furs it was the fastest route (being downstream), and therefore was used to catch the vessels before the St. Lawrence was frozen.

With the formation of the North West Company, the end of the war, and the effect of the boundary settlement on the Niagara portage, came the desire to look for any other possible routes to the west. One to which the traders turned their attention was "the abandoned trading-post and carrying place at Toronto."[29] In the summer of 1784 Frobisher, McTavish and others applied for a grant of a strip of land on the route between Georgian Bay and Lake Ontario. Apparently Frobisher was instructed to examine possible routes between Lake Ontario and Lake Huron, particu-

25. Gates, *op. cit.*, p. 191.

26. Shirley Farr, "Marbois on the fur trade" (*American Historical Review*, xxix, 4).

27. Isaac Weld, *Travels through the States of North America and the Provinces of Upper and Lower Canada during the years 1795, 1796 and 1797* (London, 1799), pp. 182, 189.

28. Cruikshank, *op. cit.*, i, 56.

29. P. J. Robinson, *Toronto during the French régime* (Toronto, 1933), p. 160.

larly by the Trent valley, but he replied that, from what he could hear of the latter, it was impracticable. He still hoped, however, that some alternative could be found to the dangerous Ottawa route, and mentioned that he had met several persons who had used the Toronto portage. This, he thought, sounded by all accounts quite hopeful.[30]

In 1788 Rocheblave, who had earlier asked for a grant of land at Toronto and along the line of the portage, petitioned for a monopoly of carrying goods from Toronto to Lake Simcoe, by a road to be made. He offered to carry merchants' stores over the thirty miles at 5/- currency per hundredweight and 5/- for every pack of furs. The land committee, to whom this request was passed, decided to refer it to the fur traders.[31] While no result appears to have come from this petition, the road it assumed became one of Simcoe's dearest projects. He went over the whole route to Lake Huron himself, and in 1796 was able to inform the council that Yonge Street was open to the navigable part of the Holland River. Thus the Toronto portage was moved from the line of the Humber east to Yonge Street, but though completed before the end of the century, there is no evidence that it was extensively used for the carriage of furs.

The characteristic tendency of this period was the steady expansion of the fur trade into the north-west and far west, an expansion which necessarily followed the main rivers. The principal routes have already been traced as far as Lake Winnipeg. From there the Saskatchewan River led south and west to join the Red Deer and Bow rivers, and the northern branch into the Rockies beyond the present city of Edmonton. To get to the more northern districts traders could ascend the Saskatchewan River to Pine Island Lake and thence up the Sturgeonweir River to Frog Portage. After crossing the portage they would ascend the Churchill River, with its many difficult rapids and portages to Portage la Loche. This portage was twelve miles long, and at its north end was the Clearwater River, flowing into the Athabasca River, which in turn led to Lake Athabasca, Slave River, Great Slave Lake, and so to the Mackenzie River. At Portage la Loche travellers crossed the height

30. *Report of the Canadian Archives, 1890.* Frobisher to Hamilton, May 2, 1785.
31. *Canadian Archives,* Q 37, p. 269.

of land from the Hudson Bay to the Arctic drainage basin. For a more northerly east-and-west route the Peace River, flowing from the Rockies to Lake Athabasca, was available.

The normal summer conveyance in the country west of Lake Superior was the middle-sized birch canoe, known as the *canot du nord*. For some sections of the west a peculiar type of canoe was used, made of wickerwork, covered with skins. These were apparently less subject to injury and could be made in areas where there was no birch, but they were quite rare. The canoes travelled in "brigades." They were carried over the portages by the bowsman and steersman, each other member of the crew carrying one, or often two, packs of ninety pounds each. John Johnston has left a short account of the mode of portaging packs:

This is done by means of leather straps or thongs the middle of which is broad and fitted to the forehead of the carrier. The first bale or piece is tied so as to lie a little above the *reins*, the second is lifted over the head and deposited, without tying, on the first, and thus loaded, the *engagés* as they are called, trot off to the place chosen for a deposit, which they call a *pose*, and which, in large portages, are from two to three miles apart. This they repeat till the whole is transported, they then set off for the canoe, which they carry on their shoulders. They so go on till night, only stopping once for their meal, and once or twice for lighting their pipes. . . . This is the mode of carrying all over the North-West, to the southward they use horses.[32]

There were two further ways of getting canoes or boats up rapids. In one, known as "tracking," a number of men, depending on the weight of the craft and strength of the current, walked along the bank with ropes, or track lines, attached to their shoulders and to the canoe or boat, while one or two remained on board to guide the craft. In the other, "handling," the men walked in the water beside the canoes.

All the fur-trading concerns used boats or canoes, but the Montreal traders continued to place their faith in the latter. The minutes of the North West Company give the number of craft used at different times. For 1806 there were to be provided 123 altogether, of which seventeen were *canots du maîtres* (for Rainy

32. Masson, *op. cit.*, ii, 165.

Lake), nine were boats, and the remainder *canots du nord*.[33] In 1810 the number was reduced to ninety-two, of which four were bateaux for Fond du Lac (Lake Superior).[34] Many of the canoes were made locally, either by Indians along the route or by the company's servants during the long winters. Some were also made at Three Rivers,

Apart from canoes and boats, other forms of transport were used to some extent. In the southern prairies horses were employed, particularly for portaging. Archibald McLeod, who was stationed at Fort Alexandria on the upper Assiniboine, makes many references to the use of horses for various purposes.[35] In the winter snow-shoes (which were made by the wintering employees or Indian women) and dog teams took the place of river travel. The sledges were made of birch. The movement of goods and furs, however, was confined almost wholly to the summer.

The conduct of the fur trade required a relatively large number of men. According to a report made by McTavish, Frobisher and Company, in 1802, there were 1,058 men employed by the North West Company alone. It is interesting to note that ninety-five of these were in American territory.

As the lines of communication lengthened, the problem of supplying food to the employees became correspondingly difficult, and the transport of food added not a little to the total bill of expense. The canoes in the interior carried food amounting to about one-third of the total load, which necessitated depending on securing further provisions *en route*. Regular supply depots were established throughout the west, and though little food was raised locally, such as there was was a help. Wild rice and fish could be obtained from the Indians, and in some areas game was plentiful. Every trading post was a hunting centre in the winter and the man in charge sometimes used far from mild methods in inducing his Indians or French Canadians to make strenuous efforts to build up a food supply. The general principles were to cut down as far as possible the amount of imported food, and not to burden the fur and supply brigades too heavily with provisions.

33. W. S. Wallace, *Documents relating to the North West Company* (Toronto, 1934), p. 222.

34. *Ibid.*, 264.   35. Gates, *op. cit.*

It remains now to examine in greater detail the inter-relation of Canadian and American traders. The Jay Treaty was followed by more restrictions on trade across the border than there had been before, in spite of the clauses in the treaty which were intended to secure freedom for the fur traders. Notwithstanding this, the Canadian companies—the Michilimackinac[36] and North West Companies—continued to trade in the Mississippi and Missouri area; and according to Astor, annually sold back to the American market furs valued at $400,000; in all, he estimated, three-fourths of the American demand was met by Canadian companies.[37] It can be deduced from this that Canadian traders were cutting into the American trade far more deeply than Americans were into the Canadian. In a memorial written in 1814 by Inglis, Ellice and Company, it is stated that in the years 1770 to 1803 the writers and their Canadian correspondents had annually imported, by way of Lake Michigan, furs to the value of about £150,000 from the Mississippi and Missouri; and £100,000 worth from the Illinois and Ohio valleys by way of Lake Erie.[38] Determined to make a vigorous attempt to control the trade of the American fur areas, Astor used his influence toward passing the Embargo Act of 1807, and founded in 1808 the American Fur Company, chartered by the legislature of New York. He hoped, by means of shorter lines of communication, to cut out Canadian competition.

In spite, however, of the patriotic argument which Astor used in getting his company incorporated, he had always had, and continued to have, close relations with Canadian traders. He offered to buy out the Michilimackinac Company (which by agreement with the North West Company traded in the southern area), but by 1810 the American regulations against British traders led to losses on the part of the Michilimackinac Company, which was in that year sold to two important Montreal firms, McTavish, McGillivray and Company, and Forsyth, Richardson and Company. McGillivray and Richardson then hurried to New York to persuade Astor

36. The Michilimackinac Company was founded about 1784 as the result of an agreement amongst the members of the North West Company to divide the territory. The Michilimackinac Company was to exploit the trade of the south-west.

37. Porter, *op. cit.*, i, 164.

38. Quoted in Davidson, *op. cit.*, p. 296.

to take a share in their new and somewhat doubtful asset. Astor, however, could now afford to starve out the Montreal firms and wait until his own terms were accepted. Gestures of independent trading in the Fond du Lac area brought McGillivray again to New York, where, on behalf of the Michilimackinac Company and the North West Company he made, in January 1811, an agreement with Astor, the result of which was the South West Fur Company.

The purpose behind the establishment of this organization was frankly stated. Some of the goods for the Indian trade could most readily be procured through New York, and others through Montreal. If there were two companies in opposition to each other, one with its headquarters in New York and the other with its headquarters in Montreal, each company would inevitably suffer losses which could be avoided by this combination.[39]

After some preliminary stages the situation would be that the North West Company would keep out of the United States and the South West Company out of British territory, the area west of the Rockies being exempted. On the other hand, the North West Company was given the opportunity of securing one-third of the share in the South West Company owned by Forsyth, Richardson and Company and McTavish, McGillivray and Company (that is, the defunct Michilimackinac Company). The proprietors were somewhat doubtful of the wisdom of this step, both as to "the Boundary Line settled with Mr. Astor" (that is, the international boundary) and to "the Companys entering into or participating in the South Trade."[40] In the end, however, the meeting accepted the proposal, but they still hankered after a more favourable frontier with the United States. In 1814 Inglis, Ellice and Company petitioned Lord Bathurst to make, if possible, some changes in the boundary at the time of the new treaty. They spoke of "errors committed in the Treaties of 1783 and 1796," and made some definite suggestions both as to cession of territory and rights of trade in American territory.[41]

The agreement of 1811 was not quite the end of the story. It appears that the outbreak of war suspended the operation of the

39. Porter, *op. cit.*, i, 253.
40. Wallace, *op. cit.*, p. 268.
41. Quoted in Davidson, *op. cit.*, p. 296.

agreement, and that the North West Company had reëstablished a considerable trade in American territory. Shortly after the war Astor made a new agreement with his former Canadian agents, Forsyth, Richardson and Company, McTavish, McGillivray and Company, and Pierre de Rocheblave to carry on trade with the United States, on joint account for five years. He explained to Monroe that he "agreed to this in Order to get a hold in part of the Trade and under the firm belief that such a law or Regulation [excluding Canadian traders] would be passed by Our Government, as soon as We are in a Situation of carrying on that Trade to the full extent. . . ."[42] It was a very pretty scheme which reached fruition in April 1816, when congress passed a law refusing licenses to any but American citizens, except by direct act of the president. Whether or not Astor inspired this law, it served his purpose well and left him free to deal with only domestic rivals.

Somewhat different was the outcome of the race for the control of the fur trade west of the Rocky Mountains, but this, like the previously described competition, also involved the Astor interests and some of the North West proprietors. The possibilities of fur trade on the Pacific coast were first revealed by expeditions which reached there by sea, but not long afterwards began the long struggle to establish an overland route. In this both Americans and Britishers took part. Alexander Mackenzie had the honour of first reaching the Pacific overland in 1793. Lewis and Clark reached the Columbia in 1804 and pursued it to its mouth. Simon Fraser, like Mackenzie, employed by the North West Company, descended the tumultuous river which is named after him, and so accomplished one of the most remarkable feats in the history of canoeing. After spending several years in preliminary exploration of its upper reaches, David Thompson, another employee of the North West Company, reached the mouth of the Columbia in 1811. By that time Fort Astoria had been built, the first and last evidence of the Pacific Fur Company. Astor had formed this company in 1810 with three Nor'Westers—Alexander McKay, Donald McKenzie and Duncan McDougall—as signatories to the agreement. Such hostages, however, did not protect Astoria from the vigorous competition of the Montreal company. From the first disasters

42. Porter, *op. cit.*, ii, 691.

overtook the Astor concern: Indian attacks, slowness of communication, starvation, Nor'West opposition, and finally the war which made it impossible to relieve the small and beleaguered garrison by sea. Before long the Pacific Fur Company was obliged to sell out its property to the North West Company which thus found itself with an effective monopoly west of the mountains.

While this was in some ways a happy position, the problem of transporting goods and furs all the way between the Pacific slope and Montreal distinctly limited the advantage of greater supply. As soon as the question of routes to the far west arose, it was discussed at the annual meeting of the proprietors in 1809 and decided

that the Trade hereafter to be carried on, to the district beyond the Rocky Mountains, known by the name of Columbia, shall be precisely on the same footing as the trade to Athabaska—that is—that the Canoes for that quarter with the Returns shall come annually to Lac La Pluye, and there take the Outfit, as otherwise it would be attended with too great an Expence to the Compy.[43]

Again in 1811 the problem of route was discussed, arising out of a suggestion by David Thompson that trade should follow the Beaver and Athabasca rivers, but it was decided that this alternative was too expensive and too difficult, and that the old route by the Saskatchewan should continue to be used.[44] From 1814 to 1821 Astoria was supplied and furs were taken out principally by sea.

3. THE ST. LAWRENCE VS. HUDSON BAY.

While the Montreal traders were carrying on an active competition with those from the south, they were, at the same time, engaged in rivalry with the Hudson's Bay Company. For a number of years there was a triangular rivalry, a competition between three outlets of the west. After the agreement between the American Fur Company and the North West Company, and the sale of the Pacific Fur Company, comparative peace settled on the southern front, and the issue narrowed down to a struggle between the bay and the St. Lawrence.

43. Wallace, *op. cit.*, p. 262.
44. *Ibid.*, p. 266.

Even before the fall of New France it had become apparent that the natural advantage afforded to the English company by the bay route to the fur country was offset by the interference of the Canadian traders in the relations between the company and the Indians. After the conquest the enterprise of the Canadians, under their new Anglo-Canadian masters, increased rather than diminished. All the old-established posts were affected by the competition from the "pedlars," and the factors saw their trade gradually being cut off at source. Fewer Indians came to the posts, and those who did grumbled at the distance and demanded higher prices. At York Fort the governor wrote that,

Ye Captains [Indian chiefs] . . . told me plainly that they thought themselves fools for troubling themselves with our goods and half starving themselves in the passage down, and up, when they could have all they wanted brought to their tent doors, and live at ease, that they expected much better payment than last Year, as the Bundles were very heavy, and very little water this Year in the river.[45]

Constant complaints came from Albany. Trade, wrote its governor, was decreasing owing to Indian wars, "and to the very great interruption the Leaders meet with from the Cursed Pedlars up Country, they are very numerous, line every Creek, River & Lake, use great force and are said to have killed several Indians who were coming to trade with us."[46] East Main and Moose were similarly affected, but Churchill, being further to the north, was longer immune. In 1770 the governor wrote that the competition was not yet serious; but five years later the trade was badly down, and the pedlars are given as the main cause of trouble.[47] The briefest description of the situation is that of the factor at Hudson's House, who, in giving an account of the Canadians, wrote: "Where ever an Indian is their are they."[48]

The old expedient of sending agents amongst the Indians to encourage them to bring furs to the bay was still employed, but was manifestly becoming almost useless. It finally became evident that inland posts must be established to compete with those of

45. Archives of the Hudson's Bay Company, York Fort Journal, 1776–1777.
46. *Ibid.*, Letters from Albany, August 28, 1769.
47. *Ibid.*, Letters from Churchill.
48. *Ibid.*, Hudson's House Journal, 1782.

the Canadians. In 1774 Samuel Hearne, fresh from his exploring expeditions to the north, led a party by way of the Hayes River to the Saskatchewan to attempt to compete with the Montreal traders who were active there, and in the course of his travels established Cumberland House. This was the first inland post that had been built by the company since Henley House was put up in 1741, but it was rapidly followed by others. Following the same route, the company built Hudson's House (1776) further up the Saskatchewan, South Branch House (1787) on the South Saskatchewan, and Edmonton House (1795) further west on the North Saskatchewan. To protect the area around Lake Winnipeg, Swan River House was established in 1790 and Brandon House in 1794. By using the Albany River entrance to the interior, the company set up Gloucester House (1777) and Osnaburg House (1786) on the river; and further to the south-east, Brunswick House (1783) and New Brunswick House (1788). Entering by way of the Churchill River into the rich Athabasca country, the company set up Nottingham House on Lake Athabasca in 1802.

This partial list of new posts will serve to indicate the speed and range of the new policy. But having launched this policy, the company was then faced with the problem of transportation. In the old days that problem had not existed, for the trapping Indians either brought their own furs to the posts on the bay, or handed them to Indian middlemen. Now it had become necessary to maintain regular communication with posts hundreds of miles from the bay. Lacking any experience or equipment for inland transportation on a large scale the company first made use of Indians, paying them for their work. In this, as in all transactions with the Indians, cost was reckoned in terms of beaver, which was a standard of value. Such means, however, proved to be most unsatisfactory, as was recognized by the staff at every post. Soon after the foundation of Cumberland House, the governor at York expressed his dissatisfaction with the system.

Bargained with, and paid most of the Indians that are to carry goods to the inland Settlement. Note, Each bundle packed up for Inland weigh on an average, sixty pounds. The lowest bargain I could make, was to pay Six beaver each bundle at the Fort, and that when they delivered their several bundles at Cumberland House (if taken proper care of) they should receive at that place three beavers more for each bundle. Last year when the Indians were totally paid at the Fort, much of your property was embezzled, I therefore thought it prudent to postpone paying the whole, 'till it were seen whether the goods were safely delivered or not. When the Indians came in to view the Bundles, they asked where the brandy was,— did I not intend to send up Brandy? I answered yes, but that the English were to carry it, as the Cags would hurt their shoulders. . . . On the bargain being made they insisted on . . . a little more Brandy. They know, nay, they say, we cannot do without them; and having neither Honour nor generosity: imposition is all they aim at, which nothing can stop except Cannoes enough can be procured with European hands sufficient to navigate them.[49]

The same complaints about the Indians were repeatedly made from the different posts. A further difficulty was that, even when the Indians were willing to carry Hudson's Bay goods, they were said to be molested by the "pedlars." Others came to the same conclusion as the governor of York: that canoes must be obtained, and white men found to paddle them. This need for canoes is stressed in almost every journal and letter of the period. It proved to be hard to get either enough birch-bark or men who were skilled in making canoes. The aid of the Indians was needed for both, and in some cases it was procured; but—seizing the opportunity— they charged high prices for their services, and were liable at any time to desert to the Canadians. Robert Longmoor, chief factor at Hudson's House, learnt the art, and in 1780 launched ten new canoes, "Nine of which is middle sized, one 28 foot long four foot five wide."[50] Small numbers of canoes were built at other posts, and some were bought from the Indians, but the supply long remained inadequate.

Partly because of the scarcity of canoes, partly from the lack of expert canoemen, and partly for their own qualities, boats were used to some extent for inland transport. On the Albany River they could be navigated with ease to Henley House, and, by passing Martin's Falls, as far as Gloucester House. The latter part of the trip, however, proved to be laborious and unsatisfactory. The Churchill River was full of falls and difficult either for canoes or

49. *Ibid.*, York Fort Journal, 1774.
50. *Ibid.*, Hudson's House Journal, 1779–1780.

boats. The main trunk line to the interior was from York Fort to Lake Winnipeg. By the time that the Red River Settlement had been established boats were used between it and York Fort. In the more southern area boats were used to some extent on the Abitibi River to connect the inland posts with Moose Fort, but as early as 1785 the chief factor suggested replacing the boats with canoes, as the boats could in any case go only a part of the way.[51] For some years there was a lively discussion as to whether the company could most profitably use boats or canoes. In the end both were retained, and used according to the character of the waterways. The boats varied greatly in size. Near the bay quite large keel boats were found to be suitable, while further inland light bateaux were better. In 1786 a boat of twenty feet on the keel was finished at Hudson's House.[52] In 1794 a boat of nine tons and a bateau of two tons burden were mentioned as in use on Hill River at York Fort.[53]

Though the problem of the crews was most acute in the case of canoes, there was at first great difficulty in getting men for inland transportation of any kind. Not only did the company's servants lack experience, but they were reluctant to leave the bay, and even higher wages did not altogether remove their objections. One effect of the scarcity of men was that it proved impossible either to get enough goods to the inland posts or to bring down the furs that were collected at them. In 1780, for example, 1,200 made beaver had to be left at Cumberland House "for want of Hands to bring them down."[54] In the same year it was calculated that Hudson's House had lost 16,000 made beaver for want of trading goods.[55] One chief factor wrote:

I am of opinion, this inland trade will be the cause of loss of Goods and great Expences for many Years, until such time as your Servants have acquired (like the Canadians) the knowledge of the Country and methods of carrying up Goods without the assistance of the Natives. The Pedlars are trained up to it, and go in bodies of twenty and thirty men with very

51. *Ibid.*, Letters from Moose Fort, September 27, 1785.
52. *Ibid.*, Hudson's House Journal, 1785–1786.
53. *Ibid.*, General letters, York Fort to London, 1794.
54. *Ibid.*, York Fort Journal, 1779–1780.
55. *Ibid.*

large Canoes. Your Servants are perfect Strangers in both these respects and have everything to learn and provide, but no doubt, in time, they will be able to do it as well as others, at least I see no reason why they should not; though almost all of them have an antipathy to that service, more especially since they have heard of the hardships the men of Gloucester House have met with.[56]

One obvious solution was to hire Canadians for the company's work.[57] Donald McKay, himself a former Nor'Wester, who entered the service of the Hudson's Bay Company in 1790, was sent to Rainy Lake in the same year to get a supply of canoes and Canadians to navigate them.[58] Although complaints were made that the Canadians who were hired were undisciplined, they proved more satisfactory than Orkneymen in work which involved canoe transport. Some years later, in 1810, Colin Robertson, who had been dismissed from the North West Company in the previous year, urged on the Hudson's Bay Company the necessity of enlarging their personnel in the fur country. He was strongly of the opinion that Canadians, though their wages were higher, were far more proficient than Orkneymen. From the tone of his letter it appears that not many Canadians had up to that time been taken into the company's service.[59]

It is quite apparent that the Hudson's Bay Company was not able to build up a transportation system as fast as posts were established in the interior. It remained, therefore, at a great disadvantage in competition with the North West Company. A contemporary account gives a picture of the situation in 1780.

The People of Canada, whose principal commerce arises from the Inland Trade, have studied everything for its convenience, and by long experience have arrived at great perfection in conducting it: having tradesmen on the spot for every branch, some packing the Bales properly for the Canoes, others making baskets, Cases, Rundlets, etc., in which the nicest attention is paid to the stowage and weight. The Canadian peasants also are brought

56. *Ibid.*, Letters from Albany to London, September 17, 1777.

57. There had been individual Canadians in the company's service, but they seem to have been few in number.

58. Archives of the Hudson's Bay Company, Letters from Albany to London, October, 1790.

59. *Ibid.*, London inward correspondence, January 17, 1810.

up to the service from their Infancy, so that a Trader may engage any number of Men ready trained and experienced to his hand. These are all great advantages which Your Honours have not: when a Servant comes first into this service, he is as awkward and clumsy as it is possible to conceive, and by the time he is render'd useful for Inland, he goes home and we have every thing to begin anew. The Canadians pack their Provisions without bone in eight-Gallon Rundlets; ours comes out with all the useless bone (which is a great weight and takes much room) and in casks of 42 Gallons which cannot be carried Inland. Their Cheese is put into wicker baskets just fitted for them, ours comes in Casks, and obliged to be carried quite open: Their Bales are covered with light raven duck, or Russian cloth; ours on the contrary have heavy rotten canvas, and not a sufficiency of that. They have proper light sails for their vessels; I have been obliged to make Sails of Duffle out of the Warehouse. They have coverings of Russia cloth or raven duck painted, to keep their goods dry in their Battaux or canoes, we have nothing at all; so that great part of the time on the journey is spent in opening and drying the Bales, and this must be done in fine weather, which is the properest time for travelling.[60]

The vigorous methods of the North West Company had serious effects on the trade of the Hudson's Bay Company. In 1770 York Fort traded 34,002 made beaver, but by 1776 the total had sunk to 11,188, and by 1785 to 3,725. At first the trade of the inland posts did little toward compensating for the loss at York and other bay forts, but gradually the totals began to rise again, though never to the previous heights. In spite of the multiplication of posts, the total trade of the company tended to fall during the period of most active rivalry.[61] The effect of competition was to some extent reflected in the dividends paid by the Hudson's Bay Company. From 1763 to 1778 there was an annual dividend of ten per cent; from 1779 to 1782 it was reduced to eight per cent; from 1783 to 1785 (after York and Churchill had been destroyed by a French squadron) no dividend was paid; from 1786 to 1800 it varied between five and eight per cent; and from 1801 until 1821 it was four per cent, except in the years 1809 to 1814 when

60. *Ibid.*, Letters from Albany to London, 1780.
61. Total trade, in made beaver, was: 1797, 95,144; 1798, 87,586; 1799, 89,289; 1800, 85,201; 1801, 94,105; 1802, 80,380; 1803, 63,328; 1804, 64,711; 1805, 68,990; 1806, 74,943; 1807, 81,007; 1808, 78,792 (Letters from York Fort to London, and Minutes)

no dividend was paid, largely on account of the loss of the European
market during the operation of Napoleon's continental system.

The Hudson's Bay Company suffered from the combined results
of competition and weaker technique inland: on the other hand,
it survived the storm better than might have been expected. That
it was able to do so was owing partly to improved technique, but
principally to its lower transportation costs. By the early nineteenth century the inland transportation methods of the two companies were similar, if not quite the same. Their total transportation systems—from England to the inland posts—were, however,
different. The North West Company was obliged to carry goods
by canoe all the way from Montreal to the fur country, whereas
the Hudson's Bay Company had the advantage of a seaway to
the interior of the continent. This difference was reflected in the
proportions which they charged to inland transportation. The
Nor'Westers drew up a schedule in 1804 which called for an advance
of 23 per cent at Kaministiquia above the Montreal price. From
there, taking the average of classes of goods carried, the advance
(that is, on the Kaministiquia price) was as follows: to Fond du
Lac department, 55 per cent; to the Nipigon department, 87 per
cent; to Rainy Lake and Lake Winnipeg, 87 per cent; to the
English River department, 113 per cent; to the Upper Athabasca
River, 123 per cent; and to Athabasca and dependencies, 130 per
cent.[62] These figures were later somewhat reduced, but continued
to be based on distance. In contrast to these charges are those of
the Hudson's Bay Company. A ten per cent advance was made on
the prices at the bay forts for cost of carriage to posts within their
districts, and a further ten per cent to any post beyond the outlet
of Lake Winnipeg.[63] William McGillivray stated that the Hudson's
Bay Company was able to carry goods to the interior at less than
half the cost of the North West Company,[64] but it also appears
that their rates were less strictly based on distance.

As the fur trade extended further to the west and north the
lines of communication with Montreal correspondingly lengthened.
This was the vulnerable spot of the North West Company, and its

62. Wallace, op. cit., p. 197.
63. Archives of the Hudson's Bay Company, Minutes, May 2, 1810.
64. Wallace, op. cit., p. 328.

members began to feel ever more acutely that they were at a disadvantage as compared with the Hudson's Bay Company. In 1794 Alexander Mackenzie again pointed out this uncomfortable fact; and before the end of the century the Nor'Westers determined to attempt—as Radisson and Groseilliers had done before them—to secure an outlet through the bay. In 1799 William McGillivray suggested to Thomas, the governor of Moose Fort, that each company should abandon certain posts in that area. After putting his request on the ground of mutual advantage, he added this threat:

If notwithstanding these our sincere wishes to fix the Trade on an amicable and advantageous footing as we conceive for both parties, it should still be the determination of your Company to persist in pushing it so much on our side; we are resolved to send Goods to Moose Fort and other Posts of the Bay next season and if from experience we find ourselves under any disadvantage from the long communication through which these Goods must pass we must have recourse to a shorter and easier mode of sending the necessary supplies of Merchandize for the Trade to the Bay.[65]

Receiving only an acknowledgment from Thomas, McGillivray wrote two or three times to the secretary of the company in London, but got no reply. Determined to cut the Gordian knot, the Nor'Westers then sent a ship to the bay in the summer of 1803, built a post on Charlton Island and made preparations to trade. Apparently, however, the venture was not a success, for they returned to the method of negotiation. Early in 1804 they obtained the opinion of two counsel that the Hudson's Bay Company's charter was invalid, on the ground that the king could not grant a monopoly of trade without the consent of parliament. Reserving this argument, the North West Company made, in 1804, through Edward Ellice, an offer to buy the stock of the Hudson's Bay Company for £103,000, but the offer was refused. Further abortive negotiations followed, and then at the end of 1805 McGillivray and Forsyth proposed these terms:

1st The North West Company will establish a communication thro' Hudson's Bay to the interior or Indian country commonly called the

65. Archives of the Hudson's Bay Company, London inward correspondence, W. McGillivray to Governor Thomas, September 1, 1799.

North West, at, or about York Factory—through which they will freely transport their effects, backwards and forwards, by land and by water, without hindrance or molestation.

2nd In consideration of which they agree to pay to the Hudson's Bay Company the annual sum of £2,000 for 7 years.

3dly They will withdraw their present posts from James's Bay, and

4thly They will bind themselves during the above period to relinquish the whole Trade of the Coast to the Hudson's Bay Company and to establish no post nearer the Sea in any direction (the above communication only excepted) than such situations as are now actually occupied by them.[66]

This offer, too, was refused, and for a few years the negotiations lapsed. In 1811 the Nor'Westers again took up the issue, though at this time they appear not to have mentioned navigation of the bay, but only a division of territory. Reinforced by authority to buy £15,000 of Hudson's Bay stock, the North West Company's agents began negotiations by offering to abandon six departments using 150 men and gathering furs to the annual value of £15,000.[67] The committee of the Hudson's Bay Company agreed in principle to a division of territory, but asked for the whole land given by their charter.[68] This impossible condition ended the discussion.

Both companies were now suffering severely from competition, but on the whole the Nor'Westers were faring worse. In 1811 their trunk line from Montreal to the west was threatened by the arrival of Selkirk's settlers, who were to be placed right across their only line of communications. Not content with this, the governor of the Red River Colony issued two proclamations in 1814, one forbidding the export of any food from the area of the Selkirk grant, and the other ordering the servants of the North West Company to evacuate their post at the forks of the Red River within six months.[69] The Nor'Westers were now threatened on

66. *Ibid.*, McGillivray and Forsyth to Hudson's Bay Company, November 27, 1805.

67. *Ibid.*, McTavish, Fraser and Company, Inglis, Ellice and Company, and Alexander Mackenzie to the Governor of the Hudson's Bay Company, June 3, 1811.

68. *Ibid.*, Hudson's Bay Company to McTavish, Fraser and Company, etc., July 24, 1811.

69. Canadian Archives, Q 133, p. 58.

all sides. They tried to drive out the settlers from the Red River by main force, and for a time succeeded. At the same time they found that their passage through Lake Superior was threatened on account of the war, and, on that ground, petitioned the British government for permission to use the Hudson Bay route. They pointed out that from Lake Winnipeg to Montreal was 2,500 miles, but to Hudson Bay only 350.[70] The petition was referred to the Hudson's Bay Company. Berens, the governor, replied in cold and pure business prose that his company had no wish to take advantage of a temporary condition, but on the other hand it was only proper that a competitor should not be allowed more than justice.

We request Your Lordship to observe that the privilege of transporting their Furs and Trading Goods through Hudson's Bay, even for the present year would be attended by direct pecuniary profit to the North West Company, as being a much shorter and easier access than they have hitherto had from Montreal by way of Lake Superior; that circuitous and difficult Route has occasion'd an annual Expence of probably more than £10,000 which they would save by passing through Hudson's Bay. The Advantages which they would derive by an Early Market for their Furs in place of having to keep them in the interior, until the route through Canada may be open, is still of greater value to them; but it is far from our intention to take the difficulties under which the North West Company labour as the measure of the compensation to which we may be entitled; Yet, as their means of opposing us in the Trade will thus be very considerably increased, we think we are bound in Duty to our proprietors to require that such compensation shall be secured to the Hudson Bay Company for the permission so granted, for the present year, as may under all circumstances of the case be considered just and reasonable.[71]

The Hudson's Bay Company held the trump card, but they would not make the mistake of holding it too long. They were feeling the strain of the competition and were ready to make a compromise. In return for a recognition of their chartered rights, and exclusive trade in that area, they were prepared to abandon the Athabasca district; moreover, they would concede to the North West Com-

70. *Ibid.*, Q 130-2, p. 281.
71. *Ibid.*, Q 130–1, p. 66, J. Berens to Bathurst, March 23, 1814.

pany passage from the bay to Lake Winnipeg in consideration
either of money rent or the relinquishment of additional territory.[72]
In the meanwhile, and further to induce the Nor'Westers toward
a conciliatory policy, Colin Robertson had gone to New York in
the spring, where he made an agreement with Astor that the latter
should harass the Canadian traders as much as possible. "An
attack," he wrote, "properly conducted on the South will enable
us to conquer with more ease in the North." "This", he added
significantly, "is the period for turning the channel of the Fur
Trade from the St. Lawrence to the Hudson's Bay therefore
nothing ought to be left undone to accomplish this Grand Object."[73]

Throughout the next five years attempts were made by both
companies to get an official decision on the validity of the charter
of 1670, and at the same time both companies expressed a general
willingness to effect a division of territory. The pace was telling
on both concerns, but more especially on the North West Company.
Peter Fidler made a report on the affairs of the latter for 1820–21
in which he expressed the belief that "they are now on their last
legs." They were, he said, feeling the competition in the Athabasca
country, and he doubted if they could keep going for four years.
"Upon the whole from their Conduct we have good reason to
think that some sudden change will take place with them."[74]

That change came soon enough. Negotiations were started in
London by Edward Ellice, Simon McGillivray and William
McGillivray with the committee of the Hudson's Bay Company.
The latter, though they had long been ready for some arrangement, were able to put the Nor'Westers in the position of having to
ask for terms; for the firms making up "the concern" were for the
most part on the verge of bankruptcy. The union of the companies
was provided for in a deed of March 26, 1821. The united company
was to take the name of the Hudson's Bay Company. Each party
to the agreement was to provide an equal amount of capital, and
bear half the expense. The "clear gains and profits" were to be

72. Archives of the Hudson's Bay Company, London inward correspondence,
"Copy of instructions to Lord Selkirk respecting any treaty with the North West
Company," August 30, 1815.

73. *Ibid.*, Colin Robertson to Wedderburn, March 14, 1815.

74. *Ibid.*, Report on Manitoba district, 1820–21, by Peter Fidler.

divided.[75] The McGillivrays and Ellice agreed to protect the governor and company against claims made by other Nor'Westers, and not to interfere with the company's charter rights. In 1824 some changes were made by a further deed, in which the co-partnership was dissolved, and the capital held by the McGillivrays and Ellice became capital of the Hudson's Bay Company.[76]

By the union of 1821 the long struggle between the North West Company and the Hudson's Bay Company was terminated, and, what is especially pertinent to this study, the competition of the two routes—by the St. Lawrence and Hudson Bay—came to an end. The reorganized Hudson's Bay Company adopted Norway House, at the junction of Lake Winnipeg and the Nelson River, as the centre of its transportation system; and while Montreal became one of the company's districts, and there remained for a time a regular canoe route by way of the Ottawa River, York Factory became the main port of entry for goods and of export for furs. The chief officers of the company were henceforth in London, and there policy was made and the affairs of the company directed.

Under these new conditions the trade in furs continued after 1821; but in the meanwhile other industries had been fast developing, and transportation was being organized in eastern Canada to meet the growing needs. The great day of the fur traders passed before the middle of the nineteenth century, but the fur trade, and all that it involved, was of great significance in the development of transportation and for the economic life of Canada in general. *Pro pelle cutem*, wrote the Hudson's Bay men with brief irony as their motto. To seek the valuable peltries generations of adventurers risked their lives in the unknown western country, and in following their profession tried out, with a speed that would not otherwise have been attempted, the network of waterways that offered the only means of travel across a great and untenanted empire.

75. The division was as follows: Hudson's Bay Company, 20 shares; North West Company, 20 shares; Chief factors and traders, 40 shares; Hudson's Bay Company (for arrangements with Selkirk's representatives), 5 shares; S. McGillivray and Edward Ellice (compensation for loss of agency) 5 shares; Hudson's Bay Company, 5 shares; North West Company, 5 shares.
76. From the original deeds in the Archives of the Hudson's Bay Company.

Many pens have in all generations written of the romance, the adventures, the triumphs and failures, the hardships, the sordidness and the glamour of the life of the men who followed the trail of the beaver. Agents have left their diaries and letters, written often in the dirt and cold of a winterer's post or on some unmapped trail that led to disaster or to success. Later, in the libraries and the archives of the world, scholars have sought to reconstruct the western scene and bring back to life an age of which only faint echoes remain. Too much stress, perhaps, has been laid on the romantic side and too little on the darker side: the reckless slaughter of the fur-bearing animals, the exploitation and debauchery of the Indians, the brutalizing influence on the white man. One reads much of the gaily-dressed *voyageur*, with his ready song and love of his work; less of the hardship, privation and death that too often attended his trips. A cheerful fellow, the *voyageur;* yet McGillivray wrote of an exhausted steersman who fell out of his canoe while asleep, and whom the following canoes callously left to drown. Lines of crosses marked the graves of *voyageurs* who had attempted to run rapids, or who had, after a portage, set their canoe back in the water too close to the suction of the falls. The discipline at the posts of the interior was often brutal, and here, too, there was more than one case of starvation. While putting it down to the pressure of competition, all the trading companies supplied the Indians with liquor, which acted as a strong drug on a people unaccustomed to it.

But be the proportions of good and evil as they may, the influence of the fur trade on the development of communications and economic growth was enormous. Opposed as they were to agricultural settlements, the traders were yet forced to initiate farming to relieve the carriage of food, and left many of their numbers in the west, who, in retirement, turned from necessity to grow their own provisions. Still more important was the opening of the country. No great settlement came until the day of the railway, but until the 'seventies transport in the Canadian west followed with slight variations the lines laid down by the adventurers of Hudson Bay and Montreal.

The triangular rivalry in the fur trade had centred around three of the great entrances to the continent. The pressure of it had forced the Montreal firms to come together in the North West Company, enabling them to carry on for a time a successful competition with both American traders and Hudson's Bay men. But when the Hudson's Bay Company carried the war into the enemy country by building up their own transportation routes into the interior, the cost of the long carriage to Montreal became more than the trade would bear. The efforts of the Nor'Westers to obtain rights on the bay having failed, they were driven into insolvency by transportation costs at a time when they were most aggressive and enterprising in the conduct of the trade. The collapse of the Montreal trade brought to an end a picturesque, and in many ways a remarkable, phase in the history of Canada. "The lords of the lakes and forests have passed away," wrote Washington Irving. In the St. Lawrence valley, the cradle of the fur traders, a new phase had already begun. Pioneer farmers and merchants were calling for new modes of transportation to meet their growing needs.

CHAPTER III

SAIL AND STEAM

1. COMMERCE AND WATER COMMUNICATION.

THE virtual disappearance of the fur trade from the St. Lawrence was a severe blow to the merchants of Montreal; and had the population and economy of Canada remained static up to 1821, it would have been a crushing blow. The forty years previous to the union of the fur-trading companies, however, had seen important additions to the population of the province and to the diversity of its commercial interests. When the first group of "pedlars" came to Canada on the morrow of Wolfe's victories they found themselves a tiny minority with interests differing from, and often clashing with, those of the army officers, British officials, and French-speaking majority. It was they who reorganized the Montreal fur trade. Following the American revolution their numbers were swelled by the *emigrés* from the United States, and the trade was conducted on a larger and more elaborate scale. At the same time came other immigrants who carved out farms or built towns in the western part of the province. As the fur trade had become more complex, firms grew up to supply the traders with the goods and provisions that they required. With the establishment of settlements such firms grasped the opportunity of building up a general trading and forwarding business, finding customers in the St. Lawrence and Lake Ontario colonists, and using the water route which they already knew well.

Immigration on a serious scale began during the American revolutionary war. After the outbreak of hostilities, and more particularly after the declaration of independence, Tories began to migrate to Nova Scotia, Canada, and other British territories. The trickle of exiles who made their way to Canada during the war grew to a steady stream immediately after the peace of 1783. Loyalist regiments were given tracts of land, and civilians came in groups or single families. For years after the treaty, immigrants continued to come from the United States, encouraged by the official policy of building up the population of the upper province. Of those who came to Canada—perhaps ten thousand in all—the greatest number were placed on land in the western part of the province (now Ontario). These United Empire Loyalists, as they came to be called, settled along the upper St. Lawrence, and on the shores of Lake Ontario. Kingston grew from its modest beginnings as the French fort of Cataraqui to be for some years the principal town of western Canada. Other towns were started at points along the lake where rivers made harbours: York (Toronto), on the site of another French fort and trading post, became the chief of these. At the western end of Lake Ontario, Newark (Niagara on the Lake) was one of the earliest towns and the first capital of Upper Canada. Between and behind the towns lay the new farms, hewn out of virgin forest, and ever pushing the frontier further back from the St. Lawrence and the lake.

Another war came to an end in 1815, and led to such conditions in the United Kingdom as favoured emigration on a comparatively large scale. The post-war depression and the industrial revolution made the lot of many Britishers so hard that they braved the discomforts of the long voyage on the often shamefully crowded immigrant ships to Quebec. On its side, the government of Upper Canada[1] encouraged immigration from Britain, partly to swell the population and partly because disloyalty in some districts during the war of 1812 led to less enthusiasm for American immigrants. In many cases families went to join friends or relatives already there, and so great became the interest in the possibilities of the new world that a whole new literature in the form of diaries, letters, and guides for emigrants, in large part still preserved, began to appear.

The growth in population was not startling: the census of 1824 shows 150,066 persons in Upper Canada. But this was not an unimpressive population for a land which had, a generation earlier, been peopled by some ten thousand inhabitants. By 1830 the

1. From 1763 to 1774 the province of Quebec stretched as far west as the Ottawa River. In 1774 it was extended to the Mississippi and the Ohio. The treaty of Paris (1783) cut off the south-western section. In 1791 the old province of Quebec was divided into Upper and Lower Canada, the boundary being approximately the Ottawa River.

numbers had risen to 213,156, and the last census of the separate province of Upper Canada (1840) shows 432,159 persons. To Lower Canada there had been little immigration for a variety of reasons: good land was not so readily available; the people, the laws, and the customs were alien to the British-born immigrants; and the official policy discouraged immigrants from stopping east of the Ottawa River. Only in Montreal and the "eastern townships" (south of the St. Lawrence) were there large numbers of British people. But by natural increase the population of Lower Canada grew rapidly. In 1831 it was reported as 553,134, and the next available figure is that for 1844, of 697,084 persons.[2]

The needs of this new population grew with its steadily increasing size, extent, and variety of interest. The economy soon became comparatively diversified; and as Simcoe, the first lieutenant-governor of Upper Canada, found in 1794, the day when all interest centred in furs was past. In that year he wrote from Kingston:

On my arrival at Kingston I found it improved beyond my expectations; many stores for Merchandize and wharfs had been built and new ones were in contemplation, I also found the language of the Merchants very much altered—The Fur Trade, as I had hoped, seem'd no longer the principal object of their attention: They look forward to the produce of their Country as the true source of their Wealth; the Lands are rising universally in price; and nothing seems to be wanting but the introduction of some British Capitals and an intercourse with other Merchants than those, who are merely conversant in the monopoly of the fur trade, to encrease the Wealth and traffic of this Country to a very important degree.[3]

Simcoe fully sympathized with the emphasis put by the early immigrants on communications. "I mean", he wrote in 1791, "to establish a capitol in the very heart of the Country, upon the River La Tranche [Thames] which is navigable for batteaux for 150 miles —and near to where the Grand River which falls into Erie, and others that communicate with Huron and Ontario, almost inter-lock."[4] His letters are laden with projects for canals, improvement of

2. See Census of Canada, 1870–1871, iv.

3. E. A. Cruikshank, The Correspondence of Lieut-Governor Sir John Graves Simcoe (Toronto, 1923–1931), iii, 228.

4. Ibid., i, 18.

navigation, and the establishment of settlements on waterways. It was, indeed, apparent from the first that water must primarily be depended on for communications. Road building was not ignored, but in a land of forests and sparse settlements, it could not be hoped that through roads could be built for some years. In any case the rivers and lakes offered an unique opportunity for water transport. Here the experience of the fur traders was only partially of value. Their canoes were not suitable for other purposes, and their pioneer transportation system in the northwest was not yet of significance to Canada. There remained the shipping on the Great Lakes, which they had done much to stimulate; and the exploration of some of the inland waterways of Ontario.

Much was written at the time, and more has since been written, on the life of the pioneer districts of Upper Canada. The farms were to a large extent self-sufficient, and a primitive-subsistence agriculture was followed which left little room for the export of products. But there was in British Canada a strong strain of North American economic growth. The tiny towns, invading a few acres of the limitless forest, were well sprinkled with men of a commercial turn, who were not content with taking in each other's washing, but looked about for profitable and expanding fields of business enterprise. To these the harbours, on which most of the towns were built, offered the essential means of communication. Even the farmers found an early export market for potash, obtained as a by-product from the burning of trees in the clearing of the land. Lumber was a natural article for export, and modest quantities of wheat began to be sent abroad. In 1788 the old province of Quebec, as shown by the customs house books, exported goods to the value of £94,870. Much the largest item in this was 200,400 bushels of wheat, valued at £40,000; next came various types of lumber, valued at £12,500, and 9,900 barrels of flour worth £11,000. Furs are not included in this list.[5]

There is a most penetrating comment on the relation between the commercial life of Upper Canada and the existing communications in a letter written by Richard Cartwright from Kingston in 1792.

5. Canadian Archives, Q 57–1, p. 53.

To what is to be ascribed the present state of improvement and population of this country. Certainly not to its natural advantages, but to the liberality which Government has shewn towards the loyalists who first settled it; to the money spent by the numerous garrisons and public departments established amongst us; and the demand for our produce which so many unproductive consumers occasion on the Spot. As long as the British Government shall think proper to hire people to come over to eat our flour, we shall go on very well, and continue to make a figure, but when once we come to export our produce, the disadvantages of our remote inland situation will operate in their full force, and the very large portion of the price of our produce that must be absorbed by the expense of transporting it to a place of exportation, and the enhanced value that the same cause must add to every article of European manufacture, will give an effectual check to the improvement of the country beyond a certain extent; the further we go, the more powerfully must these causes operate; and when we go beyond the banks of Lake Ontario, it will cost as much to bring our rude produce to market as it will be worth. . . .[6]

The main water routes followed for passengers and freight showed no changes until the period when canals were built. Westward from Montreal the St. Lawrence, in spite of its many rapids, had to be followed to Lake Ontario which offered uninterrupted navigation for two hundred miles. The Niagara portage was slow and expensive, but served as a link with Lake Erie. Northward from Lake Ontario ran the chain of rivers and lakes in the Trent valley, and further west was the old Toronto portage route leading, by way of Lake Simcoe to Georgian Bay and Lake Huron.

The types of early rowing and sailboats used in Canada fall into two classes: the open boat propelled by oars, poles and sails, and the various kinds of sailing ships that plied the Great Lakes. Open boats, again, were of two types: the bateau and the Durham boat.

Bateaux were sharp at both ends, wall-sided and flat-bottomed except for a slight inclination upward in the bottom at each end. They had generally a crew of five men, four to row and one to steer, and were equipped with square sails, oars and long poles for setting them through the rapids. The earlier type of bateau carried about three tons of merchandise or

6. Cruikshank, *op. cit.*, i, 238.

thirty-five barrels of flour. Subsequently, however, these vessels were built much larger, their carrying capacity being from four to four and a half tons.[7]

The bateau, of course, was a legacy from the French régime. The Durham boat, on the other hand, seems to have been an American invention and is said to have been introduced to the St. Lawrence in 1809. It was "a long, shallow, nearly flat-bottomed boat propelled by means of poles, and because of its larger size materially lessened the use of the bateau in the carrying trade."[8] Cousins describes them as "flat-bottomed barges with a keel or centre-board and a rounded bow," and adds that their carrying capacity was ten times that of the bateau. He says that there were, in 1835, eight hundred Durham boats and fifteen hundred bateau used in the St. Lawrence traffic above Montreal.[9]

The bateau and the Durham boat were types of river boats which could be rowed, poled, or sailed; were not unduly expensive to build; and could be used on the lakes to some extent. No doubt they varied greatly in size. Other types were found in lesser numbers. The Kentucky boat—a large, covered river boat, chiefly used on the western rivers of the United States—was at least tried in Canada. "Mr. Clark", wrote Robert Nicol to John Askin in 1801, "is building a Kentucky boat [at Kingston]—It will (I imagine) be the first Boat of the kind that ever descended the St. Lawrence and interests all the mercantile people of this part of the country very much."[10] A month later came further news: "Mr. Clark . . . arrived at Montreal with his Ark containing 340 Barrels Flour in 10 Days from Kingston, and he has proceeded with it to Quebec. He is much pleased with the Mode of conveyance. . . ."[11] The success of this voyage does not seem to have led to further "Arks" being built; but one other American type of vessel, the Schenectady boat, was used to some extent. Schenectady boats were similar to bateaux, but usually rather small.

7. Adam Shortt and A. G. Doughty (eds.), *Canada and its provinces* (Toronto, 1914), x, 489.
8. *Ibid.*, x, 490.
9. G. V. Cousins, "Early transportation in Canada" (*University Magazine*, viii).
10. M. M. Quaife (ed.), *The John Askin Papers* (Detroit, 1928–1931), ii, 343.
11. *Ibid.*, ii, 353.

The bateau and the Durham boat were particularly adapted to the rapids of the St. Lawrence, and were used exclusively before the earliest canals were opened. In these boats the United Empire Loyalists and other early immigrants were taken to Upper Canada. In neither was the voyage up the St. Lawrence an easy one. At rapids the passengers and goods had to be disembarked, and the boat propelled up by means of the setting poles, towed up along the bank on a track line, or pulled over the rocks on small logs. Any one of the modes was hard and dangerous work, and the crews required skill and strength comparable to those of the bark canoes. In coming down the river the rapids could be run, which again required great skill. In daytime the immigrants were cramped and unprotected from the sun, and at night they were put on shore, to sleep in barns or houses if they were lucky, but more often in the open. From Lachine (to which passengers from Montreal and at least half of the cargo were carried in waggons) to Kingston at the head of the river took, according to Bouchette, ten to fourteen days; and three or four for the return down stream. Bateaux and Durham boats were also the normal means of carrying freight to and from Montreal and the upper country. The voyage on these boats, both in the river and on the lakes, was slow and hazardous, as many contemporary accounts testify. It was not uncommon for the boats to break their tow lines in the rapids and be drawn into the current, or to be caught and overturned by a sudden squall on the lakes. According to Simcoe, the rates charged were "extravagant"; and from this he argued that the St. Lawrence must be improved. The cost of transporting a barrel from Lachine to Kingston was $3 to $3.50, and from Kingston to Montreal about $1.[12] As the St. Lawrence canals were opened it became a simpler task to take the boats up the river.

While the bateau and the Durham boat were well suited to the St. Lawrence, keeled and decked sailing vessels were best adapted for navigation of the Great Lakes. In the early days of English rule the control of such vessels was in the hands of either the government or the fur traders.[13] One of the first large schooners to be used for general purposes was the *Kingston Packet* of seventy

12. E. C. Guillet, *Early days in Upper Canada* (Toronto, 1933), pp. 424, 426.
13. *See above*, pp. 31-32.

tons, which was advertised in 1795 as sailing from Kingston to Niagara and other ports on Lake Ontario, carrying freight or passengers.[14] Evidently, however, the number of boats at the end of the century was still inadequate, for in 1797 Peter Russell, then acting as administrator of the province, complained that "York is . . . isolated and difficult of access, from bad roads and the reduction of the Lake Marine, which . . . can now but seldom be spared to visit York. . . ."[15] Progress was slow in commercial vessels, and until the end of the War of 1812–15 lake shipping was dominated by armed boats. It has been estimated that in 1811 the total private tonnage on Lake Ontario was only 1,100 tons; and that one-third of the vessels paying duty at Niagara and York were sailing under the American flag.[16] The end of the war, and the reduction of the navies under the Rush-Bagot Agreement, introduced a new period in which merchant shipping came into its own and rapidly increased. Sailing vessels came to be counted by the hundred.

Types of rigging and hull varied. On the whole the naval vessels used a square rig, and the merchantmen either a fore and aft rig or a compromise such as the brigantine and the barquentine. A large square sail was valuable to take advantage of the long runs down the lakes before the west wind. Some of the schooners were large and handsome. Special types of boats, blunt and shallow, were evolved for use in canals.[17] Navigation on the Great Lakes involved many hazards, particularly in early days before lighthouses and buoys had been installed. One of the worst disasters was the loss of the snow *Ontario* with all hands in Lake Ontario in 1780.

As settlement, industry, and agriculture increased, so did the number of sailing vessels on the lakes. They carried passengers, lumber, potash, and other freight; and the steady demand for new

14. *Quebec Gazette*, February 26, 1795.

15. Canadian Archives, Q 283, p. 99.

16. E. A. Cruikshank, "Notes on the history of shipbuilding and navigation on Lake Ontario up to . . . 1816" (*Ontario Historical Society, Papers and Records*, xxiii).

17. For descriptions of boats and rigging *see* G. A. Cuthbertson, *Freshwater* (Toronto, 1931), ch. xi.

vessels led to a thriving ship-building industry at many of the lake ports. Regular services were developed between Canadian, or Canadian and American ports, and vessels carrying either flag might be seen on either side of the international boundary. But travel was not without its risks and delays. One unfortunate traveller, on his way from Detroit to Montreal in 1810, picked up a boat at Niagara bound for Kingston. The vessel called at York to unload salt, whereupon the captain delayed for ten days on a visit to his wife. After this unfortunate start, they reached Kingston only to be driven to sea by an unfavourable wind and found themselves outside Oswego. There, after eight days, the captain announced that he had taken on a cargo for York, so the patient traveller embarked on an American vessel bound for Montreal. After weathering a storm, they finally arrived at Ogdensburg, but receiving news there that the price of cider in Montreal had fallen, the captain decided to turn back, and the traveller had to wait for a third boat.   At last—on the forty-ninth day after leaving Detroit —the unhappy man reached Montreal, ill and exhausted.[18]

Steamships were first used early in the nineteenth century, but it was long before they superseded or even seriously rivalled the sailing vessels. In 1863 there were 1,040 schooners on the Great Lakes, in addition to 337 boats of other rigs.[19] In the harbour of Montreal there were, in 1851, 468 river steamships with a tonnage of 91,488 as compared to 3,141 river sailing vessels with a tonnage of 221,695; and in 1866 there were 1,067 steamships with a tonnage of 196,330 as against 4,016 sailing vessels with a tonnage of 417,349.[20] In canals the steamship had many advantages, but even there the sailing vessels long held their own. In the year 1889, 820 steamships and 1,141 sailing vessels, all Canadian owned, passed through the Welland Canal. The comparable figures for the St. Lawrence canals are 3,098 as against 5,696; and for the Rideau Canal, 1,114 as against 1,120.[21]

Yet the days of the sailing ship were numbered. In recent years

18. M. M. Quaife, "From Detroit to Montreal in 1810" (*Canadian Historical Review*, xiv, 3).

19. Guillet, *op. cit.*, p. 463.

20. *Canada sessional papers*, 1867–1868, no. 8, p. 407.

21. *Ibid.*, 1890, no. 19B, p. 94.

many small schooners carried stone and coal into the ports of Lake Ontario, but those, too, have gone. Gradually the uncertain, smoky steamer was developed into an efficient and adaptable means of transportation, and the picturesque schooners faded from the scene.

2. STEAMBOATS.

The Steam Boat, which was built at Montreal last winter, arrived here [Quebec] on Saturday last, being her first trip. She was sixty-six hours on the passage, of which she was at anchor 30; so that 36 hours is the time which, in her present state, she takes from Montreal to Quebec. On Sunday last she went up against wind and tide from Brehaut's wharf to Lymburner's; but her progress was very slow. It is obvious that her machinery, at present, has not sufficient force for this River; but there can be no doubt of the possibility of perfecting it . . . and it would be a public loss should the proprietors be discouraged from persevering in their undertaking.[22]

The steamboat was the *Accommodation*, built at Montreal for John Molson and equipped with a six-horse-power motor. This first steamboat in British North America was put in the water in 1809, eight years after the first pioneer steamer in Great Britain and two years after Fulton's *Clermont* went under steam from New York to Albany. Four and one-half miles per hour is not perhaps an impressive speed down stream, but it was the possibilities in this new mode of transport that made such a strong appeal to the people of Canada. Molson, an energetic merchant of Montreal, asked for a monopoly of steamship service between Montreal and Quebec, and a bill granting it was passed by the assembly but thrown out by the legislative council. The little engine of the *Accommodation* proved too weak to push her up against the current, and a new boat, the *Swiftsure*, with a 28-horse-power engine, was launched for Molson in 1811. In the next seven years he added to his line of steamers, the St. Lawrence Steamboat Company, the *Malsham*, *Car of Commerce* and *Lady Sherbrooke*. In 1816 the steamboats made the trip from Montreal to Quebec in twenty-four hours, and up stream from Quebec to Montreal in thirty-six to forty hours. The charge from Montreal to Quebec was then $10 per passenger, but was subsequently greatly reduced. In the same year the *Car of Commerce* was reported as landing seventy passengers and 350 tons

22. *Quebec Gazette*, November 8, 1809.

of freight at Montreal on one trip;[23] and the *Malsham* carried from Quebec to Montreal a battalion of soldiers and eighty civilians, amounting to over nine hundred persons, with luggage.[24] In 1818 the *Car of Commerce* broke this record by bringing 1,380 settlers from Quebec to Montreal.[25] The *Quebec Gazette* greeted the new mode of transport:

> The Navigation by means of Steam on the Rivers and Coasts of the United States, is now become so common, and the facility of conveyance rendered so certain, that it is likely the ancient system of navigation in short voyages will before long be abolished. The bosom of the St. Lawrence already affords a striking proof, that such an idea is not ill founded. The Steam Boats have already ruined the prospects of the old River Craft, many of which long ago ought to have been condemned as unfit to receive the property of the merchant.[26]

Molson's line was opposed by one powerful rival, John Torrance and Company of Montreal, who ran the *Hercules* (100 horse-power) from 1826, and subsequently added the *St. George, British American,* and *Canada*. Further additions were made by these and other companies, so that steamship travel on the St. Lawrence became common. A steam ferry between Quebec and Lévis was also introduced, the boat giving an hourly service. There was another curious kind of craft introduced on the St. Lawrence called a "team boat," and intended as a cheaper form of ferry. A team boat was, like the steamers, operated by paddle wheels, but these were made to revolve by driving horses around in a deck house. In 1819, after a number of failures, at least one team boat, the *Edmund*, plied regularly between Cross and Longueuil.

In 1819 the first steamboat, the *Ottawa*, was introduced on the Ottawa River. She was built at the head of the Long Sault and provided with the first engine made in Canada.[27] Further steamers were added on the river, some of which used the Rideau Canal. In the same year—ten years after the launching of the *Accommodation*—the editor of the *Quebec Gazette* counted fifteen steamers in

23. *Ibid.*, June 15, 1816.
24. Montreal *Herald*, quoted in *Quebec Gazette*, August 15, 1816.
25. *Quebec Gazette*, August 10, 1818.
26. *Ibid.*, July 25, 1816.
27. *Ibid.*, October 25, 1819.

Canadian waters, three of them being American-owned.[28] The majority of these were on the St. Lawrence, but steamboats were beginning to appear on the lakes as well. The first to be built was the *Frontenac*, in 1816, near Kingston; but, although she was described as "the best piece of naval architecture of the kind yet produced in America," she at first failed to reach Prescott and had to be pushed off a rock by a detachment from the 37th Regiment.[29] After this bad start, however, she ran regularly for some years and was joined by another Canadian boat, the *Charlotte*, and two American boats, one of which, the *Sophia*, was built especially for the run between Sackett's Harbor and Kingston. In 1818 Lake Erie received its first steamboat, the American-owned *Walk-in-the-water*. Although starting somewhat later, Lake Erie did not lag behind, for in 1836 it was reported that "eleven new steamboats are now building at the different ports on Lake Erie, some of which are larger than any afloat upon the lakes."[30]

By the navigation acts only British ships could import or export merchandise from and to the provinces, or ply between the lake ports of Upper Canada. Until 1815, however, American ships were allowed to engage in both these activities, as well as to sail from an American to a Canadian port. At that time the collector of customs at Kingston seized the cargo of an American schooner on the ground that it was illegally carried from one lake port to another. A number of similar instances followed, but on the whole, and in spite of protests from interested Canadians, the collectors winked at a trade which had long been permitted. American ships were, with the above exceptions, allowed to carry on trade from one Canadian port to another. Thus the sailing ships and steamers of the United States were commonly seen in Canadian ports—so much so that it is not easy to disentangle the American from the British vessels on the lakes.

Tonnage on the lakes rapidly increased and regular services were instituted. The Upper Canada newspapers of the day were full of news and advertisements of steamships, indicating their import- ance. A few references to these advertisements will give an impres-

28. *Ibid.*, November 8, 1819.
29. *Ibid.*, September 26, 1816.
30. *Traveller or Prince Edward Gazette*, March 18, 1836.

sion of the routes and charges. In 1828 the *Queenston* was advertised to sail from Niagara for Prescott via Kingston and Brockville, returning by Brockville, Kingston and York. At Prescott connections were made for passengers to and from Montreal.[31] In 1831, the *Great Britain*, equipped with two ninety-horse-power engines, sailed every fifth day from Niagara to Oswego, where canal boats and stages left for Utica; from there she went to Kingston, Brockville, and Prescott, and returned via York. For cabin passengers the following rates were in operation:

Prescott to Brockville	£0	2	6
Prescott to Kingston	0	12	6
Prescott to Port Hope	1	10	0
Prescott to Niagara	2	0	0

Freight rates are also given:

Niagara, York or Coburg to Prescott:

Barrel of ashes	£0	2	6
Barrel of pork	0	1	10½
Barrel of flour	0	1	3
Horse	1	5	0
Ox or cow	1	0	0[32]

A list of sailings on Lake Ontario for 1834 is found in another paper.[33] The following were the ships and routes:

Saint George: Kingston-Niagara.
Adelaide: Chippawa-Amherstburg and Sandwich.
Peter Robinson: Holland Landing-The Narrows.
Cobourg: Prescott-Toronto.
Canada: York-Niagara.
Constitution: Hamilton-Rochester.
Great Britain: Prescott-Niagara.
Queenston: Toronto-Hamilton.
William IV: Ogdensburg-Niagara.
Oakville: Hamilton-Toronto.

Steamers ran regularly between Toronto and Kingston. In 1835 the *William IV* was reported as making the trip in twenty-four hours.[34]

31. Kingston *Chronicle*, April 25, 1828.
32. *Ibid.*, July 9, 1831.
33. *Courier of Upper Canada*, October 21, 1834.
34. *Bathurst Courier*, April 17, 1835.

Lakes Ontario and Erie were the centres of steam navigation. Lake Superior long remained out of the picture, and in 1845 there were said to be only two steamships and twelve sailing vessels on that lake.[35] In the 'thirties small steamships began to appear on Lake Simcoe, on the Kawartha Lakes, and elsewhere. In some places, for example on the Grand River, navigation was possible only after the completion of canals. On the St. Lawrence there was no major difficulty in steamship travel between Quebec and Montreal, or between Prescott and Kingston. In the gap between, however, lay a series of rapids. Various expedients were adopted to carry passengers and freight over this section. A common one was to use stage coaches in conjunction with the steamers, time-tables being arranged so as to make connections. Freight was sometimes carried up in Durham boats. In 1832 the *Iroquois* was built to ascend the rapids from the Long Sault to Prescott, and after her power had been increased she was able to do so.

Until 1841 all the steamships were operated by paddle wheels at the side or stern, but in the latter year the first propeller boat, the American-built *Vandalia*, was put into service. Iron hulls were introduced in a number of boats; and the sails, used as auxiliary power on all early steamships, were abandoned with the increasing strength of the engines. While improvements were steadily made in the speed and safety of the vessels, provision was also made for the comfort of the passengers. "Elegant" cabins were installed, and some of the later boats were reported as having luxurious accommodation and excellent meals. An element of risk remained in navigation of the lakes, as witnessed by the sinking of the *Lady Elgin* in 1860, with the loss of 330 passengers.

3. THE FIRST CANAL PERIOD.

The great waterways of Canada are tantalizingly near to being perfect for navigation, but there exist enough breaks in the chains of lakes and rivers to make it impossible to follow the natural waterways for more than limited distances. It was natural, there-fore, that attempts should be made to facilitate, by means of canals, the passage of the St. Lawrence and Ottawa rivers, both on

35. *Examiner* (Toronto), August 19, 1846.

the central lines of French communication. Nothing, however, came of proposals made before the Seven Years' War. Early in the British period some minor canals were made, notably that used by the North West Company at Sault Ste. Marie, and those on the Soulanges section of the St. Lawrence; but the important period of canal building belongs neither to the French régime nor to that of the fur traders, but to the new age of immigration and commercial development. An occasional energetic Frenchman might attempt the actual construction of canals, and many French and English might dream of them; but the pressure necessary to bring about their actual construction depended on a reasonably large population, including a leaven of men of enterprise, initiative and business interest in the project. One further and not unimportant factor was the military importance of adequate communications: but, as will be seen, the lines dictated by military necessity—as in the case of railways—did not always correspond with the easiest and most natural channels of trade.

The civilian English who came to the province after the conquest had an intense interest in commercial development. Their numbers, however, were not large enough to justify any attempt to improve the water communication; and in any event they were sufficiently occupied with the trade in furs, for the pursuit of which the canoe was adequate. The flood of British-born immigrants, first from the rebelling colonies and then direct from the United Kingdom, changed the complexion of affairs. The fur trade, indeed, was for some years actively continued, but it could not occupy the whole attention of the non-agrarian elements. There was real need for improved communications with the new towns and farm areas of the upper province. Even after through roads had been built, there remained the carriage of bulky and heavy articles which could only be economically undertaken by water. The water, indeed, was there, but its turbulence in essential links of the chain called for the hand of the engineer.

There arose a demand for canals both in the upper province and in Montreal—in Montreal, but not in Lower Canada as a whole. A hundred years of history had produced in Lower Canada a conservative and agrarian type which had no interest in, and no sympathy with, the economically progressive instincts of the

British American. Whatever natural talent for commercial pursuits had existed amongst the French Canadians had found little scope; and by the end of the eighteenth century there could be seen a clear line of demarcation of interest between French and English. Montreal was the centre of the English-Canadian commercial class, and while in sheer bulk the population of the city always remained French, the financial and commercial interests which found their focus there were under English control. A working alliance was bound to be formed between the English of Lower Canada and those of Upper Canada, because their interests in the economic development of the Canadas were, broadly speaking, the same. Those of Upper Canada sought an easy passage to tidewater for their goods, and those of Lower Canada were equally anxious to spread their business tentacles to the growing and progressive towns of the upper province. Hudson Bay was seen by some members of the assembly of Upper Canada as the eventual outlet for the produce of the province, but in the meanwhile it was generally agreed that the St. Lawrence was the practical route to the ocean. At times the assembly of Lower Canada, always having a French majority, was prevailed upon to make grants for the improvement of the St. Lawrence, but there was always an opposition which asked of what value such works could be to the province. The grants, moreover, could only be obtained for the lower part of the river, and the only real enthusiasm shown was for the Chambly Canal, which was entirely a Lower-Canadian affair. On the other hand it was the lower province which had the seaports, and which collected the revenue from customs duties on incoming goods—whether destined for Upper Canada or not—Upper Canada receiving only a portion and having no control over policy. Such a situation could not fail to arouse a protest, which found practical expression in 1822 with the proposal for a union of the provinces. In various towns of Upper Canada meetings of "friends of the union" were held, at all of which the question of customs revenue was prominently brought forward. In Lower Canada the union was, of course, supported only by the English element. Though an act to effect the union was drawn up it was never passed; and the revenue question was instead handled separately in the Canadian Trade Act of 1822, which introduced the principle of arbitration. It was, however, satisfactory to neither party, and the trade relation was only solved with the eventual union of the provinces in 1841. One of the most important objects of a union of the provinces was the possibility that it opened up of undertaking public works, especially canals; and it will be observed that the pace of canal building was greatly accelerated under the united legislature. The conflict between two cultures vividly coloured the political as well as the economic history of the Canadas for over half a century. That conflict as a whole is another story: it is only necessary here to point out that the different attitudes which were taken towards canal building were based on broad and divergent principles.

A glance at a physical map will show that the St. Lawrence River is one of the great natural avenues to the interior of North America. It leads directly to the Great Lakes and thus to the very heart of the continent. Of the competing entrances, the Mississippi offered special difficulties of navigation and was divided from the Great Lakes by a watershed. Further east, the Hudson was cut off from the St. Lawrence physically by rapids and politically by the Canadian border. To connect the Hudson with the Great Lakes the Erie Canal was cut through to Buffalo, a feat which, while it resulted in competition to the Canadian route, could also be taken as tacit recognition of the importance of an outlet from the lakes to the Atlantic.

The enthusiasts for canals in Canada were counting not only on their direct value to the country but also on securing a generous share of the American carrying trade, which would enrich the country through which it passed. Time after time this belief was expressed in speeches, in letters, in newspapers, and—no doubt—in conversation. If it had been altogether sound it would have meant a harvest for the port of Montreal such as the wildest optimists could hardly have pictured; for the middle west was only in its infancy in the early nineteenth century and the age of mass migration was but beginning. The argument from geography will be seen to crop up at all stages of canal development, just as it did in a later age when the railway promoters re-cast the phrases of the canal promoters and tossed them to a hungry public in the form of glowing prospectuses.

Inevitably the first part of the water route to be canalized was the central part of the trunk line to the west, that is, the St. Lawrence River between Lachine and Prescott. A modest beginning was made during the revolutionary war: four short canals (with a total of 1,700 feet) were built between 1779 and 1783 to overcome the rapids at the Cascades (where the Beauharnois Canal was later cut). They gave, however, a depth of only two and a half feet and were intended for bateaux.[36] In 1801 an officer of engineers who was sent to inspect them reported that they were in bad condition and had become inadequate for the larger boats that the merchants were beginning to use.[37] Nothing, however, was done at that time either to improve these old canals or to build new ones. Observers continued to point to the necessity of developing the St. Lawrence waterway, both as a necessary aid to the progress of the provinces and to prevent the falling of all trade into American hands. The War of 1812 brought with it a fresh argument for canals, for the movement of troops and stores proved to be slow and expensive— particularly over the first part of the route, where the cartage from Montreal to Lachine was a heavy cost. Soon after the war the increase of steamships gave added impetus to the movement toward canals, which would greatly extend the use of these boats.

The Lachine Rapids, or Sault St. Louis, were the first break in navigation, and are on the bend of the St. Lawrence where it curves south around the island of Montreal. These rapids thus block the westward route by either the upper St. Lawrence or the Ottawa: on the other hand, the double curve in the river left a neck of land some eight miles long across which a canal might be built. In 1815 an act was passed in Lower Canada appropriating £25,000 for a canal to be built as a public work, but there the matter remained. Two years later estimates were made for a canal intended for Durham boats drawing two and a half feet of water, but the plan was not acted upon, and indeed would not have been of great value. In 1819 a company, known as the Company of the Pro-

36. For historical descriptions of the canals *see Canada and its provinces*, x; W. Kingsford, *The Canadian Canals* (Toronto, 1865); T. C. Keefer, "Canals of Canada" (*Royal Society of Canada*, 1893, Sec. 3, p. 25); J. L. McDougall, *The Welland canal to 1841* (M.A. thesis, Toronto, 1923).

37. Canadian Archives, Q 290–1, p. 23.

prietors of the Lachine Canal, was incorporated, which proposed to build in three years a canal navigable by boats drawing three feet of water. In spite of generous purchases of stock by the imperial and provincial governments, nothing but preliminary work was done, and two years later the province bought out the company, and proceeded with more ambitious plans. A commission was appointed, with John Richardson of Montreal as chairman, and in July 1821 ground was first broken, an event celebrated to the accompaniment of a roast ox and beer for all. A contribution of £10,000 was made by the imperial government with the significant condition that all military stores should be passed free from tolls. The canal as completed in 1825 was about eight and a half miles long, with six locks to overcome a rise of 44¾ feet. It gave a depth of five feet, and the locks had dimensions of 100 by 20 feet. Navigation of the river was thus extended across Lake St. Louis to the mouth of the Ottawa, at which point the Cascades barred the way to Kingston. Between 1843 and 1848 the canal was enlarged so as to give a depth of nine feet and locks of 200 by 45 feet.

From the point at which the Ottawa empties into the St. Lawrence two water routes led to the west—the two traditional ones which had been used since early in the French régime. While that by the St. Lawrence provided the most direct route to Lake Ontario, it followed so closely the American border that communication along it had been interrupted during the War of 1812, and threatened to be interrupted again in any subsequent war. The authorities, therefore, decided to open a water communication from Montreal to Kingston by improving navigation on the Ottawa River and cutting a canal from near the mouth of the Rideau River (at the present city of Ottawa) along the line of that river and the Rideau Lakes. The method of dealing with the first rapids encountered, those at Lachine, has already been described. The next difficulty was met in the rapids at St. Anne's passing Isle Perrot. It was possible but difficult for boats to ascend, and various expedients were tried to facilitate the passage. A cable and windlass placed above the rapids were used by some boats. In 1821 the *Perseverance*, eighty feet long, passed the rapids in twenty minutes by means of a cable and anchor.[38] In 1816 the St. Andrews

38. *Montreal Gazette*, July 11, 1821.

Steam Forwarding Company built a wooden lock, but it was used for their own vessels only. A large lock (190 by 45 feet, depth of 6 feet) was built between 1839 and 1843. Between St. Anne's and the mouth of the Rideau River three serious rapids had to be overcome: the Carillon, Chute à Blondeau, and Grenville or Long Sault. After an examination by an officer of the royal engineers, it was decided to build canals at these points on the same scale as that at Lachine; but during construction an attempt was made to increase the dimensions to those in force on the Rideau. As completed in 1834 the three canals gave a depth of six feet, but were uneven in other dimensions. The longest, the Grenville, was five and three-quarter miles, and the shortest, the Chute à Blondeau, had only one lock.

By these means the Ottawa River was made navigable from Montreal to the mouth of the Rideau River, where there occurred the most serious problem in the Montreal-Kingston waterway. A height of land rises between Ottawa and Kingston, 292 feet above the Ottawa River. The Rideau River and a chain of lakes seemed to make possible a canalized water route. In 1816 an officer of engineers was instructed to examine the country, and reported favourably. Nothing further was done, however, until five years later, when commissioners were appointed by the government of Upper Canada to report on inland navigation, and the British government offered a loan of £70,000 towards the proposed Rideau Canal. After three years, however, the legislature decided that the St. Lawrence was a much more hopeful route. The imperial government, not willing to see their plan dropped, sent engineers to examine the ground and submit an estimate. The estimate of £169,000, although amazingly optimistic, persuaded the imperial government to undertake the work at its own expense. Construction actually began in 1826 under the supervision of Lieutenant-Colonel By of the Royal Engineers (after whom Bytown, the original Ottawa, was named). Before construction had begun By advised that the locks should be increased from the original plan of 108 by 20 feet to 150 by 50 feet, his purpose being to allow for steamboat navigation. Sir James Carmichael Smith, the administrator of Lower Canada, urged that the canal was intended chiefly for military purposes, which were as well served by the smaller locks;[39] and the master-general of ordnance argued that steamboats could not, in any case, be allowed in canals "without injury possibly to the amount of destruction of their Banks."[40] On the other hand, the opinion of Montreal, as represented in the *Gazette*, was in favour of having locks large enough for steamboats. In the end a compromise was reached, the locks being built to the size of 134 by 33 feet. It was necessary to use thirty-three locks from Ottawa to the height of land and fourteen more from there down to Lake Ontario. The depth of the canal was only five feet and was never increased.

In the meanwhile, at the end of 1827, the unpleasant news reached London that By's estimate of expenses was £474,844, or nearly three times the estimate made earlier by the engineer officers.[41] Even worse was to come, for in a tabular statement of 1849, from the office of the inspector-general of fortifications, the cost of the establishment, gates, land and "expenditure on the stations" is given as £803,774: 5: 6.[42] Tolls, as instituted in 1833, were regulated by the lieutenant-governor but were placed at the disposal of the imperial government. The charge for a cabin passenger from Ottawa to Kingston was 4/-; for wheat, per bushel, $3/4d.$; potash, 2/3 per ton; boards and planks per thousand feet, 1/6 to 2/6.[43] In 1832 the first steamboat passed through and in 1834 the Rideau Canal was finally completed, giving a navigable distance of about 132 miles. "The Rideau Canal is in very successful operation", wrote one editor. "The *Margaret* made a trip from Kingston to Bytown last week and the *Enterprise* passed up on Friday. The *Thomas McKay* and *Bytown* are expected up this morning. There is plenty of water and the boats have had full freights."[44] While the Rideau was being built, much attention had also been given to the St. Lawrence canals, and although a

39. Canadian Archives, Q 342, p. 156.

40. *Ibid.*, p. 162.

41. John MacTaggart, who made a survey under By's orders, gave an estimate of £486,060. He was a believer in the canal, and defended its cost, but was not in favour of locks as large as were built. (John MacTaggart, *Three years in Canada* [London, 1829], ii, 156, 167).

42. From a chart in the Canadian Archives.

43. E. J. Barker, *Observations on the Rideau Canal* (Kingston, 1834).

44. Bathurst *Courier*, August 29, 1834.

Toronto newspaper advised its readers that "the Rideau Canal has at length asserted its pre-eminence over the St. Lawrence rapids and seems destined for some years to be the chosen route from Montreal to the Western regions,"[45] pressure was being continually used for the improvement of the St. Lawrence. The board of ordnance regarded the latter as "*an impolitic measure*," but agreed that,

Seeing that it is an object in which the inhabitants of both the Canadas take . . . a very general and warm interest, and that its accomplishment will be attended with many commercial advantages to both Provinces, it would no doubt be considered a most ungracious act on the part of His Majesty's Government to oppose the contemplated improvements, and the Master General and Board are not prepared to recommend that course.[46]

One of the first questions to come up in connection with improvements on the St. Lawrence must have been particularly hard for the board of ordnance to contemplate with equanimity, namely, the Beauharnois Canal. If, instead of turning up the Ottawa from Lake St. Louis, travellers should proceed further along the St. Lawrence they would encounter in succession the rapids at the Cascades, Cedars, and Coteau. As has been mentioned above, small canals had been dug here by 1783; and these were widened and deepened—to three and a half feet—in 1817. Such mild measures, however, were not calculated to satisfy either the growing traffic or the expansive spirit of the times, and in 1833 commissioners were appointed to examine the conditions and report. In the following year their engineer recommended three canals on the north shore to take the place of the old ones, but no action was taken. In the meantime individual proposals were made for a single canal on the south shore, which, from the military point of view, was even more exposed. Yet it was the south shore scheme which —after many years of discussion and delay—was adopted and put into execution. Work began in 1842 and was completed in 1845. The total length of the canal was eleven and a quarter miles with nine locks, each 200 by 45 feet, to overcome a difference in level of

45. *The Patriot*, May 27, 1834.
46. Canadian Archives, Q 384–1, p. 32.

82½ feet. The depth throughout was nine feet. The cost was given as $1,331,787.95.

From the western end of the Beauharnois Canal are forty miles of navigable water through Lake St. Francis. At the head of the lake begin the Long Sault Rapids. Nothing had been done here to improve navigation except by the enterprise of an individual who had built a mill dam and a lock at Moulinette, at one of the smaller rapids. The necessity for a canal was discussed in the legislature of Upper Canada in 1816, and referred in 1818 to the interprovincial commission. A recommendation for canals four feet deep was made, but no action was taken. In 1825 the assembly of Upper Canada called for a map of that part of the St. Lawrence, and at the end of 1826 a report was laid before the legislature, giving alternative proposals for a four-foot or an eight-foot canal. The legislature was then spurred to further action by the town of Brockville, which, in 1830, itself undertook a survey of the area. A resolution in favour of a canal was put through in 1832, commissioners were appointed, and construction began two years later. Various circumstances delayed the work which was not completed until 1843. The Cornwall Canal as finished was eleven and a half miles long, and had six locks (of 200 by 55 feet) to overcome a rise of 48 feet. The depth was nine feet, which was adopted as standard. The cost is given as $1,827,249.62.

One last series of rapids between Montreal and Kingston remains to be considered—those passed by what are known as the Williamsburg Canals. The need for this work was not as urgent as in the other cases inasmuch as steamers could in any case navigate the river through the rapids. While, therefore, the canals were highly desirable they were not dug until somewhat later than the rest. A short canal with one lock of standard size and depth was finished at Farran's Point in 1847; a second, with two locks, at Rapide Plat in the same year; and a third, the Galops Canal, in three sections, a little later. The three Williamsburg canals overcame a rise of 31½ feet.

In the year after the union of the provinces canalization had progressed sufficiently to allow navigation by large steamers from Lake Ontario to below Cornwall.

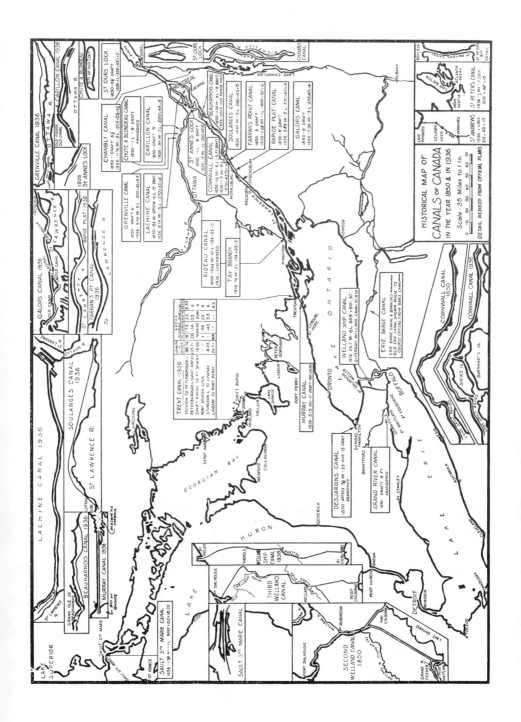

HISTORICAL MAP of
CANALS of CANADA
IN THE YEAR 1850 & IN 1936
Scale - 35 Miles to 1 in.
DETAIL REDUCED FROM OFFICIAL PLANS

. . . the inhabitants of Kingston were greatly surprised by the arrival from Cornwall of the *Highlander* . . . . Although one of the largest steamboats afloat, the *Highlander* met with no difficulty in passing through the [Cornwall] canal or locks. She left the mouth of the canal yesterday, and ascended the Rapids between that and Prescott with the greatest ease.[47]

In the same year as this memorable event, a new type of boat, the *Ericsson* propeller steam barge, was run between Kingston and Montreal, being able to pass through the old Lachine Canal. With the deepening of the latter in 1848, the whole of the St. Lawrence, from Montreal to Kingston, was equipped with nine-foot canals.

Following the trunk line westward along Lake Ontario brought travellers to the narrow but steep isthmus that separates Lake Ontario from Lake Erie. Across this isthmus runs the Niagara River, on which is the most spectacular and most complete break in navigation, Niagara Falls. The Niagara River could be navigated with difficulty from its mouth on Lake Ontario as far as Queenston. At that point even canoes had to be portaged for eleven and a half miles around the falls to Chippawa, where the river was again navigable, though against a stiff current, to Lake Erie. At the end of the eighteenth century a group of residents of the district petitioned the assembly that they should be allowed to build a canal around the falls in exchange for tolls, but nothing came of this and other early suggestions. The first effective drive toward a canal to connect lakes Erie and Ontario was begun by an energetic merchant of the Niagara district, W. H. Merritt. As a result of some amateur experiments with a spirit-level in 1818, he became convinced that a canal was feasible, and attempted to persuade the legislature of the province to undertake a survey, arguing that the expense would be "trifling," and that if this canal were built on Canadian soil it would counteract the American scheme (Erie Canal) and "take down the whole of the produce from the Western country."[48] The assembly was encouraging but apparently unwilling to undertake any action by government, so Merritt raised a fund by subscription in 1823 and engaged an engineer.

47. Kingston *Chronicle*, quoted in the *Examiner*, December 7, 1842.
48. *Journal of the House of Assembly of Upper Canada, 1818* (in *Report of the Bureau of Archives for the Province of Ontario, 1913*).

The ensuing report was hopeful but inaccurate; and, shortly afterwards, three other engineers were engaged and plans were drawn up for a four-foot canal. In the meanwhile, the Welland Canal Company was incorporated, and stock sold, both in the Canadas and New York. In Quebec a public meeting was held, where the idea was approved, and a committee appointed to help Merritt to raise money in Lower Canada. Before long, at the suggestion of the New York stockholders, it was decided to increase the size of the canal so as to admit schooners. In consequence of this the capitalization of the company was increased from £40,000 to £200,000 (currency). Of this latter amount £100,000 was taken up—more than half of it in the United States—and in 1826 the government lent the company £25,000. In the following year an act was passed enabling the government to take up £50,000 in stock, and similarly in Lower Canada the government held £25,000. The British government contributed £16,360 and 13,400 acres of land.

With the sinews of war secured, the company made considerable progress, so much so that two schooners passed through the canal late in 1829. The first canal ran from near Port Dalhousie on Lake Ontario over the height of land to the Welland River. This river was then followed into the Niagara River, which ascended to Lake Erie. There were thirty-four locks, overcoming a difference in level of 330 feet, and boats of seven and a half feet draught could pass through. The difficulty, however, of navigating the Niagara River led the directors to push the canal through to Lake Erie at Port Colborne, which was financed by a further increase of stock and another loan from Upper Canada. The new route, as finished in 1833, had forty locks with a minimum size of 110 by 22 feet, with a depth of 8 feet.

The company had shown great energy and had succeeded in completing its task, but it had met grave difficulties, both financial and engineering. It was heavily in debt, while the traffic passing through in the early years, though exciting to spectators and newspaper editors, was not sufficient to pay for the enterprise. The canal was ahead of its time and the development of the west had not advanced sufficiently for such an expensive communication. At the same time the canal had been so cheaply built that the wooden locks, inadequately protected banks, and insecure dams were constantly giving trouble and entailed repair bills which were quite out of proportion to the age or revenue of the canal.

As year after year the company appealed to the province for aid, sharp criticisms were made of its management, and there were not a few suggestions of wasted funds. W. L. Mackenzie wrote many articles in this vein: "Economy and the Welland Canal are as far apart as earth and heaven"; and a few days later: "The Welland Canal has been a hoax from first to last."[49] In 1835 he printed in newspaper form a long attack on the management of the canal, accusing the officials of keeping improper accounts, making extravagant expenditures, and so on. Many times the canal question came before the legislature, and in 1839 it was decided to buy up the stock held privately. Shortly after the union of the provinces the purchase was completed, and in 1842 enlargements were begun which were finished three years later. The alterations gave locks 150 by 26½ feet, with a depth of 9 feet.

By the end of the 'forties, then, a through communication for steamers and sailing boats had been achieved from the lower St. Lawrence through the upper river, or by way of the Ottawa River and Rideau Canal, through Lake Ontario to the western end of Lake Erie, and by way of Detroit to Lake Huron, Georgian Bay, and as far as Sault Ste. Marie. Here there was a break in navigation. No work was undertaken on the Canadian side until the 'nineties, though an American canal was completed in 1855. In addition to this great east and west highway, canals were projected or built to connect with waterways to the north and south. The Chambly Canal was intended to improve by canalization the old link between the United States and Canada by way of Lake Champlain and the Richelieu River. In the early years after the American Revolution much stress was laid on the use of the St. Lawrence as the easiest approach to Vermont and other neighbouring states. At that time the Richelieu route was the chief one to Canada from New York during the winter, and for some years the mails were brought by that way. In the case of Vermont a complicated game was played for some years after the peace of 1783 between Canadians and Americans who talked of that state

49. *Colonial Advocate*, January 18, and June 30, 1834.

becoming part of Canada on the basis of its proximity to the St. Lawrence. The first definite proposal for canalization of the Richelieu was made in 1787 by Silas Deane, a native of Connecticut then living in England, who proposed to Dorchester a canal around the rapids of St. Johns.[50] Simcoe wrote encouragingly of the plan in 1789, largely in the belief that it would ensure that at least the trade of Vermont could be captured for the Canadian route.[51] Similar proposals were made by Adam Lymburner in 1791 and by Ira Allen in 1796. The story of its actual construction is similar to that of many another Canadian canal. The War of 1812 brought the project seriously forward, and a company was incorporated in 1818 to build it. Little was accomplished, and in 1823 the legislature of Lower Canada made an appropriation for the construction of the canal by means of commissioners, who were appointed in 1829. Work began in 1830, but progressed slowly and the eleven-mile canal was not finished until 1843—and, in its improved state, until 1850. The canal had nine locks, each 120 by 24 feet, and a depth of 6½ feet. The difference in level overcome was 74 feet. Connection was possible with the Erie Canal by the Champlain Canal, running into the lake of that name. As might have been expected, the ordnance department was worried about the ease of access to Canada which the Chambly Canal would afford in case of war. In a memorandum written in 1832 they observe that the government should not have sanctioned the scheme, "being exceedingly objectionable in a military point of view." They uncomfortably visualized an attack from New York on Quebec.[52] As it proved, the Chambly Canal played no part in military affairs, and even commercially was not a success. It suffered, too, the humiliation of being the first improved waterway to be overshadowed by a railway.

A number of other canals were either built or projected. At the west end of Lake Ontario a curious relic remains in the abandoned Desjardins Canal, connecting the town of Dundas with Lake Ontario. A more realistic but almost equally ephemeral route was by the improved Grand River from near Brantford to Lake Erie.

50. Canadian Archives, Q 28, p. 160.
51. *Correspondence of Simcoe*, i, 8.
52. Canadian Archives, Q 204–1, p. 127.

More significant than any of these was the attempt to join by canals Lake Ontario and Georgian Bay, and thus avoid the long detour by Detroit. In general this was an old ambition, based on a reasonable argument that it would be a great gain to follow one side of the triangle. The Toronto portage represented one means of securing this end, but as there was no possibility of a through water communication from Toronto, an alternative route starting at the Bay of Quinté, on Lake Ontario, and proceeding by way of the River Trent and the Kawartha Lakes to Lake Simcoe, and thence to Georgian Bay, was considered. The Trent Valley Canal marked the partial achievement of this plan, but it was never completed and never became a through route. For a time it caught the imagination not only of the local settlers, but also of those further away. In 1834 the editor of the Toronto *Patriot* wrote, in terms characteristic of the period, that "the more immediate sources for the New Route will be—a great portion of Michigan—the whole North West Territory. . . ." In the middle of the nineteenth century a third route was considered, the Georgian Bay Canal proper, which was to go by way of the Ottawa and French rivers. Surveys were made, but the cost was shown to be prohibitive, and the scheme was abandoned.

4. The Canadian Waterway

Interwoven with the story of the physical growth of the means of water communication in Canada is the struggle between the competing entries to the continent controlled by Canada and the United States. It was early seen that the St. Lawrence-Great Lakes system, which ran from the Atlantic to the very heart of the continent, was a potential source not only of convenience, but of wealth to Canada. Could the navigation be so improved as to allow vessels uninterrupted passage, the cost would be reduced to such a low figure that the trade not only of Canada, but also of the growing American west, would follow the short route to the sea. Before the end of the eighteenth century a Canadian, writing to a friend in England, pointed out that Americans were already taking steps to improve their outlets to the sea, and that Canada must not allow her natural advantages to be lost. He suggested that the revenue arising from the sale of crown lands might be applied to canals, and then "that not only the produce of our own Lands, but *that* also of all those bordering on the Great Lakes, and of the many Rivers which fall into them on the southern side, must follow the same course, and centre in the Markets of Quebec and Montreal."[53]

At the end of 1801 Sir Alexander Mackenzie submitted to General Hunter, the lieutenant-governor of Upper Canada, a memorandum in which he urged that the project of the Erie Canal must not be allowed to go unchallenged in Canada; but rather that such a dangerous move must be forestalled by the improvement of the St. Lawrence.[54] The memorandum, after being sent on to London, resulted in a report by the senior engineer officer in Canada, which, however, was cautious and had no positive result. As the realization of the project of a canal to connect Lake Erie with the Hudson River became more imminent, opinion in Canada was more and more turned to the problem of competition. The situation in the state of New York was carefully watched and commented on, and in 1811 when it appeared that action was to be taken, the editor of the *Quebec Gazette* wrote:

If that great, and we must confess, praiseworthy undertaking should succeed, without corresponding exertions on our part, the prospects of prosperity and grandeur traced out by nature for the inhabitants of the navigable parts of the St. Lawrence, will vanish, perhaps, for ever. . . .

Without the trade of the Upper Countries, Canada, in ordinary times, must continue to be, what it formerly was, a drain upon the British Treasury, without any adequate advantage.

Four years later the editor of the same paper noted with satisfaction that a steamboat was to be built on the upper St. Lawrence, and asked, "Shall their [the lakes'] immense trade center in the United States or in Canada? Shall it go to support the power of Great Britain or be directed against her . . . ?" In the following year another characteristic outbreak appears:

. . . The Trade of the immense and fertile countries which surround these Lakes, will center either in New York or in Quebec, according as it is most *profitable* to the inhabitants of those countries. . . . Both New York

53. *Ibid.*, Q 57–2, p. 375 (1795).
54. *Ibid.*, Q 293, p. 120.

and Quebec have *natural* advantages; the latter a mighty river, the former a climate more favourable to navigation. The means of Canada are not to be compared to those of New York; but we have a reasonable claim on those of Great Britain. . . .

The commercial interests in Montreal took the same line as those in Quebec, urging the construction of Canadian canals before it was too late.[55]

Construction on the Erie Canal began in 1817, and Canadians argued that the St. Lawrence route was direct and better provided with water, but could only be used for part of the year, and that if it could be made easy and cheap, it would successfully rival the route to New York. Canada was poor, but Great Britain was not; and her expenditure in Canadian works for this purpose would be repaid by returns on her shipping and manufactures. Canada's progress depended on action.

The corresponding American attitude was illustrated in a pamphlet published in 1818, and partly reprinted in the *Quebec Gazette*, where it was argued that Great Britain was using Canada as the spearhead of a commercial rivalry; and that canals were being begun there which would threaten to rival "the Grand Canal," as it was called. "What immense quantities of produce would find their way to Montreal in the course of another generation, without any countervailing diversion on our part, no mind can estimate. . . ." The writer complacently referred to the annual freezing of the St. Lawrence, and predicted that the branch to Lake Champlain "will even levy a contribution on Lower Canada herself."

It was during these years in which the Erie Canal was being constructed that the international rivalry for the trade of the interior first reached its height. There was, as has appeared, more said than done in Canada. The first Lachine canal was finished in 1825, but it was more than twenty years before large boats could get through to Lake Ontario. In the meanwhile Canadian newspapers at once urged action and consoled themselves by saying that perhaps the Erie Canal would not be so successful after all. As their canals were gradually opened, Canadians began to look

55. *See*, e.g., *Montreal Gazette*, September 23, 1818.

for more successful results in competition with the Erie. The opening of the Welland in 1833, for example, led an Upper Canadian paper to argue that that forced down the tolls on the Erie Canal in the same year; and that efforts were naturally being expended by both countries "to strike the golden vein."[56] Another paper listed the canals and railways built or planned in the United States, designed "to compete with the great natural advantages offered by the St. Lawrence. . . ."[57] In 1846 the *Canadian Economist* made an examination into the relative costs of transportation to Great Britain from Canada and the United States, as a result of which they calculated that to ship wheat from Montreal cost 7d. per barrel more than from New York. They believed, however, that this difference could be absorbed in inland transport, should the canals be completed, calculating that a barrel could be freighted from Hamilton to Montreal for 1/8½d (currency) less than from Hamilton to New York.

Lord Durham was fully conscious of the importance of improved communications, both from his own observation, and from the many representations made to him. He wrote that "Buffalo, the headquarters of the robbers and pirates who have so long infested this country," was a surprisingly prosperous town, "owing to the Erie Canal which commences at Buffalo and thus makes it the Depot of all the trade of the West flowing to New York." But, he added, "all these advantages might be ours by the judicious application of not a large expenditure." In conclusion he asked for a loan from the British government. The reply was Major Philpotts' elaborate enquiry into the canal situation.[58]

Not only the engineer, but the legislator was called in to the battle over routes. For the first few years after the treaty of peace in 1783 trade between the United States and the British provinces was forbidden. Seeking to secure the carrying trade of Vermont and the Ohio Valley, both officials and merchants made representations to London as early as 1785 for the lightening of restrictions. In 1786 Dorchester appointed a committee of council to report on trade, and the merchants who gave evidence urged not only that

56. Kingston *Spectator*, quoted in *Hallowell Free Press*, April 16, 1833.
57. *Hallowell Free Press*, July 23, 1833.
58. Canadian Archives, Durham Papers, Durham to Glenelg, July 16, 1838.

American goods might be shipped through Canada, but that they should then be accepted in England as Canadian. They pointed to the possibility of milling American wheat in Canada and exporting it as flour. Subsequent to this report, limited power was given to the government of Quebec to regulate trade with the United States. The first resulting ordinances allowed trade in specified goods by the Lake Champlain route. Such relaxation of the general restrictions was largely a result of the campaign conducted by the Allen brothers of Vermont to open trade with Canada in order to make use of the St. Lawrence outlet. They painted a glowing picture of the value of goods that would move by this, their only route to the sea. The willingness of the British government to allow such trade was, perhaps, part of a general policy suggested in a memorandum found among Pitt's papers.

The only object [the writer argued] Great Britain can have in retaining Canada in a commercial view is, that as Canada extends all along the back of America, it will at all times secure to Great Britain a sale of her manufactures, and oblige the government of America to be moderate in their duties, otherwise the goods will be smuggled in upon them. . . . Encourage the back Settlers. It is from that country that we will be supplied with hemp. The settlers there will never rival us either in shipping or in sailors, nor for ages in manufactures. We will have all their trade without any expense of maintaining them—what more could you require?[59]

The Jay Treaty (1794) opened the door still wider by allowing internal trade, subject to tariffs and special exceptions, but leaving the navigation acts in force. The privileges thus granted, and which remained substantially the same for thirty years (with the exception of the war period), led to the beginnings of trade between the two countries. Huskisson's legislation of 1822 put heavy duties on goods entering Canada from the United States—an act which raised a storm of protests on both sides of the border.

The evidence of the volume of trade in these years is conflicting and scanty. A table of 1822 of goods brought to the port of Montreal in Durham boats shows only 19,633 barrels of flour and 1,836 bushels of wheat from the United States, as compared with 42,938

59. Quoted in G. S. Graham, *British policy and Canada, 1774–1791* (London, 1930), p. 131.

barrels of flour and 5,344 bushels of wheat from Upper Canada.[60] The editor regards this as a good volume of trade, but a Kingston correspondent in the same year writes gloomily of the failure of Canadians to capture the American grain trade, and says that the Erie Canal is choked with freight.[61]

The corn laws, intended to protect British farmers, virtually closed the British market to Canadian exporters, and many protests and petitions crossed the Atlantic until Huskisson, as part of his tariff reform policy, introduced in 1825 a bill by which Canadian wheat entered at a fixed rate of five shillings a quarter. Shortly afterwards this was modified in further favour of the British provinces. Such was the arrangement until 1842. Meanwhile the navigation acts remained in force, securing a monopoly for British ships; and this—so far as navigation of the St. Lawrence was concerned—was what suited the Canadian merchants.[62] Here the merchants of Lower Canada had a different interest from the farmers of Upper Canada, who were chiefly concerned with finding the cheapest outlet. There are a number of indications, too, that American opinion in favour of free navigation of the St. Lawrence was quite powerful.

Having secured themselves against competitive shipping on inland waters, and having obtained a preferential position in the British market, the Canadian merchants were in a position to handle profitably both the growing produce of Upper Canada and what wheat for the British market they could entice away from the Erie Canal. One branch of business which grew, and became increasingly profitable, was the milling of American wheat in Canada, and its export to England under the preference. In 1840 it was stated that 60,000 bushels of wheat were sent from Cleveland to Canadian ports in one week, to be there milled and shipped.[63] In the following year the *Examiner* reported that 895,550 bushels of wheat and 70,885 barrels of flour were shipped to Canada from the same city.

60. *Quebec Gazette*, December 26, 1822.

61. *Ibid.*, July 12, 1822.

62. Canadian Archives, Q 168–1, p. 70, Address of legislative council of Lower Canada to Dalhousie, February 7, 1824.

63. New York *Atlas*, quoted in *Examiner*, June 3, 1840.

This business received an impetus in 1843. Two years earlier the legislature of the newly-united province had advocated free entry of colonial wheat into England, and in 1842—as a preliminary— imposed a duty on American imports. The British government, though feeling its hand was forced, took the desired step and allowed colonial wheat to enter at a nominal duty of one shilling a quarter. Thus encouraged, the export of wheat, already increasing, bounded up to 260,000 quarters in 1844; while in the same year 67,000 quarters were exported from the United States to Canada— a gain in each case of approximately one hundred per cent over the previous year. There were other reasons for the increased growth and export of wheat, but the situation established by the act of 1843 was clearly satisfactory, and when, in 1846, the corn laws were abolished angry protests came from all over Canada. The Canadian view was fully shared by Lord Elgin who wrote to the secretary of state in 1847: "Stanley's bill of 1843 attracted all the produce of the West to the St. Lawrence, and fixed all the disposable capital in the province in grinding-mills, warehouses and forwarding establishments. Peel's Bill of 1846 drives the whole of the produce down to New York channels of communication. . . ."[64]

In 1824 the legislative council of Lower Canada, and in 1833 the Quebec merchants, had protested against any question of free navigation of Canadian waters, but with the abolition of the preference the reverse attitude was adopted. This change can no doubt be partly attributed to the passage of the first American Drawback Act in 1845, which, by allowing goods destined for Canada to cross the United States free of duty, was intended to help the Erie route; and partly to the realization that, their special advantage having been removed, Canadians must seek to promote by all means traffic on their almost completed canals. In 1847, the operation of the second American Drawback Act brought more misery to the Canadian merchants. By this act Canadian produce could be sent in bond through the United States—an arrangement which, while it might help western Canadian producers, was anathema to all those concerned with shipping.

Whatever were its full causes, there was real economic hardship in Canada in the late 'forties, and it was not unnatural that many

64. Quoted in B. Holland, *The fall of protection, 1840–1850* (London, 1913), p. 293.

Canadians should see the establishment of free trade as the cause
of their troubles. Elgin, who was usually a shrewd observer, took
this point of view, and advocated at least the abolition of the navigation acts as far as they applied to Canada. The idea, indeed,
was now fairly general in Canada that the navigation acts were a
hardship. A typical point of view is given by the editor of the
Montreal Transcript, who wrote that "it is really melancholy to
contemplate the St. Lawrence as it is, and to see its canals, constructed at an enormous expense, filling with mould for want of
trade. Whilst the Erie Canal is unable to do the immense business
of the West, we who can do it cheaper, and might have it for the
seeking, are growing desponding with hopeless waiting." The
reason given for this gloomy state was the inability of the local
government to allow American ships to use the St. Lawrence
canals. The economic discontent, combined with political causes,
led to the signing in 1849 of a manifesto calling for annexation
to the United States—a move which was met by the partial revival
of prosperity, the abolition of the navigation acts, and the Reciprocity Treaty of 1854. The last provided for the free navigation
of the St. Lawrence by American vessels, a right which has been
enjoyed ever since, with one short break.

Thus the St. Lawrence waterway had been through many
vicissitudes and had been viewed in many ways. The first optimism
which saw it as inevitably superior to the American route had
given way under experience to a belief that it must be protected
against competition. Under special circumstances the restrictions
on its use had appealed to Montreal so long as Canada had a
preferential position in the British market, and when that position
was undermined the cry was raised for free navigation.

In the meanwhile the improved St. Lawrence waterway was at
last opened in 1848, on the completion of the new Lachine Canal,
with a depth of 9 feet throughout. How now would the rivalry be
resolved? A Toronto paper found an illustration which gave it
great comfort:

The advantages of the route by the St. Lawrence over that by the Erie
Canal, were practically illustrated, in this way: Two men with their families,
and having with them two mares and foals, furniture, etc., were moving
from Western New York to Vermont. They embarked on the Steamer

City of Toronto at Lewiston, for Lachine. The passage to Lachine cost them
$15, and it would cost them about $5 more, to be forwarded from Lachine
to their destination in Vermont,—the whole of the journey from Lewiston .
occupying about nine days. Had they gone by the Erie Canal, it would
have cost them at least $60, and occupy from 17 to 20 days. The facts
speak for themselves.[65]

The completion of the Canadian canals led immediately to a
sharp decrease in transportation costs. The freight on a barrel of
flour from Hamilton to Montreal, which had been from two to
three shillings, fell by a half after 1848. The advantages of lower
rates on the St. Lawrence were partly cancelled by the fact that
Montreal was not a winter port and that New York could offer
greater possibilities of freights both in and out. Some impression
of the use of the two routes may be gained from the following figures
of the export of Canadian wheat and flour to Great Britain:

	By Montreal (Quarters)	By United States (Quarters)
1850	155,000	82,000
1851	243,000	151,000
1852	189,000	123,000
1853	255,000	161,000[66]

The glorious future predicted for the Canadian canals never
materialized, and perhaps never could have been expected to
materialize. There can be little doubt that their construction was
both wise and necessary; and they stood as a tribute both to the
Canadian provinces and to the confidence of the British government which to no small extent financed them. The St. Lawrence
canals provided what was necessary: a trunk line to the west;
and if it proved impossible to draw through them the volume of
trade which many people hoped would come, the general philosophy underlying this belief was not yet abandoned. It was held
throughout the early part of the railway age, which overlapped the
great canal age, and to some extent eclipsed it. The hopes which
had once been fixed on water transport were then diverted to the
new plan of rail transport.

65. *British Colonist*, July 10, 1849.
66. D. L. Burn, "Canada and the repeal of the Corn Laws" (*Cambridge Historical Journal*, ii, 3, p. 270).

5. THE MARITIME PROVINCES

The Maritime Provinces are well named, for not only do they face on the sea, but throughout their history their people have been builders and sailors of ships. The peninsula of Nova Scotia is from sixty to eighty miles wide, and there are few parts of it, therefore, which are far removed from salt water. Natural harbours are numerous, and in places tidal rivers run inland, and are fit for navigation at high tide by quite large boats. On the other hand, there are no rivers which are navigable for any great distances. Canalization was advocated at two points. The first of these was the strip of land between Minas Basin and Halifax, that is to join the capital to the Bay of Fundy across one of the narrowest parts of the peninsula. The scheme was brought forward in 1794 and the greater part of the canal was constructed some thirty years later, only to be abandoned before it was completed. A second plan was to cut across the Isthmus of Chignecto in order to allow navigation between the Bay of Fundy and Northumberland Strait. A survey was made for this Baie Verte Canal in 1822 and further surveys carried out in subsequent years, but no other work on it was done. Thus water transport for Nova Scotia meant coastal shipping.

The situation in New Brunswick was somewhat different, for there the St. John River was navigable from the Bay of Fundy into the heart of the province. The river was not easy for shipping because of the many currents, but it was wide, and sufficiently deep for large boats to proceed up as far as Grand Falls. Lumber was regularly rafted down to tidewater, and from early days sailboats were used for other traffic. In the early 'twenties steamers were introduced, the first two being the *General Smyth* and the *St. George*, and regular services were kept up thereafter. From St. John at the mouth of the St. John River, a steamship was run across the Bay of Fundy to Digby at about the same time.

But it was in the days of sail that the Maritime Provinces were famous for their ship-builders and sailors. Some records exist of the vessels built in the early years of the industry. In 1770 the schooner *Betsy* was built at St. John, and three years later a vessel of 300 tons was also built in New Brunswick. For Nova Scotia there are records of a brig being built at Halifax in 1751, a vessel of 250 tons in 1786, and the ship *Harriet* at Pictou in 1798. After 1800 there was considerable activity in ship-building in both New Brunswick and Nova Scotia.[67] Many of these ships were sold abroad and employed in various parts of the world. On the other hand, some of the vessels used in the Maritime Provinces were bought in New England.

It is not possible to distinguish exactly between inland and deep-water transportation in the Maritime Provinces. Situated as they were, their people made use of at least all but the largest vessels for coastal work, Atlantic crossings, the fisheries, and travel on the lower St. Lawrence. For the route between the maritime ports and Quebec sailing vessels were not found very satisfactory on account of the difficulties of the river. It was argued that if steamship services were inaugurated, trade between the two could be arranged with advantage to both parties: Canada taking Nova Scotia coal and West Indian products in exchange for flour.[68] An attempt was made in 1822 to buy a steamer with which to develop a trade so that "our accursed intercourse with the United States . . . would be instantly checked."[69] The money at first was not forthcoming until a subsidy of $12,000 offered in 1830 persuaded a group of merchants in Halifax and Quebec to create the Quebec and Halifax Navigation Company. That company then built for the inter-provincial service the *Royal William*, which made three trips until, in 1832, the cholera in Quebec rendered the business unprofitable, and the *Royal William* made her famous trip to England under steam, there to be sold.

Trade with the United States, condemned as it was, played a large part in the commercial affairs of the Maritime Provinces. The long and difficult voyage up the river to Quebec was much less tempting than the sail along the coast to the ports of New England, to those maritime provinces of the United States. Thus the transportation system between Canada and Nova Scotia, in so far as it depended on water, developed slowly, and the people of the Maritimes continued to look for trade

67. F. W. Wallace, *Wooden ships and iron men* (London, 1924).
68. *Acadian Recorder*, July 21, 1821.
69. *Ibid.*, August 3, 1822.

to the United States, the West Indies, and England. All these routes called for deep-water navigation, and on this basis the water transport of the provinces was built up. While the merchants of Canada looked west to the United States, and sought to develop the Great Lakes-St. Lawrence waterway on the basis of the carrying trade of the middle west, those of the Maritime Provinces looked south and east, with hardly more than a cursory glance toward the great river. One result of this difference was to create divergent techniques in water transportation, and another was to accentuate the traditional lack of contact between Canada and the Maritime Provinces. The people of the latter provinces, however, with their experience in and equipment for ocean navigation, sought to make the greatest use of their ports. Little here could be expected from St. Lawrence traffic—in fact the very opposite would more probably be the result. On the other hand, the maritime ports might well be developed as the termini of land routes into the interior of the continent. So long as crude roads were all that could be offered, there was not much hope in this view; but when an intercolonial railway began to seem possible, the whole picture changed, and a new vista opened.

CHAPTER IV

ROADS IN THE OLD PROVINCES

1. IN NEW FRANCE

THERE is no record of roads in Acadia before the English conquest in 1713, but in Canada the French made some headway. The waterways of the St. Lawrence valley afforded unique opportunities for transportation by water, but there were obvious limitations to these natural facilities. The original settlements were placed on the banks of rivers, but the farms later established inland could only be reached by road. There were also breaks in navigation caused by rapids, falls, or heights of land—breaks which could be only partly overcome by the Indian method of portaging. A third limitation lay in the fact that the climate forbade the use of even the Great Lakes and the St. Lawrence for some six months of the year. The Indians had been accustomed to follow narrow trails through the forest, both in winter and summer, and some of these trails were later widened into roads. In winter the eastern Indians used snowshoes and toboggans, and frequently took to the frozen rivers instead of the trails. These methods, like the canoe, were adopted by the French. They did not, however, find any roads or wheeled vehicles. Indeed, the one revolutionary change introduced by the French into land transport in Canada was the wheel, the invention of which ranks amongst the most important in the history of man. The French found no horses in the St. Lawrence valley, but the Indians of the west had begun to use them before the white explorers reached the plains. Introduced by the Spanish, horses multiplied and spread rapidly. In 1682 Tonty saw them on the lower Missouri, and by the middle of the eighteenth century they were common amongst the tribes of the prairies.[1] The Indians used them extensively for riding, but had no vehicle better than the *travois*, a triangular or square frame which dragged on the ground behind the horse, and whose shafts were attached to his sides.

1. Clark Wissler, "The influence of the horse in the development of plains culture" (*American Anthropologist*, xvi, 1).

The French brought both horses and wheeled vehicles into the St. Lawrence Valley. For these roads were needed, and were gradually built. There were great difficulties in the way: the almost continuous forests called for the heavy preliminary work of cutting trees and removing stumps; many streams made bridges or ferries necessary, and though the snow of the winter was more of a help than a hindrance, the spring brought a period of deep mud. Added to these natural difficulties were the small number and scattered settlement of the population. Yet in spite of these obstacles, a system of road-making was gradually evolved in Canada.

The administration of roads, bridges, and ferries was under an official styled the *grand voyer*,[2] the name being taken from the superintendent of roads and bridges in France during the period 1599–1626. The *grands voyers* of New France, the first of whom was appointed in 1667, were responsible for both new works and the maintenance of old ones, whether in town or country. In deciding on what roads should be built the *grand voyer* could summon a meeting of the inhabitants of the district in question, and discuss the matter with them; and if they were dissatisfied with his policy they could protest to the intendant, the principal administrative officer in the colony. The authority of the *grand voyer* was derived from ordinances issued by the intendant. While the *grand voyer* was accustomed to go over the ground himself, and while the ordinances issued on his behalf were in some detail, he had various subordinates who saw that the work which had been called for was satisfactorily carried out. There were assistants, sometimes referred to as *deputés-grands-voyers* and sometimes as *commis*, who appear to have acted on behalf of the *grand voyer* in large areas, such as the district of Montreal. The captains of militia were used in this, as in other aspects of local administration. There is an ordinance of 1730 "qui enjoint à tous les capitaines, lieutenants, et autres officiers de milice de cette colonie de faire incessament travailler aux rétablissements et réparations des chemins et ponts publics dans toute l'étendue de leurs districts."[3] In addition to this general

2. For an account of the *grand voyers see* I. Caron, "Historique de la voirie dans la Province de Québec" (*Bulletin des recherches historiques*, xxxix, 4, p. 198).

3. P. G. Roy, *Inventaire des procès-verbaux des grands voyers conservés aux Archives de la Province de Québec* (Beauceville, 1923–1932), i, 49.

admonition, instructions appear in many of the ordinances concerning particular roads for the captains or other officers of militia to see that the work is done.

Most of the work on roads and bridges was done by *corvée*, known as the king's *corvée* to distinguish it from the ordinary farm work due to the seigneurs. The general principle was that each *habitant* was responsible for the road in front of his own land, but as the frontage was never great the obligation was not burdensome. Moreover the *corvée* could be commuted for a small sum, in the manner of the later statute labour in Upper Canada. In some cases roads were constructed by wage-labour. Kalm speaks of seeing 250 men at work on a new road near Fort St. John, and says that they were paid 30 sous per day and their keep. It may be assumed that this was owing to the fact that the district was unsettled, and that there were no inhabitants on whom to levy road-work. Particularly in spring the existing roads were in need of repair, and ordinances instructed the inhabitants to work on their roads after the thaw. In many cases *habitants* refused to perform the work ordered, and for these recalcitrants fines were provided. The amount of the fines ranged from 30 sous to 20 livres, and the money was either used to pay for labour to do the work in question, or given to the local church. In 1708 the minister suggested to Vaudreuil that soldiers should be used in the construction of roads,[4] but there is no record of this having been done, although it was a common device of the British government, especially in Nova Scotia.

In addition to the ordinary work of construction and repair, the *habitants* had special duties in winter. They were instructed to mark the course of the road by placing poles (*balises*) at stated intervals. Such was the emphasis placed on these guides that corporal punishment was provided for removing them. Other duties were beating down the snow banks in front of each farm, and removing ruts and ridges of snow. One ingenious intendant ordered each farmer to lead his cattle incessantly up and down the road to trample down the snow.[5]

Roads were classified as *chemins royaux et de poste, chemins de*

4. Caron, *op. cit.*, p. 203.

5. *Edits, ordonnances royaux, déclarations et arrêts du conseil d'état du roi concernant le Canada* (Quebec, 1854), iii, 455.

communication, and *chemins de moulin.*[6] The first were the main roads or highways; the second were intended to give access to the farms not fronting on the royal roads; and the third were built at the order of the seigneur. Royal roads were supposed to be 24 feet wide with a 3-foot ditch at each side; communication roads were 18 feet wide, also with ditches, and mill roads were of unspecified width. Stone was occasionally used for the surface, and wood— "corduroy," as it was later called—was common in marshy sections. Bridges were of wood, the larger ones being built by *corvée* and the smaller by the owners of the land through which the stream ran. For the wider rivers ferries were organized by private individuals and supported by tolls.

Evidence on the number and length of the roads actually built is scanty, but what there is indicates a steady growth. Before the middle of the seventeenth century, when Canada was little more than a mission and a fur-trading post, little attention was given to roads; but after the establishment of royal government in 1663, and the increase of population that followed, it was no longer possible to depend wholly on the St. Lawrence for transportation. A modest start was made at road-building in the second half of the century, and in the eighteenth century there was, relatively, considerable activity. An examination of the number of ordinances issued on behalf of the *grands voyers* reveals at least a fairly constant increase of official interest. In the first four years, 1667–1670, there were only three ordinances; then a gap until 1683, when there were three; another gap until 1688, when there was one; one in each of the two succeeding years; a gap until 1706, when there were six. From then on the numbers are larger, so that for the period 1667–1763 there were issued in all, 864 ordinances on this subject.[7]

The two principal highways in New France were those which ran along the shores of the St. Lawrence. The river was the chief focus of settlement, and a road parallel to it would therefore serve the maximum number of people, and at the same time run through land which was for the most part already cleared. Since all the principal towns were on the north shore, the road on that side was completed first. It was, naturally, built in sections, some of which

6. For a fuller account *see* F. J. Cugnet, *Traité de la police* (Quebec, 1775).
7. Roy, *op. cit.*

were the first roads in Canada. It was, however, toward the end of the French régime before a through route was established. In 1727 Dupuy could still write that, "there is no road by land from Quebec to Montreal. This is a great inconvenience and an obstacle to the establishment of the colony. It sometimes takes a month to and from Montreal, according to the wind."[8] A few years later, under the energetic administration of the *grand voyer*, Lanouiller, the gaps were filled up, and by 1734 carriages could go from Quebec to Three Rivers in four days.[9] In 1735 Lanouiller wrote that he had driven in a carriage during the summer from Montreal to Quebec in four and a half days.[10] Franquet travelled from Quebec to Montreal in a carriole and described the road as in general "assez bon." By 1763 the north shore road was completed from Cap Tourmente to Montreal.

The road along the south shore was intended to serve agricultural areas. Like its companion across the river, it was built in sections, but was not completed in the French period. According to the map drawn up under General Murray's orders by the army engineers in 1763,[11] the completed sections were from Pointe à Caron in the district of St. Roch des Aulnaies through Lévis to a point opposite the River Batiscan, and from there were broken sections as far as the Lachine rapids. The Murray map also shows a road paralleling the Richelieu River from a point about fifteen miles south of Sorel to St. Jean. This connected with a road running across the country from Laprairie, which was begun in 1739, partly to lead to Fort Chambly and partly to open up the country. Roads, too, are shown in the neighbourhood of Montreal, and north of Quebec there was a perfect network. A road ran for an undetermined distance beside the Chaudière, and another served the St. Maurice forges. It is not easy to tell anything of the real condition of particular roads. It is evident from the ordinances and from the correspondence of the *grands voyers* that orders were by no means

8. H. A. Innis, *Select documents in Canadian economic history, 1497–1783* (Toronto, 1929), p. 396.

9. E. Salone, *La colonisation de la Nouvelle-France* (Paris, 1906), p. 372.

10. Canadian Archives, Series C 11 A, lxix, p. 110, Lanouiller de Boisclerc to minister, October 31, 1753.

11. This valuable map is in the Canadian Archives.

always obeyed. Sometimes roads which were planned were never built at all; more commonly they were built, but not according to the official specifications. Repairs were never carried out regularly, and as a result most of the roads must have been rough, except when there was good sleighing. The probability is that all but the royal roads were very crude, and that even these were rough, and probably impassable at times.

As to the use of roads there is again a lack of evidence. Some of them were evidently planned for military purposes, and most of the local ones served chiefly the farms away from the rivers. The large number of horses in Canada was an indication of the character of agriculture and of the use of roads. The first census showing the number of horses is that of 1681, when there were said to be 94 (36 of which were in Quebec). From then on the figures show a rapid increase: 156 in 1685, 580 in 1695, 5,270 in 1720, and 13,488 in 1765. The last figure represents a proportion of about one horse to every five persons. The government became alarmed lest the increase of horses should interfere with the raising of cattle, and issued an ordinance in 1709 restricting each farmer to two horses and a colt. In the following year Vaudreuil wrote to his minister that there were so many horses in Canada that the young men were losing the art of walking, with or without snowshoes. To remedy this, he says, it will be necessary to kill some of the horses; and to avoid loss they can be salted and sold to the savages "en guise de boeuf."[12]

Although the French in Canada were more concerned with road-making than has usually been represented, they always depended largely on water transport. Natural conditions made road-building and maintenance highly laborious, while travel by water was comparatively easy and cheap. The population was always so small and scattered that labour was scarce and distances great. The chief occupations were agriculture, fishing, lumbering, and the fur trade; and of these only the first was dependent on roads. Apart from a few sporadic attempts, little was done to build up other industries, and the energy that might have gone into the creation of a diversified economy was expended on the

12. Canadian Archives, C 11 A, xxxi, p. 88. Vaudreuil to Pontchartrain, November 3, 1710.

fur trade. While the fur trade offered prizes to the adventurous, it tended to draw away from the colony on the St. Lawrence the men and the resources that might have been turned to the improvement of agriculture and industry. Because of this the settlements suffered, and with them the roads.

A conflict arose between expansionism and concentrated settlement which may be symbolized by the birch canoe and the *calèche*. From early days efforts were made to prevent the colony from being spread too thin over the continent. In 1663, as soon as Canada became a royal province, Louis XIV sent one Gaudais to his colony to report on the size and distribution of the population, the fertility of the soil, the area cleared or tilled, and the prospects of iron-mining and lumbering.

The Sieur Gaudais is to understand [the instructions run] that the principal thing to be examined for the maintenance and augmentation of the Colonies of the said country is, the clearing the greatest possible quantity of land and inducing all the French settlers to live together in Villages and not at a great distance the one from the other . . . and . . . inasmuch as the Inhabitants have turned the best part of their attention to this trade [in furs], instead of applying it exclusively, as heretofore [*sic*] to the clearing and cultivation of the soil . . . the King wills that the said Sieur Gaudais inform himself particularly of the means of retaining the said Trade for His Majesty's profit. . . .[13]

Over and over again in following years the same note is struck by the home government: discovery and expansion threaten to weaken the settlements on the St. Lawrence which must be built up first. From Quebec ordinance after ordinance was hurled at the *coureurs de bois*, who, without authority, sought their fortune in the west. But all was in vain, and the process could hardly be arrested. Other factors, too, entered to weaken the colony: the immigration policy which shut out the thrifty Huguenots, mercantilism which subdued such industries as raised their heads, and the series of wars with the Indians and English that periodically took the men away from their farms. New France never developed into the well populated, concentrated, and self-dependent colony that would have driven road after road through the forests

13. E. B. O'Callaghan, *Documents relating to the colonial history of the State of New York* (Albany, 1856–1887), ix, 9.

to serve agriculture and industry. The main centres of population were Quebec, Three Rivers, and Montreal. In 1665 these three accounted for 1,627 out of 3,215 persons, and in 1754 for 12,800 out of 55,000, Quebec being still much the largest with 8,000 people. The rural population was scattered in the seigneuries along the St. Lawrence, and, as the population increased, spread a few leagues west of Montreal and east of Quebec, and also up the Ottawa and Richelieu rivers. As the frontage on the river was taken up, second and third rows of farms were established. Yet at the time of the English conquest in 1763 the population had not risen above 65,000 to 70,000 persons. Under the circumstances the achievement of New France in road-making was no mean one, and the organization that was worked out served as a model for British Canada. But the eyes of New France were fixed too much on the receding west, to which adventure and the hope of profit beckoned along the inviting waterways. In New France was born that philosophy of the empire of the St. Lawrence by which a continent was to be subdued and a golden harvest drawn down to the bosom of the great river.

2. Governmental Administration, 1763–1867.

Control of the construction and administration of roads and bridges necessarily rested in the governments of British North America, and to those governments the peoples of all the provinces looked for improvement in land communications. The need for roads was felt by a larger section of the community than that which called for the improvement of the waterways, for it embraced the agricultural as well as the commercial population. The following editorial from an Upper Canada paper illustrates a characteristic attitude:

We understand that a petition is getting up in this town and neighbourhood to the House of Assembly, praying that honourable body to make some effectual provision for improving the public roads in this province. It would indeed be a remarkable thing should the Session pass away without the representatives of the people doing something to relieve the country from the crying and degrading evil—they would stand justly chargeable with a neglect of this all important subject. The interests of the agriculturists, the tradesmen, the landed proprietor, the interest of every human being in the country will be affected, most injuriously affected, unless more efficient steps are immediately taken to form roads throughout this province, by which an easy communication between one place and another, can be effected. If indeed, poverty could be pleaded as the cause—if the want of means could be pleaded—nay if any reasonable plea could be set up, some excuse might be offered for delay, but we avow without fear of successful contradiction, that even if a million of money were to be borrowed for the purpose, the interest and the gradual liquidation of the principal to be provided for either by a moderate tonnage on all goods carried on the roads; by commuting statute labor or by a tax to be raised for the express purpose from the property of the Province, the beneficial result to every class of individuals in this colony, would be beyond our highest expectations, our circulation would be increased—employment for thousands would be found—and various kinds of property now of little use would become valuable—the farmer would no longer be at the mercy of the elements for bringing his produce to market—and the merchant would be able to obtain and furnish a regular supply of goods to the country merchants and farmers; in short, an impetus would be given to everything around us, which would advance the prosperity and wealth of the province, and of everybody and everything in the province, in a twenty fold greater proportion than would be the increase of annual expenses necessary to accomplish the improvement.[14]

Common principles ran through the machinery used in all provinces, but the methods varied in detail from one province to another and from one period to another. As in most aspects of Canadian life, one may readily trace the influence of English and American institutions, often blended into a new form.

The first part of modern Canada to become British was Nova Scotia. There, after a century of disputed possession, the British flag was finally planted in 1713. The colony, however, was not yet to remain in peace, for the struggle of French and English went on internally, the new government attempting to make English subjects of the Acadians who steadfastly resisted any legal commitment. The outcome of the conflict was the expulsion of 1755, followed by the renewal of general war on the continent. Through the years of civil struggle, Nova Scotia was governed by a governor and council, who were responsible for what little progress could be made in the building of roads. After the expulsion,

14. *Courier of Upper Canada*, quoted in *Hallowell Free Press*, January 22, 1833.

an elected assembly was created, in 1758, and from that year the ordinances of the council were replaced by statutes. The change was more than one of form. The lands of the unhappy Acadians quickly began to be taken up by the more progressive New Englanders, who were less ready to accept the local life of the Acadian farmers and fishermen. Military and economic interests alike pointed to the construction of roads.

In Nova Scotia, as later in the other colonies, the legislature made use of the judicial authorities for the administration of roads; for local government was to be delayed for many years throughout British North America. The first statute on the subject[15] orders the grand juries to appoint annually two surveyors of highways for each township. Work was to be done by statute labour, the men being summoned by the superintendent. Owners of carts and teams were liable for four days' work in the year, and all other persons for six. In the next few years the system was developed. If application were made to the quarter sessions for a new highway, or alteration in an old one, the sessions appointed two or three freeholders of the next township to report on it. If the report was favourable, the sessions then ordered the marshall to summon a jury from the next township, which was sworn by a justice to lay it out in the most convenient way. Surveyors were not empowered to alter or amend a road without the consent of three justices. An innovation was the permission given in the districts of Colchester and Pictou for the sessions to raise and spend money locally on the making or repairing of bridges. Such funds were to be laid out by commissioners appointed by the sessions.

In 1784 the old province of Nova Scotia was divided, the mainland portion being given separate existence under the name of New Brunswick. In the latter an assembly was set up, and the administration of roads followed much the same course there as in the peninsula. Commissioners and surveyors of roads were appointed by the justices at the general sessions. The commissioners were in general charge, and responsible for policy and for reports to the quarter sessions, while the surveyors superintended

15. Except where other sources are cited, the facts on governmental administration are to be found in the statutes of the various provinces. It has not been thought necessary to refer to each individual act.

the actual work. As in Nova Scotia, statutory labour provided the bulk of workers; but in both provinces provision was made for commutation, originally at the rate of four shillings a day. For the sparsely peopled districts grants might be made by the legislature to supplement the statutory labour.

In 1801 the assembly of New Brunswick began to make regular money grants for road repair and construction as supplementary to statute labor. In consequence of this it was decided to provide for appointment, by the executive government, of special comissioners to superintend the expenditure of the money granted. In 1816 a clear distinction was for the first time made between local roads and "great roads of communication." The route of each great road is described in a statute, and changes or additions were from time to time made by subsequent acts. For each great road three paid supervisors were appointed, who were to see that the work was carried out and to render accounts to the assembly. They might make use of statute labour, but were advised to let contracts.

In spite of their close relations with both England and the United States, neither Nova Scotia nor New Brunswick made much use of representative local institutions until after confederation, and consequently the machinery for the administration of roads was little changed until toward the end of the nineteenth century. Between 1879 and 1888 in Nova Scotia, and at about the same time in New Brunswick, provision was made for the incorporation of towns and counties. Elective councillors then formed a local government capable of taking over the control of those roads which were not retained as provincial.

The story in Prince Edward Island is much the same as in the other Maritime Provinces. The lieutenant-governor in council named a commissioner of highways for each district (a group of townships), and the commissioners appointed overseers of statute labour and made returns to the lieutenant-governor. By an act of 1833 the commissioners were empowered to spend money collected in commutation of statute labour or sums appropriated especially for roads and bridges. In the latter case they were obliged to advertise for tenders.

When the former French province of Canada first became a

British colony, the system of government was little changed. The council, however, assumed a more important place than it had occupied in the French régime, and it was this body which supervised the administration of roads and debated the larger questions of policy. From time to time the council appointed committees to consider the existing ordinances concerning roads, or to report on special questions that arose, such as construction of new roads. In general the council exercised a final jurisdiction over all matters connected with the use and construction of roads and bridges, and the obligation of inhabitants to work on them. Apart from the council, the scheme of administration was a modification of the old French one.[16] For each of the three districts in which the province was divided for administrative purposes—Quebec, Three Rivers, and Montreal—a *grand voyer* was appointed. This officer was instructed to visit periodically all the roads under his jurisdiction. Having decided what work was to be undertaken, he went to a justice of the peace for a written order. The actual work was supervised by bailiffs and sub-bailiffs, or by captains of militia. Minor changes were made in the system from time to time.

The system of labour remained much the same as before the conquest. An obligation rested on every occupier of land to build and maintain the roads and bridges in his neighbourhood. Fines were provided for failure to appear, and, for those who actually refused to work, a justice of the peace might give a special fine. As in the days of French rule, the *habitants* had constantly to be reminded of their duties. On one occasion the *grand voyer* of Quebec was moved to issue a public warning that,

The Roads in this district being in bad repair, those persons who by Law are bound to keep them in good order, are hereby required to mend them in ten days, in the way and manner directed by the Ordinance.

Wherever it shall be found that the necessary work has been neglected, or has been done in a slight superficial way, the Grand Voyer will employ people to do the work conforming to the Ordinance, at the expense of the person or persons heedless of the notice.[17]

16. For the administration of roads in Quebec *see*, L'abbé Ivanhoë Caron, "Historique de la voirie dans la Province de Québec" (*Bulletin des recherches historiques*, xxxix, 4, 5, 6, 7, 8).

17. *Quebec Gazette*, June 12, 1783.

With the passing of the Constitutional Act in 1791 and the division of Quebec into Upper and Lower Canada, changes appear in administration. In the lower province, which was roughly the part of Canada settled before the American Revolution, a two-chamber legislature was established to take over the legislative functions of the old council. The executive council retained some control over administration proper, but the legislature, by means of statutes, dealt with all important questions. To the legislature, also, were sent all petitions for or against construction of roads and bridges. In 1805 an act was passed establishing the first turnpike road, a new method in the province which was regarded by the governor, Milnes, as most desirable.[18] It was not, however, until after the War of 1812 that the example was widely followed. From that time petitions for the establishment of toll roads and toll bridges poured into the legislature, such petitions being usually referred to a committee of the assembly. The submission of petitions was preceded by a warning notice in the newspapers which enabled the inhabitants of the areas affected to decide on whether or not they were in favour. As in all the provinces, the legislature devoted a great deal of time to the discussion of roads, and frequently conducted elaborate investigations by means of special committees.

Statutory labour was continued as before, in spite of periodic protests against it as inefficient. The *grands voyers* were also retained, but the duties of the captains of militia were taken over by *sous-voyers* or inspectors. After the practice of parliamentary grants had been begun, three commissioners were appointed in each county to oversee the expenditure of the money so granted, and to report annually to the governor and both houses of parliament. In 1833 the powers of the *grands voyers* were transferred to the commissioners, one of whom was to be elected in each parish.

With the object of improving communications faster than the system of statutory labour would allow, the government began to undertake the construction of roads by other means. In 1806 the executive council called for tenders for a number of roads of specified width and character. The contractors were to be paid by

18. Canadian Archives, Q 97, p. 146.

grants of land adjacent to the roads.[19] Some income was derived from commutation of statute labour and from fines, which could be used to pay contractors for small undertakings. Such small sums, however, were inadequate for the growing needs of the province, and from 1815 the legislature began to make annual grants for roads. The ordinary process seems to have been that the money set aside for a given district was at the disposal of the county commissioners for internal communication, who advertised for tenders; and, having awarded the contract, kept some watch on the work to see that it was completed according to the agreement. If the contractors were negligent the payment might not be forth-coming. A procedure was probably followed similar to that used in the case of toll-bridges: that, on completion, the work was examined by experts, who swore an affidavit as to its condition before justices of the peace. Between 1815 and 1817 the sum of £63,600 was appropriated for roads and bridges, and this propor-tion was fairly steadily increased.[20]

In the newer province of Upper Canada the system of adminis-tration was based on similar principles, but differed sufficiently to warrant a separate description. The first statute relating to the administration of roads, passed in 1793, named the justices of the peace as commissioners of highways within their several divisions. Under the commissioners were the overseers of highways, who, with other officers, were elected by the inhabitants of each town-ship. The commissioners divided their parishes or townships into sections, and assigned overseers to each. In general it was the duty of the overseers to "superintend, repair and keep in order, the highways, roads, streets and bridges in their several divisions," under the direction of the commissioners. In practice this meant summoning those liable to statute labour, superintending the work, collecting sums paid in commutation or in fines, and keeping accounts which were to be handed to the commissioners. The courts of quarter sessions made decisions on the construction and alteration of local roads, levied fines on persons neglecting to do statute labour, could lessen statute labour, or suspend commutation,

19. *Quebec Gazette*, October 9, 1806.
20. G. V. Cousins, "Early transportation in Canada" (*University Magazine*, vol. viii).

appointed the commissioners from amongst the justices of the peace, decided vexed questions of surveying, classified roads as public highways, and in general controlled the administration in their several districts. In 1810 a further office was created, that of surveyor of highways; and consequent on this the process of administration was modified. Any twelve freeholders might petition for the repair, alteration, or opening of a road in their neighbour-hood; and on receipt of this petition, it was the duty of the surveyor to examine and survey the road and to deliver to the commissioners a report which was made public. If no opposition was raised, the commissioners ordered the work to be done; if, how-ever, objections were made, a jury of twelve men, whose verdict was final, heard evidence, and confirmed, modified, or annulled the report.

Shortly before the union of the provinces, special machinery was set up to provide for the administration of the macadamized roads. The trustees of the turnpike trusts in each district were to form a board of commissioners having authority over these roads "so far as the improvement of the same has been authorized by any Act of the Legislature of the Province." They were to receive no pay and might not be parties to any contract concerning the roads. They were to appoint a competent engineer or surveyor to superintend work, collectors of tolls, and other necessary officials, and to fix and pay their salaries. They were to determine the num-ber of toll-gates, which were let to the highest bidder, and fix the tolls charged. Vacancies in the board were to be filled by the lieutenant-governor.

With a few exceptions, all householders or freeholders were liable to perform statute labour, and were given three days' notice to appear with tools, and teams if they had them. The day's work of a team and waggon was reckoned as equal to two days' personal labour. The conditions of statute labour varied from time to time, but the general principle was that the number of days required varied according to the rated value of the property. Statute labour might be commuted (at a fixed rate) except where other labour could not be obtained cheaply. Commutation was compulsory for persons living in towns and liable to more than six days' work, or (after 1840) for persons living within half a mile of a macadamized road.

Such commutation fees, together with fines imposed on those who failed to appear when summoned, formed the first source of funds for expenditure on roads. Further small amounts—up to £50, or later £100—could be levied on the inhabitants of the district by the justices of the peace at quarter sessions. Absentee owners of two hundred acres or more were taxed twenty shillings per annum for roads. The largest source of revenue for the upkeep of roads and bridges consisted in grants made for this purpose by the legislature. The practice began in 1804 with a modest grant of £1,000, which rose by 1812 to £6,000 and by 1815 to £20,000. Apparently the legislature was sometimes over-optimistic in making grants, as a letter from the receiver general to the treasurer of the eastern district, printed in the newspapers, states that it had proved impossible to raise in Canada the sum granted under the act, and that he would endeavour to raise a loan in England. Between 1836 and 1840 over £100,000 was granted.[21] In the case of special grants made by the legislature of Upper Canada, commissioners were either named in the act or ordered to be appointed by the lieutenant-governor, to superintend the expenditure of the money. The assembly received a great number of petitions from various districts complaining of the state of the roads, the inadequacy of statute labour or the weaknesses of the administrative system. Such complaints were discussed; and indeed no session can have passed without considerable attention being given to the problems of roads and bridges. The reports of commissioners to the assembly were given detailed attention, in many instances their accounts were criticized, and sometimes they themselves were censured.

In 1841 the provinces of Upper and Lower Canada were brought together in a legislative union. Though elected municipal institutions were not, contrary to expectation, provided for in the act, they were created under separate instruments. This change in the machinery of government brought a corresponding alteration in the system of administration of roads. For Lower Canada municipal

21. W. H. Breithaupt, "Dundas Street and other early Upper Canada roads" (*Ontario Historical Society, Papers and Records*, xxi, 1).

institutions were created just before the union. By an ordinance of 1840 the lower province was divided into districts; and for each there was to be an elected council presided over by an appointed warden. The first session of the legislature of the united province of Canada saw the passing of the District Councils Act which extended the same system to Canada West. To these councils, strictly limited in financial freedom, were given, *inter alia*, the powers over local roads formerly held by the quarter sessions. In subsequent years the power and scope of the councils were in general increased. Certain main roads remained under the financial and administrative responsibility of the provincial government, but local roads were the problem of the councils, which, with limited powers of raising money, heard petitions and decided on the relative necessity of different projects. They were empowered to appoint a commissioner in each township in the same way that the quarter sessions had done.

Changes made in municipal government after the original arrangement in the early 'forties followed somewhat different lines in the two sections of the province. For Canada West a further act was passed in 1849 establishing wholly elected councils for townships and counties, both of which were empowered to build and maintain roads. The surveyors of roads were now to be appointed by the township councils. At the same time an act was passed which authorized the formation of joint stock companies to construct roads or bridges. The municipalities could exercise supervision over such companies and might take stock in them, or eventually buy them out. With the expansion of the country, particularly in regard to railways, the municipalities began to borrow quite heavily in London; and to provide more favourable terms for them Hincks introduced the Municipal Loan Fund Act, passed in 1852, by which the provincial government shouldered the financial responsibility. A similar course was followed in Canada East. In 1845 the elective principle was fully introduced, and this—with a brief interval—was retained. Parish and county councils had authority over roads. In 1854 the Municipal Loan Fund Act was extended to Canada East.

The federation of the provinces in 1867 made, for some years, no difference to the system of administration of roads and bridges.

Municipal government was explicitly left within the orbit of the provincial governments by the act of 1867, and the provinces retained control over roads and bridges by virtue of their assigned rights in local works. No change, in fact, was made in the provincial constitutions which would affect the administration of roads and bridges. It was not until the twentieth century that the federal government began to take any part—by subsidy or direct building —in roads in the provinces.

3. Construction and Maintenance

Until the end of the nineteenth century roads in British North America were built largely under pioneer conditions. As the frontier receded the older districts began to have metalled roads, but the number of these remained small until the next century. A road in Canada was literally interpreted as anything from a bridle-path to a macadam highway. As townships were surveyed, various types of provision were made for setting aside land for roads. In what is now Ontario two main plans may be distinguished: either a definite road allowance was left between concessions, or five per cent of each township was set aside for roads. The width of the allowance under the first plan varied from forty to sixty-six feet, the latter width being the most common except in early years. The disadvantage of leaving a definite line for a road was that it might prove to be too hilly or rocky, so that it sometimes happened that arrangements had to be made with landowners for varying the route.[22] Many through roads went from point to point, even after townships were surveyed. The first stage in road-making was to blaze a trail through the woods, following an old Indian path or taking the line from the survey. A surveyor then traced the route in detail, and was followed by men who cut down the trees and cleared the way. Sometimes nothing further was done for a time, in which case travellers had to make their way around the rotting stumps and over the soft or swampy floor of the forest. The unlimited supply of wood and the necessity of cutting down the trees in any case led to what was called the corduroy road

22. *Manual of instructions for the information of Ontario land surveyors*, issued by the Association of Ontario Land Surveyors [Toronto, 1923].

(after the durable and ridged cloth of that name). Logs were laid across the road, especially in swampy places, and provided a sound if rough foundation. If left in this state the road was indescribably bumpy, particularly when some of the logs began to rot, but it could be readily improved by throwing earth between the logs, as was commonly done. The corduroy foundation may still be seen projecting from beneath the gravel covering of many a modern Canadian road. The companion to the corduroy road was the corduroy bridge, for which unhewn logs were used both as supports and flooring. The passage of such bridges was difficult and alarming, but perhaps less so than the fords which were for long the only alternative.

The next stage was the replacement of plain corduroy by a surface of sand or gravel. Such a process assumed drainage, achieved by the sloping of the roads toward both sides and the digging of ditches—work which called for more manual labour and tools than were always available. It was barely feasible to make a surfaced road through uncleared forest, for proper drainage could hardly be secured until the clearing of the land made it comparatively dry. As the supervisors of great roads in New Brunswick shrewdly pointed out after a meeting in Fredericton in 1828,

Many tracts of land, which in a state of nature, are called Swamps, and have been studiously avoided in laying out Roads, prove afterwards, with a very little expense in draining, to be exceedingly favourable, both for Roads and for Cultivation. A dread of the difficulties which this description of wet land appears to present; and a desire to shorten the distance as much, and to finish the work as soon, as possible, are perhaps the principal causes of so many Roads having been laid out and opened over hills, or high, uneven and broken grounds, where carriages never can be driven with ease and safety.[23]

The disastrous effect of wet weather on the dirt roads, more especially in the spring, led very naturally to an attempt to provide hard surfaces. The materials ready to hand were stone and wood. In districts where stone or gravel was available, the only problem was one of expense in hauling it to the required place. It might make a very uncomfortable and rough surface, but had the

23. *Report of the supervisors of great roads* (St. John, 1828).

distinct advantage of saving vehicles from being completely bogged in bottomless clay. The macadam road was a luxury that could hardly be afforded, though a great advance on a surface of loose stone. One of the earliest roads to be macadamized was the lake shore road between Kingston and Napanee, done in 1837–1839 at a cost of $132,000. About the same time a few miles of Yonge Street near Toronto were macadamized.[24] But as late as 1863 Hind wrote that there were few properly constructed macadam roads in Canada: the turnpike trusts outside Montreal and Quebec being exceptions.[25] Even at the end of the century an observer questioned whether "there is a mile of Macadam road in Ontario outside a few towns or cities."[26]

The first plank road on the continent was laid in 1835–1836 on the road leading east from Toronto. In Lower Canada the first plank road was from Longueuil to Chambly (1841).[27] The advantage of plank roads, which became quite common in the 'forties, was that the material was present in great quantities: only a sawmill and some rough carpenters were needed. The first travellers over plank roads were, not unnaturally, thrilled at the prospect of easy transport. The editor of the *Patriot*, after a drive of six miles on the one near Toronto, wrote that the horse "seemed more in a gay frolick than at labour." In his view the problem of surfaced roads was solved. Equal enthusiasm was shown about the plank road between London and Port Stanley: "It is impossible to convey any adequate idea of the effect which this movement has already produced—several persons who were leaving the neighborhood for the West have abandoned their design—and hope and expectation are marked on every countenance."[28] In 1841, when plank roads were being introduced, a visiting engineer investigated their value with great care. He advocated four-inch planks to stand the strain of traffic, and even then gave the wood a life of only three

24. E. C. Guillet, *Early life in Upper Canada* (Toronto, 1933), p. 541.

25. H. Y. Hind and others, *Eighty years' progress of British North America* (Toronto, 1863), p. 123.

26. Guillet, *op. cit.*, p. 544.

27. W. Kingsford, *History, structure and statistics of plank roads in the United States and Canada* (Philadelphia, 1852).

28. London *Observer*, quoted in *Examiner*, January 26, 1842.

years. On the whole he sums up against plank roads, preferring
those made of broken stone.[29] In spite of this unfavourable
judgment, many plank roads were built in Ontario. Their life
depended partly on the character of the soil on which they were
placed; but at best they went to pieces under the combination of
weather and traffic, and were an interesting but passing phase
in the history of Canadian roads.

Such were the main types of roads found in the British provinces
in the nineteenth century. They were built under a variety of circumstances, and by a variety of authorities. Statute labour was
intended, in all provinces, to form the source of workers for the
majority of roads; and in spite of all the criticisms levelled against
it, the system continued. To this was added wage labour, paid, for
the most part, by virtue of individual acts of the legislatures.
In all the provinces the troops were from time to time employed in
cutting roads, which was more than justified by the military
importance of overland communication. This source of workers
was drawn on in Nova Scotia before the conquest of Canada and
for many years afterwards; it even appears that inhabitants were
enrolled as soldiers with the express purpose of turning them to
road work. Similarly the military forces in Canada were employed
on the roads soon after the capture of the colony. Simcoe's use
of the Queen's Rangers on both his trunk roads is a well-known
example.

Local roads and bridges were occasionally constructed by private
individuals; and not infrequently by public subscription. In the
former case the legislature was sometimes petitioned for reimburse-
ment, in the latter, a small group usually started the project,
subscribed themselves, and publicly invited further subscriptions.
Suggestions were made in Nova Scotia in the eighteenth century
for raising money by lotteries, but apparently these were frowned
on and never adopted. Apart from direct governmental enterprise,
the most common method of road-making was by the old English
system of turnpikes. There were a great many "turnpike trusts,"
as they were called. Though they varied widely in size, the principle
was in all cases the same: that the trusts on their side were obligated

29. Thomas Roy, *Remarks on the principle and practice of road-making, as
applicable to Canada* (Toronto, 1841).

to build and maintain a road or roads and to reimburse them they
were empowered to collect tolls from all those who used their roads.
Some at least of the turnpike trusts were organized as joint stock
companies. By the passage of the Joint Stock Companies' Act of
1849 the toll system was facilitated in Upper Canada; and after
that date a number of main roads passed into the hands of private
companies, which operated them as toll roads.

Constant criticisms were made of both public and private
enterprise. If words could have killed, the system of statute labour
would not have long survived in any of the provinces. Not all
contemporaries would have agreed that it was "worse than
useless," as one editor claimed, but many of them held that it was
inefficient and expensive; that persons unsuited to such work were
turned loose on the road; that the commutation fees would, if
made compulsory, allow for the hire of skilled workers; and that
statute labour was badly directed. While most contemporary
accounts show varying degrees of criticism of statute labour, it is
noteworthy that in the majority of replies to Robert Gourlay's
questionnaire the system is defended. This, however, may have
been due to the official element in the meetings which drew up the
reports.[30] A shocked citizen driving to Peterborough in 1835 protested solemnly against the sight of a pathmaster and all his men
"carousing on the road side."[31] One could hardly be surprised at
such an occasional scene in a province where whisky was all but
legal tender: the more serious complaints were those against the
inefficiency of the pathmasters. The engineer, Roy, who wrote in
moderate terms, suggested that " a general system of roads for the
province was not even thought of, and every separate road was
considered as a local affair," and that the commissioners "were
totally ignorant of the duties they were appointed to perform."
No general inspector of roads had been appointed for Upper
Canada to superintend the activities of the local commissioners.[32]
The editor of a Toronto paper wrote in a vein that was typical of
many such criticisms. He argued that good roads would never be
built until the system was changed: that it required skilled super-

30. Robert Gourlay, *Statistical account of Upper Canada* (London, 1822), i.
31. Cobourg *Star*, July 8, 1835.
32. Roy, *op. cit.*

intendence to construct or maintain a road. Pathmasters, he says, are appointed either because they hope for personal profit, or against their will. In either case the results are disastrous.[33] Another, and mathematically-minded editor worked out that 74,000 days of labour were annually expended on the roads of Upper Canada, which at two shillings per day would produce, by commutation, £7,400.[34]

It was inevitable that many of the holders of turnpike privileges should think more of the revenue they collected than of the care of their roads. There were constant assertions that turnpike roads were in a state of complete neglect, which was a cause of direct irritation to travellers who had to part with tolls at each gate. The toll system gradually disappeared on most of the main roads, but relics of it still remain here and there—more especially in the case of bridges. All the roads in the immediate vicinity of the city of Quebec were under the control of a single turnpike trust. Commissioners were appointed to investigate the situation, and in their report advocated the return of certain of the roads to the municipalities.

For crossing the many rivers fords and ferries were frequent. Corduroy bridges were valuable, especially if the banks of the river were high and steep. Planked bridges were a welcome innovation, and were frequently covered with a roof for protection against the weather and the weight of snow. Iron, stone, and concrete bridges belong to recent times.

Such conditions as have been sketched were, in general, natural in the pioneer stage of all the provinces. It was only when increasing population and the greater use of roads made the way easier that both provinces and municipalities developed more scientific methods of dealing with road construction and repair.

4. THE DEVELOPMENT OF ROADS

Probably every traveller who came to Canada in the first half of the nineteenth century talked or wrote of the curious kinds of roads he found and the acute discomfort of travelling on most of

33. *Royal Standard*, November 15, 1836.
34. *Loyalist*, December 1, 1827.

them. Only in winter, when the snow covered ruts and mud and stones, and made of the rivers a flat surface, could land travel be comfortable. Even then there were troubles to be met: partly frozen rivers or pools, drifts which overthrew the sleigh, thaws which spoilt the surface, cold in the day and miserable inns at night. Yet the winter was the best, as the spring was the worst part of the year, with the thaw bringing mud everywhere. So much better was the winter for travel in most districts that pleasure trips as well as much of the hauling were left until then. But, after all, snow good enough for sleighing could only be expected for a small part of the year: there was need of some provision for roads during the remainder.

The early settlers probably made use of Indian paths as the basis of a number of bridle-paths. Individuals, the mail, and supplies could be carried on horseback, and were often so carried until comparatively recent times. With all its limitations, this mode was obviously both simpler and less painful than a crude road: and most of the roads in the British provinces were crude until nearly the twentieth century. Here and there could be found a gravel, plank, or macadam road that, for a limited distance and for a limited time, was smooth; but such a discovery was the exception, not the rule. The people who used the roads were all too conscious of their defects, but neither constant complaints nor even (where it existed) a willingness to render active help, could readily solve the problem.

Conditions were not favourable to good roads. The severe climate of most areas meant a deep frost which, in the spring, broke cavities and raised humps in a surfaced road, and caused the worst form of mud on a soft road. Nearly everywhere were forests which necessitated the slow labour of cutting down trees and pulling out stumps, and made, too, many swamps which laid the workers low with ague. Rivers and lakes of all sizes meant detours, bridges or fords. In parts of the provinces hills and even mountains added acute problems of gradients. All these obstacles could readily have been overcome with the aid of plenty of money or even adequate statute labour; but the populations of all the provinces were sparse, revenues were tiny, and—in all but a few districts—a scattered population was already harassed with the task of cutting out farms or nursing some infant industry. A good deal of the blame was laid on the failure of the system of statute labour, but indeed there was little money for many years with which to hire workers. Later, when the population became relatively more numerous, and it was possible to find limited sums for road-building, the problem remained—as it remained in other forms of transportation in Canada—of finding resources for the construction of roads over a large area with a sparse population.

Nova Scotia was later than Canada in road-building, for by 1750 there seem to have been virtually no roads fit for wheeled vehicles. The earliest roads appear to have been purely local, as was to be expected. In 1754 the people of Lunenburg were reported as employed in cutting roads.[35] The first objective for a trunk road was to strike inland from Halifax, across the narrow peninsula to the Bay of Fundy. Some progress was made on this in the 'fifties, and by 1766 the important town of Windsor had been reached, although the road was mildly said to be "in an imperfect state." In the same year Francklin, the administrator, in urging upon the lords of trade the necessity of further roads, stated that only the one between Halifax and Windsor could be used by wheeled vehicles, and that other so-called roads, with the exception of the stretch from Windsor to Annapolis, could hardly even be used by horses, since the swamps and rivers had not been bridged. He describes them as "a direction to the foot travellers only."[36] Nevertheless, real progress had been made, for if a passable road existed between Halifax and Annapolis, it meant that the peninsula had been crossed, and the road carried on through one of the most fertile districts. Meanwhile, a report of 1762 spoke of a road from Halifax to Tatamagouche, and from there to Canso.[37] Governor Parr (1782–1786) was eager for the construction of more roads, and at his instigation another way was cut across the peninsula, from Shelburne to Annapolis, but it could hardly be called a road as yet. The road from Windsor to Annapolis was improved, and in Parr's régime a system of post-houses was established over the whole route from Halifax to Annapolis, a distance of 133 miles. By 1792

35. Innis, *op. cit.*, p. 214.
36. Canadian Archives, Series A 78, p. 112.
37. Innis, *op. cit.*, p. 247.

the eastern end of the peninsula had also been reached overland by a road from the capital to Pictou on the Gulf of St. Lawrence.

A generation later, in 1832, Bouchette wrote of Nova Scotia that "the roads of this province are, for a new country, inferior to none in America . . . the road from Halifax to Annapolis is very good, and kept in excellent repair. . . ."[38] He apparently refers here to the old road by way of Windsor; but by the 'thirties there was also a direct road, as planned long before by Parr. Another important highway extended from Halifax along the southern and western coasts, passing through Liverpool, Shelburne, and Yarmouth to Digby, and so to Annapolis. Similarly roads had been built to the other side of Halifax, to Canso and Antigonish. Towards the New Brunswick border roads ran beyond Truro into the county of Cumberland. In other words, there were highways radiating out from Halifax along and across the peninsula in all directions. Even if Bouchette's account of the state of the roads is over optimistic, the sum—£30,000—annually spent on construction and repairs, indicates a reasonable zeal.

In Prince Edward Island Governor Patterson (1770–1784) was an energetic road-builder, laying out the first roads of any length on the island. Shortly after his arrival he had started a road from the capital to Princetown, thirty-three miles to the east. It evidently, however, was little more than a track at that time, as a writer in a Charlottetown paper as late as 1830 recalled that, "I remember being one of the party that accompanied the present Governor to Princetown, when he drove the first four-wheeled vehicle which had ever travelled the road; and I never shall forget the difficulties which accompanied the journey."[39] Patterson also began a road to the east, with Georgetown as the objective.

New Brunswick, settled later than Nova Scotia, depended for transportation in the early years on the St. John River and its tributaries. After the War of 1812, however, more attention was given to the building of roads. The very facility of water transportation was, in Bouchette's opinion, a cause of the slow growth of roads in the province. On the other hand he also points out that

38. Joseph Bouchette, *The British Dominions in North America* (London, 1832), ii, 44.

39. *Royal Gazette*, November 30, 1830.

"almost all the great streams have . . . a road running near and nearly parallel to them."[40] One of the principal of such roads was that from St. John to Fredericton along the St. John River, supplemented in 1826 by a road between these two towns which took a more westerly line in the valley of the River Nerepis. A more northern area was opened in 1819 by a road across country from Fredericton to Miramichi; and a few years later the country on the east coast had a road from Shediac to Chatham.[41] In spite of these tangible facts, and of the many laws passed concerning roads, Bouchette held that, while roadways had been cleared in all settled parts of the province, "few of them are passable for carriages for any continuous distances, and at many seasons of the year they are wholly untraversable."

A more cheerful note is struck by Professor Johnston, who, in 1849, travelled over the greater part of the province in the course of making a report on its agricultural possibilities. Johnston is perhaps inclined to be optimistic about New Brunswick, but he travelled over 2,000 miles on its roads and found them "really good, and very creditable to the province."[42] In his report to the government he includes a statement on the condition of the roads drawn up by one of his travelling companions. This shows a total of 1,269 miles of great roads, connecting the main centres of the province. Each great road is described separately, with remarks showing that their condition varied from "good" to "as good as could be expected." "The opening and making of these Great Roads," the statement reads, "the creation of Bridges, with the allowance to explorers, surveyors and supervisors, cost the Province in the first place a sum exceeding £150,000; and an average sum of at least £10,000 per annum for the last fifteen years has been expended to keep them in repair." The by-roads, built principally by statute labour, are said to have been less well planned as to route, partly because they were built to join small settlements, or even houses, with little thought of more general considerations. Yet, in his travels, Johnston seldom had any serious difficulties

40. Bouchette, *op. cit.*, ii, 121.
41. W. F. Ganong, "Origins of settlements in the Province of New Brunswick" (*Transactions of Royal Society of Canada, 1904*).
42. J. F. W. Johnston, *Notes on North America* (Boston, 1851), i, 63.

from bad roads, and Brown, the author of the statement referred to above, sums up.

A good deal of fault has been found with the whole road system in this Province, and much has been said and written against it as tending to extravagance, political corruption, and gross mismanagement of the public money. It is, notwithstanding, an indisputable fact, that the Roads of New Brunswick, which fifteen years ago were everywhere a bye word and a reproach, are now in a better travelling condition than those of the adjoining Provinces, or the neighbouring States.[43]

More roads, of course, were needed, especially in certain areas which were inaccessible without them. Indeed the surveyor general proposed in 1849 the construction of 830 miles of additional roads at an estimated cost of £54,440.[44] On the whole the trunk roads had been built, and the work of the next decades was to fill in the gaps and to improve the grades and surfaces, as well as to build better bridges.

The overland route between the Maritime Provinces and the Canadas was a subject of constant attention both from the point of view of military communication, and because the mails which were unloaded at Halifax, when the St. Lawrence was frozen, were carried over it. Some mail came by way of New York, but the charges were heavy in passing through American territory. In the nineteenth century two routes to connect the provinces were opened up. The earliest was that which followed on the mainland the French path—the old Temiscouata portage. Starting at Halifax, the mails could be carried over the Windsor road to Annapolis by about 1785, and put on shipboard here or, later, at Digby, landing at St. John. From here there was a choice of routes. Travellers could proceed by boat up the St. John River as far as Grand Falls; or could go by land to Fredericton on a fairly good road; and even another eighty-five miles to Presqu'Isle, although this latter road was in a wretched condition, according to a report to the quartermaster general in 1819.[45] The next link mentioned in the same report is a stretch of twelve miles above Grand Falls,

43. J. F. W. Johnston, *Report on the agricultural capabilities of the Province of New Brunswick* (Fredericton, 1850), p. 19.

44. *Ibid.*, 23.

45. Canadian Archives, Q 167 B, p. 11.

"but it is at present so much neglected that even foot passengers cannot travel upon it." Worse still was a "road" beside the Madawaska, which could not even be found! However, the river was navigable and was followed by Lake Temiscouata. From the end of that lake a bad road ran to the St. Lawrence, and from there to Quebec was a road, wrote the English committee of engineers in 1825, "as good as most roads in England and certainly equal to anything that can be desired."[46]

In 1830 an extremely interesting report[47] was made by Stayner, a post office official, to Sir James Kempt on the condition of the post road between Quebec and Fredericton, with an estimate of the cost of repairing it up to a point where it could be travelled by the couriers at night. Leaving Quebec a carriage could go at five or six miles an hour along a good road. At Notre-Dame du Portage the portage road began, thirty-six miles to Temiscouata, all but five miles of which were "quite impracticable for wheels." Over the third section of forty-five miles there was no road at all, and the mails had to be carried over Lake Temiscouata. Similarly, in the fourth section of thirty-six miles, there was no road, in spite of the fact that there were a considerable number of settlers, so that the couriers took to the Madawaska River as far as Grand Falls. The fifth section was from Grand Falls to the River Aroostook, nineteen miles, where there had been "a sort of road," but not fit for use. From there to Woodstock, a distance of fifty-six miles, there was a somewhat better road, but not good enough for fast travel, or for vehicles at any speed. The last section, from Woodstock to Fredericton, sixty miles, had a fairly good road, but was short of bridges. No vehicles could be used between the St. Lawrence and Fredericton, except in the winter, when sleighing was possible over some parts. Even the courier could not travel the whole distance on foot, except in the winter with the aid of snowshoes. Stayner estimates the cost of improving the 252 miles south of the St. Lawrence at £26,700—a not inconsiderable sum.

Twenty years later, a more hopeful account is found in Johnston's report. From St. John to Fredericton the road was in good condition with safe bridges. From there to Woodstock the

46. *Ibid.*, Q 175 A.
47. *Ibid.*, Q 195–2, pp. 240 et seq.

old road, which crossed the river twice, had been rebuilt so as to run along the same bank, and was in common use. On to Grand Falls the road was on the right bank, and in places was hilly and difficult, but was nevertheless well travelled. From there to Madawaska, near the provincial boundary, the road was newer and only "pretty fair," but was apparently used. Thus no serious difficulties would apparently be encountered over the whole distance from Halifax to the Canadian border, though it may well be imagined that even a "good road" of the 'forties might offer impassable mud at times.

Emphasis was always laid on the Temiscouata route, largely because it was the only overland (and therefore the only winter) way from sea ports to the interior. During the War of 1812 it had to be used instead of the shorter road from New York; and constant complaints were made about the slowness of the mail service. In 1814, for example, letters reaching Halifax on December 3 were not delivered in Montreal until February 8. Even before the war the government of Lower Canada had had to examine into the mail service over that route. It was claimed by merchants of Montreal that the distance could be covered in six days, as apparently on one occasion it had; but even a more generous allowance of time would be considerably under a month.

In 1814 George Head, an army officer, took the journey from Halifax to Quebec in winter, and wrote a full and most interesting account of it.[48] He was in no hurry and was able to pay for what comfort there was. A sleigh from Halifax to Annapolis cost him eighty dollars, and from there to Digby, sixteen dollars. After having to wait for several days he took the packet at Digby, and got over to St. John in six hours. As soon as there was solid ice on the river he started out for Fredericton in a sleigh which he hired for twenty-eight dollars. The horses fell through the ice on the way, but were none the worse for it. Another sleigh took him the eighty-five miles to Presqu' Isle (thirty-two dollars), and from there on he had to walk on snowshoes, with the guides pulling the luggage on toboggans. It was far from being an easy journey, with head winds and blizzards and swollen feet from "*mal à raquette*";

48. George Head, *Forest scenes and incidents in the wilds of North America; being a diary of a winter's route from Halifax to the Canadas* (London, 1829).

but at Rivière du Loup he was able to get a post *carriole*, which took him the 111 miles to Quebec in two days.

The alternative interprovincial route was known as the Kempt road, named after Sir James Kempt (lieutenant-governor of Nova Scotia, 1820–1828, and administrator of Lower Canada, 1828–1830) who was an energetic road-builder. It was projected as a safer military route between the provinces, avoiding as it did the American border, and also as an encouragement to settlement on the eastern side of New Brunswick. The plan first appears in 1825, and was warmly recommended by Carmichael Smyth's commission as "the conception of a great mind."[49] In the early 'thirties it was open only in some sections, but in 1849 Johnston travelled over it.[50] The Canadian end was at Métis (reached from the west by the Taché road), and thence the line along the coast—later taken by the Intercolonial Railway—was followed. Light waggons were used. The first section across Gaspé to Campbelltown was 100 miles, a three-days' journey, and for the most part over rough and hilly surfaces through the forest. During this drive Johnston met only "the postman in his one-horse car, who passes along once a week." At Bathurst Johnston was impressed by a bridge half a mile long across the harbour. Following the general line of the coast, the Kempt road ran through more settled areas to Chatham, Shediac, and Amherst (Nova Scotia), on the Chignecto peninsula, whence, as has been seen, roads led through Truro to Halifax. But in spite of all efforts neither the Temiscouata nor the Kempt road provided adequate communication between the Maritime Provinces and Canada; only a railway could fill the long gap.

The tale of roads in Lower Canada is a longer one, stretching back to the early years of the eighteenth century. The extent and character of the roads which the British authorities found on taking over the colony have been already sketched. Increase of mileage from that time shows two general characteristics: a steady penetration of main roads into the areas more remote from the St. Lawrence, and the construction of connecting links with

49. Canadian Archives, Q 175 A, p. 201.
50. Johnston, *Notes*, 385 et seq.

the American states and New Brunswick.[51] On the north shore of the St. Lawrence roads in the interior were slow in coming. For the western district of Lower Canada it appears that as late as 1821 there was no passable road between Montreal and Hull on the Ottawa River, and that travellers were forced in places to drive on the ice of the river in winter. In 1828, however, a grant was made for the completion of the partially-built road. Between the Ottawa and St. Maurice rivers roads led northward through the seigneuries, following the river valleys; but connecting roads—apart from the old highway along the St. Lawrence—were still lacking in 1830. Much the same situation existed as far east as Quebec, while further down the river the mountains and the rough surfaces of the few roads made travelling difficult.

On the south shore of the St. Lawrence the main settled districts lay between the River Chaudière, running south from Quebec, and the western boundary of the province. The chief east and west highway was, of course, the old one along the river. The other main roads were those running through the eastern townships to the American border, serving both local and through traffic. From Quebec ran the Kennebec road along the Chaudière valley, giving access to Boston. Completed in 1830, it was said to be fit for carriages in that year.[52] A much needed communication between Montreal and New York followed the line of the Richelieu to the frontier, and though traffic went over it at all seasons, it had some bad stretches in 1830. The third of the roads connecting the St. Lawrence with the United States became known as Craig's road. Unlike the others, it was a diagonal road, cutting across country from Quebec, through the eastern townships to Richmond, and so south into Vermont. Planned in 1800, it was finished as far as Shipton in 1810 with the aid of troops sent by Sir James Craig. The *Quebec Gazette* excitedly called the road "the most important local event since this became a British Province," and made the suggestive statement that "this grand passage to the townships, will give to the City of Quebec some hope of independence, in procuring the necessary supplies for a growing Population. Hither-

51. Bouchette, *op. cit.*, ii; also Bouchette, *A topographical dictionary of the Province of Lower Canada* (London, 1832).

52. *Montreal Gazette*, October 6, 1830.

to restricted to the produce of a flinty neighbourhood, and unskilled husbandry, we have always had to look for support to the upper districts."

East of Quebec, the St. Lawrence highway ran past the beginning of the Temiscouata portage and on to a point about opposite Tadoussac. For most of this area, too, there were the usual side roads, which Bouchette says were in good condition. An important later development was the Taché road, built in the 'fifties, and affording an east and west highway in between the St. Lawrence and the American border, from south of Quebec to the Kempt road. The Taché road was intended to facilitate colonization, and from it branches were cut north and south to open up new townships. It did for the eastern end of the province something of the service that Craig's road did for the western. One of the difficulties in Lower Canada was the crossing of the St. Lawrence at Quebec. In summer this was done by a ferry; and when the river was frozen a road was cut smooth under orders of the *grand voyer*. But in the intervening period of loose ice, an exciting passage had to be made in heavy canoes which were paddled over the clear water, and dragged across the ice. Though commonly done, it was distinctly adventurous.

The early settlements in Upper Canada were made first along the upper St. Lawrence and the northern shore of Lake Ontario, and in subsequent years spread northward, taking advantage of other waterways in so far as that was possible. The first main roads, then, were built parallel to the St. Lawrence and the lake, as had been done on the lower river fifty years before. A primary need was for a highway connecting the towns of Lake Ontario with Montreal and tidewater. The Montreal end of this was built first, partly because the upper St. Lawrence was early settled, and partly because Lake Ontario offered easier navigation than the river with its rapids and falls. Sections of this had been opened in some form by 1790, but in 1796 Isaac Weld stated firmly that no one ever thought of going to Kingston by land.[53] Similarly La Rochefoucault

53. Isaac Weld, *Travels through the States of North America and the Provinces of Upper and Lower Canada during the years 1795, 1796 and 1797* (London, 1799), p. 258.

wrote in 1795 that, "although a communication by land is opened between Montreal and Kingston, and though half the road is very good, yet the intercourse between these places is mostly carried on by water."[54] The continuation of the Montreal-Kingston road was begun as early as 1798 when an American, Asa Danforth, secured the contract. At the end of three years it was said to be finished, but was probably the roughest kind of track for some years to come, without bridges over some of the rivers. It skirted the shore of Lake Ontario to Ancaster at the head of the lake, where it connected with the road to Niagara, built some dozen years before.

This "lake shore road," as it came to be known, was paralleled by Simcoe's "Dundas Street" (Canadians used the ancient practice of calling certain highways "streets"), made necessary by the military importance of establishing a communication away from the American border and leading to London, which Simcoe intended to make the capital of the province; and he set the Queen's Rangers to work in 1793 on this road, the first part of which to be opened was from Dundas, near the head of the lake, toward London, on the River Thames. In subsequent years it was continued east as far as York, following the high land away from the lake. As late as 1808 users of the road complained to the assembly that they could not cross the Credit River and the Sixteen or Twelve-Mile creeks with vehicles. East of York, Dundas Street was synonymous with the lake shore road as far as Barnard's Island, where it branched north and west to the province line.

Simcoe's other project in road-building was to link up Lake Ontario with Lake Simcoe, and so replace the old portage route to the upper lakes. He was principally actuated by military considerations (for only by this route could Niagara and Detroit be avoided), but his road was of great service, too, to settlers; and was used to an unknown extent by the North West Company in carrying their goods and furs to and from the west. Cutting of the road was begun by the Queen's Rangers in 1796, but it was some years before wheeled vehicles could pass over it with any comfort or safety. To make it fit for their bateaux, which were taken on wheels up

54. W. R. Riddell (ed.), *La Rochefoucault-Liancourt's travels in Canada in 1795* (Toronto, 1916), p. 83.

Yonge Street to Lake Simcoe, the North West Company contributed large sums of money.

Such were the main strategic routes first planned: their completion as passable roads was a gradual process. In the meanwhile the gaps were filled in throughout the province as settlement extended away from the chief water routes, and as more money became available to supplement statute labour and the efforts of the military. In the western end of the province two agencies contributed to the improvement of communication. Near the shore of Lake Erie that energetic organizer of settlement, Colonel Talbot, drove on the road-builders as he drove his settlers to clear land. In the early years of the nineteenth century the peninsula running out between Lakes Erie and Huron was traversed by a series of main roads, carrying travellers from Dundas to Sandwich *via* London, or nearer the lake shore through Port Talbot to the end of the peninsula. North of this the Canada Company showed considerable energy in having roads opened to and between their settlements. By the 'thirties Guelph could be reached from York or Dundas, and Galt from Paris or Dundas. The Guelph to Goderich road was constructed later.

To the east of the Canada Company's lands, an early highway of importance was that known as Hurontario Street, running from Port Credit on Lake Ontario to the port of Collingwood on Georgian Bay. The next north and south route made use of Yonge Street as far as Lake Simcoe, whence travellers could reach Georgian Bay either by the Severn River or (later) by direct road to Penetanguishene. East and north of Toronto was the Kawartha lakes district, centering at Peterborough, and one of the chosen spots for English immigrants. Though the lakes were valuable for transport, roads, too, were wanted. Peterborough was connected with Port Hope, but the local roads were long bad.

A general picture of the roads of Ontario in the middle of the century can be seen on a large and detailed map drawn up about 1855, and intended to show communications for military purposes.[55] The lake shore road acted as a trunk line, running from the Ottawa River to Niagara, with Dundas Street branching off to the north at each end. Most of this great length is marked as "good" or

55. This map is in the Canadian Archives.

"pretty good." Yonge Street ran to Holland Landing and then around Cook's Bay and north through Barrie to Penetanguishene. The section above Barrie is marked as "hilly and stony," succeeded by a length of "graded road," while the last part was "very bad." The west end of the province was well provided with roads: on the shores of Lake Huron they reached up as far as Goderich. From Owen Sound (then called Sydenham) a main road led to Toronto, and the Garafraxa road to Guelph. The Kawartha lakes district was by 1855 well provided with roads, though none ran immediately north of it in an area described as "bad land—no settlers." A little to the east of this was Simcoe Street, from Oshawa to Beaverton; and another road from Whitby to Beaverton and Balsam Lake. Glancing over this valuable map, it can be seen that Upper Canada roads served the southern and settled areas as well as reaching out to the northern lakes. They varied greatly in quality: some were good, many indifferent, others hilly, swampy or very bad. Not a few are marked as fit only for use in very dry weather, and some were only bridle paths.

5. THE USE OF ROADS

In the general chorus of disapproval that still echoes from contemporary letters, newspapers, and diaries, the occasional voice of praise of the roads is almost drowned. According to English standards of the day, or to modern Canadian standards, the roads of British North America cannot be given high marks. But the harvest was plentiful and the labourers few. Even now, in the settled districts of southern Ontario, many roads will be found which are almost or quite impassable for a period in the spring. The financial resources of the provinces cannot extend to all the many side roads. How much greater must the problem have been when a traveller had to drive for only a few miles from any town of British North America before reaching a wooded wilderness, broken only by the scanty clearings of the early farmers. Until well into the nineteenth century great areas of all the provinces had to be traversed in which there was hardly any local labour or local funds. Such circumstances must be borne in mind in all discussions of Canadian roads.

Many types of vehicles were used in British North America, in addition to the pack-horse which was long in common use on primitive roads. In French Canada two distinctive vehicles were found. The *calèche* is briefly described by Keefer as "a gig upon grasshopper springs with a seat for two passengers; the driver occupies the site of the dashboard, with his feet on the shafts and in close proximity to the horse with which he maintains a confidential conversation throughout the journey. . . ."[56] Used before the conquest, the *calèche* is still driven in Quebec. In winter it was replaced by the *carriole*, a sleigh with single runners and seating two persons. The lowness of this sleigh caused piling up of the snow, and the consequent *cahots*, or ridges, which were a source of constant annoyance to travellers.

In the British provinces vehicles of all kinds were found. The springless waggon was generally used for freight and sometimes for passengers. The buckboard, a carriage sprung on long and pliable boards which formed the floor, was popular in New Brunswick. In all the provinces ox-carts were once common. The most characteristic vehicle of Ontario was known as the "buggy," a light carriage with seats for two and large wheels, particularly adapted to the bumpy and muddy roads. The farmer and his family drove to church in the "democrat," a light springed waggon, drawn by two horses, and capable of carrying two or three seats. A lighter and more refined form of the democrat was known as a "surrey." When the sleighing season came wheels were discarded in favour of runners, of which there were suitable types both for waggons and passenger sleighs. The small "cutter" of Ontario corresponded to the *carriole*, but was placed higher from the ground.

Carriages of all kinds, both for town and country use, were made in blacksmiths' shops and in factories all over British North America. Here were produced most forms of English carriages, with the exception of the hansom cab. An important, and sometimes imposing, vehicle was the stage-coach. The name covers a wide variety of vehicles, ranging from an open waggon drawn by two horses to an impressive four-horse coach of the English type. Something of the latter kind is most typical of the 'thirties and 'forties when coaching was at its height. Such a coach would hold

56. In Hind, *op. cit.*, p. 111.

about nine persons, with luggage, mail, and light freight. In winter, of course, wheels gave place to runners.

It was the stage routes with which travellers from abroad were most likely to come into contact, and for that reason many descriptions of such forms of travel exist. It was, normally, far from being a luxurious experience to travel in a stage-coach. Early starts and long hours were the rule; the coach itself was often rough, cold, or leaky; the drivers, though clever and sometimes amusing, were often of a rough type and accustomed to drink too freely. In this condition they were liable to drive off the road into a ditch or worse. At least one instance is recorded of the Montreal stage falling through the ice of the river while the driver was in the post office. Led by one opportunist the passengers sailed down the river on a block of ice and were all saved. The worst enemy of the traveller by coach was the roads. Time after time travellers wrote of the terrible jolting which seemed to break every bone in their bodies; nor was it uncommon for the coach to suffer some harm which necessitated roadside repairs. In the spring particularly, but possibly at any season, the coach would stick in the mud, whereupon all passengers were called upon to lend a hand in pulling it out, perhaps with the help of rails from the nearest fence. There was a striking difference between the optimistic phrases found in the advertisements of stage-coach owners and the often painful reality.

While the traveller naturally concerned himself with comfort and expense, the historian may look more dispassionately at the system as a whole. There is no mystery about the system of stages in travel. The pages of Dickens and the pictures on Christmas cards are full of information on the subject. At bottom it was an old means of getting over the difficulty that horses—the sole form of motive power—could pull a vehicle for only a limited distance at a time, while the vehicle and the passengers were capable of going on for twelve hours or more in a day. It was therefore a natural solution to arrange for regular shifts of horses. Generally speaking, the length of each stage was based on the distance which one set of horses could travel. Thus the stage-coach, as a particular kind of vehicle, was not a necessary part of the system. In the earliest use of the stage system in Canada one- or two-horse carriages or sleighs were the rule, but later it was found convenient to enlist larger carriages. Another fundamental aspect of the stage system was that it was intended for long-distance travel, and was the only rapid means of transport by land until the railway came into being.

It was largely this fact which led to the encouragement of the stage system by the post office in British North America. No regular postal delivery system existed in the French régime, but one was quickly instituted by the British government after the conquest. Hugh Finlay, the first postmaster, made use of the existing *maîtres de poste* with whom he first arranged for the provision of saddle-horses. In the next few years he secured for the *maîtres de poste* exclusive rights as carriers between Quebec and Montreal, which made it possible for them to convey the mail at low rates. Throughout British North America something of the same arrangement was made, and thus the stage-coaches carried the royal mail under the same general conditions as did the railways in a later period.[57] In other words, there was an arrangement of mutual advantage between the post office and the owners of stage-coaches, the former providing a steady source of income for the latter. An individual, partnership, or company operating a line of stage-coaches was generally, if not always, chartered by an act of the provincial legislature, which imposed restrictions as to charges and service, and sometimes seems to have demanded a contribution toward the upkeep of the road used. In return the company received a monopoly, or at least a privileged position, in the carriage of mail and passengers.

The development of stage routes is an interesting story in itself. There was a regular stage line between Halifax and Windsor in the eighteenth century. In 1821 the proprietor of a coach called "The True Briton" advertised a regular weekly winter service between these two places, the distance being covered in a day. He further offered to provide conveyances, as required, to Horton, Cornwallis and other towns.[58] A Halifax newspaper of 1837 contains the advertisement of a stage line between Halifax, Truro, and

57. W. Smith, *The history of the post office in British North America, 1638–1870* (London, 1920), *passim*.
58. *Acadian Recorder*, January 13, 1821.

Pictou. During the winter the coaches ran only once a week. The fare from Halifax to Truro was £1, and to Pictou £1.10.0. Way passengers were carried at the rate of five pence per mile.[59]

Mention has been made of the early existence of the stage system in Canada. In 1767 several advertisements appeared of masters of the post-houses, who were ready to furnish carriages "at a minute's warning." The notices applied to both the Quebec-Montreal and Montreal-Albany services. A traveller at the end of the century writes of the regular service between Montreal and St. Johns by way of Laprairie. "Travelling in this province", he wrote, "is easy and expeditious. A public mail-stage runs from St. Johns to Quebec."[60] That all was not well in the system of post-houses in Lower Canada is very apparent from official correspondence of 1802. The inspector of provincial post-houses visited them during the summer and found many complaints that the business was an unprofitable one—so much so that many *maîtres de poste* gave up their positions—while it was hard to find men to take their place. On the other hand the travellers had something to say: that the carriages were in bad condition (an amusing touch is the complaint that "the wheels are too near the body and strike the elbows of those who are in the *Calèches*"); that they went too slowly, and were too long detained at the post-houses, and so on.[61]

The main stage line of Lower Canada was that between Montreal and Quebec. In 1811 four-horse coaches ran twice a week in the winter and three times in the summer, taking two days for the journey—but long days, for they started at four in the morning and drove until eight in the evening.[62] Two years later the stages ran six days a week.[63] In the same early years of the nineteenth century, other routes were being developed. The Albany-Montreal stage now ran three times a week.[64] Once a week a stage went from Montreal to the Long Sault on the Ottawa River, where passengers and mail for Hull were transferred to boats. In 1829 a stage line

59. Halifax *Times*, January 17, 1837.
60. J. C. Ogden, *A tour through Upper and Lower Canada* (Litchfield, 1799).
61. Canadian Archives, Q 89, p. 131.
62. *Quebec Gazette*, January 31, and April 18, 1811.
63. *Ibid.*, May 27, 1813.
64. *Ibid.*, December 28, 1818.

ran to Stanstead in two days and connected with the American lines there. In winter there was, by the 'forties, a stage line from Quebec over the Kennebec road to Portland and Boston.[65]

In the meanwhile lines of stages had begun running in Upper Canada. At least as early as 1798 one was in operation between Newark and Chippawa;[66] and, what was even better, the road was said by the surveyor general to be a good one.[67] By 1830 this road, leading to the Niagara portage, was one of the most travelled in the province. It was said in 1831 that the journey between Lakes Erie and Ontario could easily be done in a day, including a three-hour stop at Niagara Falls. Connection between Upper and Lower Canada by stage began in 1816 with a line between Montreal and Kingston, which was extended to York in the following year.[68] In 1828 Montrealers were impressed by the Upper Canada stage covering the distance from Prescott to Montreal in seventeen hours.[69] In 1831, by the "spirited exertions" of the mail contractors, the Upper Canada mail, which left Kingston early in the morning, reached Montreal on the afternoon of the day following.[70]

The first line of stages between York and Niagara began operation in 1816, charging five dollars for each passenger.[71] An advertisement of 1836 shows that by that time there was a daily service over the lake shore road between Toronto and Hamilton, and daily except Sunday by way of Dundas Street.[72] No time is given for the journey at this date, but in 1843 it appears as ten hours. In the latter year, too, the daily coach from Toronto to Kingston covered the distance in thirty-six hours.[73] Other areas in Upper Canada were gradually served with lines of stages. Yonge Street

65. R. W. S. Mackay, *Travellers' Guide to the River St. Lawrence and Lake Ontario* (Montreal, 1845).

66. *Upper Canada Gazette*, May 26, 1798.

67. *A short topographical description of His Majesty's Province of Upper Canada, in North America* (London, 1799).

68. J. J. Talman, "Travel in Ontario before the coming of the railway" (*Ontario Historical Society, Papers and Records*, vol. xxix).

69. Montreal *Courant*, quoted in *Colonial Advocate*, September 24, 1828.

70. *Montreal Gazette*, January 24, 1831.

71. Guillet, *op. cit.*, p. 553.

72. *Cobourg Star*, January 6, 1836.

73. *Examiner*, January 11, 1843.

was provided with a line in 1828 between Toronto and Holland Landing, which soon gave a daily service. Another line was chartered in 1828 to cover in four days the journey between Niagara and Sandwich (on the Detroit River). The Canada Company established a stage line from Hamilton to Goderich in about 1832 to open up their lands.[74]

Thus by the 'forties the system of stage-coaches was quite highly organized, and at the same time the carriages used became more comfortable. At no time was water transport forgotten as a supplement to that by land; and, more especially after steamers came into use, the long trips were organized (in the summer) to make use of both modes. In 1831, for example, a combination land and water route was worked out for the long journey from Montreal to Niagara, so as to take advantage of navigable water. The first nine miles to Lachine were by stage; steamer to the Cascades; stage to Coteau du Lac; steamer to Cornwall; stage to Prescott; and steamer to Kingston, York and Niagara.[75] The same system continued to be used for many years, the only change being that—except in winter—the steamers gradually took a larger share as canals progressively circled the rapids.

The objects of the system of roads in British North America need little explanation. Generally speaking they may be divided into two: long-distance routes for mail, passengers, and light freight; local roads for communication between town and country, to carry farm products to market and to ports, to supply farmers with manufactured articles, to open a way to the mills, and to make possible the settlement of a steadily-increasing area. It was very generally argued that the development of roads would benefit both agricultural communities and the urban centres they supplied. With regard, however, to the opening of roads to the American border, the editor of the influential *Quebec Gazette*, writing in 1815, was hesitant. He argued that prices of farm products were higher in the seaports of the New England states than they were in Quebec, and that the result of easy communications would raise the prices in Quebec and lower them in New England; that, in fact, they would tend to become equal. He felt that in any case the Americans,

74. Talman, *op. cit.*, pp. 9–10.
75. *Cobourg Star*, May 17, 1831.

with their ice-free ports, were already establishing a commercial ascendancy, and that easy communications would hasten the process. He would therefore limit the communication with the American states. Five years later the *Gazette* reprinted without comment a note in a Maine paper stating that cattle—"our surplus products"—were being driven over the new road to Quebec.

Some indications have already been given of the character and conditions of roads, and the problems of travel. Great emphasis was laid by officials, residents, and visitors on the importance of more and better roads. "I realy am of opinion," wrote Legge, governor of Nova Scotia, in 1774, "that this will be the most flourishing Province in North America in less than half a century. Nothing is wanting to forward it, but money to make Roads."[76] That might be taken as the text of all comments on the subject of roads for many years. An early letter in the *Quebec Gazette* gives a somewhat depressing picture of the roads near that city:

... si ... je vais faire un tour hors de ville, je suis dans une crainte continuelle, soit de me tordre le col ou estropier mon cheval, casser ma caleche, etc. . . . Que je me tourne de quel coté que ce soit dans les environs de cette ville, je me vois que des ponts cassés, des traversins qui manquent, d'autres où ils ne sont point arrêtés, et un nombre infini d'ornières.[77]

Many years later a farmer of the township of Barnston in the district of Montreal wrote that fifty-one families had left the township for the United States in the period since the beginning of the war (of 1812), largely on account of "the want of Road to the markets of the Province."[78] In 1831, complaints were still made that roads in and about Montreal were disgraceful. Two correspondents to the *Montreal Gazette* agreed that officials did nothing until they heard of a visit from the governor general. On the whole, however, the complaints about the state of the roads in Lower Canada are not so frequent as to convey the impression of a general discontent.

The wrath of English author-travellers seems to have fallen most

76. Canadian Archives, A 90, p. 4.
77. *Quebec Gazette*, July 6, 1769.
78. *Ibid.*, January 28, 1819.

heavily on the roads of Upper Canada. It was not uncommon in
that (or any other) province for a waggon to be damaged by especially heavy bumps, or even for unwary passengers to be thrown out
bodily. Mud holes were a normal hazard, and often a carriage
could not be got out without the aid of borrowed oxen. Travelling
through the bush was made a misery by myriads of mosquitoes,
and by the discomfort of the inns, which were often of the rudest.

The roads are few and poor [reads an Emigrants' Guide of 1820], but
they are moderately commensurate with the retarded progress of the
province. . . . The Conveyances, where there are any (and such of any
description are by no means universal), are generally poor; the surface
rough, the bridges wretched, and the attendance at the inns as defective,
as must necessarily be the case where there is too great a tone of general
equality and familiarity, amidst a scattered, independent, and unculti-
vated people.[79]

The information given to Gourlay in 1817 suggests a better system
of roads than is generally imagined. It may be, however, that local
pride coloured the accounts of those who answered the questions.
A letter to the *Colonial Advocate* gives a contemporary description
of the Upper Canada roads in 1825, and may be quoted here because
of its comprehensive character:

I think that by far too little attention is paid to the roads. . . . Truly
the roads are the worst feature in the country. . . . I have witnessed
vast and extensive improvements made by the settlers, not only in Dundas
Street, but even on the more remote and less frequented roads. . . . In
Newcastle district . . . is the progress of improvement in the roads apparent. . . . In the district of Niagara there are some of the best roads in
the province, especially the highway leading from Niagara through to
Queenston, Waterloo and Fort Erie. The great western road from Dundas
and Ancaster to Vittoria . . . is, with the exception of part of the Grand
River swamp, tolerably good during the greater part of the year. And
that grand undertaking the bridge across the Grand River at Brantford
has not only added greatly to the convenience of the Western country,
but has likewise given rise to the flourishing post town of that name. . . .
The Eastern district in its communication with Lower Canada has the
disadvantage of a bad piece of road which the legislature of that province
has signified its willingness to co-operate with Upper Canada in repairing.

79. C. Stuart, *The Emigrants' Guide to Upper Canada* (London, 1820).

The road through the Indian woods near Belleville, the roads below Kingston towards Gananoque, the roads near the River Trent westward, and beyond Post's Tavern to York, as also the roads from the Humber to the line where the Street enters the Gore district, and again in these woods beyond Vittoria and until we enter Talbot Street are almost impassable at some seasons of the year, and are at all times a great obstruction to the settlement and improvement of the country. The condition of the bridges at 12 and 16 mile creeks in the Gore district is deplorable and there are too many other bridges in the same condition.

It is impossible to paint a true picture of the conditions of roads of British North America, for the scene changes from year to year and place to place. Such evidence as has been presented will perhaps indicate a reasonably consistent progress in all colonies, both in quantity and quality. On the whole roads of a kind were "opened" or "cut" as they were required, but it might be a long time before vehicles could even attempt to get through. Stone, macadam, and plank roads offered brighter intervals while they lasted, and in some districts sandy soil was a guarantee against mud, the worst enemy of the traveller. By about the middle of the nineteenth century a fairly complete road system existed, and, under normal conditions, vehicles could be used with varying degrees of discomfort.

A system of roads had been essential to the settled communities of the provinces; to serve the agricultural districts as they were cut out of the forest, and to join them to the towns. In all the provinces the governments were responsible for the building of roads, but the needs of the various areas differed. In the Maritime Provinces there was no competition for government aid caused by pressure for canals—as there was in Canada. In the latter, the early roads in particular, and to some extent all roads, were designed to supplement and connect with the inland waterways; while in the Maritime Provinces the trunk roads formed a complete system of inland transportation in themselves.

The problem of providing a hard and smooth surface over the thousands of miles of the roads of British North America was one that could not, with the best intentions, be solved by the small and poor population of those vast and untamed areas. And while the people of the colonies were struggling against the odds of distance, hills, mud, and scanty resources, a series of patient inventors and engineers were in process of solving the problem in another way. Land travel, on inadequate roads and with horses as the only motive power, could never fully supply the transportation needs of the country; but the happy, if delayed, marriage of the railroad and steam locomotive promised a solution of the dual problem. And so, while roads could never be displaced for many forms of transport, their glory faded before the whistle of the iron horse. The gaily painted coach, the elaborate stage system, the innumerable coaching inns, had had their day. The road, thus displaced, came back to worry its former victor when the motor car challenged the railway train. But for over half a century the centre of the stage was taken by the noisy and exciting invention, new panacea of the problems of Canadian transportation.

CHAPTER V

THE FIRST RAILWAY ERA

1. EARLY EXPERIMENTS

"HERE we have comparatively few or no good roads, we have often to wade through mud and swamps for many miles together, and except in the sleighing season, find it almost impossible to go any distance." So wrote an inhabitant of the western part of Upper Canada in 1836, urging that railways were needed in Canada even more than in England—where good roads and canals already existed as alternatives.[1] While this picture was, perhaps, exaggerated for the sake of emphasis, and from the enthusiasm for the new method of transport, it was in part true of all sections of British North America. At that time the canals had not been carried far, and it had proved impossible to construct a system of roads anything like adequate to the needs of the population. Even when the St. Lawrence canals were finished, they provided only a partial solution to the problem of transport in Canada, since they were available for only a part of the year, and served a limited area. Canalization was of little help in the Maritime Provinces and in the inland parts of Canada. Road transport was slow; it was difficult; and it was expensive. Railways seemed a heaven-sent way of making up for the deficiencies of both water and road transport.

The steam railway came from the combination of two separate inventions: the track for carrying wheeled vehicles, used in English mines for some two hundred years; and the steam engine, an old invention developed in the eighteenth century. In 1769 the citizens of Paris were amazed to see a steam carriage puffing slowly through the streets of the city. Attempts were made further to apply the steam engine to carriages and coaches, and strange monsters appeared on English roads. By the beginning of the nineteenth century boats propelled by steam had, after many failures, been successfully built, first in England, and soon after on the Hudson

1. Toronto *Patriot*, September 13, 1836.

147

River. In 1809 the first steamboat plied the waters of the St. Lawrence. Having progressed thus far, it was simply a question of time before steam engines would take the place of horses to draw carriages on railed tracks, and experiments soon produced results which were startling in their novelty. In England, in the 'twenties, the Stockton and Darlington was the first railway to carry public goods, and at the end of the decade Stephenson's famous *Rocket* made a record run of seventy miles at an average of fifteen and a maximum of twenty-nine miles an hour. The scoffers were silenced and the steam locomotives had an assured future. Similar progress was made in the United States, where the Baltimore and Ohio Railroad reached the unprecedented length of 133 miles in 1833.

With such examples before them in the two countries from which they chiefly drew their ideas, it would have been strange if Canadians had not shown a keen interest in railways and given earnest thought to their possible application to local conditions. In all the provinces the climate was comparatively severe in the winter, and in some districts deep snow and heavy frosts must be expected. Such obstacles to railway operation had not been encountered at all in England and only in the northern states. Could steam be maintained in locomotives during the colder part of the winter? Would snow on the tracks make it impossible for trains to proceed? Not a few of those interested in railways in the early days were confident that they could be used only in the summer, while one ingenious, if impracticable, suggestion was made that the tracks should be raised from the ground so as to clear the snow. The question of grades arose, too. The more pessimistic had prophesied that smooth wheels would never grip smooth tracks even on the level, and when this doubt was dispelled by experience elsewhere it was still a question in many minds whether a locomotive could get up a hill without cogged wheels.

The Lower Canada newspapers began to write about railways in 1824, although they claimed to know little about them. They thought of the cog or rack type of rail, and assumed that railways could not be operated in the winter. As to materials, wood was present in unlimited quantities for fuel, and was for some years suggested for rails. The York *Courier*, for example, contains an

article in 1832 in which it is argued that wooden rails should be
generally adopted for the sake of cheapness and to use surplus
wood. James George (who seldom lacked ideas) proposed to the
British government that railways could be made of the "rough
trees of the Forest" at a cost of £10 per mile.[2] Gradually these and
similar notions disappeared in the light of foreign experience, and
more especially of the experience of the few Canadian railways.
Such doubts as whether an engine with flat wheels could get
traction on a flat track and whether wooden—or even metal
covered—rails would serve were answered by the working of the
little Champlain and St. Lawrence railway. Clearly a steam
engine could be made to pull cars over a track. The idea of using
wooden rails for lines with light traffic was, however, slow to disappear. In 1869 the legislature of Quebec chartered six companies
which proposed to build colonization railways with wooden rails.
Two were actually built: the Quebec and Gosford Wooden Railway, and the Richelieu, Drummond and Arthabasca. The rails
were of maple, placed on edge in notches in the ties, and held in
place by wedges. No nails or other metal were used. The Gosford
was operated for two years, but warping and other troubles with
the rails led to its abandonment.[3]

Technical difficulties were overcome in practice, but the problem
of meeting the cost long remained. At the opening of the nineteenth
century the total population (in round figures) of all the British
North American provinces was 250,000. This grew slowly in the
first decade of the century, and began to increase rapidly after the
Napoleonic wars, when hard years in the British Isles led to a more
rapid emigration. By 1825 the population had risen to some 850,000
distributed as follows: Lower Canada, 500,000; Upper Canada,
150,000; Nova Scotia, 125,000; New Brunswick, 75,000. While
this was a healthy increase, the population still remained scanty
and scattered. By the middle of the century, when railway building
began in earnest, the situation had become more encouraging.
Lower Canada had gone up to 890,260; Upper Canada to 952,000;
Nova Scotia to 276,850; and New Brunswick to 193,800. In twenty-
five years the population had considerably more than doubled, and

2. Canadian Archives, Q 170–2, p. 358.
3. R. R. Brown, "Wooden rails" (*Canadian National Railways Magazine*, xx, 7).

had comfortably passed the two million mark. Already the resources of the provinces had been strained to provide roads and canals: where would the money come from to pay for the construction and maintenance of railways? The genius of salesmen brought in subscriptions locally, and for a time the hope of profit led to brisk dealing in railway stocks; but, even when government support was added, there was not enough capital in the country to build anything but miniature railways. It was predicted that the encouragement of immigration, increase of business, and rising value of land would make railways not only pay their own way but even make fabulous profits. One writer in Upper Canada believed that land values between London and Dundas would be increased by one million dollars if a railway were built between these towns.[4] In reality, no such rapid profits came to solve the problem, and before long it became necessary to turn to the investors of England to bear the lion's share of the original cost. The very success of the appeal led to two complications: dissatisfaction in England with Canadian railway projects which too often collapsed financially, and, on the other hand, control of railways from London, which sometimes resulted in discontent in Canada.

The relation between canals and railways was a much disputed point. A first impression was that no railway should be built where it would compete with a canal. In 1832 the house of assembly of Upper Canada debated whether the proposed railway from Chippawa to Queenston would injure the Welland Canal, and opinion proved to be divided. As late as 1845, when railways were an accepted fact, an Upper Canada editor strongly urged that they would render useless the canals which were being built at great public expense. He struck a new note by prophesying that railways in their turn would but be replaced by "other schemes of locomotion, whether atmospherical or electro-magnetic."[5] On the other hand there were many expressions of the opinion that canals could never constitute a complete system of transportation, but would continue to carry heavy freight. Added to this were proposals that railways should be built instead of projected canals, as, for

4. *Western Mercury*, January 31, 1833.
5. *British Whig*, November 4, 1845, quoted in *Western Globe*.

example, on the Grand River between Brantford and Port Hamilton.[6] On the whole, railway construction was retarded by the
commitments made for canals, and by their success in the halcyon
days of the grain traffic in the early 'forties.

Connected with this question of the relation of canals and railways was that of the traffic that might be expected for the latter.
In England and the United States the first railway period coincided
with the industrial revolution and—in the case of the United States
—with a general and compelling belief in expansion. Both these
forces found an echo in the British provinces, but the fact that
industrialization in them was slower in coming meant a reduction
in potential freight traffic. The chief exports were the products of
farm and forest: wheat and flour, pot and pearl ash, timber and
lumber. Only a part of the transport business arising out of these
products would fall to the railways, for most of the timber went
at least part of the way in rafts, and the wheat was carried by
water as far as the lakes and rivers were available. Imported
manufactured products might be expected to go by rail, and a
steady source of revenue would arise from the carriage of mail.
Some attempts were made to estimate the volume of business:
for example the legislature of New Brunswick had prepared for
its information an elaborate analysis of the imports and exports
of each county.[7] Too often, however, the legislatures and the
public were swayed more by vague generalizations as to the traffic
that would arise than by exact inquiries into what existed.

The dominating motive connected with traffic was that will-o'-
the-wisp, the control of the communications of the United States.
The traffic of the railways, therefore, was not calculated on a basis
of local business only, but on the additional amount that would
arise from the position of the provinces as links between Europe
and the mid-western states. Those rapidly-growing states west
of the Great Lakes must find an outlet to the sea, and what more
natural than that this should be by the St. Lawrence Valley, the
direct route? On this hypothesis Canadian railways would not

6. *Western Mercury*, July 26, 1832.
7. *Reports relating to the project of constructing a railway and a line of electro-
magnetic telegraph through the Province of New Brunswick from Halifax to Quebec*
(Fredericton, 1847).

only pay their own way and bring profit to their shareholders, but would be the source of immense wealth to the lands through which the stream of goods would pass. Few of even the earliest schemes for railways were unrelated to this philosophy. The Champlain and St. Lawrence was meant not only to connect Lower Canada with New York, but to draw the trade of the neighbouring states to the St. Lawrence. The Halifax to Quebec or St. Andrews to Quebec projects were designed to provide a line from the winter ports of the Maritime Provinces through the St. Lawrence valley and Great Lakes to the west. The Toronto and Lake Huron railway was to make a short cut to the upper lakes, a more favourable route than the two sides of the triangle around by Detroit. The engineer engaged on the survey for this line wrote in his report,

. . . That the Toronto and Lake Huron Rail Road would attract from our neighbours a large share of the carrying trade at present almost entirely monopolized by the Hudson and Erie Canal cannot be doubted. . . . The Rail Road between Boston and Albany will bring the former into the same route as New York, and should the Rail Road between Lake Champlain and Ogdensburg be constructed, it will be another feeder to the Toronto and Lake Huron Railway. . . . When the improvements of the St. Lawrence are completed the trade to and from the route will be still more drawn in our direction and in that of the railway in question.[8]

The same idea was expressed a few years later when the Kingston and Toronto railway was under discussion, except that it was to connect with a line from Toronto to Port Sarnia. It was blissfully expected that the traffic from New York and Boston to the American west would pour over this line.[9]

Such were the reactions to the questions raised when railways were in contemplation for the British colonies. Another factor, which was not discussed but is readily apparent, is that lines of railway commonly followed the routes marked out by roads: that is to say, they were regulated largely by topographical conditions. The tale of actual construction before 1850 is a short one.[10]

8. *Patriot*, March 31, 1837.
9. Peterborough *Gazette*, October 3, 1845.
10. For general accounts of the construction of railways *see* O. D. Skelton, *The railway builders* (*Toronto, 1920*); N. Thompson and J. H. Edgar, *Canadian railway development* (Toronto, 1933); *Canada and its provinces*, x.

Discussion of a line around the rapids on the Richelieu, to facilitate travel between Montreal and New York, began in 1824. Four years later a petition was laid before the house of assembly of Lower Canada praying that this subject be taken into consideration. In 1832 a charter was granted to the Champlain and St. Lawrence Railroad Company, providing for an initial capital of £50,000 with power to increase it by £15,000. If dividends exceeded twelve per cent the rates were to be reduced on a fixed scale. Power to assume ownership on a cost plus basis was reserved to the government. Construction began in 1835, and the road was opened for traffic in the following year with a steam engine imported from England. The rails were of wood faced with iron strips: a most unsatisfactory arrangement, as the iron frequently came loose and banged against the trains. Still it was a successful start, and one graced by the usual "large and respectable gathering."

An alternative route to the American coast was that from Montreal to Portland, and for this purpose the St. Lawrence and Atlantic Railway was actually begun in 1848; but it will be best considered in relation to the great building period of the 'fifties. In the meanwhile another portage railway, similar to that around the rapids of the Richelieu, was planned to cover the eight miles between Montreal and Lachine. The Montreal and Champlain Railroad, as it was called, was opened in 1847.

In Upper Canada there was much talk but little action. Lines were proposed from London to Dundas, from Toronto to Lake Huron, along Lake Ontario, and from Cobourg to Rice Lake. Seven charters had been issued by 1841, but none of them acted on. A portage railway around Niagara Falls was attempted and rail actually laid from Queenston to Chippawa in 1839, but the grades proved to be too steep for locomotives and horse power was used until the road was rebuilt in 1854.

The Maritime Provinces had about an equal amount to show by the middle of the century. It is significant that the first steam railways were used in the coal industry of Nova Scotia, that is, in an area which was comparable in kind to those northern parts of England where railways were first built. Steam locomotives were introduced on a short coal line at Pictou in Nova Scotia in 1838. A year later another six miles of railway came into operation to

carry coal from the Albion mines to the Gulf of St. Lawrence. A
modest beginning: especially so in relation to the vast schemes
that were generally being discussed, and some of which had
reached the stage of charters and surveys: for Nova Scotia and
New Brunswick were very conscious of being Maritime Provinces,
and in a position to open a way from seaboard to Canada and to the
American states—from both of which they might then exact due
tribute.

2. The Maritime Provinces and Railways

There is something attractive about the magnitude of the railway schemes of all the British provinces. These poor and under-
populated colonies planned lines of steel from Halifax to Windsor,
in Upper Canada; from the Gulf of the St. Lawrence to New
England. It was the Yankee spirit of Sam Slick combined with a
determination so to strengthen the British colonies that they could
stand firm against the expanding power of the United States.
There were two main strategic points in the long line: one was at
the western end where Canada touched the centre of the American
west, and the other at the eastern extremity where the ports of
the Maritime Provinces held ice-free gates to the continent.

Within Nova Scotia and New Brunswick there was need of
railways for internal communication. In the case of the latter no
provincial revenues at all had been set aside for canals and in
Nova Scotia no large part. The railways in which these provinces
were particularly interested hinged on two points: St. Andrews
(or St. John) in New Brunswick, and Halifax in Nova Scotia. The
former was the first to come into the picture, for as early as 1827
a railway from there to Quebec was proposed, an advantage of this
route being that it was the shortest from the Atlantic to Canada.
The idea was given publicity by an article in the *United Service
Journal* of 1832; and in the summer of 1835 a reconnaissance of
the valleys of the Etchemin and Chaudière was made by order of
Lord Aylmer acting on the request of a committee of citizens of
Quebec. In the report of this early reconnaissance, it was frankly
proposed to go through Maine.[11] The citizens of St. Andrews

11. *Report of a reconnoissance of the vallies of the Etchemin and Chaudière.* . . .
(1835).

formed, in that autumn, the "Saint Andrews and Quebec Rail Road Association," which secured general approval for the scheme "among the best informed in this Province," as well as getting resolutions passed through both houses of the legislature of Lower Canada expressing approval and making rather vague promises of help.[12] In 1836 the railway was chartered in New Brunswick, and a cash contribution by the British government enabled the survey to be begun. Unfortunately, however, the line proposed ran through the territory in dispute between Maine and New Brunswick, and at the request of the American government proceedings were stopped. Already the editor of the New York *Express* had labelled the St. Andrews and Quebec railway as "one of the most magnificent [plans] that has yet been projected upon this continent." He pointed out that the line would make for easy transport of troops as well as of freight, and professed to "look upon the movements the British and Colonial Governments are making . . . with great anxiety and alarm."[13] By the Webster-Ashburton treaty a part of the surveyed land was lost to New Brunswick. For a decade the whole scheme was dropped, but in 1847 ground was broken at St. Andrews and a line under the name of the New Brunswick and Canada started out bravely with Woodstock as the immediate and Quebec as the final goal. Twenty years later the rails reached Woodstock, but the company was bankrupt.

In spite of the attempts by the people of St. Andrews to keep their plan to the fore, the boundary decision killed it, and attention turned to two related alternatives known as the Halifax and Quebec and the European and North American railways. The former of these called for a line through Nova Scotia and eastern New Brunswick to Canada; while the latter would take a southern route through New Brunswick to Portland, Maine, whence access to Canada could be obtained over the St. Lawrence and Atlantic. The line across Nova Scotia would be the same, but in New Brunswick there would be a material difference, depending on whether the railway went west to Maine or north to the St. Lawrence. The latter was the first to be examined. In 1844 a

12. *Prospectus of the St. Andrews and Quebec Railroad* (1846).
13. Quoted in *Prince Edward Island Gazette*, September 9, 1836.

committee was formed in London for the purpose of building the road, and the coöperation of the provinces was requested. Meetings were called in St. John and Halifax in the following autumn. The Halifax meeting was a public one; a resolution was passed in favour; and a committee set up of which Uniacke was secretary and Young, Cunard, Almon and Tobin were members.[14] In St. John a group was brought together in the office of A. L. Street and acted as a local committee.[15] The route proposed by the engineer in charge was from Halifax to Truro, thence across the isthmus to Shediac (with a branch to St. John) and near Grand Falls (with branches to it and Fredericton), turning north to Rivière du Loup and Quebec. While this was acceptable to the Halifax committee, it was far from being so to that of St. John, which urged instead a line from Quebec through Grand Falls, Fredericton, and St. John to Halifax.

What happened to the London committee is not clear, but the dispute which its proposed route aroused remained. The next step toward the railway came from the joint action of the governments of the three provinces concerned in ordering a survey; and the report of the engineer, Major Robinson, advocated neither of the ones already discussed, but one which hugged the coast of New Brunswick. "Major Robinson's line" had the advantage of avoiding the American frontier, and, partly for that reason, was that later taken by the Intercolonial. Enthusiasm waxed high in the colonies, but the home government, holding that the railway was not a commercial proposition, refused to support it financially, and not all the bait offered by the provincial governments in the form of land grants and annual subsidies could draw a grant for the cost of construction.

At about the same time that this was happening, the European and North American project began to take shape. The northern route to Quebec had been defended on the ground that it ran only through British territory, so the sponsors of the southern route wisely countered by emphasizing the spirit of international friend-

14. *Report of a provisional committee of the Atlantic and St. Lawrence Railroad* (Halifax, 1845).

15. *The New Brunswick Railway, The report of a meeting in St. John. . . .* (1845).

ship. "The spirit of peace has at last prevailed—national animosities, sectional and political hostility have disappeared between the English races, since the establishment of the boundaries of Maine and Oregon, and the contests of war have been succeeded by a noble and generous rivalry for the promotion of the arts of peace." These worthy sentiments were further expressed by intertwined flags and suitable speeches at a conference held at Portland in July 1850 to discuss the proposed railway. Delegates were present from New England and New York, Canada, Newfoundland, Nova Scotia and New Brunswick. All were in favour, and hoped to raise the necessary funds partly by private subscription and partly by governmental guarantee. Each province or state was to be responsible for its own section, while the whole would—according to its advocates—"undoubtedly prove the most popular and most frequented highway for all travellers between Europe and America," since the voyage from Nova Scotia to Ireland was the shortest. For Canada there would be access to the sea at Halifax as well as at Portland; and for New Brunswick and Nova Scotia a most enticing economic prospect was held out.[16]

Joseph Howe, fresh from his long and successful constitutional battle, seized on the building of a trunk railway as the subject of greatest interest to his province.[17] He began, accordingly, to press for action by the government as the only source of funds. Once more the British government refused to foot the bill, but it was hoped that the decision might be reconsidered, and consequently Howe was sent to London to re-open the matter. His mission, though far from an easy one, seemed to meet with startling success. In the late autumn of 1850 he sailed from Halifax, carrying a warm introduction to Lord Grey from Sir John Harvey, who had done all he could to recommend the railway plan to the home government. While Nova Scotia was ready for either the northern or southern route, the immediate purpose of Howe's visit was connected with the latter.

16. *Plan for shortening the time of passage between New York and London* (1850).
17. *See* W. L. Grant, *The Tribune of Nova Scotia* (Toronto, 1920); J. A. Roy, *Joseph Howe* (Toronto, 1935); J. W. Longley, *Joseph Howe* (Toronto, 1904); J. A. Chisholm (ed.), *Speeches and public letters of Joseph Howe* (Halifax, 1909).

I am on my way to England [he wrote to Hincks] to endeavour to negotiate a loan, on the credit of Nova Scotia, to enable us to construct our
portion of the European and North American Railroad, either with or
without the guarantee of the Imperial Government. . . . The policy on
which we are acting in Nova Scotia, is *to keep the great Highway which
must pass through our country into the United States, under the control of
the Government.* If it passes into the hands of American capitalists they will
possess an interest and an influence in the very bosom of the Province,
which sooner or later will cost the Mother Country much more than will
be required to construct the Railway. The "patronizing" at the Portland
Convention is a sign of the times which statesmen should not overlook.
Should the British Government oppose or stand aloof from the enterprise,
a dangerous state of feeling will be generated in the Lower Provinces. . . .[18]

Howe's plans, then, were for a publicly owned railway, built by
the provinces but backed, if possible, by an imperial guarantee.
He held that it was an imperial as well as a local matter, for immigration could be furthered and, what was more, it would be a step
toward that union of the provinces without which the separate
colonies must fall into the lap of the United States. He put before
Grey the argument that Nova Scotia favoured the Halifax and
Quebec scheme and was prepared to support it, but proposed as a
first step the construction of the shorter and cheaper European
and North American. By clever advocacy, and by appealing to
popular opinion, he obtained in March 1851 a promise that there
should be recommended to parliament the giving of a guarantee
for a line from Halifax to Quebec. Howe, with Chandler of New
Brunswick, visited Toronto in June to ask for coöperation in the
Intercolonial railway. The Canadian government agreed and
passed an act of parliament defining the aid it was prepared to
give. It looked like success, but a serious complication arose. In
order to meet the different interests of the three provinces, it
was agreed between them that both the Halifax and Quebec and
the European and North American should be begun. It was then
suddenly discovered that the home government would not extend—
and stated that it had never meant to extend—its guarantee to
the European and North American. How this confusion arose is
not clear. Howe was bitter, and attributed the change—if change

18. Canadian Archives, Howe Papers, vi.

it was—to the influence of English contractors. Grey claimed that he had never meant to guarantee anything but a line following Major Robinson's survey. The government of New Brunswick would not agree to the bargain if only the gulf route was to be touched. They might consent to dropping the Portland line, if the Halifax and Quebec could be transferred to the St. John Valley, but this was out of the question, as the British government would not support a railway so close to the frontier. Thus there was a complete deadlock; while the situation was made more difficult by the withdrawal of Canadian interest from railways within New Brunswick. The whole edifice, so laboriously built up by Howe, had fallen to the ground—and the pieces were not to be put together again for twenty years. From 1857 to 1864 negotiations were still carried on between the three provinces and the home government, and a survey was decided on in 1864. The accomplishment of the Intercolonial, however, belongs to the period after confederation.

So ended the grandiose plans of the Maritime Provinces in the years before confederation. Little was saved from the wreck. Howe became one of the railway commissioners for Nova Scotia, and under governmental control a line was built to Truro with a branch to Windsor (1854–1858). Nine years later the line was extended to Pictou. Thus, by the time of confederation, Nova Scotia had but 145 miles of railway, though Halifax was linked by rail with both the Bay of Fundy and the Gulf of St. Lawrence. New Brunswick also built some lines within the province. The original St. Andrews and Quebec, under the name of the New Brunswick and Canada, was pushed as far as Woodstock in 1868, which—with a branch to St. Stephen—made a total of 126 miles. Attempts were made in 1852 to push on the European and North American, but all that came of it was a line from St. John to Shediac (on the gulf), a distance of 108 miles, completed in 1860. In both provinces the construction and management of the publicly-owned railways were placed under appointed boards of commissioners, and these were given power to contract loans and issue debentures.

While the total mileage of railway was not impressive, the lines in themselves were significant in that they joined the seas on which the Maritime Provinces faced. Railways crossed Nova Scotia from the Bay of Fundy and the gulf to the Atlantic at Halifax. New

Brunswick was crossed from St. John on the Bay of Fundy to Shediac on the gulf. One effect of this was to trespass on the business of the coasting schooners and steamships, and thus to dislocate, to some extent, the economic life of peoples who had developed shipping as a major industry. This, combined with the actual expenditure on railways to create a sufficiently large financial problem in the provinces. What was, perhaps, more obvious at the time was the failure of the plans to link the ports of Nova Scotia and New Brunswick with Canada: a failure which, heart-breaking as it was at the time, was to have an important influence on the movement for the union of the provinces.

3. The First Canadian Trunk Lines

The picture of Canada in the same period was in some respects different. Canada was, for part of the year, an inland country looking for winter ports, whereas the Maritime Provinces were seeking to take advantage of the ports which they naturally possessed. Canada was, on the whole, successful in her railway projects, while those of the maritimes—equally ambitious—for the time failed of achievement. There were also factors in common. In both cases there was heavy expenditure, and in both the emphasis was on trunk lines which were designed to effect a railway conquest of the eastern half of North America.

The failure of Howe to secure English backing for his inter-provincial and intercolonial railways led Francis Hincks to turn away from these doubtful enterprises and toward the alternative plans of trunk lines within the province of Canada. There followed in the 'fifties a remarkable amount of construction of both through and local lines. Very little progress had been made in Canada before that time: in 1850 only about sixty miles of railway were in operation, in spite of all the pamphlets and speeches and meetings. The author of a pamphlet published in 1850 indicates the depression that had fallen upon the enthusiasts for railways. In the United States, he says, they build railways: in Canada we talk about it.

Old Winter is once more upon us, and our inland seas are "dreary and inhospitable wastes" to the merchant and to the traveller;—our rivers are sealed fountains—and an embargo which no human power can remove is laid on all our ports. Around our deserted wharves and warehouses are huddled the naked spars,—the blasted forest of trade,—from which the sails have fallen like the leaves of autumn. The splashing wheels are silenced, —the roar of steam is hushed,—the gay saloon, so lately thronged with busy life, is now but an abandoned hall,—and the cold snow revels in solitary possession of the untrodden deck. The animation of business is suspended, the life blood of commerce is curdled and stagnant in the St. Lawrence—the great aorta of the North. On land, the heavy stage labours through mingled mud and frost in the West,—or struggles through drifted snow, and slides with uncertain track over the icy hills of Eastern Canada. Far away to the South is heard the daily scream of the steam whistle,—but from Canada there is no escape: blockaded and imprisoned by Ice and Apathy, we have at least ample time for reflection—and if there be comfort in philosophy may we not profitably consider the PHILOSOPHY OF RAILROADS.[19]

This seems strange doctrine in a colony which had just completed, at great expense, a system of canals giving uninterrupted navigation from the lower St. Lawrence to Sault Ste. Marie; but, as plainly appears, it was the competitive spirit which lay behind the argument. Had there been no American railways, there would still have been a desire for railways in Canada, but no such pressing need for them. Just as the Erie Canal had forced on the improvement of the St. Lawrence route, so American railways hurried on the Canadian trunk lines. Somewhat strangely, as it may at first appear, the spirit of international competition was strong in the plan for connecting Montreal with Portland, Maine. In 1846 the Toronto *Examiner* remarked that "the construction of this Railroad seems to be regarded in Montreal as a question of life and death. It is looked upon as the battleground on which the fight for the trade of Upper Canada and the Western States is to be fought . . . it seems to be taken for granted that the trade of the West will flow in that direction, if the Railroad be completed. . . ." The solution of the apparent paradox is that, although trade was to go through an American port, Montreal would still be an essential link in the chain. As a seaport Montreal was hampered by climate and the difficult navigation of the St. Lawrence, and could hardly hope to overcome these obstacles

19. T. C. Keefer, *Philosophy of railroads* (Montreal, 1850).

162 of TRANSPORTATION IN CANADA

altogether. Yet she stood at the opening of the St. Lawrence canals, and at the junction of the Portland line and any other one built to the west. Thus she could secure a sound strategic position if joined by railway to an Atlantic port.

Montrealers, however, could claim little credit for the initiation of the scheme.[20] In the 'forties ideas were put forward in Boston for a railway to Montreal as a rival route to New York's Erie Canal. No enthusiasm was shown in Montreal, but the people of Sherbrooke, in the eastern townships, were heartily in favour and appointed a provisional committee in 1843. Nothing came of it at the time; but the beginning of the bonding system in 1845, which allowed Canadian imports or exports to pass through American territory in bond, put a different complexion on the situation. Montreal must now act or see the trade of Canada West pass it by. In the meanwhile an alternative route to the coast was proposed by an energetic young lawyer of Portland, Maine, J. A. Poor, who sought to make of his city the winter port for Canada. He had gone further by including in his plans a railway to Halifax, but that part of the scheme, which failed at the time, has been treated in connection with the railways of the Maritime Provinces. Thanks partly to Poor's energetic propaganda, and partly to the preference by the eastern townships for the Portland connection, it was this line which it was decided to build.

The St. Lawrence and Atlantic is said to have been the first international railway ever built. Two companies were incorporated in 1845: the Atlantic and St. Lawrence to cover the American section, and the St. Lawrence and Atlantic the Canadian. The Canadian charter provided for a capital of $2,400,000; maximum rates; and the return to the government of half the surplus profits over twelve per cent. (The latter provision in Canadian railway charters was touching but inoperative.) Having decided to build the railway, it was imperative that the Canadian company should raise money. An appeal to the government brought no response, for public funds were already earmarked for canals. The committee next turned to the Canadian public with the arguments that the railway was "to be considered as the completion of the Canadian

20. For the St. Lawrence and Atlantic Railway *see* O. D. Skelton, *Life and times of Sir Alexander Tilloch Galt* (Toronto, 1920).

efforts to obtain the trade of the West" and to save Montreal from the danger of "diverting the supply of Western Canada to New York and Boston." Even this cogent reasoning brought only £100,000 (currency); so it was decided to send A. T. Galt to England, the first of many Canadian railway financiers to seek help in that great market.

In that year, when there was an avalanche of railway charters and subscriptions, it seemed that London investors would buy stock in any railway, and Galt was highly successful in selling most of the stock of the company, for which a part of the purchase price was paid. His success, however, was almost immediately followed by a collapse of the market, and the subscribers to the St. Lawrence and Atlantic refused to pay the rest of their obligations. Although surveys were begun, the capital was still lacking, and little could be obtained in Canada. Again in 1846 Galt was sent to England, this time in the hope of selling bonds, but the mission was not a success. Great Britain had been spending enormous sums of money on railways both at home and on the continent of Europe. In 1845 and 1846 came wheat and potato famines combined with a sharp financial panic in 1847. London and North-Western Railway stock, thought to be the most solid, fell in a year from 220 to 110. There was a general retrenchment, and it was natural that export of capital should be checked.[21] As a last hope the directors again turned to the Canadian government, and after some delay an important measure was passed by parliament which was the first to provide for the construction of railways, and was intended to benefit immediately the Great Western as well as the St. Lawrence and Atlantic.

The Guarantee Act of 1849, introduced by Francis Hincks, the inspector general (an office corresponding to minister of finance), began by stating the need of government assistance in a sparsely-settled country where capital was scarce. Interest at six per cent on not more than half the bonded debt might be guaranteed for a railway more than seventy-five miles long, one-half of which had been constructed. Provisions were made to protect the government's commitment. Since Sir Allan Macnab was seeking govern-

21. L. A. Jenks, *The migration of British capital to 1875* (New York, 1927), pp. 152 et seq.

mental support for the Great Western he dropped for the moment his rôle of leader of the opposition and voted for the measure. It was the first important step in the long story of governmental guarantees and subsidies for railways.

It was necessary, however, for half of the St. Lawrence and Atlantic to be built before the act could come into effect in its favour. First an internal reorganization was necessary, and Galt was made president in succession to A. N. Morin. Then construction was pushed ahead, first under an American firm, and then by the company itself with C. S. Gzowski—soon to become a partner with Galt—as chief engineer. Richmond was reached in 1851 and Sherbrooke in the following year. By 1853 the line was complete. In evidence given before a special committee of the legislative assembly in 1857, A. T. Galt stated that the capital raised by the St. Lawrence and Atlantic was made up in this way:

Provincial bonds under guarantee act	£400,000	0	0
Montreal City bonds	102,739	14	6
Seminary of St. Sulpice	20,547	18	11
British American Loan Company	20,547	18	11
Shares	195,200	0	0
	£739,035	12	4

While the St. Lawrence and Atlantic (with its American counterpart) formed a unit in itself, it was also conceived as part of a longer line running from east to west. It was a question whether such a through route should be under one organization or several. The various sections were built independently until the Grand Trunk took over the lion's share. The individual railways first planned were the Montreal and Kingston, the Northern, and the Great Western. The special purposes of the last two require some explanation. There were two ways of reaching the west—that is the country beyond the Great Lakes—one by following the lower lakes to the American border at or near Windsor; and the other by striking north from Lake Ontario to a point on the upper lakes. Both these routes were adopted: in point of time the southern one came first, but for purposes of simplicity it will be easier to consider the northern one before examining the main route from Montreal to Detroit.

In essence the Northern railway combined two ideas: to open up the fertile country north of Toronto, and—the more ambitious purpose—to make a portage railway to Georgian Bay whence steamers could connect with the ports of Lakes Huron and Michigan, and so draw the trade of the west through to Lake Ontario. Sometimes added to this was the hope of restoring the old North West Company's fur trade route through Canada, lost since 1821. At bottom the plan was the same as that of the old Toronto portage, using rail instead of road or river. Toronto would either be the port at which goods would again be shipped in steamboats, or a junction with any railway coming from the east. The Northern (or by its older names, the Toronto and Lake Simcoe or Toronto and Lake Huron) went through the same stages as most other early Canadian railways: suggested in the 'thirties, organized in the 'forties, and built in the 'fifties. After long disputes about routes, Collingwood was finally chosen as the northern terminus, and to there the line was completed in 1855. From the little station at Toronto the curious wood-burning engines puffed their way north through what was still a sparsely-settled and heavily forested country. The forests were not altogether an impediment, for if fuel ran short crew and passengers could quickly cut more a few feet from the line. The Northern acted as a part of a combined water and rail route for grain, and apparently with some success, for in 1861 the trade at Collingwood, primarily grain from the United States, was declared to amount to $2,500,000.[22] Until the completion of the Canadian Pacific Railway the old Northern formed a link in the land and water route to the Canadian west.

The alternative, though not necessarily competing, way of reaching the west was by the southern route along Lakes Ontario and Erie. For the part of this in the western end of the province the Great Western was the chief instrument. That railway first took form when chartered in 1834 as the London and Gore Rail Road Company, but, as so often happened, no action was taken to build it. In 1845 the charter was renewed under the name of the Great Western, and at the same time the projected line was

22. H. A. Innis and A. R. M. Lower, *Select documents in Canadian economic history, 1783–1885* (Toronto, 1933), p. 494.

extended to run from the Niagara River, via Hamilton, to Windsor
and Sarnia. From the first the Great Western was seen as a factor
in competition with American routes. "The present may be
considered as an important crisis in the history of this Province,"
wrote an anonymous pamphleteer in 1836, "Internal Improvement
in the United States having proceeded with a rapidity and extent
far beyond our efforts hitherto. . . . It is conceded upon all
hands, that a Rail Road of any great extent in this Province,
must depend materially for its support and profit upon the transit
of American travel and commerce over it."[23] The Great Western,
he adds, is best calculated both for this latter purpose and for
local travel.

By the time of the second charter in 1845 a number of railways
had been built in the neighbouring parts of the United States, and a
more detailed scheme could be worked out to make of the Great
Western a part of the main western route in the United States. The
re-formed company with Sir Allan Macnab of Hamilton as president
brought out a most tempting prospectus, which reads in part:

The Great Western Rail Road is designed not only to facilitate the internal
traffic of the Province of Canada, for which its route possesses eminent
advantages, but also to form a connecting link in the great chain of Railway
from the city of Boston . . . to the Mississippi, thus drawing over it an
immense and increasing foreign traffic. . . .

The great and increasing trade of the Western country with the seaboard,
renders it therefore a matter of the highest importance, nay, even of necessity, to establish a rapid, short, and uninterrupted line of communication
between the two, by railroad, and by an examination of the map it will be
seen, that the Route of the Great Western Rail Road will possess advantages superior to that of any other for this purpose, not only from its termini
being in immediate connection with the several lines of road now in existence, but also to the fact that no other road to the northward of it can be
made, unless it shall meet the interruption of water communication, which
is closed for so large a portion of the year; neither can any road be made to
the southward of it without winding round the south shore of Lake Erie,
and increasing the distance by at least 125 miles.

For these reasons, among many others of a striking nature, the chain
of Rail Road [i.e., including U.S. ones] must ever be the chief channel of

23. *Some observations respecting a Great Western Railroad* (Toronto, 1836).

communication between the Northern and Eastern, and the Western States of the American Union, of which the Great Western Road would be the most important link. . . .

In other words the plan was to run a line from the Niagara to the Detroit River (Buffalo to Detroit), connecting at each end with American railways, and designed to form the shortest route between them in place of the detour around the south of Lake Erie. A similar plan was in the minds of those who built the Buffalo and Lake Huron, from Buffalo to Goderich (1858). From Buffalo the Great Western was intended to go by way of Hamilton to connect with Lake Ontario shipping and could be extended east to Toronto, so as to reach out to railways coming from Montreal and Kingston; and to go westward from Hamilton to London, whence the main line would proceed to Windsor, and a branch to Sarnia. Thus the Great Western was cast for a triple rôle: for the traffic of the peninsula; as part of a Canadian trunk line; and as part of an American trunk line. In 1849 the first sod was turned at London by old Colonel Talbot, who over half a century earlier had made a settlement not far away; but even a public holiday and inspiring speeches failed to bring any tangible results, and construction was not started for two years. By 1855 the line from the Suspension Bridge to Windsor was finished, connecting with the New York Central and Michigan Central. In the following year the branch to Toronto stretched out to meet the oncoming Grand Trunk.

The expression "grand trunk" had been used for some years and signified to contemporaries a main line running from east to west of Canada, and connecting on the one extreme with winter ports and on the other with the middle-western American railways. The Grand Trunk Railway Company, as organized in the early 'fifties was based on the acquisition or rental of existing lines plus new construction. The act which brought the company into being was not passed without opposition from rival interests, and it is first necessary to examine the conflicting plans of this period. Out of the various proposals for trunk roads, the Great Western and the St. Lawrence and Atlantic alone had materialized. In addition the Montreal and Kingston Railroad Company was chartered on August 31, 1851, with L. H. Holton as president and A. T. Galt as vice-president—the men who were pushing on the completion of the St. Lawrence and Atlantic. In that year, however, the larger scheme for an imperially guaranteed line from Halifax to Hamilton intervened, and the charter of the Montreal and Kingston was suspended. The unwillingness of the imperial government to support anything but the Robinson line was verified by Hincks when he went to London in 1852 in company with Chandler of New Brunswick. The larger scheme having to be abandoned, the Montreal and Kingston charter came into force in August 1852, the stock was subscribed, and the engineers were set to work. But in the meanwhile, Hincks had been exposed in England to the blandishments of William Jackson of the Brassey firm, which was seeking fresh worlds to conquer, and in May he agreed with Jackson that a company should be organized to build a railway between Montreal and Hamilton. The Brassey firm had already been active for a year in seeking contracts in the British provinces. They had approached Howe, and in 1851 C. D. Archibald wrote on their behalf an open letter to Lord Elgin urging the value—to the provinces—of bringing over this vast army of peace for a prolonged stay. The plan of campaign now was to secure control of existing companies, especially the Montreal and Kingston, and it was for that reason that the charter was revived. Jackson, however, was too slow, and the stock was snapped up, chiefly by Galt, Holton and D. L. Macpherson.

It was necessary now to try other methods, so Hincks introduced a bill to charter the Grand Trunk Railway Company, with power to build a line from Montreal to Toronto. This, of course, directly contravened the interests of the Montreal and Kingston promoters, who were not slow to protest. Meanwhile they waived their legal rights on the understanding that they would be given a fair hearing and consideration. The railway committee and the public were bombarded with arguments from both sides. The Grand Trunk group argued that capital could not be secured in Canada, and that the subscriptions by Galt, Holton, and Macpherson were unreal. The latter admitted that they did not intend to hold all the stock standing in their names, but stoutly maintained that—

while they had no objection to foreign capital—the roads should be built under Canadian control and could largely be financed in Canada. The odds were all against the Galt group, for Hincks and the cabinet were solidly behind the Grand Trunk, while Jackson fascinated legislators and public with his casual references to millions. For a time the opposition held up the plan by arranging an amalgamation of the St. Lawrence and Atlantic and the Montreal and Kingston, but were finally won over by a promise from Hincks that he would urge an alternative amalgamation of the Grand Trunk with the St. Lawrence and Atlantic and a bridge across the St. Lawrence at Montreal to connect the two. The decision to follow the Jackson plan rather than that of Galt was a momentous one. Whether or not the Montreal financiers could have found enough capital must remain an open question. The transfer of control to London, the dual position of the Brassey firm as both contractors and promoters, the inexperience of the firm in the conditions of work and climate in North America, and the expensive type of construction adopted, all combined to render this first great railway in Canada an embarrassment almost from its inception.

The legislation incorporating the Grand Trunk Railway was passed in 1853. The charters of the Montreal and Kingston, and Kingston and Toronto railways were repealed, and the Grand Trunk was empowered to build from Toronto to Montreal. The capital was £3,000,000 (sterling) and a provincial guarantee of £3,000 (currency) per mile was promised. A separate act empowered the company—under the name of the Grand Trunk Railway of Canada East—to build from Lévis to Trois Pistoles, with the same guarantee; from there to the New Brunswick border the railway might, under certain conditions, be continued with a land subsidy of 1,000,000 acres. The various new and acquired companies were then merged into a single corporation.[24] The directors included John Ross, solicitor general for Upper Canada, as president; Hincks and four other cabinet ministers; Thomas Baring and

24. For a critical but well-documented account of the origin and early years of the Grand Trunk *see* T. S. Brown, *A history of the Grand Trunk Railway of Canada* (Quebec, 1864).

G. C. Glyn. Holton and Galt were appointed but resigned. The prospectus of the company is a fine bit of optimistic imagery, and ends in this way:

The Grand Trunk Railway of Canada . . . commencing at the *débouchure* of the three largest lakes in the world, pours the accumulating traffic in one unbroken line through the entire length of Canada into the St. Lawrence at Montreal and Quebec, on which it rests at the north, while on the south it reaches the magnificent harbours of Portland and St. John on the open ocean. The whole future traffic between the western regions and the east, including Lower Canada, parts of the States of Vermont and New Hampshire, and the Provinces of New Brunswick, Nova Scotia, Prince Edward Island, and Newfoundland must, therefore, pass over the Grand Trunk Railway.

From these poetic heights we must descend to the levels of actual accomplishment. The Portland-Montreal section was acquired from the St. Lawrence and Atlantic on a 999 year lease. The core of the system, the Toronto-Montreal section, was built and opened for traffic in 1856. West of Toronto the company made a straight line for Sarnia, in spite of the protests from the Great Western directors who held that their territory was being invaded. Avoiding the southern route by Hamilton—already covered by the Great Western—the Grand Trunk went by way of the partly built Toronto and Guelph Railway, which it absorbed, through Stratford to Sarnia, which was reached in 1859. On the eastern end the Quebec and Richmond Railway was taken over, joining Montreal and Quebec by cutting south through Richmond. Further east the line was extended as far as Rivière du Loup, where it stopped. Of a number of branch lines the most important was that from Port Huron (on the American side, opposite Sarnia) to Detroit, a distance of sixty miles. The most spectacular achievement of the Grand Trunk in these years was the Victoria bridge at Montreal, built in consequence of Hincks' declared design of uniting the Grand Trunk proper with the St. Lawrence and Atlantic. The strong current and heavy ice formation made the construction of the bridge a problem from the engineering point of view, and the curious expedient was adopted of building a large, hollow tube, made of iron, through which the trains passed. The tube was 6,592 feet long, and the total distance from bank to bank 9,144 feet. Finished in 1860, the Victoria bridge was regarded as a remarkable engineering feat.

Such were the trunk lines built in Canada in the years before confederation. Before examining them from the points of view of construction and finance, it will be well to look briefly at some of the smaller railways, so many of which were chartered—and some built—in the roaring 'fifties. In Canada East there is little to record. The Stanstead, Shefford and Chambly Railway (1860) continued the line of the Champlain and St. Lawrence, and ran eastward into the townships and to the American border. The St. Lawrence and Industry (1850) covered the twelve miles from Lanorie to St. Industrie (later Joliette). The Montreal and Vermont Junction also ran south from St. John's, and connected with the Central Vermont. In Canada West there was considerably more activity. The Carillon and Grenville (1854) was a small portage railway past the Long Sault rapids on the Ottawa. Two lumber roads in the same area were built in the late 'fifties: the Ottawa and Prescott (or St. Lawrence and Ottawa), completed from Ottawa to the St. Lawrence at Prescott in 1854; and the Brockville and Ottawa, opened from Almonte to Brockville, further west on the St. Lawrence, in 1859. The use of railways for lumber traffic is a significant move, and it will be observed that they were designed to feed both the main line of the Grand Trunk and the water transport of the St. Lawrence. In the central part of Canada West were the Cobourg and Peterborough, connecting those towns in 1854; and the Peterborough and Lake Chemong, a separate company carrying the steel some twelve miles further (1861). The Preston and Berlin, Port Hope, Lindsay and Beaverton (mercifully renamed the Midland), whose original line from Preston to Berlin was abandoned a year after it was built, had by 1857 a main line of forty-three miles from Port Hope to Lindsay. West of Toronto were the Galt and Guelph (1857) with its fifteen miles of track; the London and Port Stanley (1856); and two portage roads around Niagara Falls: the Erie and Ontario (1854) and the Welland (1859).

4. Construction and Financing

By 1860 the vigorous railway building of a decade came to a stop, but in those ten years there had been added 2,000 miles of track to the mere sixty-six in operation in 1850. Iron rails were the rule at that time, which resulted in frequent cracking in cold weather. There was a difference in gauge, due partly to a disagreement amongst experts and partly to a desire to force traffic into certain channels. The St. Lawrence and Atlantic was built with a gauge of five feet six inches, and in consequence the whole Grand Trunk system followed suit. The Great Western, too, adopted this wide gauge. Some of the smaller companies used the narrow gauge of three feet six inches, the principal ones being the Toronto, Grey and Bruce and the Toronto and Nipissing. There were advocates also of the gauge of four feet, eight and one-half inches, which gradually became the standard to which all lines were in time converted. The first locomotives came from England, and some of them gave trouble as they were equipped with six wheels without the American "bogie," and proved to be unsuitable for the sharp curves and rough roadbed. Later, orders were placed with firms in the United States. The first engine used in Canada, the *Dorchester* of the Champlain and St. Lawrence Railroad, weighed between five and six tons, while the first engines used on the Grand Trunk weighed some thirty tons and had four-coupled driving wheels. All engines burned wood, and though they had a bell-shaped funnel with a screen, the sparks and cinders were unpleasant for passengers and a menace to the forests. Stocks of cordwood were kept at each station and constant re-fuelling was necessary. The cars were small, had light four-wheel trucks, hand brakes, link and pin couplings, and spartan comfort within. Night service was introduced on the Grand Trunk shortly after its completion, but Pullman sleepers were not used until 1870. Snowdrifts held up many a train, but no snow-ploughs seem to have been used. When a train finally proved to be unable to push its way through a drift, the snow was shovelled away by hand. It was no uncommon experience for passengers to be snowbound for hours or even days, often without food in the days when dining-cars were still a luxury of the future. An English officer travelling in Canada in 1857 gave a depressing account of the comfort of railway travel. He wrote that the average speed on the Grand Trunk was ten miles an hour,[25] though it appears that trains attained maximum speeds of twenty-five or thirty miles an hour at times.

Construction was carried out partly by American, partly by Canadian, and partly by English firms. The Brassey firm had the largest part of the work on the Grand Trunk, but some of this— as well as that on other lines—fell to Gzowski and Company, which included, besides the Polish engineer, D. L. Macpherson, A. T. Galt, and L. H. Holton. The St. Lawrence and Atlantic directorate took charge of its own construction by means of small contracts. Numbers of workmen were brought to Canada to build the Grand Trunk—a foretaste of the larger immigration in connection with the transcontinental railways.

The most interesting question in the construction of railways in this period was the problem of whether they should follow English or American standards, that is, whether they should be solidly built with a high original cost and low upkeep, or constructed as cheaply as possible with the expectation of improvement as revenue allowed. All the main railways followed the English practice. The Great Western, though built by a firm of American contractors, cost an average of $66,000 per mile. The authorities of the Grand Trunk, who were determined to follow the English plan of solid original construction, criticized the Great Western as jerry-built, but their costs were slightly lower at $63,800 per mile. Even so, the lack of local experience of the Brassey firm led to serious troubles, such as rails which broke in winter. Some of the other contractors scamped their work, which meant high expense without adequate return.

The total cost of building the railways of British North America up to 1867 was, for Canada, $145,794,853 for sixteen companies with 2,188.25 miles; for Nova Scotia, $6,380,000 (in round figures) for 145 miles; and for New Brunswick, $2,520,000 (in round figures) for 126 miles.[26] How was the money raised for all this expenditure? In the Maritime Provinces a large portion of the cost was met by

25. Francis Duncan, *Our garrisons in the west* (London, 1864), p. 160.

26. S. J. McLean, "The early railway history of Canada" (*Canadian Magazine*, xii, 5); Skelton, *The railway builders*.

the government, a portion raised in England, and another portion locally. The totals, however, were not large. Although the populations of both Nova Scotia and New Brunswick were small (in 1867, 330,875 and 252,047 respectively), the cost of what railways they built was small in comparison to that of Canadian railways, where the population in the same year was 2,507,657. The financial problem, then, was more acute in the province of Canada.

Public enthusiasm for railway shares was a universal phenomenon. In the United States it enabled a handful of financial wizards to buy or sell railways almost regardless of their earning capacity. In England, in 1845, shares multiplied in value in a few days and scores of new issues were successfully poured on the market. Even though this bull market was at times subject to relapse and railway shares became proverbially dangerous (so much so that Lewis Carroll's curious company threatened the life of the Snark with one), nevertheless there was normally a considerable market. In Canada, too, was the same unreasoning belief in getting rich by means of railway shares. It was possible, therefore, to raise within Canada a part of the capital required; but only a part, and the next step was to have recourse to English investors. Here began the long story which was to have an unhappy sequel in the inability of the holders of certain classes of Grand Trunk securities to obtain any returns. While efforts were made in the case of the first large railways to secure capital in England, it should be remembered that it was the pressure and unlimited promises of the Brassey firm which turned the Grand Trunk into a company that was primarily English in capital and control.

Governments of all kinds played an important part in financing Canadian railways. After the failure of the various negotiations over the Intercolonial, no imperial subsidy or guarantee was granted; but the provincial government plunged heavily into commitments. Hincks' Guarantee Act of 1849, which originally extended to any railway coming within its terms, was restricted in 1851 to the main trunk lines. An easy way of getting around the limits of the act was to return figures for the cost of construction which were much higher than the actual expenditure. It was said that the Northern Railway was built wholly under government guarantee, since the actual cost was half of what it was represented to be. Further loans were made to the Grand Trunk. By 1867 the provincial government had incurred a debt on behalf of railways as follows:

Grand Trunk	$25,607,393.53
Great Western	3,941,247.50
Northern	3,776,403.60
Total	$33,325,044.63[27]

This was far from being the whole story of government expenditure on railways, for municipalities also became heavily involved. The municipal loan fund, mentioned already in connection with roads, was intended to enable local bodies to borrow money for the support of local works at a low rate of interest. The desire to have a railway in each town and through each county led, in Canada West, to gross over-expenditure. Towns, large and small, invested in railways; Port Hope, for example, although a town with only about 4,000 people, borrowed $740,000 for investment in railways. Other towns, counties, and villages were equally optimistic. In all, about six million dollars was borrowed from the fund for railway enterprises, to which was added in Canada East less than one million. Besides borrowing from this fund, some cities also raised loans themselves in England.

When railways were first discussed in the Canadas the question arose as to whether they should be built by governments or by private companies. The precedent of the canals pointed to public ownership, especially as in several instances the governments had been obliged to take over canals from private companies which had failed either in enterprise or in finance. On the other hand, arguments familiar to all generations were advanced against public ownership. In 1847 two of the Montreal papers contained discussions for and against. The *Courier* was in favour of public ownership and management, but the *Witness* pointed out in reply that, while it favoured public ownership, the difficulty of keeping railways out of politics must be considered.

In practice it proved that in the province of Canada, unlike the Maritime Provinces, there were no publicly-owned railways before

27. McLean, *op. cit.*, p. 424.

confederation. It was recognized, however, that railways constituted a public service, to some extent monopolistic, over which
the state must exercise some control. At first the emphasis was on
encouragement rather than on restriction. Clauses were inserted
in each charter allowing the companies a maximum profit, but they
were allowed to fix their own rates on the theory that competition
would keep these within bounds. Each company was incorporated
by a separate statute, which might include any special provisions
pertinent to the case. Such statutes, however, also contained a
number of clauses which were common to all railways. In view
of this fact, a comprehensive measure, the Railway Clauses Consolidation Act (14 and 15 Vict., c. 51) was passed in 1851 to establish a
set of rules for all railways to be built thereafter. By virtue of this
act companies were empowered to receive grants of land, erect
bridges, build branch lines, and so on. Clauses were inserted to
govern surveys, valuation of land over which the line passed,
level crossings, and fences. Others concerned directors, shareholders'
meetings, and transfer of shares. Each company was still allowed
to fix its own rates.

The hope that railways could be kept out of politics was soon
seen to be vain and was negatived most curtly by MacNab's
statement that his politics were "railways." Few of the leading
or minor politicians of the day were not mixed up with private
railway or contracting companies, as well as with their official
duties in directing railway construction as a public policy. The
personnel of the Grand Trunk directorate has been mentioned,
and a similar overlap between public and private interests in the
same concerns could be found in relation to the other companies.
Myers draws an unattractive picture of members of parliament
granting charters to themselves and each other, and meeting their
special interests as landowners, lawyers, contractors, etc., by
judicious log-rolling.[28] Such a description may perhaps be tempered
by a realization that many of the men concerned were bound,
because of their private interests, to take part in the most important
economic activity of the age. One may not necessarily attribute
improper motives, but that railways did not help to purify politics
is vouched for by more than one observer. Sir Edmund Hornby,

28. G. Myers, *History of Canadian wealth* (Chicago, 1914), p. 150 et seq.

who came to Canada on Grand Trunk business, has left his impressions:

... my work was almost exclusively "Lobbying" to get a Grand Trunk Bill through the House of Representatives [sic.] . . . . The Canadian Ministers were willing enough but weak—the majority a doubtful quantity, and, although up to the last moment I felt there was a chance of getting the Bill through, I was always doubtful, since it was clear that some twenty-five members, contractors, etc., were simply waiting to be squared either by promise of contracts or money, and as I had no authority to bribe they simply abstained from voting and the Bill was thrown out. Twenty-five thousand pounds would have bought the lot, but I would rather somebody else had the job than myself. . . . I confess I was annoyed at my ill-success and had half a mind to split upon some dozen members who had been a little indiscreet in their proposals to me. As usual it was a Psalm-Singing Protestant Dissenter who, holding seven or eight votes in the palm of his hand, volunteered to do the greasing process for a consideration. Upon my word I do not think there was much to be said in favour of the Canadians over the Turks when contracts, places, free tickets on railways, or even cash was in question.[29]

Whether or not this picture was overdrawn it can hardly be doubted that some such cases existed. What is more certain, and of more lasting importance, is that Canada—from whatever motives—spent a great deal of public as well as private money on railways. Private companies they may have been, but the province had from the first a great stake in them. The preamble to the Guarantee Act of 1849, which argued that government support was necessary, had been followed in letter and in spirit.

5. THE RAILWAYS IN TROUBLE

Ten years had wrought a revolution in transportation. What did this mean to the country? First of all it meant for all those people whose districts were reached by rail the drawing aside of a curtain between themselves and the outside world. To the farming areas and backwoods towns the railway spelt a link with the main centres of population; and to the larger towns it brought easier communication with the United States and Europe. The pioneer districts of Canada West (and most of Canada West was hardly

29. Sir Edmund Hornby, *Autobiography* (Boston, 1928), p. 90.

beyond the pioneer stage) were more isolated than one can now easily realize. To these came the railway, bearing the mail and the newspapers; carrying passengers in comfort and ease—summer and winter—over long or short distances which before had meant laborious and expensive journeys. The products of the farm could now be carried to market many miles away; and to the farm came the manufactured products of the Canadian and English factories. Long before the day of the motor car and the metalled highway, the Canadian railway cut through the forested country as the Roman road ran to the outer fringes of Europe. Even now we can remember the day when the railway station was the great centre of interest in every small town. Crowds always gathered to see the daily train steam in, catching a vision, perhaps, of a wider world outside: and more than a vision, for life became less localized as people could travel with speed and comparative cheapness. But there was another side to the picture. Improved transportation extended the area open to the large industries of the cities, and so weakened or destroyed the local industries, and with them the strength of the towns. For example, the towns built up on the lake ports east of Toronto welcomed the Grand Trunk, but it proved to be a Greek gift, for in time it checked their growth or even reduced their existing populations.

The rapid construction of railways in Canada in the 'fifties brought with it economic changes that at first seemed to be wholly beneficent, but later caused dislocation and distress.[30] From the depression of the late 'forties Canada suddenly jumped into the boom of the 'fifties. Money flowed in quantities from England, and the Canadian government did not hesitate to spend freely on public works, principally on canals and railways. The debt of the province increased from $18,782,565 in 1850 to $54,142,044 in 1859. The prime cause of change was the large influx of capital from England, and this, when spent on railways, created a demand for labour and materials. Immigrants came in to meet the need for labour, which could only partially be met within the province. The existence of both capital and labour in sufficient quantities made ideal conditions for the railway companies, but the very

30. For this whole subject *see* Adam Shortt, "Railroad construction and national prosperity" (*Transactions of the Royal Society of Canada*, third series, vol. viii).

stimulus that they gave to economic life began to lead to high prices and wages, neither of which was helpful to them. The ease of travel made possible speculation in real estate, and the unnatural expenditure that is a sign of danger. In 1856 the dislocation in Europe that followed the Crimean War made it more difficult to secure further loans, while in Canada individuals, banks, and governments began to feel the strain of a prosperity that was based on too weak a foundation. The Grand Trunk, which was still incomplete, continued construction at higher costs, and required further government loans to do so. The Great Western, which in 1855 had declared a dividend of eight per cent, had fallen on evil days, partly because of the extension of the Grand Trunk into its territory. All over British North America the railways were in financial difficulties; private investors were receiving no return on their money; the municipalities were unable to meet their obligations under the loan fund; and the provincial government, which already had a large debt, was hard put to carry the railways.

The chief problem was, and long remained, the financial condition of the Grand Trunk. The original calculations had blithely produced an anticipated profit of eleven and a half per cent on the capital, but by the autumn of 1854 Grand Trunk stock was at a discount of seven and a half per cent. By 1855 the company's funds were exhausted: it could neither go on with construction nor pay interest on its debentures. A shareholders' committee in London "decided that Canada should give a five per cent guarantee for ninety-nine years upon the entire capital, as Belgium had done and India. A mission which included Brassey and Betts themselves journeyed to Canada to press the demand."[31] The Canadian government was not ready to stomach this demand, but proceeded to a series of expenditures to keep the company afloat and make possible the completion of the road. An act of 1855 provided for a loan of £900,000, secured by a lien on the whole Grand Trunk system. The directors reported that they "have not hesitated to avail themselves of the assistance thus considerately and opportunely afforded and they feel assured in this they will have the

31. Jenks, *op. cit.*, p. 202.

ready concurrence and sanction of the shareholders."[32] It may be taken that the shareholders offered no resistance. By 1856 the company was again out of funds, and the legislature again passed an act, enabling the company to issue £2,000,000 of preferential bonds with priority over the provincial lien, the proceeds to be used for construction. In the same act it was provided that, for five years, the interest on the provincial debentures issued to the company was to be advanced by the province—such advances being repaid in share capital.

In spite of governmental assistance and concessions the Grand Trunk was, by 1860, virtually bankrupt. By 1861 there was a total deficit of $13,000,000. Unless some further resources could be found the railway must cease operations. For two years a most complicated game was played, involving four groups of players: the Canadian government; Baring Brothers and Glyn, Mills; the preference bondholders; and the shareholders and owners of other bonds. In general the object of the game was, on the one hand, to force the government to grant further aid, and, on the other, to shift the burden on to the investors. An almost endless series of negotiations, plans, and lobbyings then took place in Canada. All parties used as a threat the possibility of stopping the operations of the railway; but that was a solution which the government could less easily contemplate with equanimity, for popular opinion would be bitter against them. The creditors soon began to secure judgments for debt against the company. In the autumn of 1860 A. T. Galt, on behalf of the government, obtained judgment for some £3,000,000, but did not know what step to take next. "I am in the position of the man", he wrote, "who had the good luck to win the elephant."[33]

Baring Brothers and Glyn, Mills and Company—both heavily interested in Grand Trunk stock—also got judgments against the company, declaring that they acted thus only to prevent the line from being stopped by vindictive measures. They were represented in Canada by their Boston agent, S. G. Ward, who made periodic trips to Canada, and kept them regularly informed on Grand Trunk

32. H. A. Lovett, *Canada and the Grand Trunk* (Montreal, 1924), p. 40.

33. Canadian Archives, Baring Papers, Grand Trunk Railway, S. G. Ward to Baring Bros., October 9, 1860.

matters. Ward and local associates made various gestures toward securing attachments on the rolling stock, and even talked of running it all into Maine where they could hold it for debt. Such moves brought the government to a more pliable state of mind, and brought from Ward this enlightening outburst:

. . . a great step has been taken towards converting your claim on the Grand Trunk Co. into a claim obligatory on the Government. . . .

A contest with the Government I take it for granted you would regard as I do, as out of the question. The Govt. have seen that the Road *must* go on. It would be regarded as a public necessity, and means would and could be found to evade the effect of any position you might take in Canada, and, even in the States, machinery could be devised by which the road could be run in spite of our attachments; by borrowing stock, or other means —I have never regarded any of the steps we have taken as encurring any actual security, except by acting as a lever through which assistance might be got by the aid of the Government. [34]

While it is abundantly clear from this letter what the large shareholders were seeking, Ward nevertheless had qualms, and envisaged a virtual relinquishment of the railway to the province, the latter to guarantee interest on the bonds and stocks. "Is it supposable", he wrote, "that they [the government] can be induced to advance £3,000,000 to pay your debt and other floating debt, say £2,000,000—new Rolling Stock say £400,000 and interest till the road may be supposed to earn it, say £600,000? I see no probability of this, for the Province would get no assurance that things would take care of themselves in future, nor the various classes of bondholders that they would be regularly and permanently paid."[35] Ward's work in Boston did not allow him more than brief visits to Canada, but he had a number of assistants. The most picturesque of these was George Ashmun of Springfield, Massachusetts, who had been president of the Republican convention that nominated Lincoln. Arriving in Canada at the beginning of 1861, Ashmun took up the new game with zest. He busied himself in interviewing everyone connected with or interested in the Grand Trunk and attempted to bring them to a sound point of view. By May, however, Ward had to admit that Ashmun was

34. *Ibid.*, Same to Same, October 30, 1860.
35. *Ibid.*, Ward to Baring (personal), January 21, 1861.

disappointing. He had been selected to push a measure through parliament, but there was no measure to be pushed; on the other hand he had not proved very successful in dealing with the government.

In the meanwhile the English bondholders had not been inactive. In November 1860 a committee was appointed at a meeting of the first preference bondholders, and made a report on the interest charges of the Grand Trunk. At the beginning of January 1861, at a meeting of the company, a select committee of share and bondholders was also appointed. This committee pointed out in its first report that no interest on shares had been paid since 1859, and no interest on the ordinary bonds since 1860. The shares, they stated, had for some time been at eighty per cent discount, and the ordinary bonds at fifty per cent discount. The company, they said, had debts of about £2,000,000 and needed £500,000 for engines and equipment. The causes of failure, in their opinion, were the following: the bonds and shares apportioned to Canada had not been taken up; the Crimean War; general financial troubles in England and Europe; bad harvests in 1857, 1858, and 1859; light traffic and excessive working expenses; and high-class construction in a distant country. These facts, together with a statement of the English investment in the Grand Trunk, were inserted in a petition to the legislative assembly which ended by asking for relief.[36]

In its second report the select committee made a number of specific recommendations for changes in the financial structure and the organization. The legal domicile of the company was to be in London. Bonds were to be converted into stock, and interest rates temporarily reduced. In general the proposals closely foreshadowed the legislation of 1862. The committee believed that someone should be sent to Canada to take supervision of the Grand Trunk, and agreed with the suggestion of the London directors that Edward Watkin should be chosen.[37] Watkin, who was the general manager of the Manchester, Sheffield and Lincolnshire

36. *Grand Trunk Railway of Canada: First report of the committee of share and bondholders* (London, 1861).
37. *Grand Trunk Railway of Canada: Second report of the select committee of share and bondholders* (London, 1861).

Railway, accepted the mission, and arrived in Canada in August 1861. His report to the board contains criticisms of the accounting system, the terminal facilities, and a number of other points.[38] Immediately on arrival he had a long talk with Ward, who—on Baring's suggestion—treated him "with perfect frankness", and had high hopes that Watkin's arrival might be a "turning point in the affairs of the road."[39]

The united forces of Watkin and Ward were then directed toward persuading the government to come to the rescue of the Grand Trunk. The government, however, was reluctant to move. It had already been attacked because of previous advances to the company; it had—in common with the other administrations of that period—a most uncertain majority, and claimed that it would suffer defeat on any measure of relief. Furthermore, a royal commission appointed to inquire into the affairs of the Grand Trunk brought in a highly critical report.[40] The commissioners found inefficiency in the use of rolling stock, defective management in the traffic department, fruitless competition with water traffic, unremunerative agreements with other companies, heavy grades and curves, and faulty rails. As to its future prospects, the commissioners believed that a reorganized company could secure an adequate amount of business, but must depend chiefly on Canadian traffic, which it had so far neglected in favour of American. The latter, they believed, was a dangerous and expensive policy.

From all the great markets in the west, the distance is greater to Portland by the Grand Trunk than by other lines to Boston, New York or Philadelphia; the climate makes the expense of maintenance fall heavier; and whatever may be the cause, there is no doubt, that the average load which can be taken is smaller than on most of the other roads. . . . We cannot therefore believe, when the through rates from Chicago to New York and Boston yield barely a profit, that the Grand Trunk can afford to carry from Chicago to Portland at the same rate . . . 16 per cent lower

38. *Report of the London directors of the Grand Trunk Railway Company of Canada . . . and report of Mr. Edward Watkin*, December 7, 1861.

39. Canadian Archives, Baring Papers, Grand Trunk Railway, Ward to Baring, August 16, 1861.

40. *Report of the commission appointed to inquire into the affairs of the Grand Trunk Railway* (Quebec, 1861).

than that to New York. Yet, in grasping at a large western trade, which swells the apparent traffic, and diverts their attention from a more legitimate business nearer home, without any corresponding profit, the Grand Trunk has even attempted to underbid the other roads.

The representatives of the shareholders and bondholders kept up steady solicitations, but for some time without result. They asked for a larger postal subsidy; were anxious lest the Bank of Upper Canada (which also had a judgment against the Grand Trunk) should be given a prior position; and rained plans and requests on the ministers. But the Macdonald-Cartier government, while recognizing that the railway must not be stopped, would take no action. The government was, in any case, in a genuinely precarious position. It survived the election of 1861 (in spite of Ward's refusal of an election contribution of $4,000), but fell on May 20 of the following year. "I do not think", wrote Rose to Baring, "the change can be unfavourable to the fortunes of the Grand Trunk. The *old* men were both powerless and *suspected* by reason of their antecedents. The new men *must* deal with it."[41]

And so it proved. In 1862 a bill, said to have been drafted by Watkin, and similar, as has been pointed out, to the plan of the committee of share and bondholders, became law. It was entitled "An act for the reorganization of the Grand Trunk Railway Company of Canada, and for other purposes," but the reorganization was chiefly in the financial structure. The preamble reads:

Whereas the interest on all the Bonds of the Grand Trunk Railway Company of Canada is in arrear as well as the rent of the Railways leased to it, and the Company has also become deeply indebted, both in Canada and in England, on simple contract, the various persons and corporations, and several of the creditors have obtained judgements against it, and much legislation is now pending; and whereas the keeping open of the Railway for traffic, which is of the utmost importance to the interests of the Province, is thereby imperilled, and the terms of a compromise have been provisionally settled, between the various classes of creditors and the company. . . .

The securities were changed as follows: holders of first and second preference bonds might exchange them for new issues to be

41. Canadian Archives, Baring Papers, Grand Trunk, Rose to Baring, May 23, 1862.

called first and second preference stock; the seven per cent bonds, due in October 1862, were converted into third preference stock; the remaining bonds were converted into fourth preference stock. Thus a portion of the bonded debt was compulsorily converted into stock, and an attempt made to convert the rest. By this means the company was saved from having to pay the capital value of the bonds as they fell due. At the same time the rate of interest was reduced to five per cent on first and second preference bonds (or stocks). All arrears of interest were to be paid in stock, at reduced interest, and the company was explicitly protected against legal action to recover arrears. The probability was that no interest would ever be paid on the provincial debentures, since they came ninth in order of priority, and interest on them would be paid only after that on all bonds and stocks of the company.

All receipts from postal charges and carriage of troops were to be earmarked for payment of debts, other than to bondholders or mortgage holders in Lower Canada. To provide for sidings, rolling stock, and other equipment, the company was empowered to issue bonds up to £500,000, known as equipment mortgage bonds, and forming a first charge on the property; but no allowance was made for re-investment in the property out of earnings.

It was an ingenious act, which enabled a virtually bankrupt company to continue operations; and it was presumably for the latter purpose that the province sacrificed its own investment in the railway. At the same time the control of the company was further transferred to England by making the London office a principal one concurrently with that in Montreal, and permitting general meetings to be held in London. Watkin became president, while C. J. Brydges was left in charge in Canada.

The prolonged crisis in the affairs of the Grand Trunk was the most striking event marking the end of the first great building period. It was, however, far from being the only railway to experience serious embarrassment. It remains to examine briefly the causes of this general disorder. A part may be attributed to faulty construction, a charge levelled chiefly—though not wholly—at the Grand Trunk. The existence of bad rails, deficient ballast, and heavy gradients was particularly disastrous in a railway that counted its heavy original cost as justified by the permanence of the construction. A large part of the trouble, too, arose from financial difficulties, some of which have been already indicated. All the railways cost more than the estimates, whether those estimates were made by English, American, or Canadian engineers. The Great Western, for example, which was one of the few railways that ever showed a profit, cost £1,766,563 above the estimate on the main line alone,[42] while a small railway like the Welland cost thirty per cent more than the estimates.[43] The ratio of operating cost on the Grand Trunk placed, according to English experience, at forty per cent, was in practice between fifty-eight and eighty-five per cent. The general financial stringency after the Crimean War, particularly in 1857 and 1858, made it unexpectedly difficult to raise additional funds. Dishonest as well as inefficient contractors existed, and dishonesty amongst promoters and members of parliament helped to swell the cost.

Even the estimated cost of the railways could have been met only by a realization of the calculated traffic which itself was put on the most optimistic basis. The expected traffic on the railways, however, never materialized, in part owing to the competition of water-borne freight which followed the cheaper rates. Grain especially was carried by water. The receipts of western grain at Montreal in 1862 show that only 6.59 per cent of the total went over the Grand Trunk. Competition between railways, too, helped to cut down the traffic of each. This was particularly noticeable with the expansion of the Grand Trunk to Sarnia, cutting in, as it did, into the territory of the Great Western. The Buffalo and Lake Huron Railway was a further blow to the Great Western.

The most conspicuous failure of the railways was in the struggle for their most startling aim, the securing of a large portion of the traffic between the east and west of the United States. Neither the Great Western nor the Northern lived up to expectations in this regard, for American shippers failed to see the logic of their designs. The Northern for a time did an active business as a portage railway, but at the annual meeting of the company in 1863 the directors mentioned that through competitive traffic was not as profitable

42. H. Y. Hind and others, *Eighty years progress of British North America* (Toronto, 1863), p. 230.

43. *Final report of the Welland Railway Company* (1859).

as local freight traffic. The Great Western was reduced from its high estate by competing Canadian lines, by the completion of the American lines around the south of Lake Erie, and more particularly by the construction of the Canada Southern as a direct rival. The Grand Trunk suffered from unsatisfactory western connections and a different gauge from the American railways with which it connected. On the east, too,—apart from its outlet to Portland— it was suspended in mid-air at Rivière du Loup.

The inescapable deduction was that the railways had been no more successful than the canals in capturing the long-sought prize of American trade. It by no means follows that the whole building programme of the 'fifties was a mistake. Railways there had to be for local needs and for the development of the country. They brought a revolution in the life of all the provinces—socially, economically, and politically. In the enthusiasm of the moment and in the hope of profits there had been some degree of over-building: that is to say, more building than was justified by the traffic actually available to meet expenses, and in some areas even more than was required for the needs of the community.

The railway period before confederation is marked by two main characteristics. One is the dependence on English capital—public or private—involving a greater or lesser degree of English control, personnel, and methods. The second is the continental plan on which the railways were based, in the last phase of that long struggle which began with the fur trade before the fall of French government in Canada. The lessons to be drawn from the experience of these years were not obscure. The new methods belong to the period centering around the federation of the provinces, which itself was, in a degree, both cause and effect of railway development. Though there was not a complete change, there can yet be seen in the following period a transition from English to Canadian control, and from continental to national economy.

PART II

NATIONAL ECONOMY

CHAPTER VI

FROM CONTINENTAL TO NATIONAL ECONOMY

1. CONFEDERATION AND RAILWAYS

THE decade of the 'sixties marks a turning point in the history of Canadian railways, as, indeed, it does in the whole political and economic position of the provinces. The evident failure of the Canadian trunk lines to secure such a portion of American business as would repay their generous expenditure led to a major change of policy; and the circumstances and atmosphere of the day suggested as an alternative the exploitation of national territory. Perhaps the balance sheets of the railway companies would in themselves have pointed to such a recourse, but undoubtedly the political and other economic features of the time were additional and powerful factors tending to the same end. Long before Canada became British her people had carried on a struggle for the control of the west and south-west of the continent; and so it had gone through phase after phase, by land and water. Both success and failure had attended their efforts, but in the end the attempt had evidently to be abandoned. Thus the movement toward a single British country in North America, as approached from the political point of view, coincided in time with the recognition, from the economic point of view, of the end of the continental projects. The two are in operation almost inseparable, and yet they sprang in part from different causes. It was, however, the combination of these two groups of motives that gave enough strength to the union movement to carry it to completion.

If the leaders of commerce and transportation had, perforce, to turn their eyes from the mirage of a promised land, what picture was presented by that more modest portion, the northern half of the continent? In the province of Canada nothing more encouraging could be seen than a steady increase of population with a corresponding growth of business for shippers: little here to take the place of the dreams of the Montreal merchants. To the east lay the British provinces on the sea, with their winter

191

ports. To the merchants and producers of Canada the maritime ports would afford that outlet to foreign markets which they lacked, and for the sake of which they had entertained in the early 'fifties the plan of an intercolonial railway; to the people of the Maritime Provinces a political and economic union with Canada spelt a new volume of business for their ports and an uninterrupted contact with the interior of the continent. Both attitudes assumed the construction of a railway, which became an integral part of the union scheme.

For a volume of business sufficient to justify the link between central and eastern provinces, the eyes of the people of Canada and the Maritime Provinces alike were increasingly turning to the west. For the people of the St. Lawrence valley the receding west had ever been the goal. For more than two centuries that vast land had had but shadowy political boundaries, and even in the nineteenth century the American west seemed open in an economic sense to the enterprise of Canadians. By the middle of the century the situation had materially changed. The disillusioned shareholders of the Great Western and the Grand Trunk knew to their sorrow the difference between a prospectus and a dividend. At the same time, urged on by the slogan of Horace Greeley, the people of the eastern states were hurrying to take possession of their heritage, reinforced by immigrants from abroad, many of whom spent their first years in America working on the construction gangs which were pushing the railways across the land of the Indian and the buffalo. In 1854 the steel reached the Mississippi, and in the late 'sixties the first transcontinental railway (Union Pacific-Central Pacific) was approaching completion. Apparently the people of the United States intended to develop their own country and to transport their own goods without the aid of Canadians. But would the westward flood stop at the international boundary? The close contact which had been established between the Red River settlement and St. Paul to its south worried those Canadians who were beginning to think of the future of the British territory in the west. It must not be allowed to fall into American hands, and yet for the province of Canada alone to assimilate such a great area was virtually impossible. Again the situation of the time pointed to political union.

No group of men were more vitally concerned with the future of British North America than those who guided the destinies of the Grand Trunk Railway. Having weathered the storms of the early 'sixties, secured a more favourable position in regard to their obligations, and improved their personnel, the directors were looking for that increased volume of business which alone could give them any permanent relief, and, having failed in their original design of taking traffic from the American west, they turned to the alternative of a through route on British territory. In general their plan is described by E. W. Watkin in his reminiscences:

The result of mature consideration, reasoning carefully upon all the facts I had collected, was, that, at that time, 1863, the best route for a Railway to the Pacific was, to commence at Halifax, to strike across to the Grand Trunk Railway at Rivière du Loup, 106 miles east of Quebec, then to follow the Grand Trunk system to Sarnia; to extend that system to Chicago; to use, under a treaty of neutralization, the United States lines from Chicago to St. Paul; to build a line from St. Paul to Fort Garry (Winnipeg) by English and American capital, and then to extend the line to the Tête Jaune Pass, there to meet a Railway through British Columbia starting from the Pacific.[1]

To Watkin the plan hung together as a whole—both the east and west links must be forged. "Intercolonial is . . . absolutely essential to Grand Trunk and Intercolonial is, under present circumstances in Canada, dependent upon this other movement [control of the west and communication with the Pacific]."[2] To carry it out involved a formidable series of achievements: union of the provinces, control of the Hudson's Bay Company, settlement of the north-west, and the building of the railways. All these were, in fact, accomplished. For his part in bringing about the union Watkin was knighted by the king, and thanked by Cartier "for all the *political services* you have rendered to 'Canada' in having so *efficiently helped* the carrying of the *great confederation measure*."[3] And it may be taken that Cartier, who was both the

1. E. W. Watkin, *Canada and the States* (London, 1887), p. 451. In 1864 a Montreal newspaper described this project as "an absolute certainty."

2. Canadian Archives, Baring Papers, Grand Trunk Railway, Watkin to Baring, November 8, 1862.

3. Watkin, *op. cit.*, p. 457.

solicitor to the Grand Trunk and a member of the coalition
government, knew of what he wrote. The Grand Trunk group
bought the control of the Hudson's Bay Company and publicly
declared their purposes of colonizing the western plains and establishing communication between the Atlantic and the Pacific.[4] But
it was the misfortune of the Grand Trunk Railway on more than
one occasion that others reaped where it had sowed. Neither of the
railways connected with confederation was built or controlled by
them: indeed, the Pacific link in Watkin's transcontinental railway
proved in operation to be the great rival of the Grand Trunk. The
story of the Grand Trunk interest in the Hudson's Bay Company
and the rejection of the proposed line south of Lake Superior
belong to the next chapter: it is only necessary here to notice
that the company which operated what was by far the most
important transportation agency in Canada was working with all
its energy toward a political and economic union based on a transcontinental railway. A. A. Dorion, who so often enlivened the
confederation debates in the Canadian assembly, had strong views
on the relation of the Grand Trunk to confederation.

This project [the Intercolonial, in 1862] having failed, some other scheme
had to be concocted for bringing aid and relief to the unfortunate Grand
Trunk—and the Confederation of all the British North American Provinces
naturally suggested itself to the Grand Trunk officials as the surest means
of bringing with it the construction of the Intercolonial Railway. Such
was the origin of this Confederation scheme.[5]

Later in the debate, when Cartier referred to the Interoceanic
Railway, Dorion broke in with the comment: "Yes, I suppose
that is another necessity of Confederation. . . . Some western
extension of the Grand Trunk scheme for the benefit of Messrs.
Watkin and Company of the new Hudson's Bay Company."
    The question was asked then, and has been repeatedly asked
since, whether the Dominion of Canada was, economically, an
artificial creation, built on ephemeral political considerations made
palatable by a coating of sentiment. To such a far-reaching question

    4. *The International Financial Society Limited: prospectus.*
    5. *Parliamentary debates on the subject of the confederation of the British North
American provinces, third session, eighth provincial parliament of Canada.*

there can be no simple answer, but some evidence may be adduced from the situation in the pre-confederation period. Annexation of the provinces to the United States might—though it is a moot point—have provided an acceptable economic future; but annexation was undesirable on other grounds to the people of the provinces, and probably to the people of the United States. What, then, was the alternative? The St. Lawrence entry to the continent had seemed to dominate a vast territory, but years of painful experience had proven beyond all reasonable question that the draw of the Hudson and Mississippi valleys was too strong. Yet the commercial community of Canada, as typified by Montreal its centre, was not content to rest on the local needs of a sparsely-peopled province. Rupert's Land—British, if not Canadian—had been won and lost through the fur trade, and might be reconquered for peopling and agriculture. The Maritime Provinces would form an integral part of a national economy because of their ports, while other doors to the new country were open on the Pacific and Hudson Bay.

The mutual interdependence of railways and general economic development is a theme which runs through the history of the Dominion, and one which played no small part in its creation. To make possible a stable economic structure a sufficiency of natural resources was required, and was found in the wheat and grazing lands of the west, the lumber of British Columbia and the central and eastern provinces, the fisheries of the Maritime Provinces and British Columbia, and the rich mineral deposits of the Canadian shield and the mountains of British Columbia. These, with the mixed agriculture of the east and centre, formed a basis of staples on which a superstructure of financial institutions, industrial concerns, and transportation facilities could be built. It is possible, then, to argue that confederation was not an illogical step taken by embarrassed politicians, but the fulfilment of an old dream, made possible by the linking of economically complementary areas by railways.

A number of factors combined in the 'sixties to make a federation both desirable and politically possible. The American Civil War led to friction between the North and Great Britain and emphasized the lack of unity in defence. The American objections to the addition of free soil, which would destroy the nice balance between North and South, were automatically removed by the Northern victory; and in the British provinces the fear of the force of "manifest destiny" was revived. The failure of the marriage of French and English Canada led to suggestions of a general union as a solution of political deadlock; while at the same time the Maritime Provinces were earnestly discussing a union either of themselves only or of all British North America. A few of the far-sighted saw need of action in regard to Rupert's Land lest it fall into the hands of the United States, and argued that it could be taken over only by a larger unit than the province of Canada. The British government, at first luke-warm toward the project, threw its powerful influence in favour of union, influenced in great part by the problem of defence.

In addition to this array of causes, may be added some others that have a more direct bearing on the present study. In 1849 an influential body of Canadians professed to be in favour of annexation to the United States. In so far as this was the expression of an economic grievance it was met by the Reciprocity Treaty of 1854, which established free trade in agricultural and forest products, minerals, and fish, and gave to American citizens the right to fish in the waters of Canada, Nova Scotia, New Brunswick and Prince Edward Island, and to navigate the St. Lawrence. On the whole the treaty seems to have been advantageous to both parties, but especially to the British provinces, whose exports to the United States rose steeply, especially when the Civil War created an abnormal demand in the States. Before the treaty had been in force for many years, however, it began to be attacked in the United States as a one-sided bargain, the particular complaint being that it did not cover manufactured articles. Such objections were felt more strongly when Canada began to adopt a protective tariff; and the whole arrangement was further compromised by the irritation arising out of the war. Throughout 1862 and 1863 the treaty was discussed in congress, its critics dwelling chiefly on the iniquity of the Galt tariff. At the end of 1864 it was sent to the senate's committee on foreign relations, which reported in favour of abrogation. In spite of the efforts of the friends of the treaty, the senate voted against it, and in 1865 official notification was given to the British government that it was no longer in the interests of the United States to continue the arrangement.

Neither in the United States nor the British provinces did the belief in a reciprocal trade agreement die in 1865, but for the time being reciprocity had been abolished, and the favourable conditions which had been created for colonial producers disappeared. When it was apparent that the treaty was likely to be abrogated, it became necessary to find alternative avenues of trade, the most obvious of which was that between the provinces themselves. For some years previously, and especially since 1849, arrangements had been made between the provinces providing either for mutual free trade or for free exchange in specified goods. Little had come out of this, largely owing to the lack of adequate transportation facilities, and it was hoped that a political union, together with an intercolonial railway, would compensate for the closing of the American market. A large free-trade area would thus be created, which might bring advantages similar to those in the German *Zollverein* or the American union. To tear down the tariff walls, however, without at the same time providing for adequate communications between the provinces would be manifestly ineffective; and thus the establishment of an intercolonial railway was closely associated with the plan for political and economic union. Thomas Scatcherd, indeed, went so far as to say in the Canadian assembly that "this Confederation scheme is nothing more or less than a scheme to construct the Intercolonial Railway." This may be an exaggeration, but it is evidence of strong demand for the Intercolonial by the Maritime Provinces. Prince Edward Island was an exception, and one of her delegates at the Quebec conference, A. A. MacDonald, stated that "it is a matter of indifference to our people whether the Intercolonial Railroad is built at all or not." The island was safe from invasion, and, as no plan was included for a local railway, it simply meant assuming a part of the railway debt of the other provinces.[6] Opinion in New Brunswick and Nova Scotia, however, was set on the Intercolonial. "They [the delegates from Nova Scotia and New Brunswick] will not leave the construction of the Intercolonial to the legislation of the new

6. A. G. Doughty (ed.), "Notes on the Quebec conference, 1864" (*Canadian Histo l Review*, i, 1).

Assembly—They say that the construction of this Line is the great inducement to them to go into the compact, and that its construction must be a condition precedent, or rather a base of the operation itself. . . ."[7]

Two resolutions on the improvement of communications were passed at the conference. The first concerns the Intercolonial Railway.

The General Government shall secure, without delay, the completion of the Intercolonial Railway from Rivière-du-Loup through New Brunswick to Truro, in Nova Scotia.

It will be observed that this is a definite commitment without any conditions as to cost or route. The second is less definite.

The communications with the North-West Territory, and the improvements required for the development of the Trade of the Great West with the Seaboard, are regarded by this Conference as subjects of the highest importance to the Federated Provinces, and shall be prosecuted at the earliest possible period that the state of the Finances will permit.

The west was not immediately to be a part of the Dominion; but the Intercolonial was a *sine qua non* to the people of the Maritime Provinces. No railway, no federation was in effect the attitude of their delegates, an attitude which was clearly appreciated by the Canadians. The Intercolonial had to be promised, and promised definitely, if the negotiations were to have any hope of success. On the other hand, the far west was remote from the Maritime Provinces, and, while the second resolution was phrased so as to suggest an increased use of their ports, it would not have been acceptable in the form of a binding agreement. Nor was the pressure of opinion in Canada such as to make a guarantee of western communications politically necessary.

The situation was threshed out again and again in both branches of the Canadian legislature when the Quebec resolutions were brought down in February 1865. The view of the government was ably put to the legislative council by Sir Etienne Taché on the first day of the debate. "If the opportunity which now presented

7. Canadian Archives, Macdonald Papers, "Confederation," vi, C. J. Brydges to Lord Monck, September 19, 1866.

itself were allowed to pass by unimproved," he told the council, "whether we would or would not, we would be forced into the American Union by violence, and if not by violence, would be placed upon an inclined plane which would carry us there insensibly." This note of the pressure from without was struck over and over again on the government side. There was little attempt to conceal the argument that the Intercolonial was necessary because federation was necessary—because the alternative was annexation. The political necessity of the railway was accepted, whatever might be its intrinsic merits. George Brown admitted that, "as a commercial enterprise, the Intercolonial Railway has not . . . any considerable merit," but Taché went on to find economic reasons in its favour. Canada, he said, had fine railways and canals but no seaport. She was "shut up in a prison, as it were, for five months of the year in fields of ice." The St. Lawrence and Atlantic Railway had been a boon; but now that there were threats both of the abolition of the bonding system and of the abrogation of the Reciprocity Treaty, the escape from this dangerous situation was to build a railway to the ports of New Brunswick and Nova Scotia. Much the same line of argument was taken by Cartier in the assembly. Canada had territory and population, but not a seaboard, while the Maritime Provinces lacked a hinterland and a large population.

Members of the opposition then began some well-directed sniping at the highly vulnerable position occupied by the government. How much was the railway going to cost? No amount had been given except an unofficial estimate of $15,000,000, and no maximum was indicated in the resolutions. Moreover, the burden would now be chiefly shouldered by Canada. By the arrangement of 1862 Canada was to find five-twelfths of the cost, but her proportion under confederation would be about nine-twelfths. What was to be the route of the railway? This again was not settled. How could anyone vote for a railway when neither the cost nor route were known? To these criticisms no adequate answers could be given because no definite information existed. More telling blows were struck at the probable usefulness of the Intercolonial. One point made in favour of the line was that it was needed for purposes of military defence, the general problems of which were much to the fore in the debates. It would be placed well away from the American border and could transport (from the Atlantic ports) troops and supplies that could hardly be moved by road. After some rather amateurish discussions of the use of railways in warfare, a member of the opposition pointed out that the Intercolonial would link up with the Grand Trunk, and that the line of the latter was at some points only twenty-six miles from the boundary of Maine. Here, he said, the whole communication could be cut by a hostile force.

Turning to the peace-time use of the railway members of the opposition expressed everything from scepticism to scorn of its economic value. Members of the council and assembly on the government side had defended the Intercolonial on the grounds that it would carry grain and other goods to tidewater, especially in the winter, and in general would develop interprovincial trade, but William McMaster (Midland) threw cold water on the idea that grain would move over the Intercolonial.

We are told by honourable gentlemen that the abrogation of the Reciprocity Treaty renders this road an indispensable necessity in order to secure an independent outlet to the sea-board; but, if this view of the case be correct, why do not our merchants and millers forward their produce during the winter months to New York, Boston, or Portland, by our or any of the other different railway lines which have long been open to these points? The reason is obvious. The freight by railway is so expensive that they find it to be for their advantage to pay interest, storage, and insurance on their wheat and flour until the opening of the navigation. And if they do not now avail themselves of the shipping ports referred to, neither of which are more than six hundred miles from Toronto, will they send their produce double that distance over the Intercolonial road to Halifax?

Billa Flint (Trent) drove another spike into the government's case by arguing that, assuming (as had been stated) that two cents per ton mile was a reasonable charge for freight, it would cost $2.08 to ship a barrel of flour from Toronto to seaboard—a cost which he held was prohibitive. Others in the council and assembly made similar comments: in fact the legislature was fully warned that either the Intercolonial would have to be subsidized to allow artificially low rates, or else it would not be used sufficiently to make it pay. The critics of the railway had, in fact, touched one of the fundamental problems of Canadian transportation and uncovered difficulties which were blissfully ignored half a century later.

It need not be assumed that those who voted in favour of the railway were wholly unconscious of economic arguments. The Intercolonial was not, directly, a sound financial proposition; it never was really thought to be so; and never became so. It was, however, an integral part of the federation scheme. It may not unreasonably be held that without such a communication political union would be absurd; and at least it was clear that, without the railway, no union would be accepted by the Maritime Provinces. The length of the line was dictated in large part by military considerations which were at that time pressing. In other words, both government and opposition were, from different points of view, presenting unanswerable arguments.

The question of communication with the north-west also received no little attention. George Brown was put up in the assembly to talk to this point and made a spirited and optimistic speech on what had become his favourite topic on the platform and in the *Globe*. He looked forward to the day when the fur trade would again pass through Canada instead of being "smuggled off through the icebound regions of James' Bay, that the pretence of the barrenness of the country and the difficulty of carrying merchandise by the natural route of the St. Lawrence may be kept up a little longer." Passing from this rather shaky argument to "the fertile plains of that great Saskatchewan territory," he looked forward to settlement and cultivation. Unfortunately Brown had little to say of what was going to be done about it— an omission which did not pass unnoticed by his hearers. Member after member commented regretfully, coldly, or bitterly, on the fact that the Intercolonial was given precedence over a railway to the west. Some felt that the latter would simply be delayed, and others that the cost of the Intercolonial would prohibit any further expenditure on great public works.

We find [said one] that the representatives at the Conference from Nova Scotia and New Brunswick made it a point of the proposed Constitution to construct the Intercolonial Railway, also took good care to make the opening of the North-West contingent upon the state of the finances, and the Confederation will commence life with a debt of $150,000,000. It is evident, therefore, that the North-West is hermetically sealed, as far as Canada is concerned.

Members of both parties called attention time after time to the importance of communications with the west. One member regretted that the Dominion had not immediately stretched to the Pacific, while others more modestly hoped that this would come in time. No definite suggestions were made about a Pacific railway, although the possibility of one was often mentioned.

Many references were made by the members from Canada West to canals, and sometimes with regret that they had not received more consideration at the Quebec conference. Some members thought that public funds should have been spared for the enlargement of the canals generally; others emphasized the Ottawa or Georgian Bay water routes to the west as worthy of special attention. One member harked back to the older ideas. "See the outlet we possess to the ocean," he cried, "look at the magnificent St. Lawrence. . . . Is it not possible to so improve this channel as to bring the produce of the Great Western States to market through our territory?" Presumably this was a rhetorical question, as no one troubled to tell him that the answer was in the negative. Little time need, however, be devoted to the discussion of canals in the legislature, for no plan was then seriously contemplated for enlargement or additions. With the successful conclusion of the federation movement came as its first fruits in the sphere of public works the construction of the long-talked-of Intercolonial Railway. By section 145 of the British North America Act the construction of a railway connecting the St. Lawrence with Halifax was to be begun within six months after the union.

Prince Edward Island was unfriendly toward the Intercolonial, regarding it only as a cause for additional taxation, while not solving local transportation problems, and rejected the Quebec resolutions. In 1871 the assembly passed an act providing for the construction of a railway through the length of the island, the contractors to accept debentures in payment, and in the following year a further act authorized branch lines to Souris and Tignish, with the same provision for payment. All went well for a while, and then difficulties began to arise. The original act allowed a maximum sum of £5,000 per mile for construction but contained no word as to the number of miles. The contractors extended the line (and hence the cost) unduly for the twin purposes of adding to their receipts and avoiding expensive cuttings and embankments. At the same time they either sold the debentures to the local banks or pledged them against cash advances. Both the government and the financial community (between which there was an overlap) became alarmed, and looked to confederation as the means of easing a financial situation which was becoming threatening. In spite of the remaining opinion to the contrary, therefore, Prince Edward Island joined the confederation in 1873, the Dominion taking over the partially constructed railway, and relieving the minds and pockets of both the debenture-holders and the taxpayers. At the same time the Dominion government promised to establish and maintain steam communication between the island and the mainland, thus linking the former with the Canadian system of railways.

2. THE INTERCOLONIAL RAILWAY

Throughout the 'fifties and 'sixties negotiations went on between the provinces, and between the provinces and the British government, with the indefatigable Watkin hurrying from one to the other with advice and encouragement. After a series of refusals of loans from the British government, another conference of representatives of the provinces was held in Quebec in the autumn of 1861, the delegates from New Brunswick and Nova Scotia having been transported thither by Watkin over the Grand Trunk. Again deputations went to England, interspersed by further conversations at Quebec. In the end the negotiations broke down once more. The final British terms included the establishment of a sinking fund which Nova Scotia and New Brunswick were willing, but Canada was not willing, to accept. By the end of 1862 a stalemate had been reached.

From 1863 on the situation was a peculiar one. Although the financing of the railway had not been arranged, it was decided to go on with a survey. In the course of the negotiations in London the British government had insisted on a survey being made before parliament should be asked to guarantee a loan. Accordingly the Canadian government proposed that one should be undertaken, and appointed Mr. Sandford Fleming, an engineer with considerable local experience, as the Canadian surveyor. From Nova Scotia, New Brunswick, and Great Britain came expressions of willingness to accept Fleming as their nominee also, but a series of misunderstandings and bickering between the provincial governments led to the survey being undertaken by Canada alone, with the suggestion that Nova Scotia and New Brunswick should later contribute to the cost if they saw fit. In the spring of 1864 Fleming began his task, and submitted his report in February 1865.

With Fleming and his staff hard at work between Rivière du Loup and Truro, the governments of Nova Scotia and New Brunswick began to attempt construction without waiting for Canada. The section they chose to start on was the hundred miles between Truro (to which a line already ran from Halifax) and a point on the St. John-Shediac railway. Acting on behalf of the two provinces, Watkin obtained from the British government a promise that the proposed work would be considered to come under the guaranteed loan, if such were raised. Thus encouraged, the two provinces appointed English contractors, but these failed and their successors never turned a sod in Nova Scotia, and little was done in New Brunswick. While attempting to make some progress themselves, the Maritime governments had little hope of help from Canada. The agreement to build the railway, therefore, which formed a part of the Quebec resolutions may be seen as a means of reaching a goal which had proved unattainable by other paths. After all the years of conferences, agreements, misunderstandings, hopes and failures, it is not surprising that Maritime opinion insisted on the Intercolonial being explicitly written into the British North America Act.

Would the Intercolonial have been built without confederation? That is a question to which no definite answer can be given. It may be argued that good progress was being made toward an agreement, and that the objection by Canada to the sinking fund would have been overcome by some kind of compromise. The survey would hardly have been undertaken by Canada if the railway project had been regarded as dead, although it must be remembered that by 1864 the close relation between the railway and the union was already recognized. Certainly there could have been in 1867 no confederation without the Intercolonial: there might have been an Intercolonial without confederation. The majority in the Maritime Provinces would probably have preferred railway without union, and the majority in Canada union without railway. Without confederation it would have been difficult, if not impossible, to secure a common tariff policy. Such a policy was held to be a need of the time, and was advanced as an argument in favour of federation. In practice, however, it was tied to the railway between the provinces; for, without adequate transportation, there could be little hope of extensive interprovincial trade, and without the markets and industries that could be built up behind the tariff, the railway would be hard put to find traffic. In deference to the opinion in the Maritime Provinces, the early tariffs of the Dominion were low, but within ten years they had begun to climb steeply.[8] As a source of revenue the tariff helped to finance the railways, as in the old province of Canada; and as a protective measure it contributed to creating and directing traffic.

For the thirty years or so during which a railway between the Maritime Provinces and Canada had been under discussion there had always been disagreement about the port to which it should lead and the route to Quebec. By the confederation agreement the port was to be Halifax—but there remained a choice of routes from Halifax to Rivière du Loup, the terminus of the Grand Trunk. It fell to Fleming's lot to examine the possible routes, and in his book, *The Intercolonial*, he explains the problem at some length. He was deeply impressed by the results of the boundary settlement of 1842. Had the territory in dispute fallen to New Brunswick, an almost direct line could then have been run from Quebec to Fredericton, bringing Halifax within 650 miles of Montreal, St. John within 415 miles, and leaving St. Andrews only 250 miles from Quebec.

The distance between Montreal and Halifax might thus have been lessened nearly 200 miles. St. Andrews would have taken the place of

8. S. J. McLean, "The Tariff history of Canada" (*Toronto University studies in political science*, Toronto, 1895).

Portland as the winter terminus of the Grand Trunk Railway, and would have commanded, together with St. John, a traffic now cut off from both places, and centred at a foreign port.

This, indeed, was perhaps the most fundamental problem of the Intercolonial. Not many years later the Canadian Pacific Railway built the "short line" through Maine to avoid the expensive detour, but the Intercolonial had to be built on Canadian soil. Nor was it only the position of the boundary which caused a problem in the location of the line. A hot controversy waged over the location of the line in New Brunswick. Some fifteen separate routes found advocates, but in general they fall into three main divisions: the northern route, by Bay Chaleur; the frontier route by the valley of the St. John River; and a central route in between the two running north from St. John. Around these a somewhat confusing series of arguments and counter-arguments were built up.

From a military point of view the frontier line seemed to be the least desirable, although its supporters held that any railway would be vulnerable, and that there was no longer reason to fear hostilities. The northern line—which had been chosen by Major Robinson— seemed the safest in case of war, but the central line supporters claimed that it was vulnerable from the sea. On the whole, however, there could be little doubt that the northern line was the most desirable for military purposes. The rival routes were also compared with respect to cost of construction and operation. It was said that the frontier line would have the advantage of taking over fifty-five miles of railway already built; to which the reply was that the railways in question were in bad condition and hopelessly in debt, and further that the frontier line would cost $1,000,000 more than the northern. The central line supporters produced an alternative argument: that their route could make use of existing railways by securing running rights. From a commercial point of view a case could be made out for each. The supporters of the frontier line claimed that the St. John valley was well settled, and that it offered a local lumber trade as well as that from the Aroostook district in Maine. The central route was defended on the ground that through freight could be shipped to the port of St. John. The advocates of the northern route argued that there was a high population per mile of railway, also lumber establishments, and a potential export of fish to Quebec and Ontario. Moreover, the northern route would be most useful to Prince Edward Island and Newfoundland.

The sharp division of opinion in New Brunswick was an embarrassment to all the governments concerned. "The questions of Confederation", wrote Peter Mitchell, the prime minister of New Brunswick, "are entirely subordinate to the question of *Railroad* in our province and now that the latter has become almost a certainty, the sectional interest has arisen, and a disregard of that, will do much to affect the standing of whatever government may be formed, either on the Northern and Eastern or South and Western sides of our Province for that is the way they now side off."[9] Macdonald was anxious to move cautiously, especially since opinion in New Brunswick was none too friendly toward the federation.

. . . So far as Canada proper is concerned you are aware that we have no sectional interests to serve. We want the shortest and best route. Whichever line will best secure the through traffic, and at the same time serve the purposes of New Brunswick locally, is the line we will go for. As you say, when a railway is first projected every man wants it past his own door. It certainly would appear to me, on the first impression, as the lawyers say, that it would be politic to select a St. John's River man, and a Northern route man for the Cabinet. Both interests would then have advocates at the Council table, and the government as a whole would decide after hearing both, and after considering all the evidence before them.[10]

A few days later Mitchell wrote that his party "was on the eve of disruption" from the strife of sectional interests over railways, but that he had tided over the crisis.[11]

In the end the choice of routes was made on military and commercial rather than political grounds. From a military point of view there had never been much doubt as to which was the best; and, in any case, the correspondence with the British government in the summer of 1868 indicates that financial backing would cer-

9. Canadian Archives, Macdonald Papers, "Confederation," vi, Mitchell to Macdonald, May 27, 1867.
10. *Ibid.*, Macdonald to Mitchell, June 1, 1867.
11. *Ibid.*, Mitchell to Macdonald, June 6, 1867.

tainly not have been given to the frontier, and possibly not to the central line. In February 1868 Fleming was asked to express his own opinion as to the best route, and in his reply to Macdonald he definitely advocated the northern. The chief consideration he had in mind was through traffic, for he attached little importance to local traffic on any of the proposed lines. A railway was being built from St. John to Bangor, Maine, which would be "fatal to the Intercolonial" unless the northern route were chosen; for the latter would make possible a port on the Bay of Chaleur, which would enable the Intercolonial to secure some through traffic with Europe.[12] It was one of Fleming's favourite beliefs that communication with Europe could begin at such a port, cross Newfoundland and Ireland by rail, and so cut down the sea voyage. Fortunately, however, it was not an integral part of his plan for the Intercolonial.

To avoid charges of political favouritism the construction of the railway was placed under a board of four commissioners, consisting of A. Walsh, the chairman, E. B. Chandler of New Brunswick, who had taken an active part in the earlier attempts to commence the railway, C. J. Brydges, managing director of the Grand Trunk, and W. F. Coffin of Montreal, who resigned and was succeeded by A. W. McLelan of Nova Scotia, a former opponent of confederation. Tupper had first been asked to act as chairman, but had declined on the ground that it would weaken his influence in making federation acceptable in Nova Scotia. The appointment of all officers was vested in the commissioners with the exception of the chief engineer, a position which was well filled by Fleming.

Differences of opinion arose between Fleming and the commissioners, first as to the manner of letting contracts. A number of tenders had been made for the construction and equipment of the whole road, two at the rate of $35,000 a mile (Robinson's estimate), another for $14,600,000 and a fourth for $14,800,000. The government determined, however, to let a series of small contracts by measurement and price. The commissioners concurred in the principle of contracts by sections but favoured letting each section for a bulk sum. To this the engineer objected, but was unable to have the decision of the commissioners overruled. The other

12. Macdonald Papers, "Railways," ii, Fleming to Macdonald, March 3, 1868.

subject of dispute was the materials of bridges, the commissioners preferring wood and the engineer iron. The former opinion was, no doubt, due to the influences of Brydges, who, in a private memorandum of October 1868, argued that the original cost of the Intercolonial should be kept low to correspond with the light traffic that was expected. Later, he said, more costly structures might be erected. In particular he advocated wooden bridges, which, he said, were universal in Canada, except on the Grand Trunk.[13] Fleming, however, was a firm believer in a permanent type of construction being used from the start, arguing that it would be cheaper in the end than constant replacement. In general it was a difference of opinion which has been important throughout the history of Canadian railways. In the case of bridges Fleming held that iron was not only safer and more lasting, but cost little more in the first instance. A long argument arose, the two experts—Fleming and Brydges—appealing to the privy council. In this case the engineer was upheld, and all bridges, large and small, except three which were made of wood against his protest, were of iron. It is worth noticing that the actual cost of the iron bridges when built was slightly less than the estimate for either iron or wooden structures. On the whole the Intercolonial from a technical point of view represented the triumph of Fleming's principles. The rails used were all of steel, although iron ones had originally been planned, and the road throughout was of a high standard. The cost of the whole, which both Brydges and Fleming estimated at $20,000,000, turned out to be $34,363,896.

It is a somewhat remarkable fact that it was not until after construction had begun that a decision was reached as to whether the railway should be under public or private management. As late as the end of 1870 Macdonald still apparently contemplated having the Intercolonial operated by the Grand Trunk, as the following exchange of letters suggests.

I think the time is approaching when we must take into consideration the manner of working the Intercolonial Railway when finished. I presume that the G.T.R. looks to running arrangement for the whole line, and my present impression is that that would be the most satisfactory mode, in

13. Canadian Archives, Fleming Papers, cxvii.

the Public interest, of working the railway. Still, there will be an attempt made by Brown, McKenzie and Co. to get up a feeling against any such arrangement, and we must take care the terms are such as to disarm criticism.

We may expect great and powerful resistance from the steamboat and shipping interest, who will be afraid that water borne freight to Quebec will not receive fair play, and that it will be made secondary to the through traffic on the G.T.R. It is, of course, the duty of the government to see that no preference of any kind is given, or possible, and that a barrel of flour arriving by water at Quebec will have just as good a chance as if it were sent by railway from Sarnia.

It appears to me, then, that in any arrangement with the G.T.R. that that portion of the line lying between Quebec and Rivière du Loup should be considered as a portion of the Intercolonial Railway, and that the arrangement between Government and the G.T.R. should have effect on all traffic between Quebec and Halifax. The matter is of such great importance that it will require grave consideration, & probably entail a large amount of correspondence; therefore the sooner we address ourselves to it the better. I have not yet brought it up in Council but have had a quiet talk with Cartier on the subject. It is for the interests of the Grand Trunk Ry that arrangements should be made with the present government, which is well inclined to act fairly by your company, rather than leave the matter to the uncertain chances of the future. There is little doubt that we will hear a good deal on railway matters during the next General Election.

When you are in England you had I think better commence discussing the matter with your board. Pray let me have your ideas on the subject, if you have time before you leave.

P.S. The Board should give you full powers.[14]

Brydges was apparently pleased with the suggested arrangement.

I received your letter yesterday morning, and have to-day seen Cartier upon other matters, and mentioned the subject to him.

I am glad to find you take the view you do, as to the prospective working of the Intercolonial Line. As you know, I was rather afraid of saying anything about it since my appointment as Commissioner, lest it should be supposed that I was seeking to use my position for the purpose of aiding Grand Trunk interest.

14. Macdonald Papers, Letter book 14, Macdonald to C. J. Brydges, October 31, 1870.

I have tried to do what I considered right for Intercolonial, regardless of any other consideration but its own good.

I do not see well, how, in the interests of the country, any other or better arrangement could be made than Grand Trunk working the Intercolonial; but the terms, I admit, will require very careful consideration, and considerable discussion.

I see no difficulty in accomplishing what you refer to in regard to water-borne traffic to Quebec seeking transport over the Intercolonial Line.

If you are not prepared, as I suppose is the case to purchase the line from Quebec to Rivière du Loup, on the part of the Government, I think I can suggest, without much difficulty, all the safe-guards that you are likely to require. I do not believe that Quebec will be the point where water-borne traffic for the West will find the best means of reaching the railway. It should be, I think, at Montreal. This, however, is a matter of detail, which it will not be difficult to deal with at the right time.

I should very much like to know, when you speak of the Intercolonial, what your view is in regard to the existing Railways in the Lower Provinces, which of course must be a part, practically of the Intercolonial Line. For instance, you cannot reach the two Ocean *termini* of Halifax and St. John, without including portions, at any rate, of the existing Government Lines. When, therefore, you talk of an arrangement between Grand Trunk and Intercolonial, I assume that you mean to enable Grand Trunk trains to run both to Halifax and St. John. This is an important question, because the existing lines have a certain traffic, now, the value of which is known, and the incorporation of those Lines into the Intercolonial system, would undoubtedly tend to modify the conditions upon which alone, the other parts of the whole system could be worked. If you have time, on receipt of this letter to drop me a line to say whether or not you contemplate any arrangement in regard to include the working of the existing Roads in the Lower Provinces as well as the Intercolonial, it would enable me to discuss the matter more intelligently when I am on the other side. I will come back with full authority to talk and write definitely upon the subject. . . .[15]

Unfortunately there is no means of knowing whether Macdonald clung to the idea of operation by the Grand Trunk, or whether he changed his mind. One would imagine that the cabinet was divided on the subject, for Howe had been a staunch upholder of public operation of railways, while Cartier had a close association with

15. Macdonald Papers, "Railways," ii, Brydges to Macdonald, November 2, 1870.

the Grand Trunk. Whatever may have been the decision of the cabinet, the decisive action was left to the succeeding administration under Alexander Mackenzie. Since the Liberal government contained influences hostile to the Grand Trunk, it is not surprising that the earlier scheme was abandoned in favour of governmental operation—a policy which was in any case probably more acceptable in the Maritime Provinces. In 1874 the Intercolonial was placed under the direct control of the department of public works, which assumed the powers formerly held by the commission.

The construction of the Intercolonial was principally financed by means of an act of 1867 (31 Vict., c. 13) which empowered the government to raise a loan of four million pounds sterling, the interest on three millions of which was guaranteed, or promised, by the imperial government. The loan proved to be encouragingly popular, being subscribed four times over. The sum provided by the loan was equal to the estimate, but as the cost exceeded the estimate by over $14,000,000 the balance had to be met on general account.

By 1876 the new parts of the railway were finished, and a through line was provided from Halifax to Rivière du Loup. The greater part of this was that built by the Dominion, but use was also made of the sections already completed by the Maritime Provinces. The Nova Scotia Railway, taken over by the Dominion, provided the sixty-one miles of rail from Halifax to Truro; while the European and North American contributed the few miles built from Moncton eastward and the Shediac-St. John line, which made the necessary connection with the chief port of New Brunswick. The first railway to be owned by the Dominion consisted of the "Ocean Mail Line" from Rivière du Loup to Halifax (562 miles), the Prince Edward Island Railway, together with branch lines—of which the principal were those from Truro to Pictou and Moncton to St. John—and a few side lines to wharves. Although the connection with the Grand Trunk, which had the same gauge (5 feet, 6 inches), gave the Intercolonial entry to the railway systems of central Canada and the United States, this dependent position was not altogether satisfactory. At the same time the Grand Trunk was willing to dispose of its line east of Quebec which had ceased to have any future importance, and in

1879 the line from Rivière du Loup to Hadlow, opposite Quebec, was purchased, with running rights to Point Lévis. According to the report of the department of railways and canals,

The control of the section became indispensable to the successful working of the Intercolonial Railway. The permanent way was in bad condition, and it was not possible to maintain the line established for the through Intercolonial Traffic owing to the detentions which were experienced between River du Loup and Quebec. Indeed the interests of the Inter-colonial system were throughout affected by the important link in the connection, being under independent management. The necessity for removing these difficulties was early foreseen, and the fact of such a possible transfer did not encourage the Grand Trunk Railway Company to expend more money on maintenance than could be avoided. It was also held to be of primary importance that access should be had to a landing pier on the River St. Lawrence near Quebec.

Ten years later the Drummond County Railway from Chaudière Junction to Ste. Rosalie Junction was purchased, and this, with running rights over the Grand Trunk Portland line, gave access to the Bonaventure station in Montreal. The Intercolonial was, in fact, steadily fulfilling its purpose of acting as a through line from east to west. To carry the process a step further it had been stipulated at the time of the purchase of 1879 that the sum paid over to the Grand Trunk ($1,500,000) was to be "devoted towards obtaining an independent Railway connection from Sarnia to Chicago," which arrangement "virtually confers the same advantages to the Intercolonial Railway system, owing to its close connection with the Grand Trunk." By 1916 the Intercolonial had 1,450 miles of track, acquired at a cost of $108,131,150.

It remains to consider briefly the success of this first experiment by the Dominion in public ownership of railways. Care must be taken, however, in drawing general conclusions from the bare figures of the financial returns of the Intercolonial. It is doubtful whether even its sponsors expected to see it as a paying proposition, for it was—in no sinister sense—a political railway: that is to say, it was designed to serve the political and economic needs of the state.

Considering the circumstances under which the road was built no amount of statistical analysis of surplus and deficits can prove or disprove its success.

A deficit may be an indication of success inasmuch as it results from lower rates and a more satisfactory union between Canada and the Maritime Provinces. If the road must be regarded as an essential part of Confederation, its success is measured in terms of the value of Confederation.[16]

Constructed at a high cost with a view to fast through traffic, the Intercolonial never was able to achieve a sufficient volume of business to carry this capital investment. At the same time it could not, and had not been expected to, secure adequate local traffic. The route which had been chosen carried the line in a sweeping curve through eastern Quebec and northern New Brunswick, through districts where neither people nor industries were plentiful. Even the beauty of the Metapedia valley could not compensate for the scanty population of that forested area. In general, too, it is well to remember that the greater part of the Intercolonial was in the provinces which had the smallest population and the fewest industrial centres. All this had been foreseen by Fleming, who had deliberately planned for through traffic, but that traffic proved hard to procure. Even when the Intercolonial had penetrated to Montreal, it was still dependent on competing private companies for access to the long-haul business originating in the west. Then its own territory was invaded by the Canadian Pacific Short Line to St. John—a line which was able to take advantage of the dissipation of the fears of a war with the United States.

It was to be expected that the Intercolonial would show a deficit in the first years in which it was operated. The incompleteness of the system together with the general depression of business at that time gave little chance of a surplus. Even in better times, although surpluses were shown in some years, they were not consistent. The extension to Quebec, coinciding with one improvement in general business, and the extension to Montreal, coinciding with the long-awaited period of prosperity, brought better times to the Intercolonial, but never made of it a profitable enterprise, if only the balance sheet be considered. In addition to the reasons for this which have already been indicated, were the low rates, designed to satisfy the Maritime Provinces, and to compete with water-borne traffic and with the Short Line. Management

16. H. A. Innis, *Problems of staple production in Canada* (Toronto, 1933), p. 35.

was not always efficient, nor was the railway always free from the more pernicious forms of political interference.

The building of the Intercolonial was neither the first nor the last step made by governments—before or after confederation—to meet the peculiar transportation needs of Canada. Like roads, canals, and other railways it has borne upon the taxpayer, and like them it has had compensating advantages in indirect ways. No balance can really be struck where such diverse factors exist at once. Nor was the Intercolonial the first or last railway to be subsidized by the taxpayers. And while its history throws much light on public ownership, it no more proves that public railways cannot pay than the periodic collapses of the Grand Trunk prove that private railways cannot pay.

CHAPTER VII

THE PROJECT OF A PACIFIC RAILWAY

1. Western Transportation Before the Railway

THE history of the Canadian west may be divided into three overlapping but distinct periods: that of the Indians, that of the fur traders, and, finally, that of assimilation to modern culture. From the point of view of transportation there is no marked break between the first two; but the change from the second to the third is a radical one. The building of railways from Lake Superior to the Pacific coast revolutionized conditions in that area and led to its exploitation from the eastern centres. To some extent exploitation had long been carried out by the fur traders, but in a form which, while it affected the lives of the natives, did little to introduce settlement, industries, or modern communications. The growing interest in the west, which became effective about the middle of the nineteenth century, was focused on three aims: to preserve it as British (or Canadian) territory; to people and develop it; and to establish overland communication with the far east. The last directly, and the others indirectly, called for improved transportation, which to most men of the day meant railways: railways, because any other form of transport seemed hopelessly inadequate for the purposes mentioned, in view of the size and nature of the western area. The means of travel in the west in the period before 1821 have already been examined in the first three chapters of this book. The changes after that time, however, were of sufficient moment to justify some study of the conditions prevailing in the period between 1821 and the construction of the first railway to the Pacific.

The fusion of the Hudson's Bay and North West companies in 1821 under the name of the former began a new era in the west. The bitter rivalry between the two companies had culminated in a kind of guerilla warfare; high prices and quantities of liquor had debauched the Indians; many regions were drained of furs; and both companies were in financial straits. The end of intense competition brought order into the west, and the Indians, at first suspicious, became reconciled to the new régime. At the same time as the union a grant of exclusive trade in all the territory of the west not in the British provinces or the United States was granted to the company, subject to the rights of American citizens west of the Rockies. The relaxation of the tension which had existed in the previous years and the pooling of personnel and interests enabled the company to set its house in order. Such reorganization as was carried out was due in great part to the genius of Sir George Simpson, who became first governor of the new northern department and a few years later governor in chief in America. Simpson's professional curiosity and energy knew no bounds. He covered his whole district, constantly breaking records for fast travel, and making notes on every person and thing which could possibly concern the company. His reports to London are a mine of information.

Such were the circumstances under which the last chapter of the history of the Hudson's Bay Company as a monopolistic and governing body began. In some ways the power of the company in these fifty years was greater than ever before. From Montreal to Victoria, from the Arctic to the American border, its servants dominated the scene. Just as in later years no adventurous traveller would think of plunging into the untravelled areas away from the railways without seeking the counsel and help of the nearest Hudson's Bay factor, so in the days before railways, transportation in the west on the whole was either conducted by the company or modelled on its methods.

The first major change in method which followed the union of the companies was the eclipse of canoes as the chief craft in the west—a change which coincided with the eclipse of the Montreal "pedlars" who had taken them there.

We are confident [wrote the committee in London to Simpson] that it will be found cheaper and safer to use boats in preference to canoes and that it will be practicable to do so in every part of the country except in New Caledonia and McKenzie's River. And as Orkneymen are better adapted for the constructing of boats than Canadians, and are generally more careful servants we recommend that all the Canadians, whose contracts expire this year should be discharged, with the exception of such useful men as may be in debt to the concern, or whom it may be desirable from some particular circumstance to retain in the service.[1]

Simpson agreed about the advantage of boats, but was not so happy about the Orkneymen.

Wherever Boat Navigation is practicable no other Craft I think should be used as it certainly will be found cheaper and better in regard to safety than Canoes and it is ascertained that it can be adopted in all parts of the country except New Caledonia; next season we hope to have a sufficient number for all the Establishments to the Southward of Portage la Loche and thereafter as the people become acquainted with the management of them they will be brought into more general use. Orkneymen from their slow inanimate habits would not I apprehend be found to answer the purpose for long Voyages requiring exertion to get to the Wintering grounds; it moreover takes a length of time after their arrival in the Country to give them a knowledge of Inland Navigation, whereas Canadians with proper management are active and indefatigable; one Voyage in Boats is quite sufficient to make them acquainted with the management of them and their passage into the country gives them a knowledge of the dangers of the navigation and the precautions necessary. Canadians therefore unquestionably have the preference for the Duty. . . .

Light Canoe Travelling is unavoidably attended with a heavy Expense and the Council are of opinion that in the present state of the Country it it quite unnecessary except in regard to the Columbia and Athabasca Departments. . . .[2]

A year later Simpson had begun to substitute boats for canoes and still was of the opinion that the former were better.

The advantages of Boat instead of Canoe transport are so obvious that we mean to adopt it wherever it may be found practicable; the saving in wages alone will materially exceed one-third and the property moreover will not be so liable to damage and injury on the voyage. . . .[3]

In the Athabasca department the use of boats was not altogether successful, but they were steadily introduced into other departments. When it was decided to supply the Lake Huron district from Moose Factory instead of from Montreal, for example, boats

1. Archives of the Hudson's Bay Company, General letter books, February 27, 1822.

2. *Ibid.*, Simpson's reports, July 31, 1822.

3. *Ibid.*, August 1, 1823.

were planned for the transport system. In districts near the bay, such as the Albany River, boats had always been used. In fact the Hudson's Bay Company had always believed in boats, and it was only during the period in which they were most actively competing with the North West Company in the interior that they had used canoes for some of their transport. Now they were free to return to their first love.

Types of boats varied. The best known was the York boat, a keel boat propelled by heavy sweeps or a square sail, developed after 1821 especially for use on the Hayes River between Norway House and York Factory. It was light enough to be pulled over rollers at portages, but seaworthy in the storms of Lake Winnipeg. In length it varied from thirty to forty feet. A forty-foot York boat would carry 110 pieces of 90 pounds each, with a crew of a steersman, a bowsman, and eight middlemen. On shallower waters, such as those of the Saskatchewan, the flat-bottomed bateaux were used. For the Columbia also bateaux were found more suitable, propelled, according to Simpson, by paddles instead of oars. Where canoes were still retained, they were of the same types as formerly.

Throughout the west an elaborate machinery of communications had been built up, with regular routes and time-tables. The hub of the system was Norway House at the head of Lake Winnipeg, a "Store or Warehousing Establishment, kept up for the accommodation of the interior Posts or Districts. . . ."[4] Sir Charles Piers[5] describes four main routes, centering on Norway House. The northern route led, by the Hayes or the Nelson River, to York Factory, which until the day of the American railways was the chief port for Rupert's Land. The southern route was down Lake Winnipeg and up the Red River to Fort Garry. The eastern was the old canoe route to Montreal, or rather to Lachine, which was the depot, but after 1821 this became of secondary importance. Little through traffic went by it on account of the expense, and the trade in the area near Lachine and even near Lake Huron was ruined by competition. "The only object of maintaining the posts

4. *Ibid.*, August 20, 1826.
5. Sir Charles Piers, *The Hudson's Bay Company's transportation system, 1670–1880* (address before British Columbia Historical Association, January 17, 1930).

is to keep the petty Traders in play, so as to prevent their pushing further into the interior."[6]

The longest, of course, were the western routes. From Norway House Lake Winnipeg was followed to Grand Rapids, with a portage to Clear Lake and the Saskatchewan River, which took the brigades as far as Fort Edmonton. From there a long portage was made on horseback to Fort Assiniboine on the Athabasca; up the Athabasca by boat or canoe to Henry House; from there on horseback and foot over the summit to Boat Encampment. Here the bateaux could be taken down the Columbia to the Pacific at Fort Vancouver. The brigades to the north-west left this route at Cumberland House and went by a series of small lakes and portages, over Portage la Loche, to the Athabasca River and Lake; to the Slave River, Great Slave Lake, and thence to the Mackenzie River, running down to Fort McPherson on the Peel River. These were the main trunk lines, though there were many other regular routes. The most romantic, perhaps, was the Yukon Packet which travelled 4,500 miles from Fort Yukon to Montreal, summer and winter.

The whole of this elaborate system of communication was designed for an unpeopled country, and for the carriage of standard goods and small numbers of passengers. It was dependent primarily on waterways, the sections travelled by horse or on foot being regarded as portages. It was highly complex, but made possible by the fact that all who were concerned in it were on the business of one company. Finally, it assumed one chief entrance, from Hudson Bay, and two minor entrances, Montreal and the Pacific posts, to the whole area. Two main and interdependent changes followed: the progress of settlement in Red River, and in the American states to the south of it. In Sir George Simpson's régime it became the policy of the company to utilize the Red River settlement for the production of food and whatever other supplies could be produced, to avoid the heavy expense involved in bringing everything from England and re-shipping it from York Factory to the posts. A stronger magnet in the south was in the American railways, the first of which reached the Red River in 1871, after the cession of Rupert's Land but before the Canadian Pacific

6. Archives of the Hudson's Bay Company, Simpson's reports, October 16, 1826.

touched Winnipeg. The development of agriculture and of American railways led the company to abandon the bay posts as the sole entrance to their territory, and to work out land routes to the northern department. About 1829 a "winter road" was begun from York Factory to Norway House, and although at first not successful, the plan was followed up. Rather than risk another failure (a large amount of goods had been lost in 1830) Simpson determined to go slowly.

We are, however, clearing the road, erecting stage houses, and making such other preparations connected with this object as we consider necessary, and the work is in such a forward state that, in the winter of 1834–35, I think we may safely undertake to convey 100 tons up and 100 tons down by that route. . . . This mode of transport, when conducted on a large scale, will, I am satisfied, be less expensive than what anyone, who has not given particular attention to the subject, can have any idea of. The conviction in my own mind is that it will not exceed 2/6 p. cwt. between Norway House and York, and that when large decked vessels [built at Norway House] are in use between Norway House and Red River, the transport between these places will not exceed 1/- p. cwt., making the whole charge for transport between Red River and the coast 3/6 per cwt.[7]

With the building of storehouses and stables a regular post-road was available, by means of which supplies from the Red River could be drawn overland to the northern department.

South of Fort Garry an overland route was established to St. Paul, and by 1858 Simpson was suggesting that an agency be established there. He argued that the posts could no longer be supplied only from York Factory, for the cost was too high: from York to Red River it had increased recently from 12 shillings to 28 shillings sterling per 100 pounds, whereas he calculated that the same amount could be shipped from Liverpool to Red River via New Orleans and St. Paul for about $4.50. In addition there would be a saving of interest because of the shorter period involved between shipment and use. About half the outfit should be sent this way and half by the bay. By keeping a good stock at St. Paul, it might also be possible to sell to the American traders.[8] The

7. Archives of the Hudson's Bay Company, Simpson's reports, August 10, 1832.

8. *Ibid.*, Locked letter books, Simpson to Berens, July 30 and September 25, 1858.

land route between St. Paul and Fort Garry had for some years
been followed by the Red River carts, high, two-wheeled carts,
made entirely of wood and drawn by a single ox or horse.
"Brigades" of several hundred carts made the journey each year,
carrying goods of all sorts for the merchants of Assiniboia, and
taking some twenty to thirty days. The way was made easier
with the introduction of steamboats on the Red River in 1859,
as Simpson had hoped. In the meanwhile, however, the Hudson's
Bay Company had made an arrangement with the Grand Trunk
to ship their goods via Detroit and Milwaukee to St. Paul, from
which place they would go on to Fort Garry by cart. This plan
was carried into effect, for a time at least.[9] An alternative one was
to build a road from Crow Wing (north of St. Paul) to Superior,
at the western end of the lake. An officer of the Hudson's Bay
Company succeeded in stirring up a considerable interest in the
scheme in Superior, but his suggestion that the citizens should pay
$5,000 in cash and $20,000 in city property if the company built
the road was not greeted with enthusiasm.[10] In 1871 the whole
problem of communication through the United States was simpli-
fied when the Northern Pacific Railway reached the Red River
at Brainard and there connected with the steamboats. In the same
year a stage line was started between Fort Garry and Abercrombie,
Minnesota. At first it gave a tri-weekly service, and in 1877
became daily. The mail was carried in the coaches.

To see the problems of transport between the prairies and British
Columbia before the introduction of railways, one may look
through the eyes of those who visited the country in the 'sixties
and 'seventies, men who were particularly concerned with studying
the existing means of travel as well as their possible improvement.
Two classical accounts of such expeditions may be taken, as
illustrating in the one case the approach to the west from
Minnesota, and in the other the approach from Ontario. *The
North-West Passage by Land*, written by Viscount Milton and
W. B. Cheadle, is a restrained but vivid account of an overland
journey made from the Atlantic to the Pacific by two Englishmen.

9. *Ibid.*, General letter books, August 9, 1859.
10. *Ibid.*, A. G. Dallas correspondence, N. W. Kittson to Dallas, November
23, 1863.

Landing at Quebec, they proceeded by train through Detroit and Chicago to La Crosse on the Mississippi, which was then (1862) the nearest point to Fort Garry that the railway touched. At La Crosse their adventures began. An uncomfortable stage took them across to Georgetown on the Red River, but being in doubt whether the steamer that plied between there and Fort Garry would arrive on account of low water they started on the five-hundred-mile journey in two birch-bark canoes. Paddling through uninhabited country, in leaky canoes, they were not sorry to be picked up by the paddle-wheeler which finally turned up near Pembina and landed them at Fort Garry. At the fort they made preparations for their long trek to the Pacific. With half-breeds as guides, they set out near the end of August on horseback, the luggage following in Red River carts. Passing through Portage la Prairie and Fort Ellice, they made for the valley of the Saskatchewan and got as far as Carlton House, near which they passed the winter in a home-made cabin.

In the following spring the difficult part of the trip began. Starting early in April, before the ice was out of the rivers, they made for Fort Pitt and Fort Edmonton, and beyond the latter they were in almost trackless country. Their expedition consisted of themselves, two Indian guides, with the wife and son of one, and a timorous schoolmaster who attached himself to the party and who proved a constant encumbrance thereafter. Twelve horses were taken along, six of which were to carry the provisions. Jasper House was reached with some difficulty on June 29, and from there they made for the Yellowhead Pass, minus one Indian who had deserted. The story of the journey across the mountains by the Fraser and Thompson valleys is a saga of continued hardships and daily dangers. The early part was bad enough, but the journey beside the Thompson was a struggle which nearly ended in tragedy. They had constantly risked their lives in swimming rivers, and scaling mountainsides, but now, short of food and with almost no game to be found, they literally had to cut a path through the forest with fading hopes of getting through alive. The last part of the trip was a nightmare in which exhausted men fought with the never-ending trees, staving off starvation by living on the horses they killed. More dead than alive, they staggered into

Kamloops at the end of August. While waiting to take the Cariboo Trail for Yale they were regaled with stories of other parties who had attempted to pass by the way they had come and had met death by hunger or drowning.[11]

Ten years later the same trail over the prairies and through the Rockies was taken by Sandford Fleming, but under very different conditions. Fleming, who had to examine the proposed route for the railway, took with him a party, one of whom, G. M. Grant, left a record of the trip called *Ocean to Ocean*. On July 16, 1872 the party left Toronto by train for Collingwood, where they could catch a steamer for Thunder Bay, and which they reached after a slow but uneventful voyage on July 22. From there they followed the Dawson Trail, which was part road and part water. They took waggons over a fair road to Shebandowan Lake, where canoes with Indian guides were ready for the next stage. From there to the end of the Lake of the Woods they followed the series of lakes and rivers, but even the Indians had an easy time for steam tugs towed them over all the open water. From the Lake of the Woods they drove over the trail to Fort Garry, which they reached on July 31. From Fort Garry they followed the same route as Milton and Cheadle to Edmonton, using Red River carts, buckboards and saddle-horses. Taking then to saddle and pack-horses, they reached Jasper House on September 2. Then they began the part of the journey that had all but defeated Milton and Cheadle. Not only was their equipment far better in every way, but in the intervening years a passable trail had been cut, and on several occasions they met parties of surveyors or miners on the trail. Whereas their predecessors had treasured bits of horse-flesh, Fleming and his party never lacked good fare. Near Kamloops, which they reached on September 28, they found settlers where before had been wilderness.

The main change in ten years was in the trail through the Yellowhead Pass. Neither of the two expeditions mentioned had met any

11. Another party of Canadians passed through the Rockies by the same route in the same year. *See* Margaret McNaughton, *Overland to Cariboo* (Toronto, 1896). This account is much less full. Cheadle's original diary has also been published as *Cheadle's Journal of Trip Across Canada, 1862-1863*, edited by A. G. Doughty and G. Lanctot (Ottawa, 1931).

insuperable difficulties either in getting to Fort Garry or crossing the prairie, but it can be seen that by 1872 it was possible for a well-equipped party to cross the Rockies without any untoward danger or hardship. But no part of the way from Fort Garry— or even Thunder Bay—to the Pacific slope could be passed by ordinary travellers. The time alone was a barrier, and the expense was very heavy. Even had the authors of these two diaries not expressed themselves so strongly on the subject, it might be deduced by any reader that the moral of their experiences was the need of railway communication from the Great Lakes to the Pacific.

2. The Opening of the West

It was in the interest of the Hudson's Bay Company, as it would have been of any fur-trading company, to keep the west as a preserve for fur-bearing animals, and to restrict the population to trappers and those few farmers—retired company's servants— who could raise food for the small population needed for trapping, transportation, and management. Had the company been able to maintain this position, it is probable that no number of prophets would have been able to bring within the sphere of practical politics the building of a railway to the Pacific. But, while the central prairie remained almost untouched by the plough of the settler, at each extremity civilization was advancing sufficiently to raise the question of the future of the west; and, since these advances were close to and even overlapping the American border, there loomed the danger of losing what was coming to be regarded as a Canadian heritage.

It was the fate of the Hudson's Bay Company to nurse in infancy the two settlements which were to precipitate the decision on the sovereignty of the west. After the early troubles of petty wars and grasshoppers had been passed, Assiniboia (the Red River colony) began to progress under more peaceful conditions. The population —largely made up of Métis, or French-Indian half-breeds—rose to 3,649 in 1835, and 6,691 in 1856, and then began to show resentment toward the rule of the company and especially toward its efforts to enforce the monopoly in fur-trading. Smuggling became the vogue, and the Métis openly resisted the maintenance of the company's justice. The opposition to the company was mingled with talk of a new régime. Aided by the advocacy of the first newspaper in the west, the *Nor' Wester*, a growing Canadian party preached the necessity of adding the colony to Canada—a sentiment which was warmly reciprocated in Canada itself, where the *Globe* hammered on this note for month after month.

By many such people, both in Assiniboia and Canada, there was felt to be urgent need of action because of the rival pull from the south. Since the virtual abandonment of the Ottawa route by the Hudson's Bay Company no link remained to bridge the gap of the Lake Superior region. On the other hand the development of regular communication with St. Paul by the brigade of carts or the steamers on the Red River made a connection which threatened to grow into a political one. The question came before the government of Canada in relation to postal service to Assiniboia. The extension of the American postal system to the north of Minnesota led residents of Fort Garry to establish a monthly communication with the post office there, which by 1857 had reached Pembina. Such an official link with the United States further stirred opinion in Canada West, and in the same year the Toronto Board of Trade appealed to the government to start a postal and telegraphic communication, over British soil, with British Columbia. The appeal did not fall on deaf ears, for in 1858 a postal service to Fort Garry twice a month in summer and once a month in winter was begun. During the period of navigation the mail was carried to Collingwood by train, to Fort William by steamer, and thence by canoe: in the winter dog-teams had to be substituted. These heroic measures, however, could not compete with the American route and two years later were abandoned.[12] That the residents of Assiniboia were anxious to establish communication with Canada is shown by the calling of a number of public meetings in 1863, where resolutions were passed, and a memorial addressed to the British and Canadian governments praying that a road should be built that would give access to the settlement without dependence on a foreign state.[13]

12. W. Smith, *History of the Post Office in British North America* (London, 1920), pp. 318–319.

13. Canadian Archives, Governor general's secretary, Fleming to Monck, May 23, 1863.

While this short-lived experiment represented at that time the sole contribution of Canada to the establishment of communications with the west, Americans were adopting more modern weapons for the same struggle. In 1864 the Northern Pacific Railroad Company was chartered by congress and empowered to build from a point on Lake Superior to Portland, Oregon. After some delay the banking firm of Jay Cooke and Company undertook in 1869 to raise the capital and construction began. By 1873, when the firm collapsed in the financial crisis, five hundred miles of the main line had been finished, and a new way was opened to Assiniboia—and a way which struck at its most vulnerable point the plan for linking the colony with Canada. Faced by the wide barrier of the Canadian shield, how could Canada compete with such a connection—unless it were by a railway? Yet if nothing was done to offset the economic and social pull of such a close neighbour as Minnesota, surely Assiniboia—the very gateway to the prairies—must fall into the arms of the republic?

In the meanwhile a similar problem had arisen on the Pacific coast. As in the area to the east of the Rockies, the early history of British Columbia centres around the fur trade. The monopoly of trade given to the Hudson's Bay Company in the territory west of the mountains in 1821 was seriously diminished by the settlement of the boundary at the forty-ninth parallel in 1846. In 1849 Vancouver Island was ceded to the company, subject to requirements as to colonization; but on the mainland only the trade monopoly was continued. After a short and unhappy experiment with an independent nominee, the British government appointed James Douglas, a prominent servant of the company, as governor of the island.

Such was the situation when the first gold rush began in 1858. Discovery of gold in the tableland between the Upper Columbia, Thompson, and Fraser rivers, along the Quesnel River, and in the Cariboo district forced the development of a transportation system. A number of roads were cut to the mining districts, the most famous being the Cariboo trail from Yale to Quesnel, which was converted into a waggon road in the 'sixties. In the south of the province a combination of water and land transport was used as far as possible. An important route in that area was the Dewdney trail, built in the 'sixties, and affording communication with the Kootenay country. A change in the centre of gravity of the transportation system was caused by the increase of shipping on the Pacific. The first of three vessels for the Hudson's Bay Company was built in 1836, and at least by 1847 an annual voyage was made from London. The company also used its smaller vessels for coastal work between their various posts.

The transportation system thus built up was slow and expensive, the high cost being in particular an impediment to the mining industry. Such a weakness in itself was enough to suggest the need of railways. That, however, was as yet a remote hope; while the immediate problem was what was to be the future of this land which had changed almost overnight from a fur-trading area to one rich in minerals and with a rush of population. Canadians began to take stock of this situation, too, to see whether British Columbia would remain a separate colony, enter into union with Canada, or fall to the United States. As the Pacific coast of the northern part of the continent it had a distinct importance for Canada, but, as in the case of Assiniboia, there was a strong pull toward the United States. Canada was far and Oregon near; Canada could be reached only by a harassing land journey, while Seattle was within easy steaming distance of Victoria or New Westminster. To add to this natural link came the invasion or threatened invasion of American communication systems. In 1865 the Western Union Telegraph Company placed several miles of line in British Columbia as part of a project for a cable between Europe and America by way of Alaska and Russia, though the scheme collapsed with the successful laying of the Atlantic cable in 1866. In 1867 the purchase of Alaska brought American soil on two sides of the colony; while the approaching American railways promised to draw British Columbia as well as Assiniboia toward the south.

Much hinged on the position of the Hudson's Bay Company, particularly in its chartered territories of Rupert's Land and Vancouver Island. Since the latest grant of trade monopoly was due to expire in 1859, a select committee of the house of commons was appointed in 1857, "to consider the State of those British Possessions in *North America* which are under the Administration of the Hudson's Bay Company, or over which they possess a License to Trade." To Great Britain, to the company itself, and to Canada the deliberations of the committee were of primary importance. On the invitation of the colonial secretary Canada sent Chief Justice Draper to London to appear before the committee. In his evidence Draper fairly represented the cautious ambitions of Canada in the west. He expressed anxiety that the territory should remain British, disputed the claims of the Hudson's Bay Company, and looked for an opportunity for Canadian expansion. He admitted, however, that Canada was not yet ready to govern the whole area.

I should myself propose . . . that Canada should have in the first place a free right to explore and survey, in order to ascertain the capabilities of the country; in the second place, to open communication roads in the manner pursued in that country, by putting settlers on each side of them with free grants . . . in the next place I should propose that Canada should be permitted to lay out townships, and that as fast as she did actually lay them out and settle them, those portions of the territory so settled should become incorporated with and form part of the province; I would limit it under all circumstances and at any distant period by the Rocky Mountains; I should never dream of pushing beyond them.

Draper then emphasized the need of communications with Canada since "the natural outlet of the country appears rather to be into the United States," and as Hudson Bay was open for only part of the year, the only outlet on British soil was through Canada. Draper himself did not advocate the expulsion of the company from the whole of Rupert's Land, but rather that their boundary should be pushed farther north—say to Norway House. As to the country west of the Rockies, a different situation would arise if a railway were built. His attitude on this point is rather suggestive:

I hope you will not laugh at me as very visionary, but I hope to see the time, or that my children may live to see the time when there is a railway going all across that country and ending at the Pacific; and so far as individual opinion goes, I entertain no doubt that the time will arrive when that will be accomplished. I should desire, for the sake of Canada, that permission should be reserved to her to that extent only, that if she makes a railway through her own portion of the territory, it shall go to the terminus.

John Ross, then president of the Grand Trunk, was the other Canadian to give evidence. As might be expected, his examination hinged on the possibility of a western railway; and he argued that one could be built north of Lake Superior to the Red River, and so, in time, to the Pacific. As a preliminary stage he suggested a road and a policy of settlement. The scheme involved, of course, displacing the Hudson's Bay Company from at least a portion of their territory.

The evidence showed a clear line of cleavage between the interests of the fur-trading company and those of Canada. Sir George Simpson, in the course of a lengthy examination, was surprisingly outspoken in denying the possibilities of agriculture in any but small sections of the country. The company evidently was anxious to stave off the undesired advance of civilization; and even the report of the committee, which advocated—though in equivocal terms—an agreed cession of such districts as the Red River and Saskatchewan to Canada, led only to a series of diplomatic marches and counter-marches. Vancouver Island, following the advice of the committee, was taken from the jurisdiction of the company, and the charter for trade on the Pacific coast was allowed to lapse in 1859. The appointment of the select committee, then, raised the whole question of the future of the west, and carried it some distance in the direction which Canada wished it to take. Yet the company was able to prevent for some years any decision being reached on the validity of the charter; and it may be, that if it had not been for internal developments within the company, the west might have longer remained the domain of the fur trader.

In the years 1862–1863 a strange play was being performed which involved the west, the Hudson's Bay Company, the Grand Trunk Railway, the province of Canada, and various financial groups. The *dramatis personae* were: E. W. Watkin, who played the leading rôle, the Duke of Newcastle, the directors of the Hudson's Bay Company and the Grand Trunk, Sir Edmund Head, Baring, Glyn, and a number of Canadian politicians, the last having minor parts. Unfortunately some of the scenes were acted in private, so that the course of the play is partially obscured. The general plot centres around the following circumstances: a telegraph line and a road or railway to the Pacific had been suggested, and the Grand Trunk—which was influential both in England and Canada —was anxious to secure control of any such railway. The Hudson's Bay Company was camped on the ground through which the railway must pass, but might be induced, for a consideration, either to grant a right of way or withdraw from the territory. If it withdrew, it would presumably do so in favour of Canada—or, better, a Canada federated with the Maritime Provinces.

In the 'fifties the Hudson's Bay Company, reading the signs of the times, saw that the old régime was passing, and that the west would not always remain the preserve of the fur trader; but it held a strong legal position, and while it was not unprepared to sell some of its rights, it did not propose. to give them away. "The Hudson's Bay Company," wrote Edward Ellice, "are quite willing to dispose of their territory and their establishments. It is a question of a million of money."[14] Having survived the select committee of 1857 with Rupert's Land still firmly in its grasp, the company proceeded on the one hand to spar with the British and Canadian governments over legal investigation of its charter, and on the other to await offers.

Watkin, representing the Grand Trunk group, and the Duke of Newcastle, colonial secretary, began in 1862 to force the pace. Both had, apparently, a genuine interest in the promotion of British imperial power in North America. In addition, Watkin was concerned for the Grand Trunk, which he was trying to put on its feet; and Newcastle, perhaps, was looking for the political stability of a single and united colony, strong enough to act as a barrier against American expansionism. In July 1862 the colonial office forwarded to Berens, governor of the Hudson's Bay Company, a letter from Thomas Baring, K. D. Hodgson, R. W. Crawford, G. C. Glyn, G. G. Glyn, and W. Chapman, which the colonial office supported. It proved to be a scheme for "providing a telegraphic service, and of securing the means of travelling with regularity to the British Territory on the Pacific." Would the British

14. Archives of the Hudson's Bay Company, Locked letter books, Ellice to Labouchere, September 30, 1856.

government grant a large tract of land in aid of construction?[15] As they held the land in question the Hudson's Bay Company were asked in turn if they would concede a line of territory: to which Berens replied that they would do so if adequate security were given for the completion of a road and telegraph.[16] A rather fruitless exchange of letters then took place during which the colonial office asked how much the company would grant, and the company asked for further information about the project.

At the beginning of November both Glyn and Watkin were trying to persuade Baring to sign a letter to Newcastle. "You must really help me in that Pacific matter," wrote Watkin. "If, on conclusion, you prefer not to be on the board of any company formed to *carry out* the scheme . . . I will endeavour to meet your views . . . the Pacific affair is part of our *policy*—the success of which will make—believe me—a vast difference in the value of your Grand Trunk property."[17] Apparently Baring did not refuse to act, as his name appears again as a principal. In the same letter to Baring Watkin explained that "all I propose to do . . . is to get up a Company, with a capital not exceeding £300,000." It is improbable, however, that Watkin did not then have a more ambitious plan in his mind, for at the end of a fortnight more important negotiations were under way. The following letter from the colonial under-secretary to Berens, dated November 21, 1862, was shown to the committee of the company seven months later.

With reference to your interview with the Duke of Newcastle on the 18th Instant on the subject of a proposed postal and telegraphic route from the Canadian frontier to that of British Columbia, at which His Grace understood you to express the willingness of the Hudson's Bay Company to enter into personal communication with some of the gentlemen who are desirous, under certain conditions, of undertaking the scheme and to confer with them upon the basis of forming a road through the country comprised in the Charter of your Company, or upon that of the purchase of the whole of the Company's rights, I am directed by His

15. *Ibid.*, Correspondence with His Majesty's Government, Baring and others to Newcastle, July 5, 1862.

16. *Ibid.*, Berens to Newcastle, August 11, 1862.

17. Canadian Archives, Baring Papers, Grand Trunk Railway, Watkin to Baring, November 4, 1862.

Grace to inform you that he has to-day seen a deputation of the gentlemen referred to and they on their part expressed their readiness to attend the proposed meeting.[18]

From that time—the end of November—personal conferences took the place of this rather indirect correspondence. Berens met a deputation and told them that the company would grant a right of passage. Privately he explained to Dallas that this generosity was to avoid a demand for taking the land from the company.[19] In reality he was not at all happy about the situation.

. . . The Duke of Newcastle [he wrote confidentially to Dugald McTavish] has . . . far more extended views than prudence and sound judgment can comprehend. We must therefore remain quiet, observing every move and taking care that His Grace does not steal a march upon us which I am persuaded he would do if he could. His object appears to be to favour Canada and almost at every step he takes for this purpose he is thwarted by Canada herself.[20]

A little later he avowed to A. G. Dallas, governor of the Hudson's Bay Company's territories, that "there can be no doubt but that the Duke of Newcastle is most anxious to get rid of us, and would I believe, do all he can to further this purpose. He is certainly encouraging other parties to move vigorously in the promotion of his views. . . ."[21]

During the early months of 1863 the two plans—cession of land or sale of the company—were carried forward concurrently, but there seems to have been more reality in the second. It is true that as late as May the colonial office was submitting proposals for a plan involving only a grant of land, but by that time negotiations for a sale were well advanced. The idea of purchasing a controlling interest in the stock originated with Watkin and Richard Potter, the future president of the Grand Trunk, who were supposed to be finding the capital themselves.[22] Only later did the International

18. Archives of the Hudson's Bay Company, Minutes of the committee, June 15, 1863.

19. *Ibid.*, Locked letter books, Berens to Dallas, February 5, 1863.

20. *Ibid.*, Berens to McTavish, February 7, 1863.

21. *Ibid.*, Berens to Dallas, March 20, 1863.

22. *Ibid.*, London inward correspondence, J. Maynard to Sir Edmund Head, August 5, 1863.

Financial Society appear on the scene. This society, which had been formed shortly before, came into play after a memorandum had been signed by Watkin and Potter on the one part and by the governor and committee on the other by which the first parties agreed to purchase the whole of the stock of the company at the rate of £300 for every £100, and the purchasers were to be invested with the management and control of the company.[23]

The mantle of Edward Ellice had fallen on Watkin. The sale went through, and the old board was swept away. Only Eden Colvile and George Lyall remained on the committee. Sir Edmund Head was the new governor, and C. M. Lampson (representing United States interests) deputy governor. Potter took a seat at the council table, but Watkin, the king-maker, remained discreetly in the background. With the new men in charge, the attitude of the company took a distinct change. The prospectus of the International Financial Society, in offering shares to the public, spoke of developing the company's territory, encouraging settlement, and establishing communication from the Atlantic to the Pacific. Watkin was despatched to the Red River in July, and although Head said somewhat bitterly that his report might as well have been written in London, he soon had to reprimand him for prematurely ordering telegraph wire.

In the summer of 1864 Dr. John Rae was put in charge of a survey for a telegraph across the company's territory and reported favourably. At the same time he examined the possibilities of travel by road, water, or rail. The only real difficulty he found for the construction of a railway was in the Yellowhead Pass.[24] Attached to the expedition as an assistant was an official of the Gzowski firm, who reported on the possibilities of a railway from St. Cloud (on the Mississippi, and not far from St. Paul) to Fort Garry—a project which seems contradictory to the avowed purpose of establishing communications on British soil.

There the story of the Grand Trunk-Hudson's Bay plan for a Pacific railway ends. It is the paradox of Watkin's career that his long-laid schemes were defeated by a palace revolution in the Grand Trunk itself, which caused him to resign from the presidency in

23. *Ibid.*, Minutes of the committee, June 15, 1863.
24. *Ibid.*, Telegraph survey of Dr. John Rae.

1869—just as confederation was to be completed by the addition of Assiniboia and British Columbia. And although Potter, his associate in the purchase of the Hudson's Bay Company, succeeded him as president of the Grand Trunk, that railway was soon to lose command of the western link of the transcontinental line just as it lost the eastern. Whether Watkin could have averted the disaster—for disaster it was to the Grand Trunk—must be left as a subject for speculation.

3. THE RAILWAY PLANNED

Long before the day of Watkin, books, pamphlets, memoranda, letters, and speeches had been written or spoken on the need of a railway from Canada to the Pacific. Probably the most voluble of the advocates of such a railway was Sir John Smyth, who described himself as "Baronet and Royal Engineer, Canadian Poet, LL.D., and Moral Philosopher, etc., etc., etc." In the 'thirties Smyth was sketching various railway lines in Canada, and in the 'forties had progressed to one from Halifax to the Pacific by way of Chicago. Steamers on the Atlantic and Pacific were to connect with the railway; and in a burst of generosity he added steamers and railways in Europe and the east, to complete the circle of the globe.[25] Four years later his namesake wrote pamphlets that were more imperial and somewhat more specific. His railway was to run across the prairies north of the boundary to the valley of the Columbia.[26] Other writers with imperial considerations in mind carried on the campaign: for example, Wilson and Richards in *Britain Redeemed and Canada Preserved* (1850), and Synge, in *Great Britain one Empire* (1852). In 1854 Sir Richard Broun produced a prospectus for an "Imperial British American Main Trunk Railway, Ocean Ferry and Freehold Land Company," and invited the Hudson's Bay Company to coöperate in this with the Heirs of the Hereditary Viceroy of New Scotland and the Baronets of

25. Sir John Smyth, *Railroad communication. A west proposed line of steam communication from London, in England, to China and the East Indies, etc., etc.* (Toronto, 1845).

26. *A letter from Major Robert Carmichael-Smyth to his friend, the author of "The Clockmaker"; The employment of the people and capital of Great Britain in her own colonies . . . .* (London, 1849).

Scotland and Nova Scotia. The company, however, "declined to entertain" the project in spite of the illustrious associates. In 1851 Joseph Howe, fresh from his conversations in England about the Intercolonial, told a public meeting in Halifax that "many in this room will live to hear the whistle of the steam-engine in the passes of the Rocky Mountains and to make the journey from Halifax to the Pacific in five or six days."

In the meanwhile there had been some activity in Canada. A group of men of whom Allan Macdonell was the leading spirit had a bill introduced into the Canadian assembly in 1851 to incorporate the Lake Superior and Pacific Railroad Company. The standing committee on railroads and telegraph lines reported unfavourably on grounds of feasibility, though approving of the principle. Again in 1853 and 1855 similar bills were introduced, but all were turned down. Macdonell claimed that the opposition came from the Hudson's Bay Company,[27] but efforts to persuade that company to build the railway itself did not meet with success. Three years later John Young, A. N. Morin, A. T. Galt, and J. A. Poor petitioned for a charter, but failed to get it. At last in 1858 a group which included Macdonell secured a charter for the North-West Transportation Navigation and Railway Company. The new company proposed to build from Lake Superior to Rainy Lake, where steamers would be used to Lake of the Woods, and thence by rail to the Red River. Lake Winnipeg and the Saskatchewan were to be navigated by steamers. The company proposed by this means to revive the Canadian fur trade and to supersede the Pembina outlet; capital, however, was not available and no work was undertaken.

Such schemes have a more than antiquarian interest, for they not only indicate the growth of a belief in the practicability of a Pacific railway, but served at the time to stimulate opinion in Great Britain and Canada in favour of improved communications with the west. The transition of the Pacific railway from the world of dreams to that of reality belongs to, and is intimately connected with, the period of confederation. The "Dominion stretching from sea to sea" that is supposed to have inspired the members of the Quebec conference to choose the curious name for the united

27. Allan Macdonell, *The North-West transportation, navigation and railway company. Its objects.* (Toronto, 1858).

provinces was more than a vision of a distant future, for events were rapidly developing in the settled parts of the west that made imperative some adequate communication between them and Canada—unless the hope of absorbing the west was to be abandoned for ever.

Provision having been made in the British North America Act for the admission into the Dominion of Rupert's Land, the north-western territory, and British Columbia, the new government and parliament set about the task. A formidable obstacle to the acquisition of Rupert's Land lay in the fact that it was still held by charter by the Hudson's Bay Company. That the company was willing to sell was further evidenced by its favourable reception of a tentative offer for purchase by a group of Anglo-American capitalists—a move which stimulated the activity of the Canadian government.[28] In the end the old controversy over the legal position of the Hudson's Bay Company in Rupert's Land was tacitly dropped, and both parties accepted the terms drawn up by the imperial government. The deed of surrender, signed on November 19, 1869, called for the payment by Canada of £300,000. The company was to retain all posts actually occupied, and might select blocks of land adjacent to each to a total of 45,160 acres. In addition the company might select within the next fifty years one-twentieth of the land in the fertile belt made available for settlement. Canada was to take over the materials for the telegraph at cost, and the company was to be free to carry on fur-trading.

The prairie was not conquered by legal documents alone. The half-breeds of Assiniboia saw in the invasion of civilization the end of the life of hunting and trapping which they had always known; saw the land over which they had freely roamed taken by the chain of the surveyor and the plough of the settler. They resisted with the same dim consciousness of the future that had moved the Indian tribes under Pontiac to attempt to stem the tide of white invasion just over a century before. The rebellion under Louis Riel in 1869–1870 demonstrated, if indeed any demonstration were needed, the lack of communications between Ontario and the west. The Dawson route from Thunder Bay to Fort Garry,

28. H. A. Innis, *History of the Canadian Pacific Railway* (Toronto, 1922), p. 44.

with 131 miles of waggon road between the portages, was used by immigrants in the early 'seventies, but it was at best a stop-gap, and the demand became more insistent for a railway to Manitoba and the North West Territories, as the area east of the Rockies was now to be known.

The connection between the entrance of British Columbia into the Dominion and the Pacific railway was even closer. In 1866 the colonies of Vancouver Island and British Columbia were united under the name of the latter, and the new colony showed a close interest in the federation that was about to be consummated in the east. In 1867 a resolution of the legislative council in favour of admission into the Dominion was the first formal step taken by British Columbia. For a time it appeared as if the movement would fail; but the cession of Rupert's Land, the appointment of a pro-confederation governor in Musgrave, the decline of gold-mining, and continued financial difficulties together smoothed the way, and in 1870 delegates were sent to Ottawa to arrange terms. In regard to communications, the representatives of British Columbia asked that a survey for a railway be commenced at once, and that a waggon road be completed within three years after confederation. The Dominion government, however, on its initiative shouldered the much more onerous burden of beginning, within two years and completing within ten, a railway to connect the seaboard of British Columbia with the railway system of Canada.

Why the Canadian government undertook this gratuitous obligation is not altogether clear, but a number of explanations may be offered: that the waggon road was an additional and unnecessary expense; that there was fear of an invasion of American railways; or that it was useful for the Canadian government to bind parliament to a task which perhaps could not have been attempted under any other conditions. The terms were accepted by parliament, but not before Alexander Mackenzie, the leader of the opposition, had moved an amendment that Canada should be pledged only to make surveys and to build the railway as finances might allow. The *Globe*, while reiterating its belief in a Pacific railway, was indignant at the terms: "We utterly scout the notion that a rash and may be disastrous step should be taken at the dictation of a handful of people 2,500 miles away, and to whom we are already making concessions that they may well be satisfied to accept in exchange for union. . . ." This line of argument was continued in several editorials, but a month later the editor was even more indignant with the New York *Albion*, which lectured Canadians on the foolish attempt to build their own railway, when they should use the Northern Pacific. The *Albion*, he said, was probably subsidized by Jay Cooke, and no doubt the Americans wanted to absorb the Canadian west, but Canada would have its own railway. Here the *Globe* was touching an important point, for there can be little doubt that the building of the Northern Pacific was regarded as a real danger to Canadian power in the west, and was stimulating parliament and people to undertake a herculean task.

4. THE STRUGGLE FOR THE CONTRACT

The railway to the Pacific was to be built: the Dominion was committed to it by a solemn agreement with British Columbia. The circumstances were peculiar. In the first place the population of the whole country was small for such a great undertaking—some three and a half million, of whom only 23,000 lived west of Lake Superior. Secondly, no surveys had been made of the route through the mountains of British Columbia. The Yellowhead Pass was thought to be feasible for a railway, but no way had yet been found through the Selkirks. Captain Palliser had even advised against a line to the north of Lake Superior, but in the meanwhile this had been reported as practicable.

Who was to build the railway? From the start it was intended that it should be built and operated by a private company rather than by the government. The act which was passed to implement the agreement with British Columbia (35 Vict., c. 71) stated this explicitly and provided that aid was to be granted in land and subsidies, to a maximum of fifty million acres and thirty million dollars. The gauge was set at four feet, eight and one-half inches. No company was named in the Act, the government having power to make arrangements with any one company or group within the terms of the act. This was a new subject of worry for the *Globe* (which may be taken as representing the attitude of the opposition).

The government, complained the editor, might by order in council come to terms with "any company who may be disposed in return to give their political support, or may become subservient followers, ready enough to grab the land and money; but in the end quite unable to keep faith with the country. This, of course, opens at once a door for just that political jobbery and corruption which has made the Intercolonial a great national scandal and the Grand Trunk a seething mass of political immorality." Later he saw in such a company "a monstrous and unclean offspring of the secret and immoral intrigues that call it into being." There was to be ample scope for such language before long.

While surveys under government direction were being pushed forward, the cabinet awaited a group of capitalists. For the past three years inquiries had been made by individuals or groups as to the probable terms of the contract. Alfred Waddington of British Columbia, who had shown great energy in promoting the idea of the railway, was well to the fore, but his petition for the incorporation of the Canada Pacific Railway (1871) was not seriously considered: in any case the petition was premature. C. J. Brydges was in touch with Macdonald as well as with other interested capitalists, and was officially empowered to negotiate.[29] Indeed the leaders of the Grand Trunk could hardly have been far from the scene; and, according to the *Globe*, intervened with vigour in the Ontario elections of 1871 on behalf of government candidates. The Grand Trunk, however, seem to have failed to sway the government toward their own plan of a Pacific railway, and, having failed, took no part in the scramble for the charter. Their point of view is clearly expressed in a letter from Brydges, in which he explains his refusal to join Sir Hugh Allan's group. This attitude is no doubt partly based on the strategy of the existing Grand Trunk system.

I have no belief myself in any line of railway running to Fort Garry, for a long time to come through British territory. What I believe in, and what I think must be done in the first instance is to make a connection between Fort Garry and Lake Superior in British territory, a railway west from Fort Garry, built in sections, and not attempted too fast, and a

29. Canadian Archives, Macdonald Papers, "Railways," ii. Potter to Macdonald, December 14, 1870.

branch down to Pembina to meet the United States system of railways, which will certainly get up to that point during the present year. That would give a rail connection in winter, and by Lake Superior, water connection would be had throughout the summer during the season of navigation, which, for the next 10 to 15 years will be all that can possibly be wanted. I am quite clear that railways from Fort Garry around the north shore of Lake Superior and Lake Nipissing could not be built except at a frightful cost, when built could not be worked successfully in winter, and if it could be worked would have no traffic to carry upon it.[30]

With the Grand Trunk eliminated from the race, there remained two favourites who were to run neck and neck for some months. The origin of these two companies requires some explanation. In the summer of 1871 Alfred Waddington, who was in Ottawa attempting to get a charter himself, met G. W. McMullen of Chicago, who became interested and arranged a meeting in Ottawa on July 14 of a number of Canadians and Americans: McMullen himself, C. M. Smith of Chicago, Mr. Hurlbut of New York, W. Kersteman of Toronto and his son-in-law Wood, James Beaty of Toronto, and Waddington. There were also represented by their signatures: General George W. Cass, W. B. Ogden, M. K. Jesup, T. A. Scott, Winslow, Lanier & Company, S. J. Tilden, and the Honourable G. Jackson. All the latter, except Jackson, were Americans. Three of them were directors of the Northern Pacific, and were deeply interested in the Canadian project as a possible competitor. It is probable that they sought to hinder rather than help, by working from the inside. The government, however, regarded the proposals made by the group as premature.

Subsequently Sir Francis Hincks suggested to Sir Hugh Allan that he should open negotiations with the group of Americans. "In this," commented Macdonald, "Hincks made a mistake and acted without authority, but Allan did not know that."[31] By the beginning of October the new combination was ready to discuss terms with the government, but Macdonald would go no further than to receive a memorandum. In December an agreement was drawn up in New York, and in February Allan submitted their proposal to the government. It provided for a railway from a point

30. *Ibid.*, iv., Brydges to D. L. Macpherson, March 11, 1872.
31. *Ibid.*, Letter book xviii, Macdonald to John Rose, October 18, 1872.

near Lake Nipissing to the coast, with branches to Pembina and
Sault Ste. Marie, the whole to be completed within twelve years.
For this they asked a subsidy of $15,000 and 20,000 acres a mile,
to be increased to 25,000 acres in the Lake Superior section. The
associates whom he mentions are: Andrew Allan, J. J. C. Abbott
of Montreal, Donald Smith of Manitoba, Henry Nathan of British
Columbia, A. B. Foster of Ottawa, Thomas McGreevy of Quebec,
Donald McInnes of Hamilton, and the Americans—Jay Cooke,
T. A. Scott, W. B. Ogden, J. G. Smith, C. M. Smith, and G. W.
McMullen. The company was, in fact, to be made up of the
directors of the Northern Pacific, allied with a number of Canadians. Allan affected to believe that such a connection would be
of advantage to Canada, apart altogether from its value as a
source of capital:

From Fort Garry westward to the Pacific it was intended the Road should
proceed on the route afterwards determined by the Surveys and it was
regarded as a possibility that the Northern Pacific when it got as far west
as the Missouri River might be defected [sic. deflected] so as to join the
Canadian Pacific, get the advantage of our easier pass through the mountains, and run on its track to some point west of the mountains where they
would again separate; the Northern Pacific passing south to New Westminster, and the Canadian Pacific seeking the shore of the Pacific Ocean
at such point as determined by the surveys.

I favored this scheme, because it not only gave us such a Pacific Railroad as we might desire, but also the advantage of a direct connection
with the States of Northern Michigan, Wisconsin, Minnesota and Dakotah,
the traffic and produce of which would naturally find its way to and from
the seaboard through Canada, as being much the shortest, and consequently the cheapest route, even for the traffic of New York and Boston.[32]

The latter part of this argument was not altogether unsound, as
the Northern Pacific wished to secure access to Boston via
Montreal: on the other hand, some of the Canadians whom Allan
approached had not his confidence about the western end. One
such was C. J. Brydges, whose refusal to become connected with
Allan's company has already been noticed. Brydges' decision was
important, because it meant that the Grand Trunk would not be

32. *Report of the Canadian Pacific Railway royal commission* (1882), evidence
of Sir Hugh Allan.

friendly—and in fact proved to be hostile—to the whole plan of a Canadian railway to the Pacific. Another man who was critical of the project was Senator D. L. Macpherson of Toronto, who had been a partner in the Gzowski firm. Allan approached him in February, asking him to be one of the Canadian directors. Macpherson, however, objected to the proposed organization, and "remonstrated against giving our rivals the control and owner-ship of our Trans-continental Railway."[33] He told Allan that the Northern Pacific would work it for their own purposes. He there-fore proceeded to organize a rival company, the Interoceanic. Although, of course, only one company could build the railway, in the meanwhile parliament was neutral and passed charters for both the Interoceanic Railway Company (35 Vict., c. 72) and the Canada Pacific Railway Company (35 Vict., c. 73). They are almost identical, both calling for the construction of a railway from a point at or near Lake Nipissing to a point on the Pacific coast, with branches to the River St. Mary, Thunder Bay and Pembina. The former, naming Macpherson, William McMaster, E. W. Cum-berland and some fifty other men, emphasized in the preamble that such an enterprise should as far as possible be controlled by British subjects. The other act was, of course, silent on this point. It named Allan, Abbott, Donald Smith, Donald McInnes and others. The two acts received the royal assent. In June both com-panies were officially organized. Allan was drawn toward the pro-ject of a western railway through a desire to feed his steamship line, for which purpose he had already promoted the North Shore Railway on rumours of a Grand Trunk line of steamers from Port-land to Europe. The two companies, also, represented the rival commercial interests of Toronto and Montreal. To placate both, the eastern terminus of the Pacific Railway had been placed at Lake Nipissing, a neutral point.

The government was in an awkward position. The Interoceanic directors made much of Allan's American connections, and while Allan secured a new agreement at the end of March, his company was still tainted with American capital. Nor could an exclusive charter be given to either an Ontario or a Quebec group. An elec-tion was coming on (in August), and the "friends" of the party

33. *Ibid.*, Evidence of D. L. Macpherson.

would be friends no longer if they were ignored. Allan had already shown his political power by organizing a campaign against Sir George Cartier that drove that unhappy statesman to capitulate to Allan's request for a charter. Macpherson made it quite clear that Ontario would not support the government if the charter were granted to Quebec. Macdonald, therefore, took the only course possible under the circumstances—an attempt to secure an amalgamation of the two "rings," as they had come to be called. Here again there was a stumbling-block. The rings argued about the number of directors each should have, and—worse still—Allan insisted on being president. This Macpherson would not hear of, arguing that the president would be in virtual control and should be elected by the directors. Moreover it would still leave the danger that the railway would be handed over to the Americans. "His alliance of last winter with Jay Cooke and the directors of the Northern Pacific Ry. is well known, and it is also known that he agreed with them to hand over to them our great Railway and its vast land subsidy. . . . That scheme . . . had to be abandoned and the British flag was ostentatiously hoisted by Sir Hugh and Co. This was done too late, however, to satisfy ordinary mortals that the newly professed loyalty to Canada was sincere. . . ."[34] Allan gradually drew away from his former American associates, explaining to them that Canadian opinion would not tolerate anyone connected with the Northern Pacific being concerned in the Canadian line. Macpherson, however, remained adamant, and early in October the secretary of the Interoceanic Company "declined peremptorily to enter into the scheme of amalgamation."[35] Conference after conference had failed, and finally the idea of an amalgamation had to be abandoned.

The government then approached the question from still another angle. A new charter was drawn up (February 5, 1873) the preamble of which refers to the failure to amalgamate the two companies, holds it inadvisable to agree with either, and therefore incorporates and charters a new company. In reality the change was not radical, for the new company included men from both of the old ones. The

34. Canadian Archives, Macdonald Papers, "Railways," iv, Macpherson to Macdonald, July 27, 1872.
35. *Ibid.*, Allan to Macdonald, October 4, 1872.

subscribers mentioned were: Hugh Allan, A. G. Archibald (Halifax), J. O. Beaubien (Montmagny), J. E. Beaudry (Montreal), E. R. Burpee (St. John), F. W. Cumberland (Toronto), Sandford Fleming (Ottawa), R. H. Hall (Sherbrooke), J. S. Helmcken (Victoria), Andrew McDermot (Winnipeg), Donald McInnes (Hamilton), Walter Shanly, and John Walker (London, Ont.). The company was named the Canadian Pacific Railway Company, was to have a capital of ten million dollars; and the line had to be begun within two, and—unless an extension were granted by parliament—to be finished within ten years. A railway was to be built from a point on or near Lake Nipissing to some point on the Pacific, with branches to Lake Superior and the American border. The course of the line was to be approved by the government; construction and equipment to be determined by the government and company together. The Union Pacific was to be taken as the general standard. The company was to receive thirty million dollars and a land grant of fifty million acres, with additional land grants for branches. "John A.", said the *Globe*, "has made an Act of Parliament. That which in Great Britain requires the joint action of King, Lords, and Commons, and has hitherto required in Canada the co-operation of Governor-General, Senate, and House of Commons, has been effected with a stroke of the pen by the one-man-power that has taken everything into its own hands at Ottawa. . . ."

It was, however, one thing to grant a charter and another to ensure that the company thus created could raise sufficient capital. After the connection had been severed with the American capitalists, Macdonald also refused the offer of an English group who came late into the game. At the end of November 1872 he received a cable from a certain Kersteman in London asking if he would accept an "English company of peers and commoners prepared to carry out conditions in Cartier's Act ready with one million sterling." Macdonald put him in touch with Sir John Rose, who reported that Kersteman would not disclose the names of the promoters, but was sailing for Canada. The mysterious Kersteman than submitted a memorandum offering to build the railway, but still held back the names. Macdonald's reply was that it was too late to enter into negotiations with another body of capitalists. In March representatives of the new Canadian company set sail for

England to raise money, but to the difficulties which they may have anticipated was added a new and unexpected development, known as "the Pacific scandal."

The general election of 1872 resulted in a gain for the Liberal opposition, helped by the passions raised by the Riel rebellion, dissatisfaction with the Washington Treaty, and alarm over the government's railway policy. Shortly after the opening of the session a Liberal member, L. C. Hungtington, made general charges of a corrupt relation between the government and the Allan "ring." His resolution was as follows:

That in anticipation of the Legislation of last Session, as to the Pacific Railway, an agreement was made between Sir Hugh Allan, acting for himself, and certain other Canadian promoters, and G. W. McMullen, acting for certain United States Capitalists, whereby the latter agreed to furnish all the funds necessary for the construction of the contemplated Railway, and to give the former a certain percentage of interest, in consideration of their interest and position, the scheme agreed on being ostensibly that of a Canadian Company with Sir Hugh Allan at its head,—

That the Government were aware that negotiations were pending between these parties,—

That subsequently, an understanding was come to between the Government and Sir Hugh Allan and Mr. Abbott, M.P.,—that Sir Hugh Allan and his friends should advance a large sum of money for the purpose of aiding the Elections of Ministers and their supporters at the ensuing General Election,—and that he and his friends should receive the contract for the construction of the Railway,—

That accordingly Sir Hugh Allan did advance a large sum of money for the purpose mentioned, and at the solicitation, and under the pressing instances of Ministers,—

That part of the monies, expended by Sir Hugh Allan in connection with the obtaining of the Act of incorporation and Charter, were paid to him by the said United States Capitalists under the agreement with him,— it is

Ordered, That a committee of seven Members be appointed to inquire into all the circumstances connected with the negotiations for the construction of the Pacific Railway—with the legislation of last Session on the subject, and with the granting of the Charter to Sir Hugh Allan and others; with power to send for persons, papers and records; and with instructions to report in full the evidence taken before, and all proceedings of said Committee.

The resolution was defeated on a party division, but the charge
was too grave to be ignored; and Macdonald shortly afterwards
moved for the appointment of a select committee of five, including
two prominent Liberals—Blake and Dorion. Since parliamentary
committees were not then empowered to take evidence under oath,
a bill was passed to remedy this: it was, however, disallowed as
ultra vires. Macdonald then renewed a suggestion which he had
made earlier, that a royal commission should be issued, and
offered to the committee to change their status in that way. The
Liberals, who had been anxious to keep the enquiry within parliament, resisted the commission. L. H. Holton urged Blake not to
accept. He argued that the government had from the first meant
to thwart the inquiry, and would be able to do so by adjourning the
commission or ruling out evidence.[36] Both Dorion and Blake did
refuse: the latter saying bluntly that ministers should not establish
a commission to try themselves.[37] The others refused to act without
them. Cartwright ventured the suggestion that Allan might be
summoned to the bar of the house, but it was not acted on.[38] After
this jockeying for position, a royal commission was issued on
August 14 to three judges, C. D. Day, Antoine Polette, and
J. R. Gowan.

In the meanwhile parliament and public were startled by a series
of revelations in the Montreal *Herald*. Three of the letters published
—between Allan and G. W. McMullen—were presumably contributed by the latter, who had long been indignant over the way
in which he and his associates had been thrown over.

. . . I regret to have to communicate [he had written to Macdonald] that
no offer for an arrangement has been made by Sir Hugh and it is becoming
evident that he has sacrificed our interests *and acts as if he concluded we
should let the matter rest there.* . . .

Sir Hugh Allan *came to us*, with offers of his services to secure unity of
action to two wings of the Syndicate, which had agreed to build the Canada
Pacific on the terms of the Government. *We* did not go to him. He stated
that he came to us by direction of the ministry. . . .

The Government alone had the address of our syndicate, and Sir Hugh's

36. Blake papers, Holton to Blake, June 24, 1873.
37. *Ibid.*, Blake to Macdonald, July 3, 1873.
38. *Ibid.*, Cartwright to Blake, July 16, 1873.

approach could not be viewed by us in courtesy or practically, as resting on less than direct authority from the Cabinet, and we accepted him as their representative. The Government it is understood has agreed to give the contract to another party; with Sir Hugh as the virtual head of the company, and he evidently expects to retain his position of Government contractor after a flagrant breach of faith with us. . . .[39]

It seemed at first as if Allan would be the chief sufferer from these revelations.

Sir Hugh [wrote Macdonald] as you may fancy, was in considerable distress about the publication of his letters. On the other hand I was exceedingly glad to see them in extenso. They prove Allan to be an exceedingly untruthful man; but what he would feel more they would show even to himself as he re-read them, that he had been a very foolish man. . . . Last night, before the letters came out, I told him that if they were published, as I supposed they would be, I must insist upon his making an affidavit of all the facts as to his relations with the Government, the Railway and the Elections, which he promised to do. I have held him to his promise, and Mr. Abbott, M.P., his Counsel, has prepared an affidavit. . . . This truly states his relations with the Government, so far as I am aware of them. . . . The affidavit is very skilfully drawn by Abbott. He has made the old gentleman acknowledge on oath that his letters were untrue. . . .[40]

This affidavit was published in the Montreal *Gazette*, denying that any bargain had been made with the government, and it seemed as if the storm might calm down. On July 18, however, a further blast appeared in the *Herald* in the form of a statement by McMullen, together with a number of letters and telegrams written during the election, and showing that ministers had constantly called on Allan for funds. The latter letters were copied from the originals stolen from Abbott's office.

The royal commission sat during September and the early part of October, and parliament reassembled on October 23. Attacked for alleged corruption, the government resigned on November 5. The guilt or innocence of Macdonald's government must remain a matter of opinion. There is no doubt that ministers had requested and accepted large sums of money (totalling $350,000) from Sir

39. Canadian Archives, Macdonald Papers, "Railways," vi.
40. *Ibid.*, Letter book xx, Macdonald to Lord Dufferin, July 4, 1873.

Hugh Allan, and that Allan was the head of a "ring" which hoped to get a charter from that government. On the other hand it was argued that subscriptions to election funds were common practice. In his evidence before the commission Macdonald admitted that Allan had a personal interest in the result of the election in that his steamship line and other railway interests called for a Pacific railway, which a new government might drop. But, Macdonald stated, Allan knew that his company could not be left out; and he knew that a purely Quebec group would not get a charter. An understanding had been reached between Allan and Cartier at the end of July 1872 that if the attempt at amalgamation failed, Allan's company should get the charter. This unfortunate step, which Macdonald attributed to the "failing health and waning mental faculties" of Cartier was immediately repudiated. To be exact, the company which received the charter was an entirely new one, formed after the election. It is not surprising, however, that the opposition were struck by the fact that Allan was still president.

The effects of the "Pacific scandal" on the progress of the Pacific railway project were disastrous. In the first place, the news of the early revelations reached England while the representatives of the new company were engaged in searching for capital. The delegation consisted of Sir Hugh Allan, the president, John Walker, vice-president, with Abbott and A. G. Archibald. The lack of success of earlier Canadian railways had made English investors wary of further schemes; the financial crisis of 1873 made railway securities less attractive; and the opposition of the powerful Grand Trunk group closed the doors of the English banking houses to the Canadian delegation. While, no doubt, the Grand Trunk was in any case none too friendly toward a Pacific railway in other hands, its stern opposition was accentuated or perhaps caused by Allan's personal interests, which he had tacked on to the mission. Macdonald, who was growing less and less confident in Allan ("the worst negotiator I ever saw in my life"), had foreseen some such trouble. "I fear", he wrote to Rose in telling him of the delegation, "that he will be attempting to fasten his North Shore Railway and the Northern Colonisation scheme upon the Pacific, and if he does he will of necessity arouse the opposition of all those interested in the Grand Trunk Railway."[41] In April Allan cabled Macdonald asking him to hold up a bill proposed by the Grand Trunk (the Grand Trunk Arrangements Act) as a means of putting pressure on that company.[42] On their side, the Grand Trunk officials offered to call off their dogs if the Allan lines were dropped. In Ottawa the government put what pressure it could on the Grand Trunk, but by that time the latter's efforts had been only too successful and all the ordinary channels were closed.

The only bite the delegation had in England was from McEwen, Grant and Company, a firm of financiers which had recently proposed to raise a large new issue of stock for the Grand Trunk. Alexander McEwen, who seems to have had a dashing financial career, drew up a memorandum—after discussions with the Canadian Pacific delegation in the middle of June—the purport of which was that he was ready to form a syndicate to purchase immediately $25,000,000 of bonds of the Canadian Pacific at $82\frac{1}{2}$ per cent of par value, to be followed by a purchase of a like amount at the same or a higher price, at the end of three years. As security the syndicate was to hold the government subsidy and land grant.[43] To his proposal the delegation and the directors of the Canadian Pacific agreed;[44] but the government were not satisfied either with the details or the security offered, and refused to sanction the agreement.[45] In the meantime, too, McEwen had found that his side of the bargain could not be maintained, partly, no doubt, owing to the lack of confidence which had arisen out of the revelations in Ottawa.

The decade of the 'sixties had held many important changes for the provinces of British North America. Confederation had been proposed and carried through, and with it a commitment to a railway connecting the maritime with the central provinces. In the area to the west of Ontario two colonies which the Hudson's Bay Company had planted were fast growing beyond the stage of the fur trade, and the problem of their future, long of interest to

41. *Ibid.*, Letter book xix, Macdonald to Rose, February 13, 1873.
42. *Ibid.*, "Railways," vi, Allan to Macdonald, April 5, 1873.
43. *Ibid.*, Memo. of June 17, 1873.
44. *Ibid.*, Bellefeuille to Macdonald, July 6, 1873.
45. *Ibid.*, Macdonald to Bellefeuille, August 20, 1873.

Canada, became a matter of urgent importance. Both were added to the Dominion as the 'sixties changed to the 'seventies, but it was a constitutional union which could only be given life by the establishment of adequate communications. The plan of a railway to the Pacific, called logical by its advocates and ruinous by its opponents, for a time fell foul of party politics; but as the rings, the syndicates, the companies, and the charters melted away, a new chapter began in the history of the Pacific railway.

CHAPTER VIII

THE BUILDING OF THE PACIFIC RAILWAY

1. RAILWAY POLICY OF THE LIBERAL GOVERNMENT

THE Liberal government which came into office late in 1873—
the first since confederation—was headed by Alexander Mackenzie,
who, as well as being premier, assumed the added burden of minister
of public works, which department then was responsible for railways. During the previous discussions in parliament of the Pacific
railway the Liberals had pictured it as an impossible task for the
Dominion to undertake in a short time; had urged that no additional burden be put on the taxpayer; and had encouraged its construction by private enterprise. On taking office they were obliged
to pick up the Pacific railway question in the unfortunate state
in which it had been left on the fall of the Macdonald government.
The new policy was announced in 1874: a subsidy of $10,000 and
20,000 acres of land per mile. In reality, however, there was little
hope of enticing private capital into the railway. The beginning of
a period of depression made money tight; American capitalists
would be unpopular for obvious reasons; and the British money-
market had already refused a more tempting bait. In 1876 tenders
were solicited in England and the United States for the construction
and operation of all or part of the line, but only one offer was
made, and that unsatisfactory. The opposition of the Grand Trunk
and the suspicion of English investors continued to operate as they
had five years earlier. In May 1878 Fleming wrote of a "memo.
of information for the parties proposing to tender for the whole
Pacific Railway,"[1] but it is not clear as to who these were, and in
any case nothing came of it. Whatever was done had to be done
with the aid of the public exchequer, and $2,500,000 of a loan
recently guaranteed by the British government was earmarked for
this purpose.

True to their former views, the Liberals were not prepared to

1. Canadian Archives, Fleming papers, cxc, Fleming to W. B. Smellie, May
24, 1878.

plunge into the construction immediately of a railway from central Canada to the Pacific. Indeed, in the previous four or five years, Conservatives as well as Liberals, experts and amateurs, had advocated communication to the Pacific first being established by making use of waterways and American railways. It was a reversion to this plan that the government now proposed. The most easterly link was to be made up of an existing railway, the Canada Central, from Ottawa to Pembroke, and a subsidized extension to Lake Nipissing. The line around Lake Superior was to be left for the time being, and a railway begun from Fort William to Selkirk, north of Winnipeg. A line was then to be built south to the American border, so as to connect with the American railways. Other sections were to be built as finances allowed.

The difference between the Conservative and Liberal policies in regard to a Pacific railway was essentially in the speed at which they were prepared to go ahead: the Conservative government had accepted a time limit for the whole line through Canadian territory; the Liberals were ready to accept such a line as the ultimate goal, but believed that it would have to wait. Their objection to rapid construction was partly on the ground that it entailed great immediate expenditure, and partly that haste would swell the total cost. While later generations may think of the government construction in the 'seventies as slow, to Mackenzie it seemed that the "enormous expenditure is caused by our break-neck pace. . . ."[2] In the meanwhile they proposed to provide temporary means of communication. The lines they undertook at once were portage railways between waterways or links with American lines. Neither the Conservative nor the Liberal party welcomed public ownership on principle, but both were obliged to have recourse to it in default of an alternative; and the Liberals chose public ownership for the Intercolonial, but perhaps again from necessity. The surveys were conducted by the same person and on the same principle throughout three administrations.

Defensible as it might be in the light of the conditions and knowledge of the day, the Liberal policy of cautious advance was bound to meet one obstacle in the agreement with British Columbia.

2. *Ibid.*, Alexander Mackenzie papers, Mackenzie to Lord Dufferin, May 20, 1876.

Even before the Conservative party went out of power there had been demands from British Columbia to know why construction had not been started, which Macdonald answered by saying that the survey was under way as a necessary preliminary. Even apart from accumulated irritation the Liberal party was suspect because of its determined opposition to the time limit when the terms of union were being debated. Such suspicion in British Columbia was given added strength by the known anxiety of Mackenzie to reach a compromise, and by the influence of Edward Blake which was thrown more toward financial safety than concession. The people of the province felt that the promise of a railway was the chief inducement to enter the confederation; that no real efforts had been made to implement the promise; and that the Dominion government was hostile, and attempting to evade the commitment. The Liberal government, on the other hand, faced by a period of depression, was more than ever concerned with the financial burdens which rapid construction would entail. They clung to Macdonald's argument that "ten years" was not to be taken literally—indeed it could no longer be even promised—and sought to make the best compromise they could.

A dreary period of negotiations followed. Their success was further imperilled by divisions within each party to the dispute. In British Columbia the old rivalry between island and mainland had become focused on the western terminus of the railway. By the original agreement the Dominion was bound to build only as far as the seaboard. Before the preliminary surveys had advanced far enough to justify the selection of a terminus, Macdonald had rashly fastened on Esquimalt, near Victoria. This choice complicated the issue in two ways: it led to a demand for a railway between Esquimalt and Nanaimo, to which point on the island it was expected that bridges would cross from the mainland; and it so heightened the feeling between island and mainland that any change by the provincial government in the terms of union with Canada was rendered more difficult. In the Canadian parliament there was a division of feeling in the Liberal ranks between those who followed Mackenzie in his desire for an acceptable compromise and those who followed Blake in his fear of financial commitments.

Early in 1874 J. D. Edgar was sent as Canadian envoy to British

Columbia. In confidential instructions Edgar was told to make it clear that the government was anxious to construct the railway, but that it was a physical impossibility to do so within the time set by the original agreement. He was to say that the Dominion was not bound to build beyond the coast of the mainland, and that any further extension (that is, the Nanaimo-Esquimalt line) "must entirely depend on the spirit shewn by themselves in assenting to a reasonable extension of time or a modification of the terms originally agreed to." He was further to remind the British Columbia government of the terms which they had originally proposed—terms which had been increased by the federal Conservative government only as "additional means of procuring extensive patronage immediately before the general election," even though those terms were then known to be "impossible of fulfilment."[3] After some discussion with the provincial authorities, Edgar offered an immediate railway from Esquimalt to Nanaimo, a road through the mainland, and a minimum expenditure of $1,500,000 annually on the portion of the railway in the province as soon as the road and surveys had been completed. G. A. Walkem, the premier, perhaps fearing the political consequences of a decision, questioned Edgar's right to negotiate, with the result that the latter returned to Ottawa. The next step was the despatch of a protest by Walkem to the British government, rehearsing the whole story from the point of view of British Columbia. Lord Carnarvon, the colonial secretary, had, even before its receipt, stepped into the breach by offering himself as arbitrator. To Mackenzie the offer was an embarrassment which he attempted to avoid, but in the end grudgingly accepted.[4] Carnarvon's award changed Edgar's terms in two respects: the Dominion was to spend $2,000,000 instead of $1,500,000 annually and to complete the railway by the end of 1890. Mackenzie then introduced a bill for the construction of the Esquimalt-Nanaimo Railway. In the commons the measure passed, though Blake, David Mills and Thomas Moss voted against it. In the senate the bill was defeated on a close vote, the opposition including two Liberals.

3. *Ibid.*, Mackenzie to Edgar, February 19, 1874.
4. J. A. Maxwell, "Lord Dufferin and the difficulties with British Columbia, 1874–1877" (*Canadian Historical Review*, xii, 4).

The failure of the bill produced in British Columbia an outcry, and in Ottawa a party crisis. Mackenzie felt it necessary to bring Blake back into the cabinet to heal the division in the party, but Blake would only return on a modification of the government's policy in regard to the whole Pacific railway question. R. J. Cartwright, the minister of finance, seems to have thrown his weight in the direction of the new policy advocated by Blake. Agreement was reached in September 1875. The government was to return to the meaningless formula that the rate of taxation should not be increased; the Esquimalt-Nanaimo Railway was dropped as a federal work; and "the compensation to be given them by Canada for any delays which may take place in the construction of the Pacific Railway should be in the form of a cash bonus to be applied towards the local Railway or such other local works as the Legislature of British Columbia may undertake. . . ."[5] The amount of the bonus was fixed at $750,000, but this ingenious method of at once avoiding the building of the island railway and buying off further criticisms of delay on the main line could hardly have been expected to be palatable to British Columbia.

British Columbia at once disputed the whole position taken by the Dominion government, and appealed to the colonial office. Carnarvon once more offered himself as arbitrator, an offer which Mackenzie sought vainly to escape. Having restored unity within his party, he now found himself at odds with the governor general who was taking an active—to Mackenzie's mind a too active—part in the unfortunate controversy. In the summer of 1876 the governor general, Lord Dufferin, went to British Columbia to judge the local situation. On his return he sought to transfer the negotiations to London, but to this Mackenzie was unalterably opposed and threatened to resign. Dufferin was obliged to come into line with the policy of his ministers, and Carnarvon threw cold water on the claims of British Columbia. In the spring of 1878 Walkem came back into office and celebrated his return by introducing into the legislature a resolution empowering the province to withdraw from confederation unless construction was begun by May 1879. Shortly after this a general election resulted in

5. Blake papers, lxxi, Report of a committee of the privy council, September, 20, 1875.

the defeat of the Mackenzie administration, and the Conservatives were faced with the solution of the problem that their earlier policy had caused. In the meanwhile the progress made on sections of the railway was, perhaps, greater than it appeared to the disappointed people of British Columbia. What had been done was modest indeed in comparison with the fair promises of 1870; yet through the period of economic depression and political controversy both surveys and construction on the Pacific railway had slowly but steadily gone forward.

2. GOVERNMENT SURVEYS AND CONSTRUCTION

In telling the story of the Canadian Pacific Railway emphasis has usually been laid on the period beginning with the formation in 1880 of the company which carried the project to completion. While it is true that the five years beginning with that date saw the major part of the work constructed, and that with remarkable speed, it is proper to bear in mind the necessary spadework of the previous ten years. The heaviest burden of both surveys and construction up to 1880 fell on the broad shoulders of Sandford Fleming, a Scot who came to Canada at eighteen and entered the service of the Northern Railway, of which he became chief engineer twelve years later. After the completion of this railway he visited the Red River colony—for he was deeply interested in the future of the west—and a year later was appointed chief engineer for the surveys and construction of the Intercolonial. This task was only partially completed when he was asked in 1871 to assume the additional duties of engineer-in-chief of the Canadian Pacific Railway.

The surveys were begun promptly in 1871 and continued throughout the next several years. Fleming divided the field into three regions.[6] The eastern or woodland region was from the eastern terminus to the Red River. Much of this, like the rest of the survey, was work for the explorer as well as the engineer. "No civilized man," wrote Fleming, "as far as known, had ever passed from

6. Fleming's annual reports are contained in the following volumes: *Report on surveys and preliminary operations on the Canadian Pacific Railway up to January 1877*, and *Report and documents in reference to the Canadian Pacific Railway* (1880).

the valley of the Upper Ottawa through the intervening wilderness to Lake Superior. The country east and west of Lake Nipigon was all but a *terra incognita.*" Nor was it country which looked hospitable to a railway. "All accounts of the country to be traversed by the railway, at least such portions of it as were, in any way, known, were unfavourable." In 1872 a favourable route was found north of Lake Nipigon, but this meant a long detour, and a line to the south was discovered in the following year. By a process of trial and error other portions of the route were provisionally located. (From Fort William east to Sudbury, Fleming's line was not much different from that adopted.) Attention was then directed from the Lake Superior area by the decision of the Liberal government to make temporary use of waterways. From Fort William the line chosen by Fleming ran slightly north of that eventually taken by the Canadian Pacific, and crossed the Red River at Selkirk instead of Winnipeg, as the former was thought to be the most favourable point for a bridge. In the woodland region, then, Fleming had been able to show the practicability of a line in Canadian territory, and had in fact traced the general route that was eventually followed.

The central or prairie region was that between the Red River and the boundary of British Columbia. Exploration by the imperial government indicated that no serious engineering problems would be encountered save the bridging of exceptionally wide and deep river channels. In addition to this consideration, Fleming had in mind the approach to a mountain pass, and the presence of water, timber, gravel, and land suitable for agriculture. In general he chose "the fertile belt," that is to say the northern route by the valley of the Saskatchewan River. His line at first ran from Selkirk to cross Lake Manitoba high up at the Narrows, but in 1880 this was changed to one south of the lake. From Lake Manitoba his route curved north-west to a point not far south of Edmonton, to which place it ran in a comparatively straight line. West of Edmonton he worked toward the Yellowhead Pass. Favourable gradients were found throughout. By 1880 the line through the prairie region had been sketched out, with the details of some sections to be determined. Fleming's line from Winnipeg to British Columbia was not that finally chosen for the Canadian Pacific, but blazed the trail for both the Canadian Northern and the Grand Trunk Pacific, the former following his route closely.

It was, naturally, in the western or mountain region that the greatest problems of the survey arose. They were of two kinds: one arose from local opinion which was sharply divided as to the western terminus; and the other was a straight engineering problem of how best to get from the east side of the Rockies to the Pacific coast. The chief difference of opinion in regard to the terminus was a part of the constant rivalry between mainland and island. If a southerly terminus were chosen at Burrard Inlet (Vancouver), Victoria would lose its position as the major seaport, for only a ferry could be run across the Straits of Georgia at that point. The islanders, therefore, campaigned for Bute Inlet further north, whence bridges could be built to Nanaimo. The engineers were by no means agreed on this point. Marcus Smith, who was in charge in the British Columbia section, "found out about this Burrard Inlet mania which is a huge land job in which the minister and his friends are concerned,"[7] and over this he and Fleming had a sharp difference of opinion; but the latter remained unmoved in the decision which it will be seen he reached.

As far as is known Fleming was not influenced by local interests, and based his final recommendations on the result of years of careful investigation. The general problem is stated in his account of the first year's operations (1871).

At the commencement of the Survey, all the sources of information open to inquiry with regard to the passes through the Rocky Mountains, were consulted. After careful investigation it appeared that the two passes known as the Howse and the Yellow Head possessed advantages which, taken in conjunction with the approaches to them, as far as known, best warranted further examination.

By 1873 he could report that the Yellowhead Pass was the most eligible route yet discovered between the American border and the 53rd parallel of latitude. But the real problem was beyond Tête Jaune Cache on the western side of the pass. "It was . . . evident", he wrote, "that the obstacles which intervened between the passes and the coast of British Columbia were of a very

7. Canadian Archives, Fleming papers, Smith to Fleming, December 7, 1877.

serious character, and that the selection of a pass through the
main Rocky Mountain range depended on the discovery of a
practicable line across the whole mountain region." It was soon
found that a line was practicable from Tête Jaune Cache by the
Fraser River to the North Thompson, and probably on to Kamloops
(whence Burrard Inlet could certainly be reached). Further investigation of this route, however, indicated that an "enormous outlay"
would be required, and in 1872 a search was made for alternatives.
The Cariboo range clearly barred the direct approach to the
coast, and no way could be found through it. By 1873 seven routes
were reported. Parties ranged all over the mountains, finding
possible variations and re-examining the early discoveries. In
1876 a winter survey was sent up the coast and found that of the
various inlets or fiords, Gardner Inlet was ice-bound, Dean Inlet
had been frozen for a time, but Bute Inlet not at all. By 1877
the possible routes had risen to ten. All began at the Yellowhead
Pass. Two led to Burrard Inlet, one to Howe Sound, two to Bute
Inlet, one to North Bentinck Arm, two to Dean Inlet, one to
Gardner Inlet, and one to Port Essington (Prince Rupert).

Assuming that the Yellowhead Pass was to be utilized—and this
was never seriously questioned—the routes could be reduced to
two: to Bute Inlet or to Burrard Inlet. In 1878 Fleming gave his
opinion.

Upon carefully viewing the engineering features of each route, and
weighing every commercial consideration, I am forced to the conclusion
that, if these alone are to govern a selection, if a decision cannot be postponed until further examinations be made, if the construction of the railway must at once be proceeded with, the line to Vancouver Island should,
for the present, be rejected, and that the Government should select the
route by the Rivers Thompson and Fraser to Burrard Inlet.

He was fully conscious of the responsibility he was taking, and
conscious, too, that his decision was not generally popular in
British Columbia. His advice, however, was acted upon by the
Mackenzie government, which, in the summer of 1878, accepted
the route he recommended. Shortly afterwards Macdonald was
again returned to power, cancelled the decision, and re-adopted it
in 1879. Though this line by the Yellowhead Pass was later rejected

for the Canadian Pacific, it was adopted by the Canadian Northern; while another route examined under Fleming's direction—that by the Fraser and Skeena rivers to Prince Rupert—was followed by the Grand Trunk Pacific. Eight years of pioneer work had not been wasted.

Before the surveys as a whole had been completed, construction began on those sections which had been finally located. The immediate purpose was to finish the parts which would, with waterways and American railways, afford access to the west, with a view to transporting materials for further construction and creating temporary facilities for commercial traffic. Thus work on the Pembina branch was started in 1874, and by 1878 the track was laid from Pembina to Selkirk, a distance of eighty-five miles. Amidst great excitement, a locomotive arrived at Winnipeg in 1877, having been brought down the Red River on barges. It had been built at Philadelphia and run by rail to Fargo, North Dakota, where it was put on board. The engine was primarily for construction on the Pembina branch, and was a welcome innovation, for all the early construction work was made more difficult by the impossibility of getting engines to the scene. Fort William was another strategic point, for from there the St. Lawrence could be reached by boat, or a combination of boat and rail. Contracts for portions of the line between Fort William and Winnipeg began to be let in 1875. The third section which was attacked was in British Columbia, the difficult and expensive section between Yale and Savona's Ferry, where tunnels and other heavy rock work were necessary. Presumably the start in British Columbia was intended as much to placate local opinion as from any other reason. By 1880 the following sections were built or under contract:

Fort William to Selkirk	410	miles
Selkirk to Emerson	85	"
West of Red River	100	"
In British Columbia	127	"
Total	722	"

Rails were laid for 136 miles west of Fort William, and 90 miles east of Selkirk. Regular trains were running from Emerson to Cross Lake, a distance of 161 miles.

Such was the progress on the Pacific railway in ten years. The Canadian government was a long way from living up to its promises to British Columbia. The slow speed of construction aroused constant criticism, not only from the Conservatives who (up to 1878) condemned the general railway policy of the Liberals, but also on grounds of incompetence and mismanagement. Charges were also made of irregularities and extravagance. To examine the whole situation a royal commission was appointed in June 1880, consisting of G. M. Clark, a judge, Samuel Keefer, engineer, and Edward Miall, assistant commissioner of the department of inland revenue, and its report was published in three volumes in 1882.[8] The conclusions may be quoted in part as indicating the views reached on the efficiency of work under the government.

That the construction of the Canadian Pacific Railway was carried on as a Public Work at a sacrifice of money, time and efficiency.

That in this work numbers of persons were employed as government officials who were not efficient in the positions to which they were appointed, having been selected on party grounds, irrespective of the question whether their engagement would be advantageous to the public interest.

That during the progress of the undertaking, delays occurred which would not have occurred, but for the necessity of staying operations from time to time until the necessary appropriations were made by Parliament.

That the examination of the country over which the line was located was inadequate, failing to give to the Government that information which could have been given, and which was necessary to enable the Government to estimate, with reasonable accuracy, the probable cost of the railway.

That large operations were carried on and extensive purchases made with much less regard to economy than would have happened under similar circumstances in a private undertaking.

That the practice which permits a Department to originate and enter upon transactions involving the expenditure of large sums of money, and, without other authority, to award the contracts under which such expenditure is intended to take place, is a disadvantage.

That the system under which the contracts were let was not calculated to secure the works at the lowest price or the earliest date; it pledged the Department to treat with tenderers irrespective of their good faith or financial strength, upon the single test of a deposit of money, so small as to be useless as a guarantee, the possible efficacy of this being neutralized

8. *Report of the Canadian Pacific Railway royal commission* (Ottawa, 1882).

by the invariable practice of returning his deposit to each defaulter. Such a system promises to every tenderer a position which he risks nothing to procure, and which he may at his option abandon, or retain, or sell if he can.

In his evidence Fleming stated that positions under him were filled by political patronage, and that the railway could have been constructed more efficiently and more cheaply by a private company. The total expenditure by the government from 1871 to 1879 had been $14,287,824, and it was shown that a number of the contracts had vastly exceeded the estimates. Fleming himself had been overworked, his health had suffered, and he had been obliged to take leave of absence. On his return in 1878 he found the staff demoralized and many branches of the work in a state of confusion.[9] He was, however, criticized, and finally (in March 1880) charges were made against him in the house. By an order in council of May 22 he was removed from office as engineer-in-chief, and refused to accept the position of consulting engineer, offered as a sop.[10] Probably Fleming must be regarded as the inevitable victim of a not very successful experiment in government construction by easy stages, though a comparison must not be too quickly drawn; for the very appointment of a commission may to some extent have been a party move to throw discredit on a previous administration.

3. THE CANADIAN PACIFIC RAILWAY COMPANY

For more than two years after coming into office the Conservative government continued the policy of governmental construction, but probably more from necessity than choice. Sir Charles Tupper, who became minister of public works in 1878 and minister of railways on the establishment of a separate department in the following year, seems to have consistently believed in private ownership. "I have, at some risk of separating myself from a portion of our press and party, persistently denounced the policy of constructing the C.P.R. as a Gov't work, and maintained that the terms of the Resolution moved by Sir G. Cartier relieved Canada from any

9. Canadian Archives, Fleming papers, Fleming to Tupper, February 9, 1880.
10. *Ibid.*, Same to same, June 7, 1880.

such obligation."[11] This letter was written in 1876 while his party was in opposition, and presumably he nursed the same sentiments in the years 1878 to 1880. It is probable that the new government investigated the possibilities of a private company early in its period of office, but recognized the obstacles to this course. In 1879 the government proposed to institute a commission, including representatives of the imperial government, who should hold a very large amount of land for sale, the proceeds to pay for the construction of the railway. A mission was sent to England, but the British government was not willing to take any part. So bleak was the prospect that in April 1880 D. L. Macpherson advocated stopping work in British Columbia.

Shortly after this active negotiations began with at least two groups of capitalists. One was a partly Canadian group of which D. J. McIntyre and George Stephen were the spokesmen. The tradition is that J. H. Pope suggested to Macdonald that he should get in touch with Stephen and his associates in the St. Paul, Minneapolis and Manitoba Railway. In June McIntyre received a confidential memorandum from the government to which he suggested some modifications.[12] The government, however, stuck to their terms, and McIntyre declared that negotiations were for the time being closed. The chief point of difference was that the government offered a subsidy of $20,000,000 while the capitalists they were dealing with asked for $26,500,000. Meanwhile an English group, headed by the Earl of Dunsmore and Puleston, Brown and Company, were also seeking a contract. They proposed to build the portions of the line not yet under contract and to own and operate the whole for a subsidy of $9,500 and 16,000 acres per mile.[13] The government, however, refused to come to any decision and it resolved to send a delegation of Macdonald, Tupper, and J. H. Pope to England, to receive any tenders and discuss terms. Sailing on July 10, they interviewed Sir Henry Tyler, president of the Grand Trunk, on arrival and proposed that his company should undertake the completion of the Pacific railway. Tyler, however,

11. *Ibid.*, Macdonald papers, "Tupper," Tupper to Macdonald, January 29, 1876.

12. *Ibid.*, "Railways," vii, McIntyre to Macdonald, June 21, 1880.

13. *Ibid.*, Dunsmore to Macdonald, June 30, 1880.

would not consider the proposal if it included a line from Fort William to Lake Nipissing, while the Canadians were determined to have a through rail route.[14] He clung to the old Grand Trunk argument for a line (their line) south of Lake Superior.

While the delegates were in London both the other groups of capitalists reopened negotiations. (Macdonald referred vaguely in the house of commons to other groups, but refused to disclose their identity.) The English group, who announced themselves associated with the French firm, the Société Générale, now offered to replace the subsidy with a bond issue of $65,000,000, each $100 bond to carry the right to 160 acres of farming land, the Dominion government to guarantee interest at four per cent for twelve years.[15] Apparently, however, the offer was not acceptable as nothing more was heard of it. In August McIntyre produced new terms by which he and his associates agreed to build the railway for $25,000,000 cash and twenty-five million acres of land for the 2,000 miles.[16] A confidential letter from Stephen to Macdonald, written just after the failure of the negotiations in Ottawa and just before Macdonald sailed for England, emphasized his attitude.

There are two ways by which you can get the road built and operated: one by getting up a financial organization such as Allan contemplated and such as Jay Cooke & Co. got up for the construction of the Northern Pacific Railway—with what result I need not remind you. A scheme of this nature involves the issue of a large number of Bonds . . . the outcome of a plan of this character is that the real responsibility is transferred from the Company to the people who may be induced to buy the Bonds, while the Company or the projectors pocket a big profit at the start out of the proceeds. This, in the rough, is I fear the method any English financial organization is likely to follow. . . . The other plan, and the one I should have followed . . . would have been to limit the borrowing of money from the public to the smallest possible point . . . to have looked for a return of our own capital and a legitimate profit entirely to the growth of the country and the development of the property. . . .[17]

14. E. M. Saunders, *Life and letters of Rt. Hon. Sir Charles Tupper* (London, 1916), i, 286.

15. Canadian Archives, Macdonald papers, "Railways," vii, Puleston, Brown & Co., to Macdonald, August 16, 1880.

16. *Ibid.*, McIntyre to Macdonald, August 12, 1880.

17. *Ibid.*, "Stephen," i, Stephen to Macdonald, July 9, 1880.

The government accepted the terms offered by McIntyre in London, and before the end of September the draft of the agreement was on paper. The contract was signed on October 21, and on December 10 brought down to parliament for ratification. The quality of the railway was to be that of the Union Pacific as first constructed. The gauge was set at 4 feet 8½ inches. Those sections already built were to be handed over to the company, while others under contract—that is, from Kamloops to Port Moody and from Lake Superior to Selkirk—were to be completed by the government. The remainder was to be built by the company, and the whole was to be finished by 1891. Subsidies were to be on the terms suggested in the previous summer: $25,000,000 and 25,000,000 acres of land, both payable in instalments on the completion of each twenty miles of line; but the subsidies were unevenly distributed according to the difficulty of construction. The land granted was to be in alternate sections of 640 acres each, 24 miles deep on either side of the railway between Winnipeg and Jasper House. Land not fit for settlement was to be replaced elsewhere. Additional privileges were accorded to the company. Land for the road bed, shops, stations and so on was to be granted. Materials for original construction might be imported free of duty. The railway with its grounds and buildings, "rolling stock and appurtenances" used for construction and operation, and the capital of the company were to be forever free from any taxation. The land grants were not to be taxed for twenty years, unless sold or occupied in the meantime. For twenty years no railway should be authorized south of the Canadian Pacific, except a line running south-west, but such a line might not continue to within fifteen miles of the border. Finally, the company was empowered to issue $25,000,000 in bonds secured upon the land granted. These bonds were to be held by the government, which might sell all but one-fifth and hand the proceeds to the company. By an attached schedule the Canadian Pacific Railway Company was incorporated with a capital stock of $25,000,000.

Montreal was heavily represented in the new company. The president was Sir George Stephen, who resigned as president of the Bank of Montreal to take the leading position in the railway. R. B. Angus, general manager of the same bank, became a member of the executive committee. The vice-president was D. J. McIntyre, manager of the Canada Central Railway, and his inclusion marked a further victory for Montreal since it indicated that the terminus of the Canadian Pacific would be at that city rather than at Toronto. The syndicate included no one from Ontario. There was, however, an important American connection. Both Stephen and Angus had made fortunes out of a startlingly successful enterprise in Minnesota, the St. Paul, Minneapolis and Manitoba Railway. Two of their associates in that railway, Donald Smith and J. J. Hill, were members of the original Canadian Pacific group. Smith was not at first a director because of a political quarrel with Macdonald, but he had great influence with Stephen, and continued in the councils of the company. Hill was for a time an influential director, but he never threw in his lot completely with the Canadian Pacific. His prime motive in becoming a member of the syndicate was to secure business for the Minnesota railway. From the start he opposed the construction of a line to the north of Lake Superior,[18] and when this became a reality, he found it impossible to ride two horses at once and withdrew from the Canadian railway to create the Great Northern.

There is a superficial parallel between the connection of Sir Hugh Allan with the Northern Pacific group in 1872 and of Stephen with the St. Paul, Minneapolis and Manitoba railway in 1880. The most valid objection to the first was a fear that the interests of the Americans would lead them to treat the Canadian railway as a feeder rather than as a through line. It is not known exactly what their intentions were; nor is it known whether there is any reason to suspect that such motives existed in the syndicate of 1880, except in so far as Hill may have had some such purpose in mind. It is obvious, however, that the balance of power between the Canadian and American interests was different in 1880 from what it had been in 1872; and to preserve that balance the charter provided that the majority of the directors, of whom the president was to be one, were to be British subjects. Donald Smith was born in Scotland and was only temporarily a director of the Minnesota railway. J. J. Hill was born in Canada, but remained primarily interested in American railways. Through his Great Northern he

18. J. M. Gibbon, *Steel of empire* (Toronto, 1935), p. 201.

carried on a vigorous rivalry with the American-born Van Horne, champion of the Canadian Pacific. W. C. Van Horne was born in Illinois. He became a telegraph operator in the Illinois Central at the age of fourteen; clerk in the Michigan Central; and ticket agent and telegraph operator in the Chicago and Alton. In this railway he rose rapidly, and was appointed superintendent of a new subsidiary, the St. Louis, Kansas City and Northern, with his headquarters at St. Louis. From this he became president and general manager of a bankrupt pioneer railway, the Southern Minnesota. Having restored this railway to health, he returned to the Chicago and Alton as superintendent, and thence to the Chicago, Milwaukee and St. Paul. There can have been few railwaymen in the United States with such a record of unbroken success in management. In 1881 he was recommended by Hill, whose territory touched Van Horne's, as the most suitable man to be general manager of the Canadian Pacific. It was a choice which was to be richly justified. Several other members of the original staff were brought from American railways, their experience being of value to the Canadian Pacific which was built and operated under similar conditions. But the use of Americans on the Pacific railway did not originate with the syndicate, for Andrew Onderdonk had received the government's contract for the British Columbia section. Neither in executive officers, contractors, or financiers did Great Britain play a part in the Canadian Pacific similar to that in the Grand Trunk. London, however, was represented financially by Morton, Rose and Company, and the continent by Kohn, Reinach and Company of Paris and Frankfort, and the Société Générale.

The introduction of the agreement into the house of commons in December 1880 was the signal for a long debate.[19] Tupper, who as minister of railways introduced the subject, sought to show that the terms were the best that had been obtained in the history of the Pacific railway, and by a long series of quotations from earlier speeches by leading members of the opposition attempted to take the ground from under their feet. In reality, however, no exact comparison could be made owing to the fact that a portion

19. *Debates of the house of commons of the Dominion of Canada*, 1880–1881, i.

of the railway was built or being built by the government—a point
that for some reason was not stressed by the opposition. On other
grounds the Liberals strenuously opposed the bill. Edward Blake,
now leader of the opposition, characterized it as "not merely
fraught with great danger, but certain to prove disastrous to the
future of this country." His attitude was not inconsistent with his
previous alarm about committing the country to an immediate
realization of the Pacific project. He remained opposed to a line
north of Lake Superior, arguing that it was wiser to make use of
American territory, just as Americans shipped goods through
Canada. On the whole, however, the Liberals were hampered in
debate by their act of 1874, and could only oppose individual sections of the terms under discussion. They proposed amendment
after amendment, each of which was voted down with machine-
like efficiency by the serried ranks of the Conservatives.

One or two of the points raised in the debate have more than
passing importance. An objection that was bound to arise was to
the position given to Montreal not only in the personnel of the
company, but also in the use of the Canada Central which would
give direct connection with Montreal. The old division of 1872
between the interests of Ontario and Quebec was revived, and
again a rival company—the heir of the Interoceanic—was
organized. Its directorate included many men prominent in
business, principally in Ontario: Sir William Howland, A. R.
McMaster, William Hendrie, J. P. Proctor, G. W. Cox, P. Larkin,
and a number of others. They offered to build the railway for
$22,000,000 and 22,000,000 acres of land, and to forego exemption
from duties on materials, from taxation on lands, and the clause
forbidding construction south of their line. On the face of it, it
was a much better offer, but the government claimed that it
was purely a party move, and that it was too late to change. (In
this connection it may be noted that the government had
consistently refused to reveal anything concerning the negotiations
with the chosen syndicate or any other group.) The only modification that Ontario could secure was a clause allowing to the
Ontario and Pacific Junction Railway—which corresponded in
Ontario to the Canada Central—"all reasonable facilities . . .
when their railway shall be completed to a point of junction with

the Canadian Pacific Railway and the Canada Central Railway for the receiving, forwarding and delivering of traffic upon and from the railways of the said companies." It may be deduced from this episode that the Conservative government of 1880 could charter a Quebec group when the Conservative government of 1873 could not. Or was it that the American bogey was the real obstacle standing between Allan's company and the charter? It is an interesting political study.

A side of the agreement that was to have more obvious repercussions in the future was the use of large-scale land grants in lieu of additional money subsidies, or guarantee of bonds. The Liberals fulminated against the exemption of the lands from taxation, but that was only part of a larger issue. The effect of the grant of land to the Canadian Pacific, added to the already large grants made to the Hudson's Bay Company, was to remove from the control of the government an enormous area which might have been used either for the free homestead system or as a source of revenue. It is not surprising that the vast area of the west seemed unlimited: and it was easy to argue that the land granted would be sold at low rates to settlers, whose coming in any case hinged on the existence of a railway. All this might be true, but a large portion of the fertile land found its way into the possession of two private companies.

The Liberals could not criticize the system of land subsidies as such, for this system had become an accepted method for dealing with the Pacific railway. The origin of the land subsidy policy, like not a few things connected with Canadian railways, is to be found in the United States,[20] where the idea of land grants in assistance of railways had first been put into practice about the middle of the century, and in the following twenty years some 150,000,000 acres had been granted to western railways. Opinion slowly veered against the policy, however, and by 1871 it was abandoned. This was just the time when it was first adopted in Canada, for, although grants had been earlier passed for railways, none had actually been made. With a view to grants to both the Hudson's Bay Company and the Pacific railway, power over the

20. J. B. Hedges, *The federal railway land subsidy policy of Canada* (Cambridge, Mass., 1934), pp. 4 et seq.

natural resources of Manitoba and the North West Territories was vested in the Dominion. Macdonald's Railway Act of 1872 allowed for the granting of 50,000,000 acres in aid of a Pacific railway, but the lands were to be located in large blocks instead of in alternative sections as had been the practice in the United States. The Canadian Pacific of 1873 (the amalgamated company) was also to receive 50,000,000 acres, and was for the first time permitted to refuse any land "not of the fair average quality of land in the sections of the country best adapted for settlement." Mackenzie's act of 1874 provided for the granting of 20,000 acres per mile of railway in smaller blocks, but it never became operative. On returning to power in 1878 the Conservatives obtained from parliament power to appropriate 100,000,000 acres in aid of the railway, but this act also became a dead letter. In the meanwhile the plan for allotting the land was made similar to the American practice of alternate sections.

Such was the background of the land subsidy policy which was first carried into effect in 1881. It is probable that no other expedient could have been found at the time. Apart from the importance of their land holdings to the Canadian Pacific Railway Company, the origin of the land-granting system is important, for it was carried much further before it was abandoned. But no later through line, as such, received grants of land.

The debate on the agreement with the syndicate, long as it was carried on, ended only with the passage of an act embodying the terms, virtually unchanged. In one sense it was regrettable that the Liberals, by their continued criticisms, should have been judged as hostile to the Canadian Pacific Railway Company, for out of this was to come much evil: charges of undue influence in elections, and a growing feeling in the Liberal party that a counterweight to the Canadian Pacific Railway must be found. Yet the results of their opposition were not entirely negative, for in the next twenty years they were to develop a Liberal railway policy which in some respects reflected their criticisms made in 1880.

4. COMPLETION OF THE PACIFIC RAILWAY

The tale of the completion of the Pacific railway by the company is one that has more than once been told in terms of hardships faced and problems overcome.[21] That such an approach has incidentally tended to shadow the no less great hardships and problems of the surveys and construction carried out by the government's engineers is unfortunate; but the slow progress made in the years 1871 to 1880 must pale as a story beside the dynamic energy and rapid achievement of 1881 to 1885. The rocks and marshes north of Lake Superior, the chasms of the prairie rivers, and the forbidding mountains of British Columbia were obstacles that offered battle to the stoutest hearts. Perhaps the surveyor, beset with flies and mosquitoes, hacking a way for the transit and chain, the construction gang toiling in the heat of a Canadian summer, or the superintendent harassed by shortage of supplies, may have failed at the time to see the romance of their tasks. Yet romance it was; and even these men, so beset by immediate discomfort and difficulty, must have paused at the end of a day to look upon their work and see that it was good. But since the adventurous side of the building of the railway has been told, and well told, it will be best to look at the period from somewhat different and more prosaic angles.

The contract of 1880 provided that the route to be followed was that already chosen by the government: from Callander at the east end of Lake Nipissing, over the north shore of Lake Superior to Selkirk, via Edmonton to the Yellowhead Pass, and through the North Thompson and Fraser valleys to Port Moody on Burrard Inlet. Actually only a part of this was adopted by the Canadian Pacific, and even where it was followed in general, considerable changes were made in detail. Van Horne's biographer states that Hill and Stephen had not intended that the Lake Superior section should be built as early as the rest, if at all; that in the meantime they planned a connection with a branch of the St. Paul, Minneapolis and Manitoba at Sault Ste. Marie; that it was Van Horne who encouraged the government to proceed with the Lake Superior section at once; and that it was this decision that led Hill—who had hoped to have virtual control of the Canadian Pacific

21. See, e.g., R. G. MacBeth, The romance of the Canadian Pacific Railway (Toronto, 1924); J. H. E. Secretan, Canada's great highway (Ottawa, 1924); J. M. Gibbon's recent work, Steel of empire, contains, inter alia, good accounts of construction and operation.

—to withdraw from the company.[22] If this interpretation be true of the period after the first signing of the agreement, it can only be assumed either that Hill (and perhaps Stephen) hoped to avoid building the Lake Superior section for an indefinite period, or intended to secure a change in the charter later. Either move might have received support from a number of Liberals, but it seems improbable that parliament or public as a whole would have agreed to anything but an all-Canadian route. The Conservative delegation to England in 1880 had broken off negotiations with the Grand Trunk on that issue. There is little evidence to settle the point. In making comments on the contract, McIntyre, Angus and Abbott dealt with the need of protection from foreign railways, and pointed out that traffic must run east and west. Any lines to the boundary, they wrote, would only be to draw traffic to the Canadian Pacific Railway.[23] Stephen, who was indignant at the attitude of the opposition in parliament, wrote to Macdonald that "the real control and government of this enterprise will be in the hands of Angus, Kennedy, McIntyre and myself, and I think personally I can carry with me the support of our London and Paris associates, so you see there is no danger of the control getting into the hands of our St. Paul friends."[24]

Whatever may have been the internal dissensions within the syndicate, or their private plans, it is certain that work was begun on the line west from Callander in 1882. The company's engineers found it desirable to re-locate in detail a considerable portion of this section, authority for which was secured by periodic orders in council. In 1882 some eighty miles of the way were located, a few miles of line laid, and some bridges built; but still there was suspicion that the company was not serious about its work.

I am well aware [wrote Stephen] of the *pretention* to uneasiness on the part of the (friends) of the Gov't. in Press and elsewhere, not excluding the Cabinet, lest we should turn out a pack of rogues and "lie down" on the

22. W. Vaughan, *The life and work of Sir William Van Horne* (New York, 1920), p. 78. It should be added that Hill further objected to the southern route on the prairies.

23. Canadian Archives, Macdonald papers, "Railways," viii, McIntyre, Angus and Abbott to Macdonald, January 2, 1881.

24. *Ibid.*, "Stephen," i, January 23, 1881.

Lake Superior section having made a lot of money out of the construction of the line in the central section, leave the Gov't to furnish the Lake Superior section and the Rocky Mountain section and so get rid of the thing. . . .

I take it for granted that our worst enemy will not pretend to say we have not pushed the work on the main line with energy. The *Globe* says we are building it too fast. I claim we have been equally energetic on the eastern section and have relatively accomplished as much work—real work though it does not "bulk" in the public eye. You will not forget that we had to begin de novo. The locations and surveys of the Gov't were useless to us, and I have learnt enough of Railroad building to appreciate this fact, that the moment your line is finally located, your money is gone, that is, it has only to be paid out. The *amount* is settled by your engineer when he has located the line . . .[25]

Following Fleming's advice, the Canadian Pacific Railway chose a line near the shore of the lake, rather than on the height of land. It was difficult country, rocky and marshy, and without local traffic, but allowed for rapid construction by its proximity to water transportation. Added to other difficulties was that of transportation of supplies, which Van Horne solved by shipping materials by rail to Owen Sound and thence by water. In winter rough roads were used. The progress of the Canadian Pacific Railway in the whole eastern section (Callander to Winnipeg) can best be seen from a few figures.

1883: 100 miles completed west of Callander; 35 miles completed near Port Arthur; trains running between Port Arthur and Red River (the government-built section).

1884: track laid for 403 out of 657 miles between Callander and Port Arthur; 193 miles in addition graded; train service between Callander and Sudbury.

1885: rail completed in May; passenger service in November.

The central or prairie section, from Winnipeg to Kamloops, was constructed almost entirely by the company. Here the change in route was complete, consequent on the decision to adopt a southerly line. One of the reasons given for the change was that the line could in this way be shortened, but a more fundamental consider-

25. *Ibid.*, Stephen to Macdonald, August 27, 1882.

ation was the desire to be closer to the American border. Such a position would bring two benefits: it would enable the company to compete for American traffic, and protect its American connections after the twenty-year restrictions had run out. It is also possible that Donald Smith's influence was thrown in favour of a southern route in order to protect the northern fur country from invasion. Furthermore, the company may have been influenced by the consideration that the grains then available would not ripen quickly enough to make a safe crop in the more northern part of the prairies. Thus the line was directed toward Calgary rather than Edmonton. It was commonly supposed to be a comparatively simple task to build a railway over the prairie—and was simple compared with other sections—but Stephen claimed that conditions were not so easy as they had been represented to be: "The so-called Prairie section is not prairie at all, it is a broken, rolling country, with a great deal of heavy work, and the line we are building is a very different thing from the standard fixed and costing double the price of a poor Prairie road."[26] Large parts of the prairie, however, were easy going, and the company was able to show quick results. In the first summer, 1881, only a modest hundred miles were completed, but in the second season the company was determined to build five hundred miles— an objective which seemed impossible to attain. In the summer of 1882 five thousand men and seventeen hundred teams were at work. Night gangs were put on the bridges, and to bring up the rails and lumber. The five-hundred mark was not quite reached that year, but by June 1883 the track was laid as far as the summit of the Rockies.

The choice of a southern route necessitated the abandonment of the Yellowhead Pass. In 1881 this change was decided on, and in 1882 an act was passed enabling the company to build through a pass other than the Yellowhead, provided it was not less than one hundred miles from the boundary (45 Vict., c. 53). The junction with the government-built section would, as before, be made at Kamloops. To reach this point it was necessary to cross two ranges of mountains—the Rockies and the Selkirks. Through the first a comparatively satisfactory pass, the Kicking Horse, had been found. It entailed a grade that was heavy com-

26. *Ibid.*, Same to same, August 27, 1882.

pared to the easy ascent at the Yellowhead; but the company was willing to accept this added cost of operation rather than go so far north. But on the other side of the Rockies lay the great rounded slopes of the Selkirks, through which no way had yet been dis- covered. Major Rogers, an American engineer, was sent to reconnoitre, but 1881 passed with Rogers optimistic but unsuccess- ful. In the meanwhile the railway was approaching the mountain, and unless the Selkirks could be pierced a long detour by the Columbia River would have to be taken. In the summer of 1882, however, Rogers at last found the pass (named after him) and it became possible to follow the direct line.

A good deal of heavy work—tunnels, trestles and blasting—was unavoidable through the mountains. To hasten the completion of the line the company was empowered to construct a temporary line for some nine miles. Of Van Horne, who was furiously working to get the line completed, a characteristic story is told which may be repeated here. A locating engineer was called to his office, and pointing to a profile, Van Horne said, "some infernal idiot has put a tunnel in there. I want you to go and take it out." Asked how long it would take to build, the engineer suggested a year or eighteen months. "What are they thinking about?" roared the general manager, "Are we going to hold up this railway for a year and a half while they build their damned tunnel? Take it out." Another way was found.[27]

In October 1885 the line was open for traffic up to the east slope of the Rockies, and by November rail connection was established from Montreal to Port Moody (2,893 miles). From Kamloops to Port Moody was the section constructed by the government, and part of this, near Yale, had been difficult and heavy work. During the early 'eighties, therefore, the British Columbia section was being constructed partly by the company and partly by the govern- ment. The whole was, of course, to be operated by the company: the government-built section to be handed over as part of the original agreement, the company accepting it "subject to the adjustment and correction by the Government of any defects or deficiencies in the construction thereof, if any, according to the specifications and conditions of the contracts therefor, except

27. Vaughan, op. cit., p. 87.

in so far as the same were modified by the Government prior to October twenty-first, 1880." When the section was duly handed over the company protested that it had not been built according to specifications, and to settle the dispute that arose an arbitration board was set up by order in council in January 1888. Van Horne asserted to the board that the road was not safe for use,[28] while Schreiber, the government's chief engineer, admitted, according to Van Horne's account, that the road was not as described in the contract or specifications.[29] The government, however, contended that their section was better built than that of the company; but nevertheless J. H. Pope (minister of railways) insisted that it should be examined, in accordance with the Railway Act. The arbitration proceedings dragged on until 1891, the delay, according to Stephen, being engineered by the government "to put the Company to all the loss and inconvenience that delay involves."[30] The award was made in October 1891 and named $579,255 as the sum payable by the government, representing the cost of work that should have been done on the road. The Canadian Pacific Railway had claimed $12,000,000.

While Van Horne had been directing the work of construction on the spot, and Shaughnessy[31] was in charge of sending out the enormous amounts of supplies that were needed, Stephen and Donald Smith were struggling to provide the sinews of war. Owing to the speed of construction the sums of money annually required by the company were very large and not easy to raise. Since it had been decided not to finance construction by the sale of bonds, there were left four main sources of revenue: sale of lands, sale of land-grant bonds, sale of stock, and the government subsidy. Had the first three of these consistently realized good prices there would have been no great problem, but they were far from doing so. There were a number of factors operating to

28. Canadian Archives, Macdonald papers, "J. H. Pope," Schreiber to Pope, July 22, 1888.

29. *Ibid.*, "Van Horne," Van Horne to Stephen, July 24, 1888.

30. *Ibid.*, "Stephen," Stephen to Macdonald, September 3, 1889.

31. T. G. Shaughnessy had been general storekeeper of the Chicago, Milwaukee and St. Paul Railway. At Van Horne's suggestion, he became general purchasing agent of the C.P.R.

depress prices: a lingering suspicion of Canadian railway securities; stories of the inhospitable climate, poor soil and doubtful future of the Canadian west; and the bankruptcy of the Northern Pacific in 1883. Enemies of the Canadian Pacific did their best to exploit such factors with a view to smashing or crippling the new railway. In England the wide influence of the Grand Trunk was once more directed against a potential rival, and the English public, who were more interested in Barnum's elephant, Jumbo, than in Canada, were supplied with news tending to show that the west was unsuitable for settlement.[32] (It is ironic that poor Jumbo was later killed by a Grand Trunk engine.) "The worst feature for us in Canada is that there is hardly a newspaper in the whole country which is in a position to say a word against the G.T.R. no matter what it may say or do against the country—without losing Hickson's advertizing."[33] At the same time the New York market was hostile, it is said because of the propaganda of Hill's and the other railways of the American north-west. The stock dropped from par to forty. Various expedients were adopted to keep going, but by the end of 1883 Stephen was almost in despair. "Things have gone to the d—l in New York," he wrote, "something must be done at *once* to put the company out of discredit or we better give up and let the govt step in and carry on the business of the company. . . . Things have now reached a pass when we must either stop or find the means of going on. Our enemies here and elsewhere think they can now break us down or finish the C.P.R. for ever."[34]

The cost of construction was mounting far beyond the estimates. Ten years earlier Fleming had put the cost of construction and equipment at $100,000,000, but it had become obvious that this would not nearly meet the bill. The company was thus thrown back on the government for support; and while in his more depressed moments Stephen bitterly reproached Macdonald for lack of support, the company would have failed time after time if it had not been carried over crises by public funds. But it was no

32. Canadian Archives, Macdonald papers, "Stephen," i, Stephen to Macdonald, February 26, 1882.
33. *Ibid.*, Same to same, January 4, 1883.
34. *Ibid.*, Same to same, December 15, 1883.

simple matter to provide constant loans. The cabinet was divided
in regard to the Canadian Pacific Railway. Tupper was a staunch
believer, but Campbell, McLelan, and Mackenzie Bowell were, at
least on one occasion, opposed to further relief.[35] Parliament was
equally uncertain, and Macdonald could not assume an automatic
majority for Pacific loans. An influential section of the press, too,
constantly sounded warnings of the danger of unlimited credit
to the company. There were suspicions that the recurrent crises
in the finances of the Canadian Pacific were magnified in order to
induce further governmental assistance. In the end the government always made the required loans, but it seems that Macdonald
grew wearied of Stephen's constant importunities and was not
willing to move until he was sure that it was necessary. Tupper,
on the other hand, appears to have been more ready to accept the
company's account of its own position; and when the time came
for putting loans through parliament, he was invaluable. At the
end of 1883 he was hurriedly called back from England, and
obtained from the commons a loan of $22,500,000 for four years
at four per cent, secured by a first lien on the main line. The
company subsequently (March) agreed to complete its line by
1886 instead of 1891—a declaration which was valuable to stem
the rising tide of opposition. In the meanwhile the company was
living from hand to mouth. Large advances from the Bank of
Montreal had to be covered by collateral security put up by
Stephen and Smith, and Stephen said that he was afraid to ask for
more lest there should be "a bear raid on the Bank stock, on the
ground of heavy advances to the C.P.R. without adequate cover."[36]
    One financial crisis succeeded another. The heavy expenses of
1884 brought the company once more to the end of its resources.
In December the men struck for their pay at Port Arthur. More
money was needed. Macdonald was alarmed at further demands,
for the previous loan was to have been the last, and too much
pressure on parliament would mean the collapse of the government
—and with it the C.P.R. He talked over the situation in London
with Tupper, now high commissioner, and Tupper wrote a reasoned

    35. E. M. Saunders, *op. cit.*, i, 45.
    36. Canadian Archives, Macdonald papers, "Stephen," Stephen to Macdonald,
December 23, 1883.

statement to the minister of finance, Sir Leonard Tilley, in which
he confessed that he was disappointed that further assistance was
required, but argued that either the government must take over
the road and run it—to which he was opposed—or "meet the difficulty caused by the complete collapse of the credit of the Co."
He advocated cancelling the $35,000,000 of unissued stock, and
providing for $40,000,000 of first mortgage bonds, taking
$30,000,000 in payment of the loan, giving $5,000,000 to the
company and holding the remaining $5,000,000 for future needs
of the road.[37] Sir John Rose gave much the same advice, pointing
out that it was not a good time to raise money.[38] Stephen was afraid
that "the patient will die while the doctors are deliberating on the
remedy to be applied," but managed another advance from the
bank, secured on his and Smith's securities.[39] In March he reported
that the company was still in the "greatest straits," and in April
Van Horne telegraphed that he had no money with which to pay
wages.

All during the spring it seems to have been touch and go. The
Bank of Montreal's last loan had covered the April dividend, but
the stock was driven down to 34, and complaints were being made
of wages unpaid. In March Stephen formally wrote to the prime
minister asking for terms very similar to those sketched out by
Tupper, and including the $5,000,000 loan. Macdonald was
undecided. Could he again persuade parliament? A sign was
needed, and happily provided in the ability of the Canadian Pacific
Railway to transport troops to put down the North-West Rebellion.
Until navigation opened on the lakes there was no feasible means
of getting troops rapidly to the west. Seeing the possibilities of
the situation, Van Horne offered to transport troops from Ottawa
to Qu'Appelle in eleven or twelve days. It was the kind of problem
of organization in which he revelled, and, although there were still
gaps in the line, he had two batteries at Winnipeg in four days
from the time they left Ottawa. Whether it was because of this
demonstration or other influences within the cabinet, the government finally acceded to the company's request. Macdonald got

37. *Ibid.*, "Railways," ix, Tupper to Tilley, November 28, 1884.
38. *Ibid.*, Rose to Macdonald, December 2, 1884.
39. *Ibid.*, "Stephen," Stephen to Macdonald, January 14 and February 3, 1885.

the measure through the caucus, with the loss of A. W. McLelan, minister of marine and fisheries. In July the bill was finally passed. The terms were somewhat more favourable than Tupper had first suggested. The stock in the hands of the government was cancelled, and $35,000,000 created in its place. Of this $15,000,000 was credited to the company, and the balance held against an equal amount of the company's debt to the government. The remainder of the debt—$9,880,000—was secured on the unsold and unpledged lands of the company. Of the company's share $8,000,000 was held by the government against a loan of $5,000,000 cash. The financial standing of the company was strengthened by the purchase by Barings of $3,000,000 of bonds at 90; and while only about one-half of these were taken by the public, the fact that Barings and their friends were holding the rest was not disclosed. The price was maintained at about 96.[40]

It had been a near thing, but at last the company was out of the wood, and in the summer of 1886 the entire debt to the government was paid off. With the knowledge of later years it was easy to cast scorn on the doubts of those who opposed the Pacific railway in the form in which the Conservative government had begun it, and easy to criticize those—Liberal and Conservative—who lost heart while construction was making ever-increasing demands on the exchequer. But to all but a few enthusiasts it was always, or became, a hazardous experiment. A thinly populated east, throwing a railway over two thousand miles of almost uninhabited country, was not to be taken lightly. And it is only fair to remember that the same controversy arose over the later transcontinental lines, and while the optimists again won the day, the country was later bitterly to regret a Pyrrhic victory. No little credit is due to the Canadian Pacific group—or those of them who stuck to their task—led by Stephen, Smith, Van Horne, and Shaughnessy, who had the courage to risk their fortunes and their reputations in what not once, but many times, seemed a hopeless cause. And credit, too, is due to the government which (in the face of strong opposition, and under the shadow of disastrous failure,) made it possible for the railway builders to complete their work. Perhaps it was partly fear of the political consequences that led the majority

40. *Ibid.*, Same to same, October 3, 1885.

in the cabinet to keep their hand to the plough; yet Macdonald, with as keen a political sense as has been seen in Canada, feared a hostile vote in the house of commons. The completion of the most daring enterprise undertaken by the Dominion was made possible only by a successful (if somewhat tempestuous) marriage of private enterprise with public support. Without the first the railway had languished: without the second it must have crashed into bankruptcy.

November 7, 1885. "The first train from Montreal is approaching Yale, within a few hours of the Pacific coast. The last spike was driven this morning by Honourable Donald Smith at Craigellachie, in Eagle Pass, some 340 miles from Port Moody. On reaching the coast, our running time from Montreal, exclusive of stoppages, will be five days, averaging twenty-four miles per hour."

And so a prophecy was fulfilled. By the writer, surveyor, navvy, politician, financier, and engineer, it was brought to pass that they should have dominion from sea to sea.

CHAPTER IX

CONSEQUENCES OF THE PACIFIC RAILWAY

1. EFFECT ON THE GENERAL POSITION

THE first train that ran from Montreal to the Pacific coast was the herald of a new era in the history of Canadian railways, an era that was marked by two main characteristics: the development of transcontinental traffic across Canada; and active competition between large companies, which in the course of that competition absorbed the smaller lines. From these twin impulses came a growth in railways that was all the more remarkable in that it came under conditions which were far from being uniformly favourable. Broadly speaking, the period from confederation to the turn of the century saw a series of economic depressions, the spaces between which were all too brief. Population increased at a sedate pace from 3,689,257 in 1871 to 4,833,239 in 1891. The number of immigrants, which was only 27,773 in 1871, and never reached high figures in the next ten years, jumped to over 100,000 in each of 1882, 1883, and 1884, that is, the years in which the main work of construction on the Canadian Pacific Railway was under way. Canada was still predominantly an agricultural country, sixty-eight per cent of the population living outside towns in 1891. The area of occupied farms increased from 36,046,401 acres in 1871 to 58,997,995 in 1891—the increased rate of settlement corresponding to the rise in immigration, both of which were primarily due to the opening of farming areas in the west. By 1891 the annual value of mineral production was still slightly less than $19,000,000, and the lumber trade was steadily advancing. Although the larger part of the population was still rural, the chief change that was taking place in the Canadian economy was the gradual increase of urban areas and of the industrial concerns on which they depended. The "national policy" of 1878 was designed to raise the tariff against imports sufficiently to protect infant industries, and this policy was modified rather than altered by the Liberal administrations after 1896. In the twenty years from 1870 to 1890 the gross value of manufactured goods mounted from $221,617,773 to $481,053,375.

The growth of railways did not spring from an existing prosperity but from a belief, generally held, that Canada could only progress if an adequate transportation system was built up. This belief was translated into concrete terms by the willingness of the legislatures to render financial assistance. Cities made substantial grants. The provinces of Quebec and Ontario adopted, in 1869 and 1871 respectively, policies of subsidies to local railways, either in money or in land. In 1882 the Dominion government introduced its own subsidy policy, which in effect replaced those of the provinces. The measure provided for a grant of $3,200 a mile (the cost of steel rails) to selected railways distributed amongst the four original provinces. Two years later the system was extended to the western provinces, land taking the place of cash. Payments made under the subsidy policy, which were in some cases higher than the general rate, averaged one million dollars a year. A drawback to this method of encouragement was that it tended to be directed by sectional or party interests rather than by genuine needs. A further objection was that investors were mistakenly reassured by the stamp of government approval apparently involved in a subsidy. A company which received $400,000 in subsidies stimulated the sale of $500,000 of its bonds in England by a statement that the capacity of the road was taxed to the utmost. The equipment of the company consisted of two engines, one passenger car, two box cars, fifteen flat cars, and a snow-plough![1]

Government support, however, did not mean government owner-ship. The experience of governmental construction on the Pacific railway had not been a happy one, and for a time discouraged all further experiments except in additions to the Intercolonial. Both the Grand Trunk and Great Western offered to sell out to the government, but their offers were firmly refused. "We have a sufficiently big elephant in the Pacific Railway," wrote Blake, "without undertaking to become the proprietors of other lines. . . . Mr. Childers [president of the Great Western] may be right in his view that Canadian credit will suffer somewhat by calamities

1. O. D. Skelton, *The railway builders* (Toronto, 1920), p. 171.

overtaking private corporations, but I am sure it would suffer much more by our purchasing great railways which are known to be in very great straits."[2] The tendency was toward private companies assisted by public funds. Such companies, however, were subject to an increasing degree of regulation. The first federal statute applying to all railways chartered by the Dominion, the Railway Act of 1868 (31 Vict., c.68), was modelled on the province of Canada act of 1851. In addition to provisions similar to those of the latter, the act of 1868 included new ones: any company might make special traffic arrangements with another, but must also afford reasonable facilities to the remaining companies without discrimination. The interests of the country in a national emergency were protected by a clause which reserved for the government, when necessary, the exclusive use of both telegraphs and railways. Various penalties were provided for persons interfering with or damaging the property of a railway, and for officers of the company who contravened its by-laws.

For the continuous supervision of the private railway companies a special body was set up, the railway committee of the privy council, to consist of not less than four members, and whose particular duty it was to ensure the safe operation of the railways. No railway or portion of railway might be opened for traffic without a month's notice to the committee, which might then have an inspection made by the department of public works, and if necessary the opening of the line could be delayed. The committee might also have any railway examined when in operation, and—with the consent of the governor in council—condemn all or part of it. The inspecting engineer might also on his own authority stop the operation of a railway and report his action to the committee. Every railway was to contribute an amount, to be fixed by the committee and not to exceed $10 a mile, to the railway inspection fund. It must also make returns twice a year of all accidents. In 1886 the control of rates, which up to that time had been left to free competition (with the exception of maxima set in some of the early charters), was assigned also to the committee.

For the first twelve years after confederation there was no separate minister or department within the federal government

2. Canadian Archives, Mackenzie papers, Blake to Dufferin, January 6, 1876.

to deal with railway matters, which were in that period handled by the department of public works. With increasing mileage, however, and particularly with the construction of the Pacific railway, the work became important enough to justify the establishment of the department of railways and canals in 1879, with a minister holding that portfolio alone.

The progress of railway building in the generation after confederation was rapid, though not nearly so rapid as the granting of charters. In 1867 the total mileage of railways operating in Canada was 2,278, having increased by only 200 miles in ten years. By 1881 it had risen to 7,331, which included the Intercolonial, but only a small part of the Canadian Pacific Railway, and by 1900 it was 17,657. More than 15,000 miles of railway were brought into operation in thirty years. Increased traffic led to the necessity of double tracks and the acceptance of a standard gauge (four feet, eight and one-half inches). Larger engines were procured, and coal was gradually adopted as a more efficient fuel than wood. Snowploughs reduced the loss of time due to drifts, and night travel was made more attractive by the introduction of Pullman sleeping cars in 1870. More elaborate stations were built to take care of growing traffic, such as the Union Station at Toronto (later replaced)—an unhappy example of the architecture of the age—which was opened in 1873, and described as "capacious and elegant."

Running through this general story of growth may be seen the attempt of the Canadian Pacific Railway to secure control of a complete transcontinental line, and to make that line pay by providing enough traffic for it. In the pursuit of this aim the company was determined to secure some hold over southern Ontario and Quebec, the area in which railway activity was already most conspicuous. Companies, large and small, were adding to their mileage; but already the tendency was for the absorption of the smaller by the larger. The picture there is important both in itself and as the main field of battle of the two great companies. In the western part of Ontario the Wellington, Grey and Bruce was built in 1870–1874 from Guelph northward, breaking into two forks to the ports of Southampton and Kincardine on Lake Huron. On completion it was absorbed by the Great Western. A railway with

a similar name and in the same area was the Toronto, Grey and
Bruce, the main line of which ran (1873) from Toronto to Owen
Sound, thus covering the portage route between the lower lakes
and Lake Superior. A branch ran north-westerly to Teeswater on
the Wellington, Grey and Bruce. From Wingham, near Teeswater,
the London, Huron and Bruce ran south-west to London. The
Hamilton and North Western was built in 1878 from Hamilton to
Barrie and thence to Midland on Georgian Bay. In 1879 it amal-
gamated with the Northern. A railway which was important
because of its place in the C.P.R.-G.T.R. struggle was the Credit
Valley from Streetsville to Orangeville, and the longer line from
Toronto to St. Thomas (1881). These, with the lines of the Grand
Trunk, the Great Western, and the Canada Southern, made up
the chief railway services in the western part of the province.

In central Ontario there were two important railways in addition
to the Grand Trunk: the Northern and the Midland, the latter of
which had only reached Lindsay before 1867. It was carried on past
the east side of Lake Simcoe to Midland. The Northern, a
railway built before confederation as far as Collingwood,
expanded into a considerable size in the 'seventies and 'eighties.
Taking over the Hamilton and North Western in 1879, its
name was changed to the Northern and North Western (which
was perhaps just as well as its affairs became so suspicious that a
royal commission was appointed to examine it in 1876, and found
that improper payments had been made from its funds.) Its tracks
were from Port Dover, through Hamilton and Barrie to Collingwood and Meaford; and another line from Toronto to Barrie,
where it forked to Midland and Gravenhurst. In 1884 it had 377
miles in operation. In 1886 it reached North Bay.

Between Port Hope and Kingston there were few railways except
the main lines of the Grand Trunk and Canadian Pacific. From
Kingston the Kingston and Pembroke ran north into Lanark
County. The Brockville and Ottawa was extended to connect with
the latter city, and, as the Canada Central, to the north-west
as far as Callander (1882), just after having been purchased by the
Canadian Pacific Railway in the previous year. Across eastern
Ontario, from the Ottawa River to Georgian Bay, was the Ottawa,

Arnprior and Parry Sound Railway (1896), taking a northerly line through a sparsely settled part of the province.

In the province of Quebec a new railway with an imposing name and an important strategic position was the Quebec, Montreal, Ottawa and Occidental. The North Shore, as this was more briefly called, was a combination under the provincial government of two private companies which had failed to raise enough capital to carry on construction. One of the reasons for failure was the opposition of the Grand Trunk, actuated by the knowledge that the whole scheme was intended to draw western traffic to the city of Quebec. By 1879 the line was complete from Quebec to Ottawa, and branches were added in the next few years. An important pioneer and lumber road was the Quebec and Lake St. John, which ran nearly two hundred miles north from Quebec to Roberval on the shore of the lake. Completed to that point in 1888, it was extended eastward to Chicoutimi on the upper Saguenay in 1894. To the south of the St. Lawrence the Atlantic and North West, which absorbed the International, ran from Lachine through Sherbrooke and Megantic to the border of Maine, and thence easterly to Mattawamkeag. Leased from 1886 by the C.P.R., it became a part of the Short Line to St. John. From Sherbrooke to Lévis was the Quebec Central (1884).

Such were the most important railways in the central provinces, with the exception of three which have a peculiar interest. In western Ontario the Great Western was the pioneer trunk line. One of its purposes was to handle local traffic in a well-settled country, and to carry out this policy it expanded its lines built in the 'fifties by absorbing the London and Port Stanley (1875), the Wellington, Grey and Bruce, and the London, Huron and Bruce in 1876, and the Brantford, Norfolk and Port Burwell in 1878. But the search for local traffic was the least of the ambitions of the Great Western, for it was designed, too, to act as a trunk line serving not only Canadian, but also American through traffic. In this it met two obstacles: the competition of the Grand Trunk, which had invaded its territory, and a further threat from an American railway, the Canada Southern, completed from Windsor to the Niagara River in 1873. The prospectus of the Canada Southern explains that the railway is "to form with other Roads a cheap line of Traffic between Chicago and New York, so located and constructed as to reduce the cost of transporting the products of the Interior to the lowest limit." The line is said to be "practically level and straight to tide water." It is to connect with other railways at each end, and "will thus be a connecting link between two great systems of roads, which can now supply to it, at either end, a traffic equal to its utmost capacity." This reads strangely like the original prospectus of the Great Western. To meet this last challenge the Great Western built an "air line" (that is, one taking a comparatively straight course) from Fort Erie, near Welland, and cutting across the southern part of the peninsula to join up with the main London-Windsor line at Glencoe. The air line, however, was not a panacea. The Great Western, and the Grand Trunk as well, began to suffer heavy losses from rate wars with each other and with competing American lines. In 1869 the two Canadian companies agreed to maintain equal rates and to pool competitive Canadian traffic; but this, with other similar agreements, did not prove to be lasting. Following the failure of the attempt of each company to sell out to the government, amalgamation of the two roads began to be discussed in 1876, but it was not until 1882, when competition from the C.P.R. created a pressure, that it was accomplished.

The condition of the Grand Trunk, which had been so critical in the 'sixties, was still such as to give alarm to its directors and shareholders. In general the position had not materially altered; revenues were low, expenses high, shareholders clamorous for dividends, and there was a crying need for expenditure on the property. It is unfortunate that most of the available comments on the history of the Grand Trunk are from hostile or at least unsympathetic pens, but the causes of what was a general unpopularity are not far to seek. Although the railway had done essential pioneer work in the development of Canada, it had never been a Canadian enterprise. Foisted on a dazed legislature and public by the ingenuity of Hincks and the spell-binding of Jackson, its management had been steadily removed from Canada, while at the same time it had called—and successfully called—for privileges and subsidies from the Canadian government. On the other side of the Atlantic the Grand Trunk was conceived of as a distant enterprise for earning dividends on the capital that had been poured into it; and when it failed to earn dividends it met with no sympathy.

The Grand Trunk had a heavy capital structure, and while an effort had been made by the Arrangements Act of 1862 to reduce the bonded indebtedness, there was a constant pressure to take the scanty operating profits for dividends instead of improvements, and to add further issues of stocks or bonds. Secondly, the railway had been built at great expense, but defects were constantly appearing in the line itself and the equipment, and the executive were never able to secure sufficient funds to repair these weaknesses. The revenues from operation were not enough to justify the expensive machine that had been built up. The Grand Trunk was primarily designed for through traffic, but had never been able to secure a sufficient volume. The plan of using its road as part of an American through route was, as has been shown, not a success; and the Grand Trunk consistently refused to build into the Canadian west unless allowed to go south of Lake Superior. Finally, it may be noticed that the directors in England were handicapped by a lack of understanding of Canadian conditions, and the divided rule introduced a complicated relation with executive officers resident in Canada. The Grand Trunk was served by individuals of considerable ability, but from the circumstances of its organization was never able to develop an *esprit de corps* or a continuous personnel: the latter partly because of periodic and acute differences of opinion between presidents, general managers, directors and shareholders.

After one such difference, Sir Edward Watkin retired as president in 1869, and was succeeded by Mr. Richard Potter, chairman of the Great Western Railway of England. Potter spent three months of the year of his appointment in Canada, going over the property. On his return he stated his belief that "the only safe and prudent course as a matter of account keeping and as a matter of policy is that when a railway is maintained all renewals which do not add to the extra accommodation of the railway properly belong to revenue."[3] He pointed to ballasting, new rails, and new cars as proper objects for the scanty surplus. But Potter received little support, and the revenue was still diverted to dividends. In 1872

3. H. A. Lovett, *Canada and the Grand Trunk* (Montreal, 1924), p. 83.

the president inspected the road in company with Mr. Allport, general manager of the Midland Railway of England; and Allport's impression was gloomy: "I am bound to say that it has not been my experience, I think, ever to have gone over a worse line,—a line in a worse condition than a great portion of the Grand Trunk."[4] To the heavy expenses of laying steel rails in place of iron ones, re-ballasting, and other necessary works, was added a new financial difficulty. The Arrangements Act of 1862 created a "suspense period" of ten years during which the first and second preference bonds and stocks would pay only five per cent, and no legal action could be taken in respect of these securities. In 1872 that period would come to an end and the capitalization of dividend and interest would cease.

Potter's comments on the state of the road were as grave as Allport's. He reported that some six hundred miles of the line were in a dangerous condition, and that two hundred and fifty miles did not pay working expenses. The whole position of the company he regarded as critical, and—after consultation with the board and some of the proprietors—made the following suggestions for financial adjustment: that there should be issued an additional £600,000 of equipment mortgage bonds, a re-issue of £410,000 of Atlantic and St. Lawrence guaranteed stock, and an extension of the Arrangements Act. To this Mr. Baring and Lord Wolverton had agreed, after a last attempt to protect the bondholders. There now appeared on the scene a syndicate who were ready to issue a large amount of common stock. The men concerned were Alexander McEwen, a Scot, and Baron (Albert) Grant, both of whom had had colourful financial careers. Whether they first approached the Grand Trunk, or the Grand Trunk them, is not clear; but it is certain that they offered to issue £10,000,000 of common stock.[5] After an agreement had been reached between the Grand Trunk executive and the syndicate, an act was passed through the Canadian parliament in 1873 (36 Vict., c.18), extending the suspense period for three years, but raising the rate of interest to six per cent. The company was empowered to issue second equipment mortgage bonds up to £1,100,000 and common stock

4. *Ibid.*, 89.

5. Joseph Nelson, *The very latest Grand Trunk scheme* (London, 1873).

DOMINION OF CANADA

SHOWING THE RAILWAYS AS THEY EXISTED IN 1886

A description of the different lines, showing under which system they were operated, and from whom acquired.

Number on map	Name of Railway
	CANADIAN PACIFIC RAILWAY
	composed of:
88	Own original roads.
54	Brockville & Ottawa.
55	Canada Central.
89	Dominion Government.
	South Eastern
36	Own original roads.
33	Mississquoi & Clyde River Railway.
38	Lake Champlain & St. Lawrence Jc.
39	Montreal, Portland & Boston.
47	Quebec, Montreal, Ottawa & Occidental (North Shore).
73	Credit Valley.
53	Ottawa & Prescott (St. Lawrence & Ottawa).
	Ontario & Quebec.
57	Original roads.
72	Toronto, Grey & Bruce.
91	Manitoba South Western Colonization.
	Atlantic & North West Railway.
31	International Quebec.

Number on map	Name of Railway
	GRAND TRUNK RAILWAY
	composed of:
75	Own original roads.
	Champlain & St. Lawrence.
42	Own original roads.
43	Montreal & Champlain.
	Northern & North Western.
69	Northern Railway of Canada.
71	Hamilton & North Western.
83	Buffalo & Lake Huron.
	Great Western.
74	Own original roads (Galt & Guelph, 1852).
81	London & Port Stanley.
86	Welland.
76	Wellington Grey & Bruce.
79	London, Huron & Bruce.
85	Brantford, Norfolk & Port Burwell.
	Midland.
64	Own original roads.
	Toronto & Nipissing.
67	Own original road.
68	Lake Simcoe Jc.
66	Whitby, Port Perry & Lindsay.
65	Victoria Railway.
59	Grand Junction.
61	Belleville & North Hastings.
	Grand Trunk, Georgian Bay & Lake Erie.
78	Own original roads.
82	Port Dover & Lake Huron.
77	Stratford & Huron.
44	Montreal & Champlain Jc.
45	Montreal & Sorel.
	Canada Southern

Number on map	Name of Railway
84	Own original roads.
87	Erie & Ontario.
48	St. Lawrence & Industry.
63	Cobourg & Peterborough.
51	Carillon & Grenville.
37	Central Vermont (Leased from Stanstead, Shefford & Chambly).
41	Montreal & Vermont Jc.
32	Connecticut & Passumpsic Rlwy. (Massawippi Valley).
46	Quebec & Gosford.
35	South Eastern.
34	Waterloo & Magog.
29	Quebec Central.
28	Levis & Kennebec.
58	Napanee, Tamworth & Quebec.
52	Canada Atlantic.
56	Kingston & Pembroke.
93	Manitoba & North Western
92	Portage, Westbourne & North Western.
94	North Western Coal & Navigation Co.
49	Great Northern Railway of Canada.

Number on map	Name of Railway
	INTERCOLONIAL
12	Own original roads.
	Nova Scotia.
4	Own original roads.
9	European & North American (a part).
17	Chatham Branch.
8	Cumberland Railway & Coal Co.
3	Halifax & Cape Breton Railway & Coal Co. (Eastern Extension).
27	Grand Trunk.
14	Petitcodiac & Elgin (Elgin, Petitcodiac & Havelock).
13	Albert.
15	St. Martins & Upham.
	New Brunswick Railway.
24	Own original roads.
22	New Brunswick Railway Construction Co.
23	New Brunswick & Canada.
	St. John & Maine.
18	European & North American (a part).
21	Fredericton.
6	Windsor & Annapolis.
5	Prince Edward Island.
2	Sydney & Louisburg.
	Aroostook River Railroad.
25	New Brunswick (part).
7	Western Counties (later Yarmouth Annapolis).
19	Grand Southern.
16	Kent Northern.
62	Central Ontario.
62	Prince Edward County.

to a maximum of £10,000,000. The bonds and preference stock were again re-arranged so as to create stock instead of bonds, and thus postpone a reckoning. The effects of the reorganization of 1873 were twofold: on the one hand important improvements were made on the road in the laying of steel rails and new ballast, and changing the gauge to standard; and on the other the capital structure was made even more top-heavy. It was apparently a year or so after the act of 1873 that the company was offered for sale to the government, so that it was not yet in smooth waters.

Potter was not long to remain in office to watch the effects of his planning, for in 1876 he was forced to retire after a break with Joseph Hickson (the new general manager) and the board. The new president was Sir Henry Tyler, an engineer who had been a member of the Grand Trunk board. In the year in which Tyler took office, General M. B. Hewson, an engineer with Canadian and American experience, set out to find the causes of the difficulties of the Grand Trunk. The trouble, he believed, was not due to over-building, for Ontario had less mileage of rail in proportion to population than Maine or Michigan, half that of New Hampshire and one-third of that of Minnesota. Nor was the climate more rigorous than that of several American states. The receipts from traffic per mile compared favourably with American roads, but not the working expenses. The following comparison illustrates the latter point:

	Mileage	Operating ratio
All lines in Michigan	1,904	62.5%
Great Western of Canada	444	59.7%
Grand Trunk	1,377	80.4%

Finding no other cause, the author attributed the troubles of the Grand Trunk principally to faulty management, citing such instances as the building of the Victoria bridge, leasing the Buffalo and Lake Huron Railway, leasing the bankrupt Montreal and Champlain Railway, and the Atlantic and St. Lawrence on unfavourable terms. He calculated that the Grand Trunk had hired 4,291 freight cars while needing only 1,222. Finally he criticized the centralization of the management at Montreal, arguing that it was impossible for the general manager to exercise real supervision over the whole road.[6]

6. M. B. Hewson, *The Grand Trunk Railway of Canada* (Toronto, 1876.)

Yet, if the Grand Trunk was suffering from problems of finance and management, it did not pause in its growth. By 1881 the Rivière du Loup section had been disposed of to the government and a line to Chicago acquired. Amalgamation with the Great Western in 1882 gave it valuable new lines and obviated expensive competition. The addition of the Midland and other smaller railways gave a total mileage of 2,856 in 1884. The company began to lay double tracks on its main line in 1888, and completed the work between Toronto and Hamilton in 1892, between Montreal and Toronto, and Hamilton and Suspension Bridge in 1903. The important communication with Michigan was greatly improved by the boring of a tunnel under the St. Clair River, from Sarnia to Port Huron, begun in 1889 and completed two years later. Such growth and improvements were largely inspired by the threat from the expanding Canadian Pacific Railway.

2. Expansion of the Canadian Pacific in the East

The charter of the Canadian Pacific provided for the construction of a railway from Callander on Lake Nipissing to the Pacific Ocean, but it was manifestly impossible that a railway could remain poised in mid-air in northern Ontario: the question was how connections were to be established with the ports and industrial areas of eastern Canada. The terms of the charter also empowered it to acquire the Canada Central and "to obtain, hold, and operate a line or lines of railway from Ottawa to any point at navigable water on the Atlantic seaboard, or to any intermediate point." With these comprehensive powers, the company began a rapid and calculated policy of eastward expansion. The Canada Central was bought in 1881, and its completion taken in hand. In the same year the Brockville and Ottawa was acquired, and in 1884 the St. Lawrence and Ottawa—the latter being a direct line between Ottawa and Prescott.

By these means the Canadian Pacific Railway had reached two important river ports as well as the capital, but it was also considered essential to extend to Toronto and the south-western part of the province on the one hand, and to Montreal and tidewater on the other. The first object was secured by building a line (at first under the name of another company) from Smiths Falls on the Canada Central through to Toronto. The territory west of Toronto was covered by the acquisition of the Toronto, Grey and Bruce, the Credit Valley, from Toronto to St. Thomas, and an extension from there to Windsor. To reach Montreal the C.P.R. bought from the province of Quebec the western section of the North Shore Railway (from Ottawa to Montreal), and later—by threatening to build a parallel road—the eastern section to Quebec from the Grand Trunk.

It remained to secure a direct line from Toronto to Sudbury, to tap the eastern townships, enter the Maritime Provinces, and secure a winter port. For a time the company contemplated following the example of the Grand Trunk and acquiring a line to Portland. That municipality was ready to sell its interest in the Portland and Ogdensburg Railroad, and so in the autumn of 1883, Stephen and Abbott (the company's solicitor) visited Portland and discussed with the city council the possibility of purchase by the Canadian Pacific Railway. "It is not unnatural," Stephen said to the council, "having reached Montreal, and, as you are well aware, Montreal being only a six-months port, we should be looking to the question of reaching the Atlantic, and it is not unnatural that our eyes should be cast upon the most direct way. . . ."[7] Nothing came of the negotiations, however, and as an alternative the company proceeded to secure a route to the American border only. In 1883 they obtained possession of the South-Eastern Railway, which ran from Farnham to Newport, just across the border; and from Farnham to Montreal opened a new line. At Newport connections were made with American railways to Boston and Portland.

Access to American ports over American railways was not enough for the Canadian Pacific, or to satisfy opinion in the Maritime Provinces. In a letter to Tupper, Van Horne wrote that "we were pressed into the 'Short Line' scheme by the Government to meet the wishes of the people of the Maritime Provinces,"[8] but it seems improbable that the company would in any case have been content

7. Anon., *Canadian Pacific Railway: correspondence and papers shewing the efforts the company has made to secure Portland for its winter port* (Montreal, 1884).
8. Canadian Archives, Macdonald papers, "Stephen," Van Horne to Tupper, July 30, 1888.

to leave the Atlantic provinces untapped, or to be without a direct line to a winter port. It was part of the scheme that the Canadian Pacific Railway line to the maritimes should run in conjunction with a new and fast Atlantic service of steamships. It may well be, however, that it was the pressure from the government and from public opinion that led to the choice of St. John rather than Portland. The Short Line, as it was called, was planned to cut across Maine, and so avoid the long loop by the northward. The route which it should take was the subject of a controversy only less active than that over the Intercolonial. The rival claims of Halifax and St. John as termini were put forward by chambers of commerce and city engineers, and various alternatives and compromises were suggested. Finally it was decided that the line should take advantage of railways built or in course of construction; that the terminus should be at St. John; but that running rights should be secured to Halifax. The lines acquired by the Atlantic and North-West Company, described above, were leased in perpetuity to the Canadian Pacific Railway, which thus reached Mattawamkeag in Maine. The eastern section of the Short Line was made by the New Brunswick system of railways, leased for 999 years to the C.P.R. In 1890 the Canadian Pacific reached the port of St. John.

The company, however, was dissatisfied, or affected to be dissatisfied, with its latest extension. The line of fast steamships did not materialize. Construction of the new sections was more expensive than had been anticipated and business was light. The company —rightly or wrongly—attributed this unhappy state of affairs to sins of omission and commission by the government. The Intercolonial was accused of discouraging passengers from going by the Short Line, of making connections as inconvenient as possible, and of charging excessive rates for the haulage of C.P.R. cars. Stephen expressed his woes in a characteristic letter to Macdonald.

As to the "Short Line," you know what the influences were that induced me to touch it. Tupper had a political object to serve; Pope had, in addition to that, a personal advantage to gain; and that, I am free to say, weighed with me quite as much as the former. Further, at a meeting of the Maritime Members,—which I have since learned originated with Pope,— under the threat that they would not support one of our life-and-death measures then before the house unless I agree to build the Short Line. Tupper and Pope repeatedly said, by way of inducement to undertake the work, that, on the opening of the Short Line, the I.C.R. would be run as a local road, that the through business would all come over the Short Line, that the I.C.R., worked as a local road, would be just as useful to the people of the country traversed by it; and the annual loss to the Government would be much less than by operating it as an expensive fast through line;—and much more to the same purpose. Can any sane man suppose I would have touched the Short Line unless I felt certain that the C.P.R. would have every facility for its short line trains reaching Halifax and doing business there as well as at all intermediate points along the line between St. John and Halifax? In this, as in many other things, I have been the victim of my own credulity and of my criminal confidence in the Government,—especially in the then Minister of Railways—and the C.P.R. is to-day suffering the consequences.[9]

This, and a similar letter from Stephen a week later—embracing other sore points as well as the Short Line—brought a cool answer from Macdonald. "I shall do my duty to the country according to the best of my judgment, and suffer even the threatened hostility of the Company, if need be." Stephen, who had used phrases about a possible breach in the friendly relations of government and company, hastily denied that there was any threat implied in his words. He was not blaming the government for the lightness of traffic on the Short Line: only asking for a fair share of what there was.[10] Some twenty years later an independent outlet to Halifax was secured by the lease of the Dominion Atlantic Railway, and a steamship service from St. John to Digby.

The expansion of the Canadian Pacific Railway into central and eastern Canada necessarily brought with it competition with the Grand Trunk: a competition, which, while it was in large part inevitable, was bitterly resented by the older company. In Stephen's view, there was bound to be competition as soon as it was decided that the C.P.R. should build from Montreal north of Lake Superior, for the C.P.R. would naturally try to take the western business over their line, and the Grand Trunk to take it by way of Chicago.[11]

9. *Ibid.*, Stephen to Macdonald, September 3, 1889.

10. Joseph Pope, *Correspondence of Sir John Macdonald* (Toronto, 1921), pp. 454–457.

11. Canadian Archives, Macdonald papers, "Stephen," Stephen to Macdonald, January 4, 1883.

The first phase of Grand Trunk opposition had taken the form of an attempt to discredit the whole project of a railway through Canadian soil to the Pacific, and an embarrassingly successful blockade of the London money market against Canadian Pacific loans. Such activities were, of course, never admitted by Grand Trunk officials, but there can be little question that they took place; and certainly they were not forgotten by the harassed management of the Canadian Pacific. Overlapping these moves, and carried out in the open, was a campaign to prevent the Canadian Pacific Railway from cutting into Grand Trunk business east of Lake Superior. The Grand Trunk executive took the attitude that the C.P.R. should be confined to its line from Callander west, and tacitly argued that it should find an outlet over the lines of other companies. More especially were they opposed to C.P.R. expansion between Toronto and Windsor, an area in which the Grand Trunk was already trying to remove competition by absorbing the Great Western and other smaller companies. The Grand Trunk argument was that construction of additional competing lines was extravagant and unnecessary; that their cost fell both on the Grand Trunk and the taxpayer; and that the C.P.R. was being enabled by public money to compete with a private concern.

For years a literary warfare was waged by the partisans on both sides. Shareholders were informed of the iniquities of the rival company; pamphlets on the subject poured from the presses; newspapers took up the issue; and the heads of both companies deluged the prime minister with statements, cajolements, and veiled threats. The chief spokesman for the Grand Trunk was Joseph Hickson, who had succeeded Brydges as general manager. He claimed that his company was not unfriendly to the Canadian Pacific as long as the latter kept within its legitimate sphere, but that it was being allowed to trespass beyond that sphere.

It seems to me not only the height of folly, but vicious, and in the highest degree detrimental to the interests of Canada to have two Railways built alongside each other for eighty miles and practically within the same fences —Mr. Stephen and his friends are building a road from the neighbourhood of Peterboro to Perth, alongside the Midland Railway practically constructed. . . . Mr. Stephen and his friends with the power of the Government at their back, and with the funds which they are obtaining from the

Government, are constructing the Ontario and Quebec line to the serious injury of commercial investments, and perhaps without much benefit to themselves in the long run. . . .[12]

Macdonald sent the letter on to Sir John Rose in New York, where Rose was trying—vainly as it proved—to reconcile the claims of the two companies. He was not altogether happy about the extent of the commitments in "collateral projects" which Stephen was making, but vigorously denied Hickson's statement that Stephen was fighting the Grand Trunk with public money.[13] Hickson, however, continued to harp on that theme. In forwarding a cabled protest from his directors against subsidizing lines outside the Canadian Pacific charter, he took occasion to enlarge on the argument in a letter which was later printed.

If that Company [Canadian Pacific] had been incorporated and its transactions conducted on the ordinary basis of a Joint Stock Corporation, it is probable that the Directors of the Company would not have thought it necessary to address any remonstrance to the Government, as the usual conditions attaching to the investment of private capital would have afforded them all the protection necessary, or that they could expect:— but as practically the money to build the railway is being supplied out of the public revenues, largely increasing the burdens of this Company, which is directly and indirectly at present the largest separate taxpayer within the Dominion, the operations of the Canadian Pacific Company assume an entirely different aspect. When in addition the fact is taken into consideration that the funds provided by the Canadian Government, more than sufficient in themselves to complete the Pacific line, and the resources of the Canadian Pacific Company, obtained through the assistance and credit of the Government, have been and are being diverted to the promotion of lines in direct antagonism to the company,—lines which are either not needed in the public interest, or where needed should be supplied entirely by private enterprise,—it becomes a duty incumbent upon those who have charge of this Company's affairs to protest against the course being pursued.[14]

The whole stand of the Grand Trunk in the matter of public assistance was, of course, disputed by the Canadian Pacific.

12. *Ibid.*, "Railways," viii, Hickson to Macdonald, August 17, 1882.
13. *Ibid.*, Rose to Macdonald, August 31, 1882.
14. *Ibid.*, "Railways," ix, Hickson to Macdonald, February 7, 1884.

Writing in 1890, when the controversy was still active, Van Horne attempted to turn the argument by showing that the Canadian Pacific Railway had spent, since 1882, a total of $28,296,000 on lines toward which no subsidy had been granted. On the other hand, he said, not a single important work had been carried out by the Grand Trunk in the same period without governmental assistance. As an extra dig, he added that the Grand Trunk had no more reason to complain of the original subsidy to the Canadian Pacific Railway than the latter had to the loans made to the Grand Trunk, which "became practically a gift."[15]

The phrases used by both sides have a modern ring, and a modern parallel which will be easily recognized. In reality, of course, the parties in the case were both private companies, both heavily indebted for their success to the assistance of the state. If on the one hand the Grand Trunk was seeking to prevent what it held to be improper competition, on the other hand the partisans of the Canadian Pacific raised the cry of monopoly (a cry of which they were soon to tire in another connection). The Grand Trunk, Stephen told his shareholders, cannot monopolize railway enterprise in Canada. And from Toronto came a blast from E. B. Osler, addressed to the members of parliament representing that city, protesting against the attempt of the Grand Trunk to establish a railway monopoly in Ontario by blocking the C.P.R. Once that was accomplished, the company "could, and would, at once put up rates from one end of the country to the other."[16]

Where did the Conservative government stand in the face of this fire from both sides? To Hickson and to Stephen, Macdonald long protested that the government was impartial, and the subsidies show that both companies were generously assisted. But when pushed too far he was forced to remember that the Canadian Pacific Railway was a child of the Conservative party. "My own position as a public man", he wrote to Stephen, "is as intimately connected with the prosperity of the C.P.R. as yours is, as a railway man."[17] And a few months later: "We have been showing

15. *Ibid.*, "Van Horne," Van Horne to Macdonald, September 26, 1890.

16. *Grand Trunk Railway versus Canadian Pacific Railway* (Toronto, 1884).

17. Canadian Archives, Macdonald papers, Letter book xxvi, Macdonald to Stephen, September 17, 1889.

such preference for the C.P.R. that Hickson has declared war—what we will, I dare say, survive."[18] The Canadian Pacific Railway, on its side, remembered the affiliation when election time came. "Our canvass is nearly complete and the C.P.R. votes will be practically unanimous—not one in one hundred even doubtful. My letter to Drummond was intended to show our men on which side their interests lie and it has had the intended effect with them." An enclosure from the general manager of the Dominion Express Company (a subsidiary of the C.P.R.) was also encouraging: "I have all hands at work, two men I sent west of Toronto changed thirteen votes yesterday. I have no fear of our men and think they will all work for the Company's interest when they have the way pointed out to them."[19]

Honours were pretty equally divided between the two companies, and in the following years the process of competitive expansion continued both by new construction and the absorption of smaller railways. The effect was to leave two great companies in possession of the greater part of the railway mileage of Canada. In central Canada they served roughly the same areas, but on the east the Grand Trunk cut down to Portland, while the Canadian Pacific ran through to St. John. On the western side the difference between their positions was more significant. The Grand Trunk, by extending to Chicago, consistently followed the theory that the approach to the west should be to the south of Lake Superior. If it could secure a direct connection with the Canadian west by the Red River Valley, that would be a serious threat to the C.P.R. The position in the west, then, was that the Canadian Pacific was free from the rivalry of the Grand Trunk and was partially protected from competition. As long as it could maintain an uninterrupted flow of traffic over the Lake Superior section its pioneer venture was likely to be increasingly fruitful.

3. Competition or Monopoly in the West

The dominating theme in the project of a Canadian railway to the Pacific had always been that of a line through Canadian territory, reaching both Atlantic and Pacific ports, and serving

18. *Ibid.*, Same to same, June 3, 1890.
19. *Ibid.*, "Van Horne," Van Horne to Macdonald, February 28, 1891.

as a link in a British route from Europe to the Orient. Despite early differences in the syndicate concerning the Lake Superior section, the company officially took over this whole conception of its purpose, adding a private rider that it would one day have its own steamships on both oceans. To carry its plans into effect, the company bought and built its way to the ports of Montreal, Quebec, and St. John on the east, and to Vancouver and Victoria on the west. The completion of the transcontinental line, together with the necessary feeders, would produce a railway which would have the benefit of through traffic, and would be able to pay its way in spite of the existence of unprofitable sections.

From the first the chief officers of the company took the attitude that they must be enabled to reach the more populated areas of central and eastern Canada, and that they must be protected—for a time at least—from competitors tapping their line at any point. Both these demands were partially met in the charter. To enable the company to extend eastward from its specified terminus at Callander, the clause was inserted which permitted acquisition of the Canada Central and other railways. As defence against the inroads of rivals, the "monopoly clause" read as follows:

For 20 years from the date hereof, no line of railway shall be authorized by the Dominion Parliament to be constructed south of the Canadian Pacific Railway, from any point at or near the Canadian Pacific Railway except such line as shall run South-West, or to the Westward of South-West; nor to within fifteen miles of latitude 49. And in the establishment of any new Province in the North-West Territories, provision shall be made for continuing such prohibition after such establishment until the expiration of the said period.

Such was the wall built round the Canadian Pacific Railway by the original charter. In general an attack might be expected at one of several points: in northern Ontario, at Sault Ste. Marie, in the Red River Valley, or on the Pacific coast. In any case the object of the attack would be the same: to tap the long trunk line of the Canadian Pacific and divert traffic to rival roads. The company held that any such attack was not only dangerous, but that it was unfair: dangerous because it threatened their ability to make the whole line carry the sections with no local traffic, and unfair because they claimed to have built north of Lake Superior only on the understanding that they should not be attacked from the rear. The attacks came, however, and each varied according to the area.

In northern Ontario the Canadian Pacific main line ran to Callander, this point having been chosen so as to favour neither Montreal nor Toronto. The C.P.R. succeeded in obtaining its own approach to Montreal over the Canada Central and North Shore, but in regard to Toronto they were forestalled by the Grand Trunk, which, by absorbing the Northern and North-Western, gained control of what had been the Northern and Pacific Junction from Gravenhurst to North Bay.

The objects [wrote Stephen] which the G.T.R. have in view in securing the control of the Northern and Nor Western Railways are now clear to me, and may be so to you. Having secured the control of the Northern System they thereby cut off the C.P.R. connection with Ontario. Seventy-five per cent. of the C.P.R. business to and from the Nor West is with the Province of Ontario, and to save a share of that business it is perfectly clear to me that the C.P.R. will be forced to build a line of its own from Toronto to Sudbury.[20]

It was not, however, until some years later that the Canadian Pacific Railway was able to counter by building its own line.

The second vulnerable point was at Sault Ste. Marie, where the transcontinental line first ran near to American territory. The C.P.R. had early planned to connect the Canada Central with Sault Ste. Marie, with the immediate purpose of reaching Lake Superior navigation while their main line was under construction, and with the further purpose of drawing in traffic from the neighbouring state. The problem was to make sure that their "Soo" line was drawing in rather than letting out business. The only way to secure this end seemed to be to gain control of adjoining American roads.

Smith and I are off this afternoon to New York and to try and devise means of saving the line from the "Soo" to Minneapolis from falling into the hands of the Vanderbilt system. If we fail, the result will be the loss

20. *Ibid.*, "Stephen," Stephen to Macdonald, January 29, 1888.

for ever of that traffic to the St. Lawrence route to Europe, and the permanent diversion of the traffic into the existing American channels. The Minneapolis traffic including that of the Nor Western States would be captured by the Michigan Central Line, which on reference to the map you will see runs direct north from Detroit to the Straits of Mackinaw, at which point there is a railway transfer ferry in operation, and the whole traffic taken east to the seaboard over the Vanderbilt lines, without a pound of it ever getting on the Canadian lines at the "Soo." . . .

There was even worse to come, as Stephen read the signs of the times, for the Grand Trunk spectre was also to be seen.

. . . The G.T.R. with the Northern in their hands will at once build a line from some point on their line between Gravenhurst and Callander, westwards to the "Soo," connecting at the "Soo" with the Duluth and South Shore line which runs direct along the lake shore from the "Soo" to Duluth, where a connection will be made with the Northern Pacific and with the St. Paul and Manitoba lines, both of which will sooner or later have independent connection with Winnipeg as well as with other points westward on the C.P.R., and so giving the G.T.R. a through connection with the whole Nor West to the Pacific Ocean *through American territory.*[21]

There was the rub. If Stephen and his fellow officers allowed this Grand Trunk scheme to go through they would lose not only their anticipated American traffic, but also the traffic of the Canadian west. These alarming results, however, never came: rather the boot was on the other foot, for the C.P.R. at that time began to establish a very powerful position in the middle western states. They bought control of both the Minneapolis, St. Paul and Sault Ste. Marie Railway and the Duluth, South Shore and Atlantic Railway Company. On completion of the system, the C.P.R. had a line from Sault Ste. Marie, through Duluth to Winnipeg; and another from Sault Ste. Marie to St. Paul, and north-west to meet the main line at Moosejaw. Together with branches, these railways made a network which formed an ample barrier against the invasion of rivals—Grand Trunk or American.

So far the Canadian Pacific had registered one failure and one success in the struggle to protect its trunk line. The battle waged at the third point of danger had less definite but more far-reaching

21. *Ibid.*

results. For some years the chief outlet for Manitoba had been south by the Red River valley to the border of Minnesota, where use could be made of American railways. The news of the formation of the syndicate in 1880 was received with mixed feelings in Manitoba. In general there was satisfaction that progress in the building of the Pacific railway was to be made, but the personnel of the syndicate was not altogether acceptable. The presence of a group from the St. Paul, Minneapolis and Manitoba Railway suggested a connection with American lines, and a consequent lack of competion which might keep down freight rates. To create the competition that it wanted, the province began to charter railways itself: the Winnipeg South-Eastern, to run to the American border; the Emerson and North-Western Railway Company, from Emerson (on the border of Minnesota) to the western edge of the province; and the Manitoba Tramway Company.

Such action was bitterly resented by the Canadian Pacific Railway Company, which had, even before the charter was discussed in parliament, given notice that they could not have any competing line running to the border, for this would "strangle" them.[22] The federal government then disallowed the charters. The reason given for this and later disallowances was that railways to the American border would divert traffic from the C.P.R. At first it was said in parliament that this policy would be continued only until the C.P.R.'s line north of Lake Superior was completed, but in practice the policy was retained for some three years longer. This change of policy, together with the earlier statements that Manitoba had the right to charter railways led to a long controversy between the provincial and federal governments. Disallowance was not on the grounds that the Manitoba charters contravened the act chartering the Canadian Pacific, for that, being a Canadian act, could not override the British North America Act. The disallowance was rather based on the fact that the federal government had power to veto provincial acts which were not in the general interests of the Dominion. Legally this power was indisputable, but in practice it was continually opposed by Manitoba.[23]

22. *Ibid.*, Same to same, October 18, 1880.
23. Sessional papers, 1888, No. 58B; house of commons debates, 1887, pp. 543 et seq.

The force behind the resistance of Manitoba was resentment against the freight rates charged by the Canadian Pacific Railway. The freight rates were undoubtedly high in comparison with those either in eastern Canada or on American railways. The difference was defended on grounds of higher cost of operation, to which it was answered that the C.P.R. had been subsidized just because it was not at first expected to pay. Moreover, the rates were increased in 1883, and it was felt that the whole development of the province was being retarded by the high cost of moving commodities. A few figures taken from a pamphlet issued by the Winnipeg Board of Trade illustrated the difference in freight rates on wheat between east and west.

Local Rates

C.P.R., Brandon to Winnipeg	133 miles	20	cents per 100 lbs.
G.T.R., Stratford to Bowmanville	131 "	13	" " " "
C.P.R., Moosejaw to Winnipeg	398 "	34	" " " "
G.T.R., Brantford to Montreal	403 "	17½	" " " "

Through Rates

C.P.R., Winnipeg to Toronto	1,287 "	50	" " " "
G.T.R., Ingersoll to Halifax	1,283 "	31½	" " " "

The rate on wheat on the St. Paul, Minneapolis and Manitoba Railway from St. Paul was 10 cents for 100 miles and 30 cents for 525 miles; on the C.P.R. from Winnipeg, it was 17½ cents for 100 miles, and 39 cents for 525 miles. J. H. Pope, who was not unfriendly to the C.P.R., wrote that ". . . Stephen and Hill . . . are charging such exorbitant rates from St. Paul to Emerson that it is almost ruinous to shippers and operates very much to prejudice the public against our policy, as they say if you had allowed another road to be built from Winnipeg to the boundary there would have been a competing line to the St. Paul and Emerson road."[24] No matter how conscious the people of Manitoba may have been of the advantage of having a transcontinental railway, and even of the problems of operating it in a sparsely settled area, it is not surprising that they continued to protest against the cost of transportation. They believed—not altogether correctly—that the high cost was due to a monopoly, and a monopoly based on an

24. Macdonald papers, "Pope," Pope to Macdonald, August 24, 1882.

unreasonable use of federal powers. They therefore proceeded to break the monopoly by the establishment of competing lines.

Stephen claimed that the agitation for another railway was really for the benefit of speculators who did not care about the province, and that there was an annexation element in it; but there seems to be every indication that the campaign against monopoly, led by the *Winnipeg Free Press*, represented a very wide body of opinion. More convincing was the argument that the real danger lay in the continued opposition of the Northern Pacific to the Canadian Pacific, and a threat to divert the traffic of the Canadian west to the south at Winnipeg. "Now if he [Villard] can manage to tap our traffic from Winnipeg West before it has become fully developed or got into its own proper channel we might as well give him the line east of Winnipeg to Thunder Bay and save our money on the North Shore Line."[25]

The Ottawa government was impressed by the general danger to the C.P.R. and for a time held to its policy of disallowing the provincial charters on grounds of general interest. In the meanwhile the legislature of Manitoba grew more reckless. Not content with railways to the border, it chartered and subsidized a railway to Hudson Bay, of which forty miles of track were actually laid. It then turned back to the border railway. The Manitoba Central, Winnipeg and Southern, and Red River Valley companies were all chartered in 1887, and all disallowed. The first of these was designed to connect with the Northern Pacific, and on the act being disallowed the government determined to carry on the undertaking itself. On the constant buying and selling, chartering and disallowing of Manitoba railways there is no need to dwell in detail. The point of importance was the clear-cut issue between the province and the Dominion as to railway policy. Feeling ran high, and at one moment there was danger that the struggle might end in tragedy. The provincial government was building a branch of the Red River Valley Railway from Portage la Prairie to Winnipeg, and to do so had to cross a branch of the C.P.R. Van Horne ordered resistance. An old engine was ditched in the line of the oncoming track and two hundred and fifty men were brought by the C.P.R. superintendent to hold the fort. A volunteer army of

25. *Ibid.*, "Stephen," Stephen to Macdonald, August 27, 1881.

three hundred men was rushed out from Winnipeg and took up a position near by. In the night a "diamond" crossing was laid, and promptly torn up by the defending force. Reinforcements were brought by both sides, and it was only a growing sense of reasonableness in both groups of partisans that prevented a fight.

For a year or more the struggle continued to be waged between the Dominion government and the Canadian Pacific Railway on the one hand and the province on the other. The British North America Act, the charter of the Canadian Pacific Railway, and Hansard were read and re-read, interpreted and re-interpreted. The C.P.R. claimed that the attempt of Manitoba to divert traffic to the south was a breach of faith, and threatened to transfer its western shops to Fort William. The executive council of Manitoba formally protested against the policy of the federal government, and the latter answered with a charge that Manitoba was acting against the general interest of the Dominion. Macdonald privately told Rose that Manitoba was running toward bankruptcy, and asked him to discourage the floating of her government's loans in London.[26] In Ottawa, however, it was gradually being recognized that the game was not worth the candle. Thomas White, the minister of the interior, advised Stephen that the policy of disallowance was a mistake.[27] The Winnipeg Conservatives clamoured for the abolition of the policy, and formed an association to present their views. In the meanwhile the Canadian Pacific officers found that the agitation against the company both in Manitoba and Ontario was destroying their credit. Stephen told Tupper and Macdonald that the Canadian Pacific Railway could not remain in the position of an unpopular monopoly, and would have to face competition. But there was an urgent need of cash—"$15,000,000 will be required within the year 1888. . . . If the capital cannot be secured the company must collapse and go into bankruptcy. . . ." Lack of revenue made the need acute.[28]

The government, by adding two and two together, found the solution to an intolerable situation. By an act of 1888 (51 Vict., c.32) the monopoly clause was repealed, the policy of disallowance

26. *Ibid.*, Letter book xxiv, Macdonald to Rose, June 25, 1887.
27. *Ibid.*, "Stephen," White to Stephen, May 18, 1887.
28. *Ibid.*, Stephen to Macdonald, November 11, 1887.

was implicitly abandoned, and the government was empowered to guarantee the interest on a loan of $15,000,000 to be issued by the company. The battle was over, but who had won the victory? The federal government got peace, the C.P.R. fifteen million dollars, and Manitoba freedom to build or charter other lines. But the real object of the struggle was not gained by the province, for the freight rates remained much as they were. The Northern Pacific built a number of lines in Manitoba, but instead of conducting a rate war with the C.P.R. divided the traffic with that company. Continuing complaints from the west led to a series of inquiries into freight rates.[29] A royal commission of 1888 reported against any fundamental changes and its views only led to increased powers in the railway committee of the privy council. Another commission was appointed to investigate the question, but this reported in 1895 that the C.P.R. gave lower rates than American railways operating under similar conditions; and that, while local rates were higher than in the east, they were necessary on account of the greater cost of transportation. No relief came to the west until 1897 when the Crow's Nest Pass agreement was made between the Dominion government and the Canadian Pacific Railway. In consideration of a subsidy to a line through the pass the company agreed to a general reduction.[30] Finally a comprehensive consideration was given to the whole question of rates in an inquiry made by Professor S. J. McLean. His two reports, presented in 1899 and 1902, made definite criticisms of the railway committee on the grounds that it was political as well as administrative, was not sufficiently permanent or expert in personnel, and did not travel about the country.[31] He also proposed an alternative method of handling consideration of freight rates, a plan which was written into the Railway Act of 1903 (3 Edw. vii, c.58). There was to be a board of three (later six) commissioners appointed by the governor in council for ten years. To this board a permanent staff

29. D. A. MacGibbon, *Railway rates and the Canadian railway commission* (Boston, 1917), pp. 80 et seq.

30. H. A. Innis, *History of the Canadian Pacific Railway* (Toronto, 1923), pp. 183–184.

31. *Reports upon railway commissions, railway rate grievances and regulative legislation* (Sessional paper No. 20A, 1902).

of experts was attached. The commission took over all the powers of the former committee, but, unlike the committee, its activities were largely in the regulation of rates, and for such purposes it was to act as an informal court of law. Appeals from its decisions lay to the governor in council, while appeals on points of law might, with the consent of the commission, be carried to the supreme court of Canada.

A less tangible result was the continuing and rooted objection to railway monopoly which existed in Manitoba and in the west generally. Whether or not the Canadian Pacific had taken advantage of its monopolistic position, and whether or not the appearance of other Canadian and of American lines in the west affected the height of freight and passenger rates, there was a very strong feeling that never again must the west be exposed to the monopoly of a single railway. It was the existence of that sentiment, which, probably more than any other single factor, set opinion in the west against any amalgamation of the Canadian Pacific and the heir to the other railways, the Canadian National.

The cancellation of the monopoly clause in the Canadian Pacific charter hastened a struggle that had already been foreseen with American roads. The old bogey was the Northern Pacific, but the Northern Pacific expanded into the prairies and did no great harm. In any case it was a failing force. After his phenomenal success in the St. Paul and Pacific and the St. Paul, Minneapolis, and Manitoba, Hill for a time was associated with the Canadian syndicate, but before long withdrew and devoted his great energies to the building up of a new transcontinental line, which he called the Great Northern. It was primarily this railway which Van Horne had to fear when, in 1892, he became president on the resignation of Lord Mount Stephen (as he now was). The two men—Hill and Van Horne—the one a Canadian in charge of an American railway, and the other an American in charge of a Canadian railway, were worthy antagonists. Indeed, their love of battle might have led them further than interest demanded had it not been for the shock-absorber put in by Mount Stephen and Strathcona, both of whom had remained at once influential directors of the Canadian Pacific Railway and large shareholders in the Great Northern.

There was a clear clashing of interest between the American

and Canadian roads, for both hoped to penetrate beyond the national boundaries and draw business in to their main lines. Both believed in the offensive as the best form of defence. The personal attitudes of the presidents toward the struggle may be illustrated by two remarks. Hill, on hearing that Van Horne was determined to build the Lake Superior section, had burst out—"I'll get even with him if I have to go to hell for it and shovel coal." And Van Horne, in connection with Hill's intention of invading Canada, had remarked, no less picturesquely: "Well, if he does, I'll tear the guts out of his road."[32] Van Horne's measures of protection were, in the main, two. The Minneapolis, St. Paul and Sault Ste. Marie was joined up with a branch running north-west to meet the Canadian Pacific main line at Moosejaw. The object of this was to make a shorter route between the Pacific coast, St. Paul and Chicago. The extension from Port Moody to Vancouver also assisted in the development of traffic with the Orient, a side of their business which the Canadian Pacific were anxious to encourage. A mail subsidy from the British government in 1889 was followed by the building of Canadian Pacific steamers, and the full operation of a trans-Pacific service by 1891.

The second measure of defence was to run lines through the southern part of British Columbia, that is, in the boundary or Kootenay country, into which the Great Northern had made its next raid. In the late 'nineties the Crow's Nest Pass line was begun, partly by acquisition of local railways and partly by construction. Running close to the border, the new line, together with branches, forestalled serious incursions of the Great Northern, and at the same time enabled the Canadian Pacific to take advantage of the development of mining in the boundary country. In British Columbia as in Manitoba the cry of "monopoly" was raised. In 1897 the provincial government announced an impressive number of subsidies to be granted, one of them for a railway into the Kootenay country. In 1898 the government made a contract with Mackenzie and Mann for a railway from Vancouver to Penticton, on Okanagan Lake, and on to Midway, east of Rossland. The election of the same year led to the cancellation of the contract. Nothing further was done until the accession of the Dunsmuir

32. W. Vaughan, *Life and work of Sir William Van Horne* (New York, 1920), p. 229.

government in 1901, when it appeared that the Canadian Pacific Railway was to receive the contract, and in public meetings and in newspapers protests were voiced against monopoly and against the influence of the Canadian Pacific in politics.

Broadly speaking, the Canadian Pacific had succeeded in protecting its trunk line against the threats of either American or Canadian rivals. Theoretically it gave up its monopoly in 1888 but the absence of any real competition for many years rendered that concession nugatory. It was not until the opening of the new century that the tardy appearance of the Grand Trunk Pacific and the formation of the Canadian Northern showed that the days of the absolute rule of the Canadian Pacific in the west were numbered.

CHAPTER X

THE LATER TRANSCONTINENTAL RAILWAYS

1. THE COMING OF PROSPERITY

WITH the turn of the century there came the long-awaited prosperity in Canada. The years from 1898 or 1900 to 1913 saw a rapid recovery throughout the world from the doldrums of the 'nineties, and the economic expansion which resulted was nowhere so marked as in North America. In spite of all efforts, Canada—and particularly the Canadian west—had only progressed in short spurts, though there was a rooted belief throughout the country that it was only a question of time before Canada would grow in population and wealth as she had already done in territory. That belief seemed to be justified when the new century brought a flow of immigrants, capital, and orders for foodstuffs. It was seen as the dawn of a new day. Since, it was argued, the land of the American west was nearly taken up, the tide of European emigration must be diverted to Canada, which would then go through a similar stage of rapid development. Out of such comforting thoughts arose the expression, "Canada's century." It was in this atmosphere of optimism, and with tangible signs of the better days, that the third great forward movement of Canadian railways was imagined and begun.

The basic need of the Dominion was for more people. Immigration, which had materially increased in the 'eighties, owing principally to railway construction and the opening of the west, had fallen off badly in the 'nineties and reached a low mark of 16,855 in 1896. From there it began to recover, passing 50,000 in 1902, 100,000 in 1903, 250,000 in 1908, and reaching a maximum of 382,841 in 1913. Allowing for emigration, there was a loss until 1901, and while emigration remained important, there was a net gain of over 200,000 persons in 1913;[1] and the rate of growth of population in the years 1900–1910—thirty-five per cent—was

1. *See* R. Wilson, "Migration movements in Canada, 1868–1925" (*Canadian Historical Review*, xiii, 2).

higher than in any other country. The United Kingdom quota of immigrants was in most years the largest, with the United States second. Other European countries contributed, too, more especially when the search for immigrants by the Canadian government, led by the energetic minister of the interior, Clifford Sifton, was definitely extended into Europe, in the belief that the English-speaking countries alone could not provide all the people that were needed. Eastern Canada absorbed a portion of the new-comers; but they migrated chiefly to the scantily-populated prairies. Those settling in the east found their livelihood in the industries which were springing up or increasing, and helped to swell the movement to the towns, and the consequent relative gain of urban over rural population; and those going to the west were absorbed in wheat-growing or ranching, and so participated in the produc-tion of foodstuffs for export. Many of these latter newcomers found temporary or seasonal work in railway construction—some-times supplementary to independent farming.

Imports of capital on a large scale accompanied immigration. Since only a small amount of capital could be found within the country, public and private bodies turned to the United Kingdom, the United States, and European countries. After a long period of industrial expansion England was possessed of a large amount of exportable capital. The general prosperity of the early twentieth century brought a willingness to lend large sums abroad, while the bright prospects in Canada, combined, perhaps, with the revival of imperial sentiment, created an almost unlimited credit for Canada in London. The United States was the second largest lender, and other countries combined to make a poor third. The total investments in Canada in the period 1900 to 1913 have been calculated as follows:

Great Britain	$1,753,118,000
United States	629,794,000
Other countries	162,715,000
	$2,545,627,000[2]

2. J. Viner, *Canada's balance of international indebtedness, 1900–1913* (Cambridge, Mass., 1924), p. 139.

This capital financed new railways and the industrial and agricultural development of which railways were at once the cause and result.

The heavy expenditure on railways in the early twentieth century was defended partly by glowing phrases about the future and partly on the grounds of tangible needs. For the former, illustrations will be found in plenty in the orations of the day; for the latter, a few figures may be quoted to indicate the rate and distribution of economic progress, though it must be remembered that in the period covered railway construction synchronized with, rather than followed, the development of agriculture and industries.

	1901	1911
Area of occupied farms, in acres	63,422,338	108,968,715
Production of wheat, in bushels	55,572,368	132,077,547
Value of live stock	$268,651,026	$615,457,833
Exports of wood and wood products	$33,099,915	$56,334.695
Mineral production	$65,797,911	$103,220,994
Gross value of manufactured products	$481,053,375	$1,165,975,639[3]

Agriculture gained slightly or remained stationary in the eastern and central provinces, but showed a marked increase in the west, where the rapid expansion of livestock and wheat-farming strained the resources of the existing railways. Manufacturing was centred almost entirely east of Lake Superior, and its growth signified urbanization and a more mixed economy. The industries which increased most rapidly were those connected with building materials, iron and steel, and transportation equipment.

The prime motives in building the two later transcontinental railways were to provide more adequate transportation facilities for the west, and—on the part of the companies concerned—to share in the traffic that was being created there. Such traffic was both in the exports of the west and in the carriage of supplies, lumber, and other goods to the settlers. "Railways and continually improving transportation were as essential as rain and sun to progressive settlement on the Canadian prairie. Nearness to railways and to projected railways was of first importance to

3. *Canada Year Book*, 1934–1935.

the settler."[4] In the prairies and foothills grain and livestock could be grown for export. Since it has been calculated that, under most circumstances, grain could not be profitably hauled more than ten miles to a railway,[5] main or branch lines were needed if the west were to have more than a narrow belt of settlement. Railways and immigrants went together to the west, each dependent on the other. The following table indicates the growth of population.

| Province | 1901 | | 1911 | |
	Total population	Immigration	Total population	Immigration
Manitoba	255,211	11,254	461,394	34,289
Saskatchewan	91,279 }		492,432	40,076
Alberta	73,022 }	14,160	374,295	44,091
British Columbia and Yukon	178,657	2,600	392,480	52,786
Totals	598,169	28,014	1,720,601	171,242

Canada had a great pioneer area—"the last best west"—for neither the United States nor any other country could any longer offer free lands to large numbers of immigrants, and every effort was made to exploit this advantageous position. No further grants of land were made to railways after 1896, and the land was used instead for the free homestead system. Governments—federal and provincial,—railways, and private organizations sent agents and literature to the United States, England, and the continent of Europe to advertise the attractions of settlement in western Canada, and to make smooth the path of the immigrant. By 1912 there was little land still available for homesteads in the southern half of the provinces. Added to those who came from the United Kingdom and foreign countries were thousands of others from Ontario and the eastern provinces.

4. W. A. Mackintosh, *Prairie settlement: the geographical setting* (Toronto, 1934), 46. *See* also the valuable series of maps in this work showing the relation of railways to the distribution of rural population in the prairie provinces (pp. 48–52), and the spread of settlement (pp. 60–73). It is equally true that settlers were vital to railways. One estimate sets the annual potential revenue to the railway of each farm as $282.56 (Robert England, *The colonization of western Canada* [London, 1936], p. 310).

5. Mackintosh, *op. cit.*, p. 55.

Farming was the chief occupation of new and old settler alike, and wheat played the leading part. Manitoba, as the first part to be settled, was for some years the chief centre of wheat production. A crop of a little over a million bushels in 1880 rose to nearly seven millions in 1885, to eighteen millions in 1900, and to nearly thirty-three millions in 1905. Alberta and Saskatchewan, meanwhile, had passed the Manitoba total, increasing from five million bushels in 1900 to thirty-five millions in 1905. These are small figures compared with those of ten years later, but they already represented a considerable surplus for export and at times strained the existing railway system. In the late nineteenth and early twentieth centuries the variety of wheat most commonly grown in the west was Red Fife; but as settlement spread northward it became increasingly necessary to develop another type which would ripen earlier, and so escape the frosts. The result of a long series of experiments was a cross named Marquis, which was first distributed in 1909, and soon came to be the dominant variety.

Wheat was by no means the only crop, but it produced the acute problem for the railway. Oats and barley were grown in considerable quantities, and cattle raising was an important industry, the latter especially in Alberta where the foothills of the Rockies offered ideal conditions. The largest part of the wheat crop had to be moved to eastern ports shortly after it was harvested. The period involved was very short, and every box-car and engine that could be spared had to be put into this service. Gaunt elevators rise at intervals beside the track, and whether on the main or on local lines, had to be cleared by the railways, and the crop started on its long trip eastward. At the beginning of the century the grain had to be moved from Winnipeg, the hub of the system, over the single line of the Canadian Pacific Railway to Fort William, where water transport began. In that link there were stoppages in 1901 and 1902, and the movement of grain was interrupted, a state of things which affected all those who were directly or indirectly concerned with the sale, financing, and export of the crop. It needed no more than one or two such examples to cause a re-examination of the railway situation in the west.

In 1900 the only railway with any considerable mileage west of Fort William was the Canadian Pacific. From its main line branches

ran north to Saskatoon and Prince Albert in Saskatchewan and to
Edmonton in Alberta. South of Winnipeg were a number of
branches running to the border or parallel to it. From Calgary
a line ran south to Macleod, and Lethbridge, on the Crow's Nest
Pass line, was reached from the main line further east. In addition
there were numerous shorter branches. Besides the Canadian
Pacific there were only the lines of the Great Northern to the
south and west of Winnipeg, the nucleus of the Canadian Northern,
and a few other local railways.

Faced by the rapid growth in the population and traffic of the
west, the Canadian Pacific made efforts to keep pace with the
demands upon it, and further branches were continually thrown
out. These branches in turn threw a heavier burden on the main
line. It was not, however, to be the fate of the Canadian Pacific
to maintain a virtual monopoly in the west. All the forces were
moving toward the building up of further railway systems. First
there was an obvious need for greater mileage. Not only did the
overloading of the Winnipeg-Fort William line indicate the necessity of duplication, but also the frontier of settlement was steadily
being pushed northward. With the discovery of great tracts of good
agricultural land and the perfection of varieties of wheat maturing
early enough to escape the frosts, the incoming settlers moved to
more northerly districts until they reached the rich Peace River
country. The current view was that, as the settled belt was
widened, railways should be established to serve the new areas
as the Canadian Pacific served the longer settled area in the south.
All degrees of optimism were evinced as to what the future of the
west would be, but there was general agreement that the one
railway was not enough.

The opportunity for new business was seen by other railway
companies as well as by detached observers. The Canadian Pacific,
instead of failing to pay for its own axle grease, had been a financial
success. So long as the west developed slowly there was, perhaps,
no room for another railway to share in the same harvest, but now
that prosperity had come others might expand into that field.
There were two companies interested: the Canadian Northern,
possessed of a few small lines in the prairies, but with unlimited
ambition; and the Grand Trunk, which, having failed to confine

the Canadian Pacific to the west, was now thinking in terms of transcontinental traffic. Both companies were under energetic and enterprising management.

Lastly, the pressure for additional railways came from the people of the west themselves. They wanted, naturally, to ensure adequate facilities for the export of wheat, and lines to be extended as settlement spread; but they did not want the whole transportation system of the west to be in the hands of one corporation. The memories of the struggle over monopoly in Manitoba were fresh. That province had never ceased to exhibit a readiness to charter and assist independent companies, or even to operate railways as public works. Throughout the west, too, there continued to be dissatisfaction with the rates charged and a belief that they could be lowered through competition. Shippers claimed that they were in the hands of a monopolistic company which charged whatever the traffic would bear and which gave little thought to their convenience. It was, therefore, certain that further railways would be built. Whether there should be one or more, where and how they would find outlet in the east, and how they were to be financed, were all matters to be decided.

2. The Liberal Railway Policy

The policy adopted at the beginning of the century, of allowing the construction of two additional transcontinental railways, marks a turning point and crisis of Canadian railway development. After a long sojourn in the wilderness, the Liberals came into power in 1896, on the eve of the great years of prosperity. With a rapidly filling treasury and a good working majority in parliament, the government was in a strong position to carry out the popular policy of rapid expansion of railways. It was also in a strong position to steer a judicious course between a timorous refusal to bank on the growth of the west and a prodigal disregard of caution. No Liberal government had held office at Ottawa since that of Alexander Mackenzie. The memories of that administration and of the opposition as led by Edward Blake would, in so far as they concerned railways, have been willingly forgotten by the Liberals of the twentieth century. The cautious policy of Mackenzie and Blake had as its fruits the slow and partial construction of the

Pacific railway; while the criticism of the arrangement with the syndicate of 1880 had been popularly interpreted as opposition to the whole plan. The Conservative government had then, by taking a risk on the success of the syndicate, completely eclipsed anything that had been done by the Liberals, wiped out the memory of the Pacific scandal, and gained the credit for the completion of the much-desired Pacific railway. It came to be accepted by both the government and the Canadian Pacific Railway Company that they were mutually dependent; and it was not surprising that the company formed a tacit alliance with the Conservatives in the years immediately following the completion of the road.

It is not an unreasonable deduction that the Liberal administration was ready to sponsor a fresh railway enterprise which would cancel their former mistaken, if honest, belief in the inability of the west to maintain a railway. They were now in prosperous days instead of in days of depression. They had in Wilfrid Laurier a leader who could catch and exploit the public optimism in the future of the country. Moreover, it had been demonstrated that there was room and business for another railway across the west. All the signs, in fact, pointed to action: the question was as to the exact form that that action should take.

There was not, as there had been a generation before, a clean sheet on which the government could write a new railway policy, for there existed two powerful companies, neither of which had a transcontinental line and both of which felt it necessary to secure the benefits of long-haul traffic. The Grand Trunk had a network of lines throughout Ontario and Quebec, a seaport at Portland and an entry to the middle west at Chicago. Although the company had more than once refused opportunities of building into the Canadian west on Canadian soil, its officers and directors had now become satisfied that such a step was necessary. The Grand Trunk had not been able to settle its relations with the Canadian Pacific on the basis of a division of territory, and therefore turned to the alternative of competition as a through road. A much younger railway, the Canadian Northern, was geographically in the opposite position: it had lines in the west but none in the east. With a number of lines in Manitoba and Saskatchewan, it had (in 1902) built to Port Arthur, where the wheat which it gathered on the prairies could be delivered to lake boats; but it had no other access to the east, and was anxious to remedy the defect.[6]

The logical solution for the problems of both companies was amalgamation or coöperation. Negotiations to this end were conducted, but such a veil of mystery shrouds them that it is impossible to know the whole truth. It is said that the Grand Trunk offered to purchase the Canadian Northern in 1902, and that the latter eventually agreed to sell on a basis of about $30,000 per mile— a price which the Grand Trunk refused to pay.[7] In evidence before the royal commission of 1917, E. J. Chamberlin, president of the Grand Trunk, threw some further light on the negotiations:

They [the G.T.R. executive] tried to buy the Manitoba lines, but they could not get together, Mr. Hays told me at one time, and Mr. Wainwright told me also. I asked him why they did not buy out the Canadian Northern. They said they had had meeting after meeting with them, and that the best terms they could get were that they assume all obligations, all bonds and everything else, and give $25,000,000 for the common stock for that little bunch of lines up around Winnipeg.

But Sir Donald Mann's later account of the situation, given in evidence before the arbitration board (1918) does not entirely bear out the statement that the Canadian Northern was willing to sell.

Both companies [C.P.R. and G.T.R.] wanted to buy us out and neither was friendly. Of course the Grand Trunk made no bones about it. The Government sent for us and we had a session at Ottawa, and they (the Grand Trunk) wished to buy us out and always were in the hope they would buy us out. We offered to build a joint section from Port Arthur to North Bay, and we would develop the west and they would develop in the east. That was before the Grand Trunk Pacific was built and they refused and would not do anything but buy us out. We were too young and ambitious to sell out at that time. That was the year they got their charter . . . and we were running to Port Arthur at the time.[8]

6. For more detailed accounts of the Grand Trunk and Canadian Northern *see* sections 3 and 4 below.

7. H. A. Lovett, *Canada and the Grand Trunk* (Montreal, 1924), p. 129; L. T. Fournier, *Railway nationalization in Canada* (Toronto, 1935), p. 13.

8. *Canadian Northern Railway Arbitration* (1918: mimeographed), Evidence, p. 2683.

Another attempt to bring the railways together was made, apparently in the winter of 1902–1903, by Laurier, who called the heads of the two roads to Ottawa and suggested a general plan by which each company should be the complement of the other, the Canadian Northern in the west and the Grand Trunk in the east. It is fairly clear that the reason for the failure of discussions was the refusal of both sides to give up their separate ambitions. It is not at all clear, however, why the government gave way, since neither railway could proceed without a charter and financial assistance from parliament. Various explanations of the weakness of the government in this connection may be guessed at: divisions in the cabinet; fear that too much pressure would result in no railway at all; a failure to appreciate the significance of the issue. To the last may be added the excuse that the general optimism of the period supported an almost unlimited expansion of railways. The government of the day was no more foolish and—unfortunately —no wiser than the public, the companies themselves, and business men, eminent and otherwise, who were using extravagant terms about the boundless possibilities of Canada and the necessity of double-tracking all the railways. Nevertheless the willingness of the government to take the line of least resistance committed the country to a system of railways that was ill designed for its needs and greater than it could support without strain.

After the failure of the negotiations for coöperation the government turned to alternatives, the first being the plan proposed by the Grand Trunk. In November 1902 that company offered to build a railway from North Bay (its terminus in northern Ontario) to the Pacific coast, at or near Port Simpson, and asked a subsidy of $6,000 and 5,000 acres per mile, with tax exemptions. This represented half the amount of land and three-fifths the cash paid to the Canadian Pacific syndicate, but the offer was not acceptable. Judging by the generosity of later subsidies it is evident that the amount was no obstacle, although it would have had to be wholly in money since no more large land grants were to be made.   The chief reason given for the refusal of the terms was that the traffic gathered by the road would be carried to Portland instead of to a Canadian port. The Grand Trunk's expressed willingness to connect with the Intercolonial was apparently not credited, and the government was still labouring under the delusion that grain would be carried to the sea by rail by way of the direct line that they proposed.

During the greater part of 1902 and 1903 the cabinet may be imagined as wrestling with the railway problem. No doubt there were frequent consultations of all sizes, involving ministers, railway officials, and financiers. No doubt there was the usual lobbying by interested parties. But what came out of it all was that the railway fathered by the Liberal party was to be no mere extension of the Intercolonial and Grand Trunk into the west, but a completely new transcontinental line, stretching from New Brunswick to the Pacific. The change from the original Grand Trunk proposal to the plan adopted was explained by W. H. Biggar, the company's solicitor, in a letter written to the royal commission of 1917.

In the early months of 1903, conferences were from time to time held between Mr. Hays and Mr. Wainwright on behalf of the company and Sir Wilfrid Laurier and members of the Cabinet, as a result of which Mr. Hays was asked to have the Bill amended to provide for the construction of a line from North Bay to Quebec. Not only do I personally know this to be the fact, but it is corroborated by a letter written to Sir Charles Rivers Wilson by Mr. Hays on March 16, 1903, in which he stated that at the request of the Government we have amended our Grand Trunk Pacific charter, taking powers to build a line from Quebec to North Bay. . . . When the Bill first came up for discussion before the Railway Committee of the House of Commons, such strong opposition developed that practically no progress was made at that meeting nor, in fact, at several subsequent meetings of the committee. While the Bill was thus under consideration, several members from the Maritime Provinces insisted that the eastern terminus of the line should not be Quebec, but a point in the Maritime Provinces. So strongly was this view pressed that in the end the Government acquiesced and directed that the Bill be further amended to include the construction of a line from Quebec to Moncton. . . . Moncton was decided upon as a compromise, regard being had to the fact that both Halifax and St. John could be reached from there by the Intercolonial. . . . That his [Hays'] original intention was not carried out was, to my personal knowledge, not due to a change of view on his part but because he came to the conclusion that the Government aid essential to the construction of any Grand Trunk Pacific line could only be secured upon the terms set forth in the agreement of July 29, 1903.[9]

Laurier was unable to secure unanimous approval by his cabinet of the plan which was finally adopted. A. G. Blair, his minister of railways and former premier of New Brunswick, resigned in July 1903 rather than agree to the proposed railway. The announcement of Blair's resignation, which Laurier made to the house of commons on July 16, was the first official word on the government's railway policy, although it was known that plans were afoot. It was not a happy beginning to have to tell the house that the minister most directly concerned felt so strongly against the measure that he was determined to leave the government. Although it was not revealed at the time, Clifford Sifton was also opposed, and before leaving for England on the Alaska boundary case had given to the prime minister a memorandum in which he urged that the Canadian Northern and Grand Trunk should be "required" to come to an arrangement by which the two formed a "perpetual traffic contract," neither building into each other's territory, the boundary of which would be at Port Arthur. But, because he was in England when the decision was reached, Sifton swallowed the unsavoury bill, being able to distinguish, as a friend remarked, a hearse from a band waggon.[10] Blair's arguments, as expressed by his and Laurier's speeches in the house and by their letters printed in the *Debates*, are clear as far as they go.[11] His "decided preference" was for "a Government owned and government operated railway across the continent." This he was prepared to forego, but was opposed to a "hybrid scheme involving the compromise of two antagonistic principles." In particular he disbelieved in the Lévis to Moncton section, which, he held, would parallel the Intercolonial; and in building the Quebec to Winnipeg section before the character and conditions of the country had been more fully explored. He accused Laurier of discussing with other ministers, and allowing those ministers to discuss with Grand

9. *Report of the royal commission to inquire into railways and transportation in Canada* (1917), xxviii.

10. J. W. Dafoe, *Clifford Sifton in relation to his times* (Toronto, 1931), pp. 265–271.

11. *House of commons debates*, 1903, pp. 6735, et seq.

Trunk officers, plans for the transcontinental railway without informing him, although he was the minister of railways. Laurier's answer to this last charge was put in such general terms as to be an admission of its truth. This is most suggestive, for it seems to indicate either a general lack of confidence between Laurier and Blair or else a fundamental difference on railway policy. It has been asserted that Blair was more friendly to the Canadian Northern than to the Grand Trunk;[12] yet it is curious that Blair made no reference to the Canadian Northern in his letters to Laurier— curious because the paralleling of lines was the weakest joint in Laurier's armour, as Blair himself made clear in reference to the Intercolonial. Sifton had expressed himself vigorously about the avoidance of such overlapping. Either Blair failed to appreciate fully the significance of this point, or else he hoped that the government would come to terms with the Canadian Northern rather than with the Grand Trunk: that is to say, he would adopt the Machiavellian tactics of scotching the first plan and then producing the second. Again, however, there is mystery about the motive.

In spite of the protests of the opposition, nothing further was revealed concerning the new railway policy until July 30, when the prime minister moved for leave to introduce a bill for the construction of "a National Transcontinental railway,"[13] thus again arousing resentment amongst members of the opposition, who had not yet seen the bill. The scheme was an ambitious one, envisaging a completely new transcontinental railway from Moncton in New Brunswick to the Pacific coast. The eastern section from Moncton to Winnipeg (the National Transcontinental) was to be built by the government and on completion leased to a new corporation, the Grand Trunk Pacific. The route was to be from Moncton to Edmundston, near the American border, and thence midway between the border and the St. Lawrence to Quebec. The western section, to be built by the Grand Trunk Pacific, would follow a northerly route to Winnipeg and thence through the Yellowhead Pass to Port Simpson.

12. O. D. Skelton, *Life and letters of Sir Wilfrid Laurier* (Toronto, 1921), ii, 189.

13. As first used, the phrase "National Transcontinental" applied to the whole line from Moncton to Prince Rupert, but to avoid confusion it will hereafter be used in its later connotation, i.e., the government section (Moncton to Winnipeg).

In introducing the measure Laurier emphasized the necessity
of immediate action.[14] Unless Canada could provide for the trade
of her own west it would be captured by "an ever vigilant competitor." This led up to the theme of the national character of the road,
which was his chief defence of the section east of Quebec. The
Intercolonial followed too circuitous a course, and the Canadian
Pacific line went through Maine. The old bogey of abolition of the
bonding privilege was once more trotted out, and the words of
Andrew Carnegie and President Cleveland (in 1888) quoted to
show the sinister intentions of the United States. Against the
Quebec-Moncton section the opposition protested time after time.
Blair, who took a leading part in the debate, denied that the
Intercolonial was unsuitable for through traffic and claimed that the
National Transcontinental would be a parallel and unnecessary
road. From the experience of the Canadian Pacific, R. L. Borden,
leader of the opposition, argued that little grain would be moved by
rail east of Port Arthur. He also sought to show that the Grand
Trunk would secure virtual control of the Intercolonial, whose
lines it would need to use from Moncton to St. John or Halifax.
Or, as J. G. Haggart, minister of railways in the former Conservative government, put it.

With the experience we have had in connection with the Intercolonial
Railway—an expenditure on capital account of nearly $43,000,000 and
a loss to the people for the last six years, putting it at a moderate amount,
of $2,500,000 per year—we are asked to build a road which will destroy
the traffic of the Intercolonial Railway from Quebec to Moncton . . .
for the purpose of saving a distance of fifty or sixty miles in the carrying of
traffic from the North-West Territories and Manitoba to St. John and
Halifax. Did a more insane idea ever take possession of any one? The ports
of the North-West and the ports of Manitoba are at the head of Lake
Superior, and I believe will in the future be at Hudson Bay.

The remaining part of the National Transcontinental, from
Quebec to Winnipeg, was to be in northern country which was,
for the most part, unexplored. There were two obvious arguments
in favour of this: to provide a direct line for through traffic, and to
widen the area available for agriculture, mining and lumbering.

14. *House of commons debates*, 1903, pp. 7658, et seq.

The validity of the first hinged on the volume of through traffic, which was, to say the least, problematical. In regard to the second, one can either praise the optimism or question the temerity of building a colonization railway to the standard of the best trunk lines. It is said that Laurier was induced to choose Quebec city as the St. Lawrence terminus by political pressure from the province; and, further, that the province was willing to accept the National Transcontinental in lieu of a projected railway to the northern area. In any case, given Quebec rather than Toronto or Montreal as the chosen point on the east, it was inevitable that the line should run rather far to the north, rather than slant down toward Montreal and Ottawa. The National Transcontinental from Moncton to Winnipeg was to be constructed out of public funds under the supervision of a board of three commissioners appointed by the governor in council, but the Grand Trunk Pacific Railway Company was to approve of the specifications. On completion, the National Transcontinental was to be leased to, and operated by, that company, on terms of no rent for the first seven years, and three per cent per annum on the cost of construction for the remainder of the fifty-year term.

The situation was paradoxical. On the one hand the government section was to be built as part of the Grand Trunk Pacific— that part which the company was not prepared to finance itself, would be operated by the company, and to all intents and purposes would become a part of the Grand Trunk system. On the other hand, to the National Transcontinental was ascribed the rôle of a common highway for those western railways which had no eastern outlet. It was in these terms that Laurier described it to the house of commons.

But why did we keep this section of the road in our hands? Why did we not give it to the company to build as the other section? We did it because we want to keep that section of the line which is to be the exit of the productive portion of the west, in our own hands so as to be able to regulate the traffic over it. The prairie section will be teeming with business, as we know; it will be teeming with activity as we know. Already there are three lines of railway, the Canadian Pacific Railway, the Great Northern and the Canadian Northern; and this one will be still another. Other roads are also going to be built there to meet the increasing wants of the people.

The Canadian Pacific Railway has its exit on the north shore of Lake Superior; those other railways have no exit. It is our intention that this road shall be kept and maintained under our supervision, so that all railways may get the benefit of it, so that the Canadian people may not be compelled to build another road across that section of country.

This is a curious statement. In the first place, the government only undertook construction because the Grand Trunk was either unwilling or unable to do so; in the second place, the Canadian Northern had completed its line to Lake Superior; and in the third place the line was to be handed over to one, not all, of the western railways. Moreover what the house of commons should first have been discussing in 1903 was whether Canada could maintain two transcontinental railways in addition to the Canadian Pacific. In the previous session, in 1902, an act (2 Edw. VII, c.50) had been passed allowing the Canadian Northern to extend its lines from Port Arthur to Montreal, Ottawa, and Quebec. And yet in 1903 the prime minister (who had failed to bring the Canadian Northern and Grand Trunk together) was talking about a common highway to Winnipeg! Yet no real consideration was given to this preliminary problem, although Laurier had seen the unwisdom of two additional lines north of Lake Superior.

Members of the Conservative opposition were free to point out the weak spots in the government's plan. This they did at considerable length: the debate in the commons occupies several hundred pages of Hansard. Speaker after speaker attacked the Quebec-Moncton line from every possible point of view. Further criticisms were levelled at the decision on the construction of the Quebec-Winnipeg section without adequate surveys. A number of members showed the unlikelihood of grain being carried to seaboard by rail. The financial burden of the whole project on the country was viewed with alarm by others. On the whole relation of the great Canadian railways to one another there was less clarity. Haggart and others called in question the arrangement by which any company might have running rights over the National Transcontinental, holding that this was in principle no exceptional privilege, and in practice would be unworkable. Members on both sides of the house were strikingly silent about the future of the Canadian Northern. At one stage of the debate Borden suggested that the government should buy the Canadian Pacific line from North Bay to Fort William, improve it, and allow running rights to the Canadian Pacific, Canadian Northern, and Grand Trunk Pacific. Similarly he suggested that the latter two companies should build one common line through British Columbia to the coast. He added that the Intercolonial should be extended to Georgian Bay.

In the light of later events it is easy to conclude that it was this failure to see the railway question as a whole that was the weakness of the plan of 1903—a failure that was to bring much trouble to the next generation. It is hard now to recapture the optimism of that period, when parliament, the press, and business men all were thinking in terms of progressive prosperity and rapid expansion. It was this spirit which gave a grandiose character to the plan for providing additional railway facilities; and some additions, it must be remembered, were genuinely necessary. The nature of the plan adopted was determined not only by this general attitude but by a number of special considerations as well. The Conservatives were associated with the Canadian Pacific whose national character coincided with the federalist tendencies of that party. If new railways were to be built the interests of all the provinces had to be considered, more especially as the Liberal party leaned toward the support of provincial rights. The main pressure in this connection came from three sources: the opposition to monopoly in the west, the insistence by Quebec on a colonization railway in her northern territories, and the determination of New Brunswick to obtain as her part a line through the centre of the province.

Having failed to secure voluntary coöperation between the Grand Trunk and the Canadian Northern, and being unwilling or unable to force that coöperation, the government was then driven toward a compromise scheme which had both advantages and disadvantages. It had the weakness of a plan designed to satisfy all parties. The National Transcontinental was needlessly expensive for a colonization railway and proved to be too heavy for the Grand Trunk to carry, while in New Brunswick it imperilled the through traffic of the Intercolonial. The west secured unlimited competition at the cost of over-building. For scores of miles west

of Edmonton the Grand Trunk Pacific and Canadian Northern
were built side by side, only to be unified in a later day. While,
therefore, the nature of the railway policy of 1903 may be understood, its defects are glaring. The Canadian railway problem did
not begin in 1903, but it was greatly accentuated by the decisions
taken at that time.

3. THE GRAND TRUNK PACIFIC

The Grand Trunk Pacific was the Grand Trunk writ large. The
old company, in spite of a staggering debt and periodic crises,
had amazing powers of recovery. One period of recovery happily
began just before the early 'nineties had run their gloomy course.
In 1895 Sir Henry Tyler retired from the presidency after an
exciting but expensive period of office. He was succeeded by an
even more exciting and considerably more expensive régime. The
new president was Sir Charles Rivers Wilson, who, as an eminent
civil servant, had significantly had charge of the national debt and
been a member of the international commission of liquidation
for Egypt. As general manager, Wilson immediately secured the
services of Charles M. Hays, an American, who in his early thirties
had pulled the Wabash Railway out of difficulties. With the exception of a year when he returned to the United States Hays was
general manager of the Grand Trunk until 1909, and president
from then until he was drowned on the *Titanic* in 1912.

The new administration began to show promising results. A
valuable rental was obtained from the Wabash for the use of some
five hundred miles of Grand Trunk tracks; similarly running rights
over the Toronto-Hamilton line were leased to the Canadian Pacific.
The Chicago extension, a separate company, was put into receivership, and reorganized as the Grand Trunk Western with a considerable reduction of interest charges. By these and other measures an
operating deficit was changed into a respectable surplus in 1902.
Not that this was of much help to the general manager, for any
revenue that could thus be collected went into the insatiable maw
of the bond- and stockholders. During twelve years under the new
management the business of the company had grown substantially.
Compared with 1806 gross earnings were up by 99 per cent, net

earnings by 85.7 per cent, and total tonnage moved increased by 111.9 per cent, in 1907.[15] In 1902 and 1903 curves were reduced and grades improved in a number of places, thus reducing the cost of operation. Engines and rolling stock were increased in numbers, size, and power. The lighter rails were replaced by others weighing eighty or a hundred pounds per yard.[16]

The most far-reaching plan of the Grand Trunk was to tap the growing business of the west and secure the advantages of a long haul. Now that the Canadian Pacific had had such good success, and the west was beginning to fill up, Hays was anxious that no more opportunities should be let slip. For purposes of construction and operation a new company was incorporated, known as the Grand Trunk Pacific Railway Company, with a capital of $45,000,000. This company was to construct the "western division," from Winnipeg to the Pacific, and to complete it in five years. It was to be built to a standard "not inferior to the main line of the Grand Trunk Railway Company of Canada between Montreal and Toronto, so far as may be practicable in the case of a newly constructed line of railway." The decision to achieve immediately the standard of a first class railway was based on the belief that the cost of original construction would be more than offset by lower operation and maintenance charges, a policy in marked contrast with that of the Canadian Northern.

No such railway could, of course, be built without generous assistance from the public exchequer. Although the government were not willing to provide land or cash subsidies, they were ready with guarantees and—later—with loans. On the prairie section, from Winnipeg to Wolf Creek, Alberta, the government guaranteed first mortgage three per cent bonds to the amount of $13,000 per mile, and on the mountain section, that is, the remainder, similar bonds to the extent of seventy-five per cent of the total cost, whatever that might be. For seven years the government was to pay the interest on the bonds which it had guaranteed. The balance of the cost of construction was to be met by the sale of bonds, these to

15. *Grand Trunk Railway System, 1896–1907.*
16. W. McNab, *Historical narrative of the inception and development of the Grand Trunk Railway of Canada* (Montreal, 1923, typed), pp. 54, 61.

be guaranteed by the parent company. The Grand Trunk also was to acquire and hold not less than $24,900,000 of the common stock of the Grand Trunk Pacific.

The eastern division, from Winnipeg to Moncton, was to be built by the government, on the same high standard that was set for the western. When completed, the eastern division was to be leased for fifty years to the Grand Trunk Pacific, rent free for the first three years, and at the rate of three per cent per annum on the cost of construction thereafter. The whole line, from Prince Rupert to Moncton, was to be equipped with "modern and complete rolling stock," and to be operated by the Grand Trunk Pacific. The agreement also provided that the lease of the eastern division should contain articles designed to implement the general principle of the government that the whole railway was to have a national character. The articles were to reserve power to the government, in respect of publicly-owned railways, of running rights over both the eastern and western divisions; and power to grant running rights to any railway company over either division. How these provisions might have been worded in the lease, or how effective they might have been, is a debatable question, for, as it proved, the lease never came into operation. At the time they were treated with scant ceremony by the opposition in parliament on the grounds that they secured little more than was already in the Railway Act, and that the rights which they seemed to convey could not in practice be exercised. A further clause was included in the agreement of 1903 which read as follows:

It is hereby declared and agreed between the parties to this agreement that the aid herein provided for is granted by the Government of Canada for the express purpose of encouraging the development of Canadian trade and transportation of goods through Canadian channels. The Company accepts the aid on these conditions, and agrees that all freight originating on the line of the railway, or its branches, not specifically routed otherwise by the shipper, shall, when destined for points in Canada, be carried entirely on Canadian territory, or between Canadian inland ports, and that the through rate on export traffic from the point of origin to the point of destination shall at no time be greater via Canadian ports than via United States ports, and that all such traffic, not specifically routed otherwise by the shipper, shall be carried to Canadian ocean ports.

The proposed railway was to run through a greater proportion of unsettled and presumably unproductive territory than either the Canadian Pacific or the Canadian Northern, both of which cut down into southern Ontario as soon as possible. Therefore it was designed for through traffic to the sea, either at Quebec or at St. John and Halifax. What goods could be carried? The chief export of the west was grain, but grain, as had been demonstrated over and over again, would take the cheaper transport by lake carriers. There is some question as to whether the last quoted article was intended to cover combined land and water transport. As far as grain was concerned, the real pull away from Canadian ports was not to Portland, but to American ports by way of Buffalo. It seems a reasonable conclusion, therefore, that the ports of the Maritime Provinces would benefit no more from the National Transcontinental than from the Intercolonial; for the small saving in mileage would not materially affect the movement of grain. From the company's point of view Chamberlin claimed (in evidence before the royal commission of 1917) that it was impossible to carry freight to Halifax at the same rate as to Portland or Boston, and that it had always been recognized as impossible.

The work of construction on both the eastern and western divisions began in 1905. The criticisms of the Moncton-Quebec section had no deterring effect and the line was built as planned. At Quebec the St. Lawrence had to be bridged. The Dominion government undertook to provide a bridge independently, without charge to the railway, and engaged a firm of engineers to erect it. The plan was ambitious, calling for the longest cantilever bridge in the world, and providing for electric railways, a road, and pedestrians as well as for the trains. Construction began and about half the bridge was in place, when in August 1907, with only slight signs of weakness showing, the completed portion collapsed so suddenly that the men on it were carried into the river. This catastrophe, bringing with it a terrible toll in lives and money, led to a modified and less ambitious plan, which was carried out at a cost of $22,616,898, and the bridge was opened for traffic in 1917.

From the city of Quebec the railway followed its lonely course through northern Quebec and Ontario, unconnected by branches with Montreal or Toronto, except with the latter by the Temiskaming and Northern Ontario. Shunning Lake Superior, the main line ran to the north of Lake Nipigon, with a branch to Fort William. No railway surveys had previously been made and no accurate maps existed, so that the engineers were also explorers. Much of the country through which the line ran caused difficulties in construction. The first contract was let in 1905 and the battle began with the rock and muskeg (swamp) of the north.[17] The last spike in the eastern division was driven late in 1913, but at that time the Grand Trunk Pacific refused to carry out the agreement by which they were to lease the road, being not unnaturally staggered by the fact that the cost exceeded the estimate by approximately one hundred million dollars, or two hundred per cent.

No friend of public enterprise can fail to be embarrassed by some aspects of the story of the National Transcontinental. Charges of widespread corruption in the letting of contracts were never proved, but the public continued to believe that fire existed as well as smoke. The opposition in the house of commons was vigilantly looking for irregularities in contracts. In 1909 a minor sensation was caused when the chief engineer of the National Transcontinental, H. D. Lumsden, resigned on the grounds that the assistant engineers were not following his instructions. He charged them with showing more rock-cutting than existed. In the debate that followed in the house, Houghton Lennox pointed out a number of contracts in which common excavation had been turned into rock-cutting—to the profit of the contractors, and hinted at collusion with the commissioners.[18] The cost of the road was so enormous—about $88,600 a mile—that a royal commission was appointed to investigate. It reported that neither the Transcontinental Railway commission nor the Grand Trunk Pacific had encouraged economy; and that the instructions for low grades had been laid down without information as to the real cost of

17. For accounts of the surveys and construction on the National Transcontinental and Grand Trunk Pacific *see* F. A. M. Talbot, *The making of a great Canadian railway* (London, 1912), and N. Thompson and J. H. Edgar, *Canadian railway development* (Toronto, 1933).

18. *House of commons debates*, 1909 1910, pp. 2335 et seq.

construction.[19] A more legitimate reason was the rise in cost of materials and labour.

The western section, that built by the Grand Trunk Pacific, followed in general the route long since chosen by Fleming. Running somewhat south of the Canadian Northern, it passed through Edmonton, pierced the Rockies at the Yellowhead Pass (although it had been earlier intended to use either the Peace or the Pine River Pass), and took one of Fleming's alternative routes by the Fraser and Skeena rivers to the Pacific, where a new port was established at Prince Rupert. The whole division was opened for traffic in September 1914. By that time, however, the Grand Trunk Pacific was in such a parlous condition that it could not long stand on its own feet.

4. THE CANADIAN NORTHERN RAILWAY

Unlike either the Grand Trunk or the Canadian Pacific the Canadian Northern Railway began not with a trunk line, or any plans for a trunk line, but with a few small and local roads. That it grew rapidly into the third of the great railways of Canada was due to the ambition and enterprise of its two architects, William Mackenzie and Donald Mann. After experience as contractors on the Canadian Pacific and other railways, the two men formed a private partnership under which they operated until 1902 when they incorporated a joint stock company, Mackenzie, Mann and Company. From the beginning of their acquisition of railways they associated with them Z. A. Lash, who, besides being their solicitor, became a director in the company. The interest in the company was equally divided between Mackenzie and Mann, Lash holding a qualifying share.

In 1896 Mackenzie and Mann bought their first railway, the Lake Manitoba Railway and Canal Company—or rather bought a charter passed by the legislature of Manitoba in 1889 but never acted on. The times were propitious. The spread of settlement in the west offered opportunities for such grain-gathering railways as the partners first acquired. The sentiment of Manitoba, too, was friendly towards railways in competition with the Canadian

19. Fournier, *op. cit.*, p. 21.

Pacific. The position at that time, as he saw it, was later summarized by D. B. Hanna, one of the first employees of the Canadian Northern.

The Canadian Pacific Railway . . . then [1896] practically controlled the province [Manitoba] in its operations, and it might be said that it entirely controlled it regarding any traffic moving between the East and West of Canada. It is true that the Northern Pacific and Manitoba, a subsidiary of the Northern Pacific of St. Paul, Minnesota, had a few hundred miles of railway in operation in that province, but there was a friendly arrangement between the two companies—not necessarily put on paper, but in such a way as to be a gentleman's agreement . . . that the traffic coming to the West from Eastern Canada should not be poached on by the Northern Pacific, and in the same way the Canadian Pacific Railway respected the territory of the American line for business passing into the United States. So that to all intents and purposes the province of Manitoba at that time was subject to the control of the Canadian Pacific Railway. So that it follows that any demand that might be made for reduced rates or fair treatment received the usual consideration when one enterprise has the traffic by the throat.[20]

The charter of the Lake Manitoba Railway already carried a valuable federal land subsidy of 6,000 acres per mile for 125 miles, and to this the provincial government added a guarantee of bonds up to $8,000 per mile for the same distance. The charter gave authority to build to Hudson Bay, but its new owners began in a modest way. From Gladstone (thirty-six miles north-west of Portage la Prairie) they built to Lake Winnipegosis by way of Dauphin. Running rights over the Manitoba North-Western enabled them to come as far south as Portage la Prairie. Operation began in 1897 as a pioneer road, with mixed trains twice a week, using second-hand or borrowed cars, and stopping wherever there were passengers or freight.[21] East of Winnipeg construction was started on the Manitoba and Southeastern Railway, the first section of which—forty-five miles from St. Boniface to Marchand—paid its way by hauling firewood. In the next few years additions

20. *Canadian Northern Railway Arbitration*, Evidence, 395.
21. For an interesting account of this and other early Canadian Northern lines *see* D. B. Hanna, *Trains of recollection* (Toronto, 1924). Details of lines built or acquired will be found in E. W. Oliver, "History of construction" (C. Price-Green [ed.], *Encyclopaedia, Canadian Northern Railway* [1918]).

were rapidly made in both directions. By 1902 there was a through connection between Winnipeg and the Dauphin country, and in the same year the Canadian Northern (as it was called after 1899) reached Port Arthur by construction under the charters of the Manitoba and Southeastern and the Ontario and Rainy River railways, and by the acquisition of the existing track of the Port Arthur, Duluth and Western. In 1901 the Canadian Northern secured the Northern Pacific lines in Manitoba, which had been taken over by the provincial government on a 999 years lease, and were sought by both the Canadian Pacific and the Canadian Northern railways. The latter paid to the government a sum equal to the rental paid to the Northern Pacific, and gave reductions in freight rates, which, for competitive reasons, led to a similar reduction by the C.P.R. The most important of the lines thus added were those from Winnipeg to Emerson, and from Morris, on that line, to Brandon. In all the new mileage totalled 350.

In 1901, also, the first move was made in eastern Canada by acquiring a three-mile line from Parry Sound to a junction with the Canada Atlantic Railway. Two years later development in the east began in earnest. In Quebec the Canadian Northern absorbed the Great Northern Railway of Canada and the Chateauguay and Northern Railway. The principal lines thus obtained were from Rivière à Pierre Junction to Hawkesbury, Montreal to Joliette, and the Montfort branch. Taken together, these formed the nucleus of the Ottawa-Montreal-Quebec line. In Nova Scotia the company acquired the Central Railway, from Lunenburg to Middleton (that is, across the peninsula), and a branch to Caledonia. The Canadian Northern had 344 miles of track in eastern Canada at the end of 1903, and a total of 1,706 in east and west together.

At the time of the parliamentary debates on the new railway policy the Canadian Northern was rapidly extending its lines in both eastern and western Canada. What reason was there to suppose that it would grow into a transcontinental railway? There was the charter of 1902, but that might have been interpreted as a precautionary measure rather than as a definite intention. The Canadian Pacific and the Grand Trunk Pacific both announced their intentions at the outset. Sir Donald Mann was questioned on this point by the counsel for the Canadian Bank of Commerce, and the following answers were elicited.

Hellmuth: . . . perhaps you would tell me about the time when you came actually to consider and eventually accomplish the building of the road through to the Pacific coast?

Mann: That was much after this date [1903] we were considering it; but I always maintained we should not build east or west until we had about five thousand miles in operation in the prairies, which would feed the lines east and west; and my judgment then was that there was sufficient through traffic to make the road pay. . . . I discussed it with the late Mr. Hill. . . We were in the west and we were bottled up; anything we had to send there or get from the east had to go over our rivals' railway.

Commissioner Harris: The Canadian Pacific Railway?

Mann: Yes. I tried many times to make a satisfactory arrangement with them, but they were not friendly and could not do it.[22]

The fact that Laurier attempted to persuade the Canadian Northern not to build eastward, and—still more—that it refused to consider the suggestion, indicates that the final objective was a transcontinental railway.

Whatever may have been their views as to the final position of the Canadian Northern, there is no doubt that Mackenzie and Mann continued their policy of expansion. By the end of 1905 the Canadian Northern ran from Winnipeg to Edmonton, and from Winnipeg almost to Prince Albert. To the eastward there was through connection to Port Arthur, and beyond that the lines between Ottawa and Quebec. To make a connected system two long and expensive sections would have to be filled in: from Ottawa to Port Arthur, and from Edmonton to Vancouver. In other words Mackenzie and Mann had devoted their attentions first to the areas where construction was relatively cheap and a paying business might be expected. Such a procedure was in accord with their general principles. They built relatively inexpensive lines which were intended to make some revenue before being improved to the condition of a first-class road. Freight was always the chief concern of the Canadian Northern, and its passenger traffic was never heavy. The Lake Superior and mountain sections would

22. *Canadian Northern Railway Arbitration*, Evidence, p. 2603.

involve expensive work and run through country where there was little or no local business.

In 1908 surveys were begun through the Yellowhead Pass to Vancouver, following the line traced out by Fleming. Building had begun toward the pass from Edmonton when it was found that the Grand Trunk Pacific, which had seemed to be heading for either the Pine or Peace River Pass, also was making for the Yellowhead. To avoid the duplication of expensive construction, Mann suggested to Hays that the Canadian Northern should get trackage rights from the Yellowhead Pass west, and the Grand Trunk Pacific similar rights from Port Arthur to north of Lake Nipigon. He also, he said, offered rights from North Bay to connect with the main line. Hays, however, refused without giving any reason.[23] Thus the two railways ran side by side through the pass, although the Grand Trunk Pacific continued westward to Prince Rupert while the Canadian Northern turned down the valley to Vancouver. Good grades were obtained throughout the mountain section, enabling trains to be pulled through without the aid of extra engines. This condition was particularly desirable in that the heavy grain trains could be hauled over the mountains without great expense. The Pacific ports, being open throughout the year, were valuable outlets for the export trade. In distance Vancouver was 1,237 miles nearer to Saskatoon than was St. John by land.

During the same prosperous years before the war the greater part of the Lake Superior section was built. To avoid the long detour by Toronto, a straight line was followed from Ottawa to Capreol, and thence in a northerly curve—between the Canadian Pacific and National Transcontinental—to Port Arthur. In September 1915 the last spike was driven in the transcontinental line, and before the end of the year a regular passenger service was established from Quebec to Vancouver. While the main line was under construction a considerable number of branches were added, especially in the west. One—based on an acquired railway—ran from Prince Albert down through Saskatoon and Regina to Brandon. From near Edmonton another was built down to the coal mines at Drumheller, and thence to Saskatoon. A single

23. *Ibid.*, 2684.

invasion of American soil was made by a branch from Fort Frances to Duluth. In 1915 the Canadian Northern, with its affiliated companies, possessed 9,362 miles of track.

In spite of some unfortunate results, it is hard to avoid admiring the performance of the Canadian Northern group, for the creation of the railway was the most astonishing feat in the history of Canadian railways. A pioneer in the northern parts of Manitoba with a total staff of thirteen, it ended as a line from tidewater to tidewater. Two peculiar features have already been mentioned: the patchwork way in which it was put together, and the cheapness of the original construction. It has been said that the track had a regrettable tendency to jump up and hit the trains from behind, but much might be forgiven to a pioneer. A third feature of the Canadian Northern—and one that was to bring grey hairs to many an accountant—was its original and tortuous methods of finance. The methods of raising capital for construction and equipment for the other two transcontinental railways may readily be understood, but the Canadian Northern had no such virtues of simplicity. In the first place it consisted of a number of companies separately incorporated, which gave to its accounts a striking variety. The sources of its capital were many. There were cash subsidies from the federal, provincial, and municipal governments. A second source of funds was in grants of land; for, although the policy of making land grants to railways was abandoned shortly before the Canadian Northern was started, some of the old charters which it acquired carried such grants with them. Thirdly, the Canadian Northern obtained loans from the Dominion government. Its fourth, and main source of revenue was the sale of bonds, of which there were a large number of issues, a considerable portion being guaranteed by the federal and provincial governments. It will thus be observed that the Canadian Northern received substantial assistance from public bodies, although such assistance was rendered piecemeal over a period of years. Few railway builders have had more success than the Canadian Northern group in extracting financial aid from governments, though for the most part they were fortunate enough to make their appeals in times of optimism and prosperity. However badly they may have been in need of funds from time to time, Mackenzie and Mann never parted with their common stock, by the possession of which they retained control of the voting shares.

The Canadian Northern, with the Canadian Pacific and Grand Trunk Pacific, made three transcontinental railways in Canada. The two later ones belong to the period of rapid economic expansion in the early twentieth century, a period which came to an end as abruptly as it began. At the end of 1913 and in the early part of 1914 the pace slowed up and signs of a change were unmistakable. In the summer the war broke out; and while this led in time to an artificial stimulation of industry, at first it did nothing but harm to the new railways, then incomplete. Immigration ceased, British investment stopped, and the new railways—outward and visible signs of the belief in the Canadian millenium—were left stranded without sufficient funds or traffic. From the vantage point of later years the mistakes in policy seem clear enough. First in importance was the decision to build two additional and complete transcontinental railways, instead of adopting one of the compromises suggested. Secondly, the expensive construction of the Grand Trunk Pacific and National Transcontinental, and the route of the latter, were hostages to fortune. These were, indeed, mistakes which were to cost the country dear, and to form one of the most important contributory causes to what has come to be called "the railway problem."

CHAPTER XI

NATIONALIZATION OF RAILWAYS

1. RAILWAYS AS A PUBLIC PROBLEM

THE early years of the twentieth century saw a rapid development of railways in a period of marked prosperity. The total mileage in operation almost doubled in the years from 1900 to 1914; and in that period two great transcontinental systems were added to the older one. Between these three companies there were significant differences. The Canadian Pacific Railway had overcome its earlier financial difficulties and was able to carry out a policy of gradual expansion built on a foundation that was strategically sound. The report of the company for 1913–1914 showed an operating surplus of some eighty million dollars, and—after making provision for replacements and contingencies—a large surplus on the total account. A handsome profit was being made on the company's lands, for in that year 259,371 acres were sold at an average price of $17.80 an acre.

An early dream of the Canadian Pacific directors was realized when the company's steamships plied on both Atlantic and Pacific, joining Canadian ports with England on the east, and Japan, China, and Australia on the west. Whether or not the ocean steamships were independently profitable, their prime purpose was to feed the transcontinental railway; for Canadian Pacific officials never forgot that their success or failure depended on that long line, to protect which they had fought many a battle. Increased traffic made it necessary and possible to effect improvements. On the east the position of the C.P.R. was strengthened by the lease of the Dominion Atlantic Railway in 1912, which, with a steamship service between St. John and Digby, gave access to the port of Halifax, and also made possible a steamship connection from Yarmouth to Boston. Increased business in the prairies brought the steady building of branches, and the traffic from these, together with larger through traffic, made it desirable to double-track the main line, most of the section between Winnipeg and Swift Current being so improved by 1914. Heavier traffic in the west put further pressure on the rest of the main line. The section between Winnipeg and Fort William carried not only through rail traffic, but also the grain and other goods that followed the rail and water route, and consequently was double-tracked in 1907. A start was also made on the section from Fort William to Sudbury, which, however, carried lighter traffic. From Sudbury there were two main routes to Montreal: the older and more direct line by the Ottawa River, and another line by way of Toronto. This latter was connected with the Great Lakes transport by a branch from Port McNicoll on Georgian Bay to Bethany Junction near Peterborough (1910). There was now an additional strain on the Toronto-Montreal line, which was relieved by an additional and more southerly track from Toronto to Glen Tay, and double tracks from there to Montreal. In the far west improvements were made by running a connecting link from the main line by way of the Columbia River valley to the Crow's Nest line, and by reducing the grades through the Rockies by means of spiral tunnels between Hector and Field.

For railway companies, as for armies, the offensive may be the best means of defence. The Canadian Pacific was now carrying on a war on two fronts, with American and with Canadian rivals. To broaden its front on the Pacific, it secured running rights through Spokane to Portland, Oregon. To compete with the Canadian Northern and Grand Trunk Pacific in the northern area a branch was cut off the main line at Portage la Prairie and extended to the Calgary-Edmonton line, just south of the latter city. Between this new line and the American border the network of rail was steadily filled in. By means of its control of the Minneapolis, St. Paul and Sault Ste. Marie Railway and the Duluth, South Shore and Atlantic, the C.P.R. could retain some command over the two southern routes between the Canadian prairies and eastern Canada, by way of Sault Ste. Marie and Chicago—the latter being made possible by a lease of the Wisconsin Central to the Minneapolis, St. Paul and Sault Ste. Marie, and by traffic arrangements between Chicago and Detroit. The practice of utilizing existing lines was also followed in southern Ontario. Control of the Kingston and Pembroke Railway made a connection between Lake Ontario and the transcontinental line at Renfrew, and the lease of the Tilsonburg, Lake Erie and Pacific Railroad gave access to Lake Erie at Port Burwell.

The other great private companies were in a very different position from the Canadian Pacific. At the outbreak of the war in 1914 neither the Grand Trunk Pacific nor the Canadian Northern had completed the laying of rails, far less had an opportunity of improving the new line, building branches, or in general establishing the traffic which was their life-blood. Apart from the fact that some sections of the Canadian Northern had been in successful operation for some years, the two new transcontinentals may be compared to the Canadian Pacific of twenty-five years before. They were, in fact, approaching that stage, found in many enterprises, in which a heavy capital expenditure must soon be relieved by income. It was the misfortune of both companies to reach the final and most expensive stage in their development at an unfavourable time—most expensive because they were carrying the accumulated burden of borrowed capital and were engaged in construction in the mountains of British Columbia.

A steady rise in wages since the beginning of the century increased the labour costs of the railways during the period of construction, but there was an ample supply of men.

Index Number of Wages (1913=100)[1]

1901	67.8	1916	105.7
1906	78.7	1917	117.5
1911	92.5	1918	139.8
1914	101.4	1919	160.4
1915	101.4	1920	192.1

Materials for construction, rolling stock, and equipment of all kinds increased in price. The index number of wholesale prices shows a rise from 84.5 in 1901 to the basic 100 in 1913, to 102.3 in 1914, 109.9 in 1915, and to much higher levels in later years.[2]

The rise in wages and prices was accompanied by a corresponding increase in prosperity, and by private and governmental optimism which made railway construction accepted as part of the general

1. *Canada Year Book, 1922–1923*, p. 733. It covers building trades, metal trades, coal mining, printing trades, electric and steam railways.
2. *Canada Year Book, 1934–1935*, p. 861.

progress of the country. Apart from the first panic at the outbreak of hostilities, the war stimulated rather than depressed business. Unemployment and other indications of depression that existed in 1914 were soon cured by an increasing demand for men and goods. Immigration fell off, and production was encouraged by the sudden demand for natural products and manufactured goods in Europe. The effect of the war on traffic and income of all Canadian railways is evident in the following table.[3]

Year (ending June 30)	Passengers	Freight (tons)	Gross earnings	Operating expenses	Ratio of expenses to receipts
			$	$	%
1911	37,097,718	79,884,282	188,733,494	131,034,785	69.43
1912	41,124,181	80,444,331	219,403,753	150,726,540	68.70
1913	46,185,968	106,992,710	256,702,703	182,011,690	70.90
1914	46,702,280	101,393,989	243,083,539	178,975,259	73.63
1915	46,322,035	87,204,838	199,843,072	147,731,099	73.92
1916	43,503,459	100,659,088	261,888,654	180,542,259	68.94

The height of the good years before the war came in 1913 and income declined in 1914 and in 1915. The ratio of expenses to receipts scarcely changed in the first year of the war (1914–1915), and went down materially with better traffic in 1916.

The last spike in the National Transcontinental was driven in November 1913. The Grand Trunk Pacific refused to implement the agreement by which it was to lease that railway, and it was operated by the Canadian Government Railways from June 1915. The Grand Trunk Pacific, from Winnipeg to Prince Rupert, was opened for traffic in September 1914. The rail on the Canadian Northern was completed in January 1915, and passenger traffic established by November. For both of the latter railways a large amount of work on the track remained to be done, and the Grand Trunk Pacific particularly required extensive branch lines.

At this critical time in the history of the two companies the flow of capital began to diminish. The London money market had for some years been ready to meet their needs, but in 1912 began to be less responsive, and a Canadian Northern issue raised in the spring of 1914 proved to be the last. The company was then

3. *Canada Year Book, 1922–1923*, p. 627.

obliged to turn to New York, but loans could only be floated at low prices and higher rates of interest.[4] Parliament had long been a main source of capital, and in 1914 it again made loans to one or both companies. When in 1916 it was proposed that further advances should be made, it became apparent that it was time to take stock of the position of the government in regard to these railways and to consider the formulation of a policy for the future. Sir Thomas White, the minister of finance, told the house of commons that,

with improving financial conditions and with better earnings in prospect, it was hoped that no material assistance would be required in addition to the aid which was given in 1914; but it is now clear, from the statements presented by the railway companies in question, . . . from the financial conditions which still prevail, and from the fact that the war is still raging, that relief is absolutely necessary if these two railway companies are to continue as solvent and going concerns. It has been the policy of the Government since the outbreak of the war to maintain stability and to promote confidence in the financial and economic condition of Canada. We have, therefore, . . . looked with growing concern upon the financial condition of these two great transcontinental enterprises whose affairs have become so intimately connected with the public credit both of the Dominion and of the provinces of Canada. Securities to the amount of several hundred millions of dollars have been issued by both these companies and have found their way into the hands of investors in Great Britain, the United States, and Europe. Any financial crisis in their affairs could not but react seriously upon the general credit of the Dominion in the eyes of the outside world.[5]

The minister went on to examine in detail the financial position of both railways, in the course of which he quoted from a letter from A. W. Smithers, chairman of the Grand Trunk, in which Smithers stated that "we are at the end of our tether with regard to Grand Trunk Pacific financing." Having laid bare the facts, White then sketched the three alternative policies which might be followed. The first was to withhold aid and allow the companies to go into receivership. Such a course would endanger the position of the Grand Trunk itself; would, in his opinion, be a serious threat

4. D. B. Hanna, *Trains of recollection* (Toronto, 1924), p. 240.
5. *House of commons debates*, 1910, p. 8564.

to the credit of public and private bodies in Canada; and would result in the dismemberment of the Canadian Northern, the provinces taking over the constituent companies which they had guaranteed. The second alternative was

to permit default and take physical possession of the two railway systems in question; that is to say, foreclose the mortage which we hold. In that event the Dominion Government would take over the mortgaged premises and hold them as it does the Intercolonial railway. If it continued to hold them and operate them without a receivership or liquidation it would mean that it would have to pay all the interest on all the securities of these companies at present outstanding. It would have to provide the amount of temporary aid which we are now proposing and in addition it would have to provide for the future financing of these roads.

The third alternative, and the one which the government advocated, was to give such temporary financial assistance as would enable the two companies to continue operations, and to delay any decision on policy until an investigation of the whole railway situation had been made by experts. A royal commission was appointed in July 1916, consisting of A. H. Smith, president of the New York Central Railroad (chairman), Sir Henry Drayton, chief commissioner of the board of railway commissioners for Canada, and W. H. Acworth, an English authority on railways. (Mr. Acworth was appointed to replace Sir George Paish, who had resigned on account of ill health.) The terms of reference covered the general problem of transportation in Canada, the status of the three transcontinental railways, and reorganization or acquisition of any of these. In the case of acquisition, the commissioners were to give an opinion on the most effective system of operation. During the autumn the commissioners toured Canada, taking evidence as they went. At the same time they had a physical examination of the Canadian Northern and Grand Trunk Pacific made by engineers under the supervision of Professor G. F. Swain of Harvard.

The commission reported in 1917, Drayton and Acworth presenting a majority, and Smith a minority, report.[6] The disagreement

6. *Report of the royal commission to inquire into railways and transportation in Canada, 1917.*

between them was not on the necessity of governmental aid, but as to the extent and character of that aid. All commissioners agreed that the Canadian Pacific was able to stand on its own feet and needed no governmental assistance. The only way in which this railway entered into any plan that might be adopted was in relation to the avoidance of discrimination against it, for example, by means of uneconomic rates. The majority of the commissioners recommended that the Grand Trunk, Grand Trunk Pacific, and Canadian Northern "be assumed by the people of Canada." Having decided on this, they considered "how this control should be exercised."

In our judgment it is not in the interests of Canada that the operation of its railways should be in the hands of the Government. We know no country in the world, where a democratic state owns and operates its railways, in which politics have not injuriously affected the management of the railways and the railways have not had an injurious influence on politics. We do not think Government ownership of the Canadian railways would tend to reduction of rates, but rather in the contrary direction.

Somewhat paradoxically, the commissioners maintained, as an argument especially applicable to Canada, that government ownership and operation of other railways would be unfair to the Canadian Pacific, since rates might be lowered; so that, if the Dominion operated the other railways, "it would be morally bound to offer to purchase the Canadian Pacific also." A second particular argument against government operation was adduced from the fact that the railways in question had a considerable mileage in the United States; and a third was that Canadian resources were fully needed for the conduct of the war.

The commissioners, it appears, objected not only to government operation, but to government ownership. At the same time, the three companies were to "pass into other hands"; but not by way of receivership, for that course would involve danger to Canadian credit.

We think the question, whether there should be one body or more, is answered by the facts that we have already recited. The Canadian Northern is weak in the East. The Grand Trunk, with the inadequate prairie branches of the Grand Trunk Pacific, would be almost powerless to compete in the West with the Canadian Northern and the Canadian Pacific. The natural tendency of the Grand Trunk and Canadian Northern organizations, if left separate, would be for each to invade the territory of the other. Remaining separate, the Canadian Northern system would need to spend many millions of dollars to obtain an adequate hold on the East in competition with the Canadian Pacific and Grand Trunk. Remaining separate, the Grand Trunk and Grand Trunk Pacific system would need to spend many millions of dollars on new branches in the West, in order to hold its own with the Canadian Pacific and the Canadian Northern. And this money would be needed at once, for till it was spent neither organization would possess a complete system. Canada cannot afford all these new railways, and does not need three competitive systems. We recommend therefore that the three undertakings, the Canadian Northern, the Grand Trunk, and the Grand Trunk Pacific be united in one system.

It had been suggested to the commission that the Canadian Pacific should acquire the other roads and operate them as partner with the government, and again that the government should acquire all the roads, including the Canadian Pacific, and operate them as a unit, but both of these suggestions were rejected in the majority report, largely on the grounds of opposition to monopoly on the one hand and to state ownership on the other. Believing that a commercial company could not be formed to take over the three railways which were in trouble, the commissioners then turned to the solution which they favoured. A board of five trustees should be constituted by parliament and incorporated as "The Dominion Railway Company," in which the ownership of the Canadian Northern, Grand Trunk and Grand Trunk Pacific railways was to be vested. The Intercolonial (including the Prince Edward Island Railway), and the National Transcontinental were to be "handed over" to the company, and the whole five to be operated as a single system. For its part, the government was to assume responsibility for the payment of interest on existing securities.

In order to secure its independence, the board of trustees was to be permanent and self-perpetuating. It should be made up of experts in railways, finance, and labour, and must not even be suspected of assuming a political complexion. This was the great danger that the majority commissioners saw in their plan, and time after time they reiterated their opposition to state operation. "We do not recommend the transfer of the three companies at all," they wrote, "unless our recommendations as to the method to be followed are also substantially accepted."

In a brief but able minority report, A. H. Smith explained the reasons for which he differed from his colleagues.

> They insist that this board is to be permanent and self-perpetuating. I do not know by what means one Parliament can bind its successors to a given policy, especially in so simple a matter as changing the organization of a government board. My friends seem to avoid government owner-ship and operation, in fact condemn it as inadvisable, but propose a plan which contains so many elements of danger in the direction which is sought to be avoided that I am unable to join them.

Their plan, he added, would add about a billion dollars to the Canadian debt. It left out some of the railways, and discriminated in the methods by which properties were to be acquired. Centraliza-tion of control, Smith believed, would not ensure good service. In place of the plan suggested, he proposed another, which he sum-marized as follows:

> Let the Canadian Pacific alone; let the Grand Trunk operate the eastern lines now held by that company and the Canadian Northern; let the Canadian Northern operate the western lines, now held by that company and the Grand Trunk Pacific system; let the government operate the con-nections or procure their operation by private companies.

Smith realized that his plan would not do away with the con-tinuance of public aid to some of the railways, but believed that that aid would be reduced to a minimum, and would be concentrated on those lines which were not self-supporting and could not, for many years, be expected to be self-supporting.

2. NATIONALIZATION OF THE CANADIAN NORTHERN

The report of the royal commission was presented to parliament in the spring of 1917, and at the beginning of August the govern-ment announced its policy.[7] The gravity of the situation, as por-trayed by the report, was accepted; and it was assumed that some steps must be taken immediately which would ensure the maintenance of an adequate transportation system, avoidance

7. *House of commons debates,* 1917, pp. 4015 et seq.

of a dislocation of credit, protection of the governmental investment in the companies, and some degree of permanence in the solution. In regard to the Canadian Northern the policy was simplicity itself. The government should be empowered to acquire that portion of the common stock of the railway which it did not already hold, the value of the stock to be determined by a board of arbitration. Holding the common stock, the government would then be in a position to control the company, whose credit would be restored by the very fact of acquisition.

The debate on the plan was long and, at times, bitter. After two weeks of debate G. P. Graham, who, as a former minister of railways, naturally became chief spokesman for the opposition, moved an amendment that parliament should take over the Canadian Northern without any compensation to the holders of common stock. The amendment was lost, but the issue continued to be debated. Objections to the bill were based on a number of grounds. Some members objected to it because they disbelieved in government ownership on principle. A more consistently expressed argument was that, since the Drayton-Acworth report had found the stock to be valueless, the proposed arbitration was unnecessary. A number of members sought to show that the government was influenced by financial interests. Persistent questioning elicited from the minister of finance the fact that, of the $58,614,000 of common stock standing in the name of Mackenzie, Mann and Company, $51,000,000 was pledged to the Canadian Bank of Commerce against advances. The minister, however, was not prepared to state the amount of those advances. One member asked baldly: "Would not the object [of the bill] also be to save from bankruptcy the Canadian Bank of Commerce, which is said to be responsible for all the Canadian Northern's liabilities since its very inception?" A second member, though making no charge, said that "the conclusion is borne in upon the mind of any man who thinks that unless this stock is given some value the Canadian Bank of Commerce may have trouble in getting repayment of their loan."[8]

8. On this question *see also* the pamphlet, *Railway question in Canada: Liberal legislation from 1896–1911* (Publication No. 30, 1915); W. S. Wallace, *The memoirs of the Rt. Hon. Sir George Foster* (Toronto, 1933), pp. 155–161.

Again and again the bill was attacked and defended. The debate ran through the whole of August, and it was only by vigorous use of the closure that the government was able to bring it to an end before another month began. The act (7 & 8 Geo. V, c.24) was brief indeed as a result of such major campaigning. It empowered the government to acquire the 600,000 shares which it did not already hold, at a price to be determined by arbitration. When the transfer of shares had taken place, the government might assist the Canadian Northern to the extent of $25,000,000 without further authority from parliament. In the agreement of October 1, 1917, between the government, Mackenzie, Mann and Company, and the Bank of Commerce, for the purchase of the shares, it was stated, under the authority of an order in council, that no more than $10,000,000 should be paid for the stock.[9]

The die was cast, and it only remained to determine the value of the shares. The board of arbitration as appointed consisted of Sir William Meredith, chief justice of Ontario, as representative of the government and chairman of the board; Wallace Nesbitt for the stockholders; and R. E. Harris, justice of the supreme court of Nova Scotia, as the neutral member. The hearings began at Toronto on January 18, 1918. A galaxy of legal talent was ready to argue the case: W. N. Tilley for the government, Pierce Butler, of the Minnesota bar, for Mackenzie, Mann and Company, I. F. Hellmuth for the Canadian Bank of Commerce, and F. H. Phippen for the Canadian Northern Railway, were the leaders. The hearings continued, with some protracted breaks, until the middle of May, and covered and re-covered almost every possible aspect of the value and operations of the Canadian Northern. The mass of evidence brought forward, together with previous examinations of the railway, afford an opportunity of analyzing the position of the Canadian Northern system at that time.

The Canadian Northern was built at a low cost with the intention of effecting improvements as income permitted. That this was in general the case was never seriously questioned by its friends or its critics. Both D. B. Hanna and Sir Donald Mann, men who knew the road intimately, in evidence before the board of arbitra-

9. Sir Clifford Sifton's comment on this is quoted in J. W. Dafoe, *Clifford Sifton in relation to his times* (Toronto, 1931), p. 434.

tion, argued that the Canadian Northern was in all essentials the best transcontinental railway in Canada. They referred to the superior grades and curvatures which had been obtained; and Mann, when questioned about the relative standards of the Canadian Northern and Canadian Pacific, pointed out that people had forgotten what the latter was like when first built. He admitted that the Canadian Pacific in 1917 was better in some places than the Canadian Northern, but that difference, he said, could be made up: on the other hand the Canadian Pacific could never get such a favourable route through the Rockies or between Nipigon and Sudbury. Other witnesses told of deficiencies which they had found. G. R. Balloch, one of the engineers employed by Swain, made the general comment: "It is the cheapest line. The most cheaply-constructed line, with more temporary structures which will depreciate in time, rapidly in fact. The time is maturing now for a lot of things and in another fifteen or twenty years will mature on the others."[10] In detail he said that the roadbed was narrow in places; that the line was undulating; that the ballast was in some cases inadequate; and that light or worn rails were not uncommon. He pointed to wooden bridges, trestles, culverts, and water-tanks —all of which would have to be replaced. H. A. Drury, engineer for the board of railway commissioners, stated that he had found the line along the Kaministiquia River to have a dangerously narrow embankment, and a track that was rough and out of line.

Further impressions may be gained from the report drawn up at the request of a group of New York financiers by a commission composed of E. E. Loomis, president of the Lehigh Valley Railroad, and J. W. Platten, president of the United States Mortgage and Trust Company, and employing as consulting engineers the New York firm of Coverdale and Colpitts. In the report, dated March 1917, it is said that "the entire transcontinental line is well located and well built. As to grades and alignments, it is superior to its competitors. . . ." The roadbed on both main and branch lines was described as "adequate," but portions of the latter were said to require ballasting. The only real criticism was directed at the inadequate supply of locomotives and rolling stock. As compared with other evidence, the Loomis report seems to give too favourable

10. *Canadian Northern Railway Arbitration*, Evidence, p. 3347,

a picture. Leaving this as one extreme and the stories about trains sinking into the mud as the other, it may probably be taken that the Canadian Northern was well planned and located, and economically built, but maintenance had been inadequate, and it contained a good deal of temporary work that would sooner or later have to be replaced. The amount of replacement necessary had an important bearing on the value of the property.

All those who examined the Canadian Northern, whether officers of the company or not, laid stress on the route it followed, not only as regards grades but also in relation to the traffic which it either had or might expect to have. The line, with its feeders, through the northern wheat belt had proved a great success. Besides grains, forest products and coal were carried in satisfactory amounts, as well as the usual freight of a settled area. In the prairies, where the Canadian Northern had originated, adequate branches and terminals existed; but in 1917 such developments had not been more than started in the east and far west. Lack of terminal facilities at Vancouver meant that little use could be made of the railway for exporting wheat. In the east the situation was worse. Terminals had yet to be established at many centres, notably at Montreal. Spur lines to factories did not exist in sufficient numbers to allow competition on even terms with the other railways which were in a position to secure freight and route it over their own lines. Another weakness was the lack of American connections. The company intended to build west from Toronto, *via* Hamilton to Niagara Falls, but had not yet been able to do so. Largely to this condition was attributed the small amount of passenger traffic, especially in the east. Over the whole system the revenue from passenger traffic was very slight: in 1915 the Canadian Pacific's earnings per mile on passengers were $2,468, while the corresponding figure for the Canadian Northern was $843.[11]

As seen from the Canadian Northern point of view the problem was that financial considerations made it impossible to complete a programme by which it had been hoped to create a profitable railway; and it was a lack of capital rather than a breakdown in operation that caused the crisis of 1917. Part of the difficulty of

11. "General passenger business" (C. Price-Green [ed.], *Encyclopaedia, Canadian Northern Railway*, [1918]).

disentangling the accounts of the Canadian Northern arises out of the number of companies that made up the system as a whole. In order to secure provincial aid, separate companies had been created in almost every province. The transcontinental line was made up of the Canadian Northern Pacific, Canadian Northern, Canadian Northern Ontario, and Canadian Northern Quebec, and in addition there were a score or more affiliated companies. The cost of construction was met by the sale of bonds and debentures, of lands granted in aid of construction, and by direct subsidies. The common stock of both the Canadian Northern proper and of the affiliated companies was held almost entirely by Mackenzie, Mann and Company, in payment for their services as contractors and promoters and in exchange for lands which they had received as contractors on the roads making up the early Canadian Northern.

As owners of the voting shares Mackenzie and Mann were able to control the policy of the Canadian Northern, and to act quickly without notice to the public. Such a position was valuable, for example, in the case of the acquisition of a railway which rival interests might want. Although no dividend was ever paid on the common stock, their ownership of it was the only means by which Mackenzie and Mann could expect a return on their expenditure of time and money. The arrangement by which all expenses were met out of securities calling for a fixed interest was advantageous from the point of view of management, but it had drawbacks in other ways. This was a point emphasized by Tilley in his argument before the board of arbitration.

The Canadian Pacific Railway [he said] has a certain flexibility to its capital because it has the shareholders' money, and if they cannot pay a high dividend they can pay a lower dividend. They can get some return, but with the Canadian Northern you have the whole expense of the road in its fixed charges, you have got no flexibility at all. If you do not get the money, you just accumulate your debts, and instead of being able to say to the shareholders, now, we will cut off your dividend, the debt keeps on accumulating and piling up, because everything is in that fixed charge, and it goes on, and that must be paid. . . . The capital stock itself represents no cash investment. Nothing has gone into the property for it.[12]

12. *Canadian Northern Railway Arbitration*, Evidence, p. 6306.

The last remark is hardly accurate, because in fact Mackenzie and Mann never charged the company with their services as contractors; but the main point is an important one. Mackenzie and Mann had followed a financial policy directly contrary to that followed by the Canadian Pacific, with its small fixed charges, and they ran into difficulties. On the other hand, the use of bonds for construction expenses may be partly explained by the willingness of both federal and provincial governments to guarantee such bonds in preference to helping the company by land grants—a change of method which dates from after the building of the Canadian Pacific.

In a small compass it is impossible, even if it were otherwise practicable, to recount the intricate financial history of the Canadian Northern. As an indication of the trend, however, a portion of D. B. Hanna's evidence in 1918 may be quoted.

. . . for 18 years up until the 30th June, 1914, the road not only paid all its fixed charges, interest on all its equipment purchases, but it did something more, it paid for four years dividends out of its net income after paying all its fixed charges, dividends on the 5 per cent. income charge convertible debenture stock. That stock was sold subject to dividends based upon net income, and in 1911 that stock sold to the extent of 15 million dollars. It paid out of its surplus income after all fixed charges, including interest on equipment securities, $312,892.05. The surplus for that year before paying these amounts out being $1,007,696.80. In 1912 the surplus after paying all fixed charges, including interest on equipment securities, was $1,250,200.99. It paid out that year on income charge account $674,804.11. In 1913 we had sold the additional 10 million dollars of the 5 per cent. income charge convertible debenture stock increasing the amount to 25 millions. That year the surplus was $1,832,943.78, after paying all the fixed charges and equipment securities interest; and they paid out of that surplus on income charge account, $988,214.49. In 1914 the surplus for that year was $1,554,505.41. Out of that surplus the railway paid $1,250,000 on income charge convertible stock. . . . In 1914 . . . the depression came along, and the war aggravated that situation, and business fell away, and we have not paid anything since 1914.[13]

The financial stress forced the company to look to the Dominion government for help. In years past it had received, like all Canadian

13. *Ibid.*, 435.

railways, public aid from several sources and in several ways. Now that it needed more, the government was unwilling to commit itself further without receiving consideration in return. Already this process had begun, for by an act of 1913 (3 & 4 Geo. V, c.10) subsidies to the Canadian Northern Ontario and Canadian Northern Alberta were granted on condition of the transfer to the government of $7,000,000 (par value) of the stock of the Canadian Northern. The total stock issued at that time was $77,000,000. When further funds were needed in 1914, a new arrangement was made by an act (4 & 5 Geo. V, c.20) under which the total authorized capital of the Canadian Northern was limited to $100,000,000. At the same time $33,000,000 of stock was transferred to the government as against a guarantee of the capital and interest on $45,000,000 of bonds. In this way the government secured forty out of a total of one hundred millions of the stock of the company. The greater part of the remainder was nominally held by Mackenzie, Mann and Company, but all but a small portion was pledged to the Canadian Bank of Commerce. The ownership of the common stock helps to explain the process of the transfer of the company, and accounts for the parties to the arbitration; it also affected the freedom of action of the company. It was a curious twist of fortune that the concentration of the voting shares in the hands of Mackenzie and Mann, which was intended to give them control over the destinies of the company, made it possible for them to lose control to the government just when they most needed it.

In spite of governmental assistance—or perhaps because of its limitations—bankruptcy began to loom on the horizon. Sir William Mackenzie, who had already secured loans in New York after the closing of the London market, hoped to make some more permanent arrangement there which would tide the company over its financial difficulties. In 1916 a syndicate headed by Bertron, Griscom and Company had under consideration the furnishing of a large amount of capital. To acquaint themselves with the value and character of the property, they appointed Messrs. Loomis and Platten to investigate, and they in turn arranged for the report which has already been described. Unhappily for this plan, however, the royal commission of 1916 intervened and, by raising the possibility of nationalization, prevented any further steps being taken. A second way out of the difficulty was cautiously mentioned by Mann in his evidence before the board of arbitration. He stated that the company had an opportunity to sell its whole property a year before the act was passed which provided for the arbitration. As the company controlled only sixty per cent of its stock, and the government would not sell its forty per cent, the party refused to buy.[14] Pressed on this point later, he stated that there had been negotiations with "connections of the Canadian Pacific Railway"[15] —which was presumably the "party" he had previously mentioned. It is interesting to speculate on the course of later history had the negotiations with the Canadian Pacific resulted in a sale. It is also interesting to speculate on the reasons for the government's action in blocking the sale. While such reasons can only be guessed at, it is worthy of note that the government, by blocking the sale, might be judged to have undertaken a moral commitment toward the holders of the securities. A third attempt to avoid receivership was made by inviting the provinces to pay the interest on the bonds they had guaranteed. This, according to Mann, was accepted in principle by British Columbia and one other province, but the process was interrupted by the decision of the Dominion government to buy the road.

The government would not dispose of its minority interest, and thus nullified the plans of the company's directors to escape receivership—whether or not these might otherwise have been successful. It decided to buy the majority interest, which stood in the name of a holding company but was actually held by a bank, and, as a final curiosity, provided for arbitration to decide the value of the majority stock, but set a maximum figure which might be paid.

In approaching its task the board of arbitration very naturally turned to the report of the royal commission of 1916. Drayton and Acworth had used three methods of arriving at the value of the Canadian Northern. From the point of view of cash investment they reached a figure of $370,000,000 as the "maximum possible cost of the Canadian Northern system as at present existing."

14. *Ibid.*, 2708.
15. *Ibid.*, 2812.

Secondly, by making use of Swain's investigations, they were able to arrive at an estimate of the cost of reproducing the property new, at pre-war prices. Allowing for depreciation, they put the cost of reproduction at $402,749,663. Considering that the outstanding liabilities were about $400,000,000, they would appear to be about equal to the reproduction cost; but because of the minority holdings in some of the Canadian Northern enterprises, the commissioners subtracted $10,000,000 from the assets. Thirdly, the commissioners considered the value of the property for sale as a going concern. On the basis of earning power, they believed that no purchaser would pay a price equal to the total liabilities. By means of these three arguments Drayton and Acworth arrived at the conclusion,

that the shareholders of the company have no equity either on the ground of cash put in, or on the ground of physical reproduction cost, or on the ground of the saleable value of their property as a going concern. If, then, the people of Canada have already found, or assumed responsibility for, the bulk of the capital; if they must needs find what further capital is required; and if they must make up for some years to come considerable deficits in net earnings, it seems logically to follow that the people of Canada should assume control of the property.

The arbitrators, of course, did not accept without question the Drayton-Acworth report. Early in the proceedings both Phippen, as counsel for the Canadian Northern, and Hellmuth, as counsel for the Bank of Commerce, protested against the Drayton-Acworth calculations on the ground that they left out of consideration a number of assets, such as money in banks, and land, involving an error of $52,000,000. Whether or not this was accepted by the arbitrators is not clear. The statement accompanying their award was general in the extreme, and gave little indication of the weight which they put on the mass of evidence that had been submitted. The relevant part of it reads as follows:

As to whether or not there was a surplus of assets over liabilities was naturally a subject which engaged much time and consideration. It is of course not a conclusive test as to the value of the stock but it is an element which cannot be ignored. Its importance was perhaps emphasized by the fact that a Royal Commission had reported the assets and liabilities of the Company to be about equal. This report which was made in a proceeding to which the company and its shareholders were not parties, was admittedly made on a misconception of some of the facts, and there were omissions of both assets and liabilities. It should also be pointed out that the work of the Royal Commission has reference to a date anterior to the first day of October, 1917, and there were changes in the interval.

In arriving at the surplus of assets over liabilities, the report of Professor Swain as to the reproduction cost of the physical property based on pre-war prices, and also his estimate of the depreciation has been adopted and after a careful examination we found the surplus of assets over liabilities of the Company on the first day of October, 1917, on a conservative basis to be not less than twenty-five million dollars after deducting the full amount of depreciation found by Professor Swain and making such reduction in the value of the land grants and other assets as seemed reasonable.

It is to be pointed out that a valuation of the physical property of a railway company by the reproduction new method, less depreciation, is not to be regarded as an ascertainment of the actual value. It is only a means to that end, but as it was the best, and in fact the only estimate available, it has been adopted as a basis for the foregoing calculations.

While the surplus of assets over liabilities is an element for consideration as has been already pointed out, it is not conclusive as to the value of the stock of the company. The prospective earning power is perhaps more important than any other element in ascertaining such value. And in arriving at a conclusion we have given careful consideration to the past history of the company, the location of its lines and their construction, the rate of interest on the funded and other debts of the company, the probable future growth of the population and business of the country, and all other factors which seemed to us to have any bearing upon the question.[16]

The award, which was signed by all three arbitrators, was that the value of the six hundred thousand shares in question was $10,800,000. How this figure was arrived at is not disclosed, nor its relation to the $25,000,000 of surplus assets. The value set on the shares was very close to the sum fixed as a maximum in the agreement ($10,000,000).

The award did not in any way affect the status of the Canadian Northern, which had already passed into the hands of the govern-

16. The award and explanatory statement were not printed. The above extract is taken from a copy in the records of the department of railways and canals.

ment. In September 1918 the government appointed a new board of directors, and in November charged it with the management of the Canadian Government Railways in place of the general manager. In December a further order in council authorized the board to use the designation "Canadian National Railways" for the lines which they operated. For the time being, however, the Canadian Northern was preserved as a separate entity: the final organization of the Canadian National awaiting the nationalization of the Grand Trunk and Grand Trunk Pacific.

3. NATIONALIZATION OF THE GRAND TRUNK.

When in 1917 parliament was asked to pass a measure to take over the Canadian Northern it was also obliged to recognize that the Grand Trunk Pacific was in difficulties. At that time, however, it was not possible to take steps in regard to the Grand Trunk Pacific parallel to those taken in regard to the Canadian Northern. The government's policy, as explained to the house of commons, was to make temporary provision for the Grand Trunk Pacific pending further negotiations.

. . . the situation is complicated by the fact that the Grand Trunk Railway Company is . . . largely involved by its guarantee of the Grand Trunk Pacific securities. It is, therefore, not possible for us, even if we were disposed to do so, at this time to deal with the Grand Trunk Pacific Railway Company in the same manner that we propose to deal with the Canadian Northern Railway Company, because a long negotiation would be necessary with the Grand Trunk Railway Company, in order that the public interests might be safeguarded before the Grand Trunk was relieved from any or all of its liabilities in connection with the matters which I have mentioned. Our policy with regard to the Grand Trunk Pacific for the time being is this: we propose to make a demand loan, repayable at six per cent, secured by a mortgage to the amount of $7,500,000. We shall take the power to constitute the Board of Directors of the Grand Trunk Pacific as we see fit.[17]

So much for the present necessity. As to the future, the government apparently looked forward to acquiring the Grand Trunk Pacific, though whether they would go as far as the Drayton-

17. *House of commons debates*, 1917, p. 4017.

Acworth proposals by adding to it the Grand Trunk was not yet disclosed. White continued:

Personally I would look forward to the Government some day acquiring the Grand Trunk Pacific system, because with the Canadian Northern system belonging to the Government, as we propose, the two systems could usefully co-operate in the West. . . . It is not our intention to release the Grand Trunk Railway Company from their obligations in respect of the Grand Trunk Pacific Railway Company. . . .

The last remark referred to the Grand Trunk's suggestion, first officially made at the end of 1915, that the government should take over the Grand Trunk Pacific and the liabilities of the Grand Trunk to that company. To this suggestion the royal commission was firmly opposed, as the government subsequently proved to be. The government already had the National Transcontinental on its hands and was unwilling to become the owner of any other lines with such distant prospects of financial success. The divergence of opinion served to complicate and prolong the negotiations with the company.

In May 1918 the prime minister told the house of commons that if the Grand Trunk Pacific were taken over, "that practically involves the taking over of the Grand Trunk Railway as well."[18] This he believed desirable in order to give eastern connections to both the Grand Trunk Pacific and the Canadian Northern; because the Grand Trunk might be crippled if it had to meet its obligations to the Grand Trunk Pacific; and, while it had "no bright future prospects" without its western connections, it might do well if amalgamated with the Grand Trunk Pacific and Canadian Northern. Confidential negotiations, he told the house, were being conducted with the Grand Trunk. These had, in fact, been in train for some months. In January the government asked the Grand Trunk on what terms that company and the Grand Trunk Pacific could be acquired by the Dominion. The terms proposed in reply were that the government should assume all the liabilities of the Grand Trunk, pay an annual amount of $5,287,000 for dividends on guaranteed and preferred stock, and an amount sufficient to cover dividends on the common stock at a rate rising annually

18. *Ibid.*, 1918, p. 2004.

from one to two and one-half per cent. After refusing this optimistic offer, the government expressed its willingness to take over the assets and liabilities of the Grand Trunk and Grand Trunk Pacific and pay annually to the shareholders $2,500,000 for the first three years, $3,000,000 for the next five, and $3,600,000 thereafter. This met with no more success than the first proposal, and the correspondence continued. In July the government renewed its offer, together with an alternative one that the whole question of remuneration be referred to a board of arbitration. This again was refused, and a further offer made.

In February 1919 the company notified the government that they expected to have to default on March 1 in respect of the interest on securities falling due in London, and indicated that a serious situation would arise if funds were not found to prevent such an unfortunate occurrence. The minister of finance replied that no further sums would be voted as long as negotiations "remained in their present unsatisfactory condition." The interest was paid; but a few days later, "without any previous intimation or discussion at all," notice was received by the government that the Grand Trunk Pacific could not be operated after March 10, on the ground that the freight rates in the west were not high enough to allow operation without loss. This the government regarded as a threat designed to bring the desired loan;[19] but instead of taking that action they appointed the minister of railways and canals as receiver under the authority of the War Measures Act— holding that the exchequer court was not competent to act in such a case. The Grand Trunk Pacific, with its telegraphs, steamships, hotels and other undertakings, was operated under receivership from March 10, 1919 until September 1, 1920, at which date its management was entrusted to the board of directors of the Canadian National.[20]

It still remained to come to an agreement with the Grand Trunk, which continued to be held responsible for its obligations to the Grand Trunk Pacific. At long last that agreement was reached in October 1919. Two acts (10 Geo. V, c.17, and 10 and 11 Geo. V, c.13) and an agreement between government and company

19. *Ibid.*, 1919, p. 664.
20. The receivership was not technically terminated until 1926.

covered the acquisition of the Grand Trunk and its subsidiaries. All the capital stock was to be taken over with the exception of the issue of four per cent guaranteed stock, and on that the government agreed to pay interest. To determine the value of the stock a board of three arbitrators was to be appointed, and they were limited to a maximum award of $64,166,666.66.

After some delay, the board of arbitration met on February 1, 1921. Sir Walter Cassels, justice of the exchequer court, was chairman; Sir Thomas White represented the government; and Mr. W. H. Taft, formerly president of the United States, represented the company. The proceedings were similar to those adopted for the Canadian Northern, but in this case only the government and company were represented by counsel. For each party there were a number of distinguished lawyers: W. N. Tilley appearing again for the government, and Eugene Lafleur for the company. The arbitrators were asked to determine the value of the first, second, and third preference stock and of the common stock. As in the previous arbitration, the board examined in some detail the physical and financial condition of the railway; but, since the majority of the board refused to accept evidence bearing on reproduction value, less evidence could be adduced on physical condition. Because the arbitrators failed to reach an unanimous decision, each wrote his reasons for coming to certain conclusions; and these three arguments throw light not only on the arbitration but also on the condition of the company.

At the time when the board met, the Grand Trunk system had not taken over the National Transcontinental, and had lost the Grand Trunk Pacific. Nevertheless, for purposes of estimating the value of the stock, the G.T.P. was included in consideration, because of the financial relation between the two companies. This outlet to the Pacific, on which Hays had pinned his hopes, had proved to be a disastrous failure, as was most clearly evident from the efforts of the parent company to get rid of it. As a matter of policy the line to the Pacific had been built to a high standard, and the large capital expenditure inevitably involved was enhanced by the rising prices of labour and materials in the pre-war and war years. The expected traffic never materialized, partly because the west did not develop as had been hoped, partly because the G.T.P.

was supplied with an inadequate system of feeders, and partly because of competition from the spreading Canadian Northern lines. The Grand Trunk claimed, with some apparent justice, that the Canadian Northern had been supported by the government after the agreement concerning the G.T.P.; and that this unexpected competition had upset the calculations concerning traffic. An additional reason, which might or might not have changed with time, was that Prince Rupert was a new port, with no established ocean traffic and no facilities. It was more like a dead end than an outlet to the far east.

For purposes of profitable operation, therefore, the Grand Trunk was confined to its old territory in central Canada and the eastern and mid-western states. An interesting analysis of these lines was made by Mr. Taft, whose attitude toward the company was friendly but not uncritical.

The Grand Trunk System has been burdened with a very great number of branch lines, and with some lines parallel to its main trunk line, which it acquired to avoid competition, and which are not a source of profit. Many of the branch lines of course are feeders, but it is quite apparent that they are in some respects a burden. In a degree the same thing has been true of branch lines acquired in Michigan, but the marvellous growth of business in that State in the centres reached by the Grand Trunk is likely to make them very profitable. With much care and wisdom the business of the Grand Trunk System has been nursed into a large through traffic between Chicago and the Atlantic Seaboard. While the amount of business done in the United States by the Western Lines and the New England Lines of the Grand Trunk System is not more than one-third of the Grand Trunk Railway of Canada, the business which has come to the Grand Trunk is perhaps 70 per cent. due to its business from and to the United States, to and from Canada, and to other business from and to points in the United States through Canada to and from other points in the United States.[21]

The Grand Trunk had in reality continued to rely on its original policy of operating as a through road for New England, central Canada, and the middle west. Nevertheless—and in spite of the financial failure of the Grand Trunk Pacific—it need not be assumed that the general idea of expansion into the west was a mistake.

21. *Grand Trunk Arbitration: the award and reasons for the award* (Ottawa, 1921), p. 39.

One of its prime difficulties was that it missed the profits accruing from long-haul traffic. In 1920 the Grand Trunk, operating 4,775 miles of rail, moved 33,026,658 actual net tons, for which it was paid $80,686,623. The Canadian Pacific, operating 13,402 miles, moved 29,919,645 tons, and was paid $143,878,185. Thus the Grand Trunk, moving 3,100,000 tons more freight than the Canadian Pacific, was paid $63,191,562 less for services. The Grand Trunk received $2.44 for each ton and the Canadian Pacific $4.81. The difference may largely be attributed to the fact that the Canadian Pacific carried each ton an average of 463 miles and the Grand Trunk an average of only 212 miles.[22]

Mr. Taft paid a high tribute to the efficiency of the local management in Canada, and believed that if policy, as dictated from London, had been equally enlightened, the fate of the railway would have been different. On the physical condition of the property there was, not unnaturally, considerable disagreement.[23] H. G. Kelley, who had been president of the company since 1917, testified that the road was in good operating condition and could carry a fifty per cent increase in its business without heavy expenditure. He can hardly be taken as an impartial witness, more especially as he had, in 1917, when the company was anxious to exhibit poverty, reported that the road was in need of large expenditure for maintenance. Two inspections were made of the Grand Trunk, one on behalf of the company by J. B. Berry, an American railway engineer of considerable experience, and the other for the department of railways and canals by engineers under Colonel Montserrat. Berry prepared a report on reproduction value less depreciation, but it was not allowed as evidence. His report, according to Taft, was that "the railroad does not show deferred maintenance, but on the whole is in excellent condition." Taft attributed to Montserrat "an enthusiasm of condemnation," and criticized him, and the department, for "calculating the cost of producing a perfect road without regard to economical considerations." On the Grand Trunk Pacific, Sullivan, an engineer and witness for the government, and Berry were in general agreement

22. Sir Joseph Flavelle, *The Canadian National Railway System: letter addressed to the Rt. Hon. Arthur Meighen* (Toronto, 1921).

23. The opinions which follow are taken from the Grand Trunk *Award*.

that a number of wooden trestles would soon have to be replaced by permanent structures.

In their statements in explanation of the award Cassels and White laid great emphasis on the financial condition and future financial prospects of the railway. When the decision was reached that reproduction cost was not relevant to the value of the stock of the company, it was also agreed that "the essential fact to be ascertained was the earning power, actual and potential, of the system." The following table, based on the statement of the company's auditor, indicated the results of operations. The Grand Trunk Pacific and Central Vermont are not included.

Year	Surplus (+) or Deficit (—)	Add surplus on other subsidiary companies
1910	+$3,617,876	$83,360
1911	+ 4,188,783	267,865
1912	+ 4,482,448	249,196
1913	+ 2,874,592	484,648
1914	+ 2,014,176	71,132
1915	+ 5,755,730	245,924
1916	+11,319,341	732,834
1917	+ 3,402,540	270,540
1918	− 3,872,344	492,588
1919	− 6,488,918	166,932

To obtain a view of the real position of the railway the sums lost by the Grand Trunk by reason of its support of the Grand Trunk Pacific should also be considered. Apart from the sums lent from time to time to the G.T.P., there remained an absolute guarantee of $2,292,760 annually for interest and a further guarantee of $1,395,170 annually, conditional on the parent company having a surplus after paying its own running expenses and interest on funded obligations and guaranteed stock. It is no wonder that the Grand Trunk had made spirited efforts to rid itself of a company which had a deficit of $30,845,828 by January 1, 1920: and equally not surprising that the government persisted in holding that the Grand Trunk's guarantee was still binding.

The Grand Trunk executive had always suffered from the demands of stockholders for dividends, and had very often had to face the problem of whether profits should be used for interest on an over-capitalized system, or to meet obligations to the government, or go back into the road. At the beginning of the explanation of his award, Cassels refers to two points raised by the government's counsel: that the accounts of the railway had been manipulated, and that dividends were paid "when"—to quote Cassels' words—"to the knowledge of the chairman, there were no earnings applicable to the payment of such dividends; and those moneys so paid were diverted from paying claims due to the Government, which should have been paid, leaving the Government claim unpaid to the present time." The latter point is well reinforced by a series of cables between the chairman and the president of the company.

In a case involving the value of any railway, and particularly a railway with such complicated finances as the Grand Trunk, it was not unnatural that there should be differences of opinion. A. W. Atwater, in his argument for the company, took as a fair period the years 1912 to 1916, and showed that during that time there was an average of two and one-half million dollars annually available for dividends on the preferred and common stock, and that the operating ratio was approximately the same as that of the eastern rate group in the United States. In 1920, he said, the Grand Trunk operating ratio was higher than that group, so that if the transportation act of the United States operated, as it was intended, to produce a return, the Grand Trunk would have $2,800,000 available for dividends on preference and common stock.[24]

In September 1921 the official award was made, Cassels and White both holding that there was no value in the shares in question. The latter summed up his conclusions as follows:

(1) The actual earning power of the Grand Trunk Railway Company of Canada before, during, and since the war, and, so far as can be estimated, for the future does not justify the assumption that any profit would, from the date of the acquisition by the Government of the preference and common shares, viz., May, 1920, ever have been available for distribution to the holders thereof, after providing for the contingent liability of the com-

24. *Grand Trunk Arbitration* (1921), Evidence, p. 7260.

pany in respect of the Grand Trunk Pacific securities guaranteed by the company and dividends upon the "guaranteed stock."

(2) Having regard to its own continued heavy deficits, the necessity for making provision for deferred and extraordinary maintenance and capital construction, and its heavy liabilities in respect of securities of the Grand Trunk Pacific Railway Company of Canada bearing its guarantee, the Grand Trunk Railway Company of Canada, but for the financial support of the Government since May, 1920, must have been forced into a receivership.

Upon these conclusions I find that the preference and common stock of the Grand Trunk Railway Company of Canada has no value. Any question as to compassionate consideration of the shareholders must be for the Government and Parliament of Canada to deal with and not for the Board.

In a dissenting judgment Taft analysed the earnings of the past and estimated earnings for the future, which enabled him to rate the value of the stock at not less than $48,000,000.

In the light of the actual history of the Grand Trunk Railway since 1920, either under separate management or as part of the Canadian National system, one is tempted to believe that the majority of the arbitrators were right in their conclusion. But, taking into consideration all the circumstances, it is not surprising that there was a strong feeling generated in England against the award and against the government's acceptance of it. A parallel was at once drawn with the arbitration on the stock of the Canadian Northern. In the Drayton-Acworth report the stock of the Canadian Northern was held to have no value, but the subsequent board of arbitration found a value of $10,800,000. In the case of the Canadian Northern arbitration a basis of "reproduction new" was allowed as the principal test of value, while no evidence bearing on that point was admitted by the board in the case of the Grand Trunk.[25] Furthermore, the Canadian Northern was a Canadian company, whose stock was largely in the possession of a Canadian bank; while the Grand Trunk was an English company, whose stock was widely distributed throughout England. Neither

25. There was some justification in making this distinction on the ground that the Canadian Northern was well located, but had had no opportunity of demonstrating its earning power; while on the other hand the Grand Trunk had shown that its earning power was insufficient.

the appeal to the privy council on a point of law, nor that to the Canadian government for equitable consideration, met with success, and a sense of grievance was left to flourish.

In general, the English point of view was that a great deal of capital had been expended on this pioneer railway in Canada, and that the investment had been jeopardized primarily by the insistence of the Canadian government on its own plan for the Grand Trunk Pacific. It was felt that the attitudes of both government and board of arbitration were biased against the railway, and that they were willing to sacrifice the shareholders because they were not Canadian. On the other hand the point of view held in Canada was that the railway had always been operated too much for the shareholders; that its losses were due in large part to mismanagement from a distance; that it had not been forced to undertake the Grand Trunk Pacific; and that its recent history showed a consistent attempt to trick the government out of a repayment of the sums which had been advanced. A last act of the English directors made a bad impression in Canada. On the date of the ratification by the shareholders of the acquisition agreement, they voted a year's salary to the leading officials (a total of $306,000) out of the company's fire insurance fund, and five years' salary to the directors ($167,800). A royal commission later severely criticized the president and vice-president as responsible for this misplaced generosity.[26] Between the English and Canadian positions it was hard, if not impossible, to build a bridge; and the result was that a railway which had done much for Canadian development passed out of separate existence amidst protests and recriminations.

The Grand Trunk did not at once become part of the Canadian National organization. A temporary arrangement was first made by which a board of management, consisting of C. A. Hayes and S. J. Hungerford, representing the Canadian National, W. D. Robb and Frank Scott, representing the Grand Trunk, and H. G. Kelley as chairman, operated the railway from the end of May 1920. A year later, on the expiration of the legal term of the board of arbitration, a further act was necessary to continue the arbitration; and in this act provision was made for the resignation of

26. *Canadian Annual Review, 1923,* p. 366.

the English directorate of the railway and the establishment of the head office in Canada. The new board nominated by the government consisted of Sir Joseph Flavelle, Toronto, chairman, H. G. Kelley, Montreal, A. J. Mitchell, Toronto, E. L. Newcombe, Ottawa, and J. N. Dupuis, Montreal. Kelley remained the president of the company for the time being.

Following the award of the board of arbitration and the dismissal of the appeal to the privy council, the process of consolidating the Grand Trunk and the Canadian National began. By the end of January 1923 the two had been united under a single board, and the act to incorporate the Canadian National Railway Company brought into effect. The head offices of the company were established at Montreal, and a new president, Sir Henry Thornton, a man with a successful record in American and English railways, was appointed. So ended the long revolution by which the Dominion became possessed of a great system of state railways.

4. The Canadian National Railways

To those who see in a great railway something more than steel and wood, offices and balance sheets, there must come a moment of sentiment at the loss of its corporate soul and the passing of a name which has stood for the hopes and labours of its servants and a link with the outer world for hundreds of communities. The history of the Grand Trunk and the Canadian Northern Railways spans the long years from the first bold attempt to provide railway transportation for what was then settled Canada, through the rush of expansion of the early twentieth century, to the time when it was tacitly acknowledged that optimism unrealized must at last yield place to the harsh facts of deficits. But the mood of the time in which the Canadian National Railways were born was more critical than sentimental; more conscious of the burden that was to be carried than of the ambitions that had been foiled; more censorious of the sins of the fading companies than proud of the achievements they had made. "For half a century on this continent", Sir John Willison reminded an audience, "the clamour against railways after they have been constructed has been almost as vociferous as the clamour for railways before they were

constructed."[27] Unemotional painters hurried to erase the names
of the old companies, and to write on locomotives and cars the new
emblem, "Canadian National."

The new name was symbolic of a new era in the history of Canadian railways: a new tradition had to be evolved to replace the
old. The people of Canada had not launched into this great expansion of public ownership by design but from the pressure of existing
facts. Here and there, in parliament and press, voices were raised
in support of public ownership as a principle; but on the whole
it was undertaken with no enthusiasm, and from necessity rather
than from choice. Alternative proposals were made but not adopted.
Lord Shaughnessy proposed in 1921 that the then government
lines should be operated by the Canadian Pacific in conjunction
with their own lines. Sir Thomas Tait, on the other hand, argued
that the whole railway system of Canada should be operated by a
new corporation, in which fifty-one per cent of the capital would be
subscribed and owned by the Canadian government. His plan
provided for guarantees to holders of Canadian Pacific securities.
W. F. Tye, an engineer, propounded a similar solution to "the
railway problem," with the difference that the government should
hold only forty per cent of the stock. The government, however,
continued to hold at least to the general terms of the Drayton-
Acworth report: the Canadian Pacific to be left as it was, and the
remaining railways to be owned by the Dominion, but operated
by a semi-independent body.

The Canadian National Railway Company was evolved by
degrees. When the Canadian Northern was taken over in 1918 a
small body of directors, with Mr. D. B. Hanna as president, was
appointed to administer it. In the same year the Canadian
Government Railways were placed under the same board, and in
1920 the Grand Trunk Pacific was added—the whole being now
known as the Canadian National Railways. In October 1922 this
board resigned, and its place was taken by a new one, with Sir
Henry Thornton as president and chairman. The new board also
took the management of the Grand Trunk Railway, the provisional board of that company having also resigned. The formal

27. Sir John Willison, *The railway question in Canada* (speech to the Canadian
Club of Montreal, 1921).

unification of the Canadian National and the Grand Trunk was made in January 1923 by an order in council, which also brought into effect the act of 1919 (9 & 10 Geo. V, c.13) incorporating the Canadian National Railway Company. The act provided for a board of not more than fifteen directors, appointed by the governor in council, and empowered the board to issue securities against its mileage, except on the former Government Railways, any deficit on which was to be met out of the consolidated revenue fund.

The first period of re-organization (1918–1922) was faced by Mr. Hanna's board. It found a heavy problem in deferred maintenance, which had to be met at a time when wages and prices were high and freight rates stationary. "If the National Railways," wrote Hanna, "were to be managed as a business, and not as a makeshift, the Board felt that there should not only be a thorough rehabilitation of the property, but that all possible costs should be charged to revenue so that there could be no mistake about the strictly businesslike character of the whole administration. That meant requests for vast sums of money, and the charging of them against revenue, which in turn meant the declaration of huge, and to the short-sighted, terrifying deficits."[28] Holding that the Canadian National could not only never pay, but that part of it would fall into complete disrepair unless it were put into better condition, the board approached the government, which proved to be ready to provide the money required. Put in the form of figures, the results of this policy seem depressing enough, but in Hanna's view the figures of earnings and expenses justified the policy adopted.

Canadian National Railways, 1919–1922[29]

	1919	1920	1921	1922
Gross earnings	$105,036,176	$125,641,753	$126,691,456	$120,135,957
Operating expenses	125,349,797	162,484,723	142,784,358	129,872,275
Operating deficit	20,313,621	36,842,970	16,092,902	9,736,318
Deficit after fixed charges	49,004,545	67,505,060	56,673,934	51,103,297

28. Hanna, *op. cit.*, p. 278, and chaps. xv and xvi *passim*.

29. L. T. Fournier, *Railway nationalization in Canada* (Toronto, 1935), p. 77. Fixed charges do not include the Canadian Government Railways. *See* the whole chapter (vi) on the Canadian National from 1919 to 1922.

The new national railway company was rich in physical property, if in nothing else. By 1923 there had come within its management the Canadian Government Railways, including the Intercolonial, Prince Edward Island, National Transcontinental, St. John and Quebec (leased) and Hudson Bay railways; the Canadian Northern system; the Grand Trunk Pacific; and the Grand Trunk Railway, including the Grand Trunk Western (American) line and the Grand Trunk New England lines. For purposes of operation this great system was divided into four divisions: (1) the Atlantic region, comprising all lines in the Maritime Provinces as far west as Rivière du Loup, and Monk on the Transcontinental—a total of 2,760.08 miles. The headquarters were at Moncton. (2) The central region, comprising all lines west of the Atlantic region as far as, but not including, Port Arthur, and Superior Junction on the Transcontinental. It included the Portland line, and amounted to a total of 7,830.91 miles. The headquarters were at Toronto. (3) Grand Trunk Western lines, comprising Grand Trunk lines west of the Detroit River—a total of 991.69 miles, headquarters being at Detroit. (4) Western region, from Port Arthur and Superior Junction to the Pacific coast, including Vancouver Island—a total of 10,268.21 miles. The headquarters were at Winnipeg.

The executive officers were appointed to the several divisions, each of which had a general manager and superintendents. The central office in Montreal was headed by the president and five vice-presidents, the latter being assigned to the following departments: operation, maintenance, and construction; finance; insurance, immigration, development, lands, express, and telegraphs; legal affairs; and traffic. With the exception of the president, the officers of the company were drawn from the component railways of the national system, a policy which called not only for tact in establishing precedence, but also for the creation of an *esprit de corps* amongst men who had formerly belonged to competing organizations.[30]

Even more formidable was the task of bringing some unity out of a number of railways that had been deliberately built to rival each other. Hundreds of miles of parallel tracks, with the

30. *Report of the department of railways and canals, 1923–1924*, p. 5.

corresponding terminals and other equipment, were nothing but a liability to a single company. The company was empowered by the act of 1919 to abandon operation, with the approval of the governor in council and on the recommendation of the board of railway commissioners, on lines on which operation and maintenance had "become unnecessary or inexpedient through duplication, or other economical considerations," and to dismantle or dispose of these lines with the consent of shareholders representing the majority of securities; but, while such drastic measures might make for economy and efficiency in operation, they would leave a dead weight of debt to be carried by operated lines. To parallel lines and a mountainous debt was added the ogre of deferred maintenance. Whatever may have been the exact degree to which the component railways had been allowed to deteriorate, there was no doubt in the minds of Canadian National executives that there was a crying need for expenditure on the road. The Canadian National company was visited with the sins of the private companies, but the railway map was a reflection too of national policies, wise or foolish: the Intercolonial, the National Transcontinental, the Grand Trunk Pacific.

The calendar year 1923 was the first in the history of the Canadian National system after the addition of the Grand Trunk. By bringing in that railway, with its profitable business in eastern Canada, the general operating ratio was brought down to 92.06— a figure which, though higher than the agreed danger mark, was lower than had obtained on some portions of the National system. For the year 1923 the revenue was $254,926,456.04 and the expenses $234,689,892.95, leaving net earnings of $20,236,563.09. The latter amount, though it might be regarded as a good start by the management, looks small indeed when set against the whole financial position of the company. An impression of its position may be gained from the headings from the consolidated balance sheet as of December 31, 1923. This covers all parts of the Canadian National except the Central Vermont.

The burden of fixed charges could not be fully met by increased earnings, more especially since the total continued to mount as further loans were made by the government to effect improvements in the property and pay interest on the securities held by the public. A suggestion was made that the capital of the railway should be written down to a point where it bore some real relation to possible earnings, but no action was taken at the time.

Assets

Investments	$1,899,407,586.74
Current assets	101,724,097.90
Deferred assets	12,683,832.93
Unadjusted debits	8,400,169.71
	$2,022,215,687.28

Liabilities

Stock	$270,230,913.70
Government grants	16,204,520.40
Long term debt	1,937,282,331.65
Current liabilities	59,018,478.92
Deferred liabilities	3,287,585.83
Unadjusted credits	19,582,262.25
Corporate surplus	283,390,405.47 deficit
	$2,022,215,687.28

Since the administrators of the railway could do nothing to modify the capital structure, they devoted their attention to reducing the cost of operation and securing more traffic. Such additional business might come from a general development of the country, based on immigration and prosperity of agriculture and industry; or it might be diverted from the Canadian Pacific. The creation of the national system left the Canadian Pacific as the only important rival and the only large private railway company in Canada. Built on a consistent plan, and ably managed, the company was making a large revenue and paying handsome dividends on its preferred and common stock. At the same time the railway and equipment had not been allowed to depreciate. It appeared, therefore, to the Canadian National executive that they must bring their property at least up to the standard of the Canadian Pacific, if they were to compete successfully with that well established company. This was exactly the kind of task which Thornton knew, and he threw himself with great energy into it. Before many years had passed the pace was accelerated by the economic prosperity which swept all business forward in a torrent. There thus arose the latest, and perhaps the last great period of railway growth in Canada.

CHAPTER XII

RAILWAYS IN SUNSHINE AND SHADOW

1. A New Era of Expansion and Competition

THE history of Canadian railways in the dozen years since the organization of the Canadian National System is so obscured by a cloud of controversy, by personalities, and by political entanglements, that it is difficult to see the whole significance of the period. The experience of public ownership on a large scale and violent fluctuations in national prosperity have bulked so large in the picture that they tend to hide a background that on closer examination proves to have changed little from earlier days. *Plus ça change, plus c'est la même chose.*

As long as the frontier continued to be pushed northward the pioneers called for railway connections, and were little impressed by a superabundance of lines in older parts of the Dominion. It meant little to compare the total population with the total number of miles of railway, much as this ratio might signify for the public purse. For those living in regions already served by railways there arose the perennial question of freight rates. It was not that the Canadian railways charged an exorbitant rate per mile, but that the number of miles normally to be covered was large. Whether for internal or for export trade the Canadian producer or manufacturer had ordinarily to count on heavy transportation expenses, which fell unevenly according to geographical position. The alternative means of relief in spreading the burden more equally were to to develop shorter routes, especially to tidewater, and to favour certain districts by adjustment of rates.

The solution of these general problems was influenced, in the period with which this chapter is concerned, by the existence of the Canadian National Railways and the operation of the trade cycle. The lines included in the Canadian National were already built: the expenditure was made and the plant ready for use. The creation of the Canadian National did not aggravate but rather eased the situation in some respects, for it made possible the

377

abandonment of unnecessary track and equipment. Although much duplication still remained, the position was manifestly sounder in this way than it would have been under the two private companies which had expected to operate the lines. But there were also drawbacks. The Canadian National included two railways designed to compete with each other, and these, with the previous government lines, were to be welded into one system. In practice the duplication looked worse than it otherwise would have done, although it was actually less wasteful.

A new element in the situation was the nature of the relations of the Canadian Pacific and Canadian National. The two were very different in composition. One was a private and the other a publicly-owned company. One was designed on a unified plan, and the other was a congeries of separate railways, in many places arranged as rivals. One had prestige, ample resources, and was in excellent physical condition; the other was deficient in all these respects. All but a small portion of the railway mileage in Canada was in the control of two companies, and the process of absorption of the smaller companies continued to take place.

Competition there had always been, and competition, said the public, there should still be. But it was to be competition of a type that the Canadian Pacific had not known since it had been harried by the Grand Trunk in the 'eighties and 'nineties, for, instead of poor companies skating on the edge of bankruptcy, came this new one that had behind it the long purse of the government. Hanna had done the spadework of re-organization and rehabilitation, but there was a new note struck from the outset of the Thornton régime. It was Sir Henry Thornton's belief that a character had to be created for the Canadian National: it must stand in the public eye not as a monument to the past, but as a vital force of the present. In the years immediately preceding their nationalization no one of the constituent companies had a reputation comparable to that of the Canadian Pacific. Grand Trunk trains were proverbially late; the Canadian Northern was cheaply built; the Intercolonial was part of the cost of confederation; and the National Transcontinental had been spurned by the Grand Trunk Pacific. If there had been a great wave of enthusiasm for public ownership the past might have been buried beneath the tide, but there was no such enthusiasm. The public had been warned over and over again that public ownership was at best a doubtful expedient for meeting an unfortunate situation, and for once was inclined to believe what it was told.

Thornton, who was rather like Van Horne in his flair for building up a decayed property, set about the task of improving lines and equipment, reducing expenses, and offering improved service. Since his competitor was necessarily the Canadian Pacific, that must also be his standard, and because he had to gain prestige for his railway, he forced the pace. He would not merely copy the Canadian Pacific: he would show the public that the Canadian National was even better—hence the improved passenger cars and faster schedules. When, in 1924, the National cut the running time to Winnipeg, and the Canadian Pacific had to follow suit, it was evident that the new railway had taken the initiative.

The presidents of both railways became peripatetic, explaining to audiences all over Canada their respective opinions on the railway situation. Mr. (later Sir) Edward Beatty, appointed president of the Canadian Pacific in 1918, necessarily adopted a defensive position. The Canadian Pacific, a private corporation, felt itself menaced by the vigorous opposition of a rival which seemed to have the unlimited resources of the government at its disposal. Leaving in abeyance for the present the question of amalgamation, Beatty adopted a formula which has since become familiar, a legacy—if an unconscious one—from the Grand Trunk.[1]

It is a peculiar anomaly that the less profitable the operations of the National System, the greater the taxes of the C.P.R., while if the National Railways prosper through diversion of traffic from the C.P.R., we lose in revenues more than we gain in taxes. . . . This company has every reason to hope for the success of the National Railways, provided it is accomplished without withdrawing from us traffic which we have taken so many years to build up and secure. The greatest factor which will contribute to the National Railways' progress is the development of Canada. . . .[2]

Thornton made a series of barn-storming expeditions, telling the people of Canada that the National railway was going to be

1. Cf. pp. 298-299.
2. Speech of January 10, 1925, quoted in *Canadian Annual Review, 1924-1925*, p. 114.

all right, that it was going to pay both its expenses and overhead charges. He, too, stressed the importance of the progress of the country, from which indeed he had as much to hope as had the rival orator. In his first report as president (1922) he made this brief but discerning remark: "The success of the National System . . . is not entirely to be obtained by methods generally applied to Railways which are not producing returns, viz., improving the physical condition and operating methods—it is a matter of building up the country to support the Railways."

Competition in services was inevitable, and the determination of the Canadian National's officers to obtain a good share of the traffic meant that that competition must assume a particularly active character. Its origin, therefore, was not dependent on any tangible signs of better times, but it was given a great impetus by a period of prosperity that was comparable in effect to, if greater in degree than, the rich years at the opening of the century. The depression which followed the war was succeeded in the latter part of 1925 by a "boom" which rapidly began to assume unprecedented proportions. For Canada it meant expanding markets for natural and manufactured products, ample supplies of capital, and a revival of immigration. The following table[3] will indicate the trend.

Net Value of Production
(000 omitted)

Industry	1924 $	1925 $	1926 $	1927 $	1928 $
Agriculture	1,140,895	1,382,598	1,400,244	1,522,948	1,501,271
Manufactures	1,256,643	1,360,879	1,519,179	1,635,923	1,819,046
Total (including other industries)	3,018,182	3,364,824	3,640,356	3,901,505	4,122,509

Between 1923 and 1929 foreign investments in Canada increased by $1,337,000,000.[4] Owing partly to changed conditions in Europe, and partly to the completion of construction work on the Canadian transcontinental railways, immigration never again approximated

3. *Canada Year Book*, 1931.
4. H. A. Innis and A. F. W. Plumptre (eds.), *The Canadian economy and its problems* (Toronto, 1934), p. 226.

to the volume it had reached just before the war. It did, however, show a marked increase within this period. The low figure of 67,446 in 1923 was changed to 145,250 in 1924, and reached 167,723 in 1929. Business was what the railways most needed, and the general rise of prosperity reacted favourably on them.[5]

Year	Gross earnings $	Ratio of expenses to receipts %
1922	440,687,128	89.39
1923	478,338,047	86.52
1924	445,923,877	85.77
1925	455,297,288	81.70
1926	493,599,754	78.91
1927	499,064,207	81.68
1928	563,732,260	78.53
1929	534,106,045	81.08

Once again in Canadian history a forward movement in railways paralleled a general economic advance of the country. The determination of the directors of the Canadian National to secure more traffic led to a considerable movement in the railway world before the dawning of general prosperity. The advance of the railways was then caught up by the national economic expansion, which carried it along on the flood tide of optimism. It is not to be wondered at that the railways should have shared in the epidemic of capital expenditure that was characteristic of the four or five years before the collapse of 1929. Always they had been in the van in periods of expansion, and more was demanded of them as a public service when prosperity seemed to have no bounds. Faster and more frequent passenger trains, new outlets for grain, branch lines into progressing districts—all these were called for by the public, contractors, and the companies themselves. In years when factories were built for an imaginary future demand, when precarious fortunes were based on watered stock, when municipal bodies mortgaged the future, and when hardly a voice was raised against senseless gambling throughout the community—at such a time it was not to be expected that the railways, whose profits depended on a capacity to undertake the business that was offered, should alone have adopted a wise and conservative policy.

5. *Canada Year Book*, 1934–1935, p. 704. All Canadian railways are included.

Without attempting to describe all the additions made to railway mileage and facilities in these years, some indication may be given of the most significant moves. One was the provision of railways for the steadily broadening belt of settlement. The Peace River country, far to the north of Edmonton, and centering in the river valley, was the frontier area which made most progress in the years just before and after the war. Here was a district of some millions of acres of good agricultural land, with a climate that allowed for the growing of wheat and other field crops; and here was re-enacted the never-ending story of pioneer farming. The fur traders, who had first discovered the Peace River, used their accustomed system of water transport, but for the farmer who sought to send his crops to a market governed by a world price, the labour and expense of hauling overland was so slow and expensive as to eat up the profits in a most discouraging way. Hence he called, as generations before him had called, for railways.

Three related railway companies, at first under private ownership, built into the Peace River country and eastward of it. From Edmonton, then the nearest point, the Edmonton, Dunvegan and British Columbia Railway took its solitary course north along the Lesser Slave River, and past the south shore of Lesser Slave Lake to McLennan (1915)—a distance of 245 miles. From there it was built another hundred miles westward to Roycroft (1916), on to Hythe, and over the boundary of British Columbia to Pouce Coupé. From this trunk line the second company, the Alberta Great Waterways, branched off near Edmonton, and ran northeasterly for a distance of three hundred miles to Waterways on the Athabasca River (1921). The third company, the Central Canada, built from McLennan to Peace River, and west to Fairview (1928). All three companies were operated together, and in 1920 were leased to the Canadian Pacific. In 1929, after prolonged negotiations with the Alberta government (which had taken over the railways) they were bought by the Canadian Pacific and Canadian National and operated jointly as the Northern Alberta Railways.

Besides requests for further branches in the Peace River country, there developed a number of plans for a direct outlet from that area to the Pacific. A joint board of engineers of the Canadian

Pacific and Canadian National undertook an examination of the question and made a report in 1925. "The reason this subject is being discussed," they wrote, "is the general opinion of the settlers in the Peace River district, who, without any study or thought as to whether or not their business can afford the cost, believe that if there was constructed a shorter railway to the Pacific coast that they would be entitled to, and would obtain lower freight rates."[6] The board expressed the opinion that it would be "more economical to handle the business, regardless of the rate received, over the existing lines until the traffic was many times the present," but nevertheless reported the results of their study of routes. The one which they regarded as most feasible involved joining the Central Canada to the Canadian National at Obed, east of the Rockies, and so using Canadian National lines to Vancouver or Prince Rupert, the cost being estimated at $80,000,000. An alternative was a line through the Monkman Pass, and to Vancouver over the Canadian National or Pacific Great Eastern or via the Canadian National to Prince Rupert. A second alternative was by the Peace River Pass and direct to the coast at Stewart (north of Prince Rupert), or over existing railways as before.

In spite of the board's disapproval of even the Obed connection, and in spite of a reduction of freight rates from the Peace River to the head of the lakes in 1924 and 1925, the Pacific outlet continued to be urged by local members in the house of commons. Mention of a new railway to a new port on the Pacific gave rise to a project, entertained by a group of English capitalists, for building a railway from Stewart to join the Peace River railway, a plan which had once before been attempted but dropped after a few miles of rail had been laid. Such a northern route, or that by Obed, was held to be unsatisfactory in British Columbia, where much concern was felt for the future of the Pacific Great Eastern Railway. In 1912 a private company was chartered by provincial statute to build from North Vancouver to Prince George, and two years later was further authorized to extend its line to the Peace River block. Securities to the extent of $42,000 per mile were guaranteed by the province

6. *Report on various proposed railway routes for a western outlet to the Pacific from the Peace River district, by a joint board of engineers of the Canadian National and Canadian Pacific Railways* (Ottawa, 1929).

over a distance of 480 miles. The purposes in building the railway were twofold: to open up and develop central and northern British Columbia, and to effect a junction with the Grand Trunk Pacific at Prince George. To ensure the latter connection an agreement was made between the two companies the gist of which was that the Grand Trunk Pacific would route its Vancouver traffic over the P.G.E. Construction went forward, and by 1921 the line was in operation from Squamish at the head of Howe Sound to Quesnel, a point on the Fraser River seventy-eight miles from Prince George. Completion of the line was delayed partly because of the difficult nature of the country between Quesnel and Prince George. In the meanwhile fate had been unkind. The Grand Trunk Pacific was taken over by the government of Canada, which already owned the Canadian Northern, and the latter's line to Vancouver was used by the consolidated companies. In 1918 the P.G.E. fell into the hands of the British Columbia government, and proved to be an embarrassing possession. There was, it is true, a not inconsiderable traffic in lumber and from the gold mines of the Cariboo district, but the direct connection with a transcontinental railway had not been made, and there was little hope that the line could be operated without loss on the scanty local traffic of a sparsely-settled area. The only hope that seemed to remain for profitable operation was in linking up with the Peace River lines. For a time there appeared to be a possibility that the Pacific Great Eastern could be sold to one of two or three groups of capitalists that considered the property, but in the end none of them went further than preliminary negotiation. The provincial government, therefore, sought to deposit the foundling on the federal doorstep.

If the eyes of British Columbia and Alberta were turned toward the Pacific, those of Manitoba and Saskatchewan were fixed on Hudson Bay. As long as the province of Manitoba had existed there had been talk of a railway to the bay, which would mean a far shorter land journey than to Montreal and even a slightly shorter voyage to Liverpool. Throughout the 'eighties and 'nineties there was much interest in this project, stimulated by the hope of offering competition to the Canadian Pacific and thus reducing freight rates to Montreal. Beyond the formation of a company no steps to realize this ambition were taken until Mackenzie and

Mann acquired Hugh Sutherland's charter, with its land grant, for their Lake Manitoba Railway and Canal Company and began to build northward on the west shore of Lake Manitoba. This line, however, turned westward to Prince Albert and left the bay project still to be completed. In 1906 it was carried a step further when the Canadian Northern began an extension northward from Hudson Bay Junction to the Pas, the line being put into operation in 1911.

At that point the activity of private companies ended, and it was left to the Dominion government to complete the work. Nothing loath, the government began in 1910 the erection of a bridge over the Saskatchewan River, and, in succeeding years, the laying of track. Progress, however, was slow. Late in 1913 passenger service was opened for fifty-six miles to Scott, but the outbreak of war slowed up and finally stopped further construction. When work was stopped in 1918 track had been laid to within ninety miles of Nelson, but over one hundred miles of this had never been operated. During the period of eight years (1918–1926) in which construction was suspended, maintenance also ceased, so that considerable repairs became necessary. After the war the Hudson Bay Railway was debated vigorously in parliament and in the newspapers. The legislatures of Manitoba and Saskatchewan urged completion of the road, as did a number of newspapers such as the *Manitoba Free Press* and the *Regina Leader*. In 1924 the On-to-the-Bay Association was inaugurated with a mass meeting at Winnipeg, with representatives from the three prairie provinces, and from North and South Dakota. In eastern Canada there was less support and even active opposition, particularly in Montreal. For a few years little was done, except to repair a portion of the line earlier constructed, and to run the "Muskeg special" for a part of the way.

Hesitation as to the wisdom of completing the railway was due to a number of considerations. It was questioned whether further outlay would be justified by the volume of traffic, especially in view of the growing importance of Vancouver as an alternative outlet for grain. There was doubt as to the practicability of navigating Hudson Bay and Hudson Strait. The Hudson's Bay Company had done so for some two and a half centuries, but not without difficulty and during a very short season. Expert opinion differed widely as to the length of the season of navigation which could be regarded as assured. Furthermore, there were doubts as to the wisdom of selecting Port Nelson as the terminus, although such a decision had been made in 1912. In spite of the greater distance to Churchill (some eighty-seven miles) it was argued that it would be a better terminus, since it was a better harbour. In 1920 a committee of the senate, to which the question was referred, gave the opinion ". . . that the Government should not make further important expenditures at this Port [Nelson] without first making a new and thorough examination into the relative merits of Churchill and Nelson as a terminus for the railroad." In January 1926 the government announced its intention of providing for the completion of the railway, and a year later Frederick Palmer, an English engineer, was requested to make a report on the two harbours. In October of the same year Palmer expressed strongly his preference for Churchill,[7] and in the meantime government surveys had shown that there were no serious obstacles to the continuation of the railway there. The route of the railway was, therefore, changed to turn north at Amery on the Nelson River, and preparations were made for developing a port at the old Hudson's Bay post. Whatever could be moved of the considerable works already undertaken at Nelson was then transferred to the new terminus. By the summer of 1931 the new part of the railway was completed, and the old, much of which had fallen into disrepair, was restored. A grain elevator, with a capacity of two and one-half million bushels, had in the meanwhile been built, and in September 1931 two cargoes of wheat were shipped to Europe. From 1920 to 1926 the Hudson Bay Railway was included in the Canadian government railways. In the latter year it was returned to the department of railways and canals until completed, and subsequently was operated with the other government railways on behalf of the government by the Canadian National.

Once more the bay had recovered its old position as an outlet for western Canada, and the ghosts of generations of fur traders looked amazed at the tall elevator, great wharves, and puffing

7. F. Palmer, *Report on the selection of a terminal port for the Hudson Bay Railway* (London, 1927).

engines. Whether it was a triumph for economic principles of transportation remained to be proved. Completed at a time of depression, the bay route came into operation under unfavourable circumstances. There was the problem of insurance rates, which remained high relatively to the St. Lawrence route. In 1931 the insurance rate for the bay route was two per cent and in 1936 it was reduced to one per cent. For the St. Lawrence the rate was almost stationary at a quarter of one per cent. The railway from the Pas to Churchill, together with the facilities at the port, cost some fifty million dollars. The argument that other railways could not handle the through traffic in wheat had ceased to be valid before construction had even begun, but the mining area north of the Pas had already provided some local traffic. The Hudson Bay route, however, has not been open long enough to test its permanent value. In 1934 four million bushels, and in 1935 two and one-half million bushels, of grain were exported from Churchill. For 1935 the operating loss on the railway was $336,000.[8]

Further to the east, too, rails were being laid to James Bay. At the beginning of the century the Ontario government had begun a colonization railway, known as the Temiskaming and Northern Ontario, from North Bay into the clay belt. The discovery of mines added greatly to the business of the road, and this encouragement—combined with the oncoming National Transcontinental—led to an extension as far as Cochrane, where it joined the line of the other new railway. The distance thus covered was 252 miles, and there for a time the railway halted. After the war the legislature decided to carry out a plan which had once been considered for private enterprise, to build on to James Bay, nearly as far again as from North Bay to Cochrane. The object of this adventurous move was apparently more to open up the northern part of the province than to reach tidewater, but when completed in 1932 the T. & N.O. constituted another outlet to the sea. The terminus was at Moosonee at the mouth of the Moose River, and although it could not be used by ocean-going vessels, it gave to Ontario a door on the ocean.

The new railways that have thus far been traced show a development in marked contrast to the policy of earlier years. From force

8. *House of commons debates*, 1936, pp. 465 et seq.

of necessity the first emphasis had to be laid on the provision of
railways from coast to coast, serving a relatively narrow belt.
This accomplished, branches were thrown out from the trunk lines,
intended at once to facilitate settlement and create traffic. By this
means the area served was gradually widened. A third phase came
with the trunk lines to the north, which modified the east and west
conception of railway growth. The Peace River railways, the
Hudson Bay Railway, and the James Bay line all made possible
development of the country through which they passed; but they
did more than this, for they could be combined with other methods
of transportation to serve the whole northern area. With the
completion of the line to Moosonee, the Hudson's Bay Company
supplied the James Bay district by rail. The railway to Churchill
gave an entrance to the minerals of the northern pre-cambrian
shield, and formed a base for further transport by tractor and
aeroplane. In conjunction with steamships on Hudson Bay, the
railway also provided a route to the eastern Arctic alternative to
that by the Mackenzie River. From Churchill ships can carry goods
to Wager Inlet, and tractors have been used to portage the cargo
over the neck of land to Cockburn Bay at the mouth of Backs
River.[9] In 1937 the Hudson's Bay Company brought the eastern
and western Arctic even closer together by way of Bellot Strait.
The old problem of the north-west passage is thus in course of
being solved by a series of links with the south, and an integration
of rail, water, and air transport.

At the same time the transcontinental trunk lines, with their
established termini and ports, remained the basis of the Canadian
railway system. In this field the governing factors were the general
economic expansion, competition between the two large companies,
consolidation of the Canadian National lines, and problems of
freight rates. On the main lines there were steady improvements,
such as ballasting and double-tracking, made necessary by the
increasing speed and weight of trains. These sufficed for the
Canadian Pacific, but more complex adjustments were required
for the Canadian National, which was faced with the problem of
unifying as far as possible the lines which it had inherited. One

9. H. A. Innis, "The Hudson Bay Railway" (*The Geographical Review*, xx, 1);
H. A. Innis, *Problems of staple production in Canada* (Toronto, 1933), pp. 82 et seq.

drastic expedient was to tear up one set of rails where two Canadian National lines closely paralleled each other, such as part of the old Canadian Northern line between Toronto and Napanee, at which latter point the lines branched, the Canadian Northern turning north to Ottawa. On a longer stretch from Edmonton to the Yellowhead Pass, the Grand Trunk Pacific and Canadian Northern track had been built side by side, and no difficulty arose in unifying them. A little over a hundred miles of Grand Trunk Pacific track was torn up as early as 1917 and the rails sent to France. Similarly a hundred miles of Canadian Northern track was torn up in other parts of the stretch. At Red Pass Junction, near Mount Robson, the line forked, leaving the former Grand Trunk Pacific line to Prince Rupert and the Canadian Northern to Vancouver. The National Transcontinental was left intact, but an ingenious combination was made between it and the Canadian Northern by the construction of the Longlac cut-off, thirty miles in length, which made it possible to route through trains between Toronto or Montreal and Winnipeg by the Canadian Northern as far as Longlac and thence to Nakina and over the Transcontinental straight to Winnipeg. By avoiding the long loop south to Port Arthur a saving of 102 miles was made.

Nothing more was done—and little more could be done—to unify the Canadian National main lines. In New Brunswick there remained the National Transcontinental and Intercolonial, but to abandon either of these would be to leave a part of the province without railway communication. Similarly the National Transcontinental from Quebec to Winnipeg was a pioneer railway for northern Quebec and Ontario, even if built to the standard of a trunk line. On the other hand the National Transcontinental was too far north to replace the Canadian Northern for regular western trains, except for the portion from Nakina west, which was thus utilized; as was, for a time, the line west of Cochrane, in conjunction with running rights over the Temiskaming and Northern Ontario. In the mountain region, where traffic was light, something had been done to avoid duplication; and the only other possible step was to abandon the Prince Rupert line, a step which would shatter the hopes of any development of the northern part of British Columbia.

A railway depends for profits on its branch or "feeder" lines as well as on its trunk lines: particularly in Canada, where urban centres are few and far between, and where the railways look to agricultural, mining, and lumbering districts for freight. In the ten years from 1924 a programme of expansion of branch lines which was startling in its magnitude was approved by parliament. Including new work on the Hudson Bay Railway, a total of 4,198 miles of branch lines was projected, which, as was pointed out by the deputy minister, was "considerably greater than the trans-continental mileage between Halifax and Vancouver. From this, it is apparent also that new mileage of the two chief railway systems of Canada is being added to at an average rate of more than a mile a day."[10] Not all of this work was actually carried out, but even that it should have been planned, and partially built, shows that the country was prepared to add materially to its railway system. Given two competing railway companies, it was inevitable that in some at least of the branch line projects the motive of building for the needs of an area should be mixed with an element of rivalry. In many places the borders of the territory of one company were not recognized by the other: and, particularly in the prairie provinces where new settlements were constantly being made, there were invasions and counter-invasions that added unnecessarily to the costs of the companies. That such cases existed, however, should not be allowed to conceal those others where new branches were beneficial both to the company concerned and to the public.

Saskatchewan and eastern Alberta were the chief scenes of activity in branch lines. New lines were built both in the northern areas, and to those other districts throughout the provinces which were still far from any railway. In the pursuance of their respective programmes for branch lines in the west the Canadian National and the Canadian Pacific became involved in a long dispute. In 1929 the presidents of both railways issued statements decrying wasteful competition, but there was no agreement as to which should give way, or as to the limits of spheres of influence. The bulk of the new mileage in Alberta and Saskatchewan was intended primarily to serve agricultural districts, but elsewhere branches

10. *Report of the department of railways and canals*, 1928–1929, p. xxii.

were built to recently developed mines, as, for example, those to the Flin Flon and Sherritt-Gordon mines in northern Saskatchewan and Manitoba, and to the Rouyn mine in Quebec.

The following table will indicate the location and extent of new railway mileage. With the exception of the Hudson Bay Railway, the greater part of the new mileage may be attributed to branch lines. The discrepancy between the additional mileage and the totals is explained by the abandonment of certain existing lines, and to other minor factors such as reclassification.

| Province | Miles opened for operation during the year | | | | | |
	1925	1926	1927	1928	1929	1930
Prince Edward Island	—	0.06	—	—	—	9.95
Nova Scotia	4.22	0.13	0.04	—	—	0.02
New Brunswick	—	0.26	0.01	—	—	0.01
Quebec	22.37	22.88	91.55	52.18	22.99	3.86
Ontario	32.83	2.48	1.48	52.17	20.33	70.27
Manitoba	22.48	47.01	0.04	0.16	1.07	126.16
Saskatchewan	123.94	215.04	94.56	194.71	215.46	406.64
Alberta	154.40	85.90	127.60	171.68	243.84	94.13
British Columbia	145.51	1.89	0.06	11.97	0.36	1.97
Total new mileage	505.75	375.65	315.34	482.82	504.05	713.01
Total miles in operation	40,352	40,352	40,572	41,024	41,382	42,049

Important developments were made in terminals during the period. After some delay, the Union Station in Toronto was opened in 1927, together with the elevated tracks leading into it from both directions. While both companies made use of this, the Canadian Pacific also rebuilt its North Toronto station on the northern track, which eliminated the gradient from the edge of the lake to the higher ground east of the city. A larger project was the Montreal terminal undertaken by the Canadian National. For some years the Bonaventure (Grand Trunk) station had been considered unsatisfactory because of the level crossings involved, and with the growth of the Canadian National the management of that railway was anxious to secure a central terminal which would both obviate this difficulty and give to the railway a stronger position in Montreal. The plan which was evolved was to build a single passenger station at the site of the Canadian Northern's tunnel station. Before sanctioning this plan the government engaged the English engineer, Mr. Frederick Palmer, to examine its desirability. Mr. Palmer reported favourably, adding, however, the suggestion that the proposed terminal should also be used by the Canadian Pacific.[11] As it proved that that company was unwilling to participate in the scheme, holding that the Windsor Station was capable of expansion, authority was given by parliament in 1929 for its commencement by the Canadian National alone. Work was therefore begun, but a halt was later called on the ground of expense. In Halifax a new hotel was built by the Canadian National, which also inaugurated a steamship service to the West Indies for the carriage principally of passengers and fruit. In 1928 the first of the five "Lady" boats was put into service, and the completion of the others followed.

The conditions of Canadian geography created unequal economic opportunities for the various areas. On the one hand the areas remote from tidewater sought relief from the heavy transportation charges on their exports; and on the other hand the provinces or districts possessing seaports wished to secure the maximum volume of business through those ports. The development of Vancouver, the railway to Churchill, the projected Peace River outlet, improved facilities at Halifax, and the car ferry to Prince Edward Island (with standard gauge on the Island railway) were— together with the improvement of the St. Lawrence-Great Lakes waterway—means of attaining the aims of the two interests. There was, however, a limit to the results that could be achieved in this way, for there must remain sections, like the central prairies, still distant from tidewater. Furthermore, the provision of further outlets as a solution to the problem as a whole involved inherent contradictions. The more the traffic of the centre was drawn to west and north, the more the ports of the far east would suffer. New Brunswick and Nova Scotia had come into the federation with hopes that their ports would carry a large portion of the business of central Canada, and to make this possible the Intercolonial Railway became an integral part of the federation scheme. Bitter experience had shown, however, that Montreal and American ports took the lion's share, and "maritime grievances" were the result.

11. F. Palmer, *Report on railway terminal facilities at Montreal* (Ottawa, 1929).

Out of this complexity of factors had long since arisen the device of modifying the charge on freight with lower rates on certain routes.

A great many factors, such as competition from water and highway transport, and from American railways, bear on freight rates; but without attempting to analyze the complicated rate structure of Canada,[12] two aspects of it which affect the point under discussion may be mentioned. The first of these is the most noteworthy attempt to compensate for geographical position by the reduction of freight rates. Complaints in the Maritime Provinces that railway rates were too high to allow trade with the rest of Canada led to the appointment of a royal commission under Sir Andrew Duncan. In its report, presented in 1926, the commission in general accepted the point of view of the Maritime Provinces, and advocated a reduction of twenty per cent on all freight originating on the Atlantic division of the Canadian National (which division was to be enlarged for the purpose), without prejudice to the Canadian Pacific. The proposals were, in the following year, embodied in the Maritime Freight Rates Act, with the provisoes that the lower rates were to be operative on all railways in the area, and that the loss to the companies was to be made up by the government. In other words, all freight from the Maritime Provinces was subsidized to the extent of twenty per cent at the expense of the taxpayers as a whole. Another case in point is the continuance and expansion of the operation of the Crow's Nest Pass agreement. Passed originally to relieve the shippers of western Canada, the lower rates were suspended in 1918 and revived in 1922. In 1925 the Crow's Nest Pass rates on grains and grain products were extended to cover shipments to Vancouver; and subsequently to cover shipments of grain over the Canadian National to Quebec at the request of those interested in that port.

While such reductions were intended to benefit shippers, and in general to compensate for the peculiarities of Canadian geography, they could hardly be viewed with anything but apprehension by the officials of the railway companies. Shortly after his

12. On this subject *see* W. T. Jackman, *Economic principles of transportation* (Toronto, 1935).

appointment, Thornton indicated the views of his company in regard to the burning question of freight rates:

Railway freight rates in Canada are and have been for many years the lowest in the world. The average freight receipt per ton per mile for Canadian Railways in 1914 was 0.742 cents. War time increases forced this unit of earning up to a point approximately 75 per cent. over the pre-war level. The series of reductions which began on January 1, 1921, have substantially reduced this average so that in 1923 it stood at 0.980 or 32 per cent. above the pre-war level. In contrast to this the average prices of labour, material and supplies prevailing in 1923 were somewhat in excess of 90 per cent. over the pre-war scale. . . . There is no way by which freight and passenger rates can be continually reduced and net earnings at the same time increased; and, moreover, restricted net earnings must inevitably mean additional taxes to provide for annual deficits. . . .[13]

A similar note was struck by the president of the Canadian Pacific Railway:

. . . The Canadian producers suffer from a geographical disability due to the great distance their products have to be hauled. This difficulty has always existed and cannot be entirely eradicated. The remedies which are suggested are for the most part artificial and of doubtful soundness. A general lower scale of rates is not possible without grave unfairness to the transportation companies through increase of traffic in consequence of greater population and development in the country itself. . . . In public discussions of the subject the value of the work of the transportation companies . . . is frankly recognized, but the fact that their work can only be carried on successfully under a fair scale of rates is overlooked. . . .[14]

It will be obvious that the public and the private companies were in somewhat different positions, but both had an eye to profitable operation. The simple economic facts to which the presidents referred set natural limits to the use of rate changes for the solution of the problem of shippers.

2. THE DEPRESSION AND THE RAILWAYS

In the autumn of 1929 feverish selling and tobogganing prices on the New York stock exchange heralded the end of the hectic period of prosperity and the beginning of a severe depression. The

13. *Report of the department of railways and canals, 1923–1924,* p. 17.
14. *Annual report of the Canadian Pacific Railway,* 1924.

resultant contraction of general business had an almost immediate effect on the railways. The following table[15] shows the rapid decline from the maximum figures of 1928.

Year	Total train miles	Passengers carried	Freight carried (tons)	Gross earnings
1928	125,034,253	40,592,792	141,230,026	$563,732,260
1929	117,645,670	39,070,843	137,855,151	534,106,045
1930	107,620,076	34,698,767	115,229,511	454,231,650
1931	93,443,731	26,396,812	85,993,206	358,549,382
1932	81,291,028	21,099,582	67,722,105	293,390,415
1933	73,938,707	19,172,193	63,634,893	270,278,276

Both passenger and freight traffic were cut in half, as were the gross earnings. The number of passengers carried in 1932 was less than for any other year since 1902, at which time the railway mileage was about forty-four per cent and the population about half of the 1932 figures. In the case of passengers, and to a lesser extent of freight, the decrease was due partly to the competition of motor vehicles, which, however, increased only slightly in numbers during the same years. Export of wheat, a principal source of income for the railways, was exceedingly high in 1929, low in 1930, fair in 1931 and 1932, and better in 1933. It is not possible, therefore, to attempt to establish an exact correlation between the decline of traffic for the railways and any single factor: rather it would be more accurate to say that the railways suffered from the general shrinkage in business, in both export and internal trade.

The railways thus were caught—as most industrial and financial organizations were caught—by a severe and unexpected depression at a time when they were in the process of expanding their services in both quantity and quality. Their losses were alarming when the national income was declining and an era of extravagance was giving way to one of retrenchment. Individuals suffered from a reduction of dividends on the stock of the Canadian Pacific Railway, but the greater part of the stock was held outside Canada, and in any case there was no direct charge on the public funds. The Canadian National had been steadily showing a better net revenue and there was hope that this would soon meet a fair pro-

15. *Canada Year Book*, 1934–1935, p. 704.

portion of the fixed capital charges, but the depression changed the surplus into a loss, and the fears, scarcely stilled, that the national railway would be a greater financial burden than could be borne, quickly revived.

The loss to the public on the Canadian National, because it could be expressed in figures, was a reality in a way that watered stock, overbuilt factories, and personal extravagances could never be. Viewed in a depression atmosphere, the mounting debt and declining revenues of the company took on the rôle of a national bogey, and the railway problem once more was dominated by its financial aspect. E. W. Beatty decided that "the time would be opportune for an enquiry into the whole question of transportation in Canada by an independent tribunal."[16] and suggested to Thornton that he make the proposal. Thornton accordingly, on June 25, 1931, put forward the idea of a royal commission to the select standing committee on railways and shipping, which in turn recommended it in their report. In November the royal commission was appointed. Instead of three commissioners, as in the commission of 1916, there were now seven. The Right Honourable L. P. Duff, justice of the supreme court of Canada, was chairman, and the other members were: Lord Ashfield, chairman of the London Underground Railway; L. F. Loree, president of the Delaware and Hudson Railroad; Sir Joseph Flavelle, a financier, of Toronto; Beaudry Leman, general manager of the Banque Canadienne Nationale; W. C. Murray, president of the University of Saskatchewan; and Dr. J. C. Webster of Shediac, New Brunswick. Each area in Canada was thus represented, while there were also experts from England and the United States.

The commissioners were empowered to "inquire into the whole problem of transportation in Canada, particularly in relation to railways, shipping and communication facilities therein, having regard to present conditions and the probable future development of the country, and report their conclusions and make such recommendations as they think proper." The usual procedure of taking evidence from officials of the two principal railways and from other persons in different parts of the country was followed.

16. E. W. Beatty, *Canada's railway problem and its solution* (Speech before the Canadian Club, Toronto, 1933).

In spite of the broad implications of their terms of reference, the commissioners seem to have concentrated on two points: the seriousness of the existing financial situation in the railways, and the cure of this disease. While undoubtedly these were the aspects of the problem that required most immediate consideration, they might have taken a somewhat different colour if placed against a background of the fundamental geographical, economic, and political problems of the Dominion in respect of transportation. Such phenomena as over-building, light traffic, and even competition have significance only in relation to past, present, and future conditions. All forms of transportation in Canada have always involved public subsidies of some kind, whether in land, money, or guarantees. Periodically there came a day of reckoning in which an attempt was made to balance the national services of transport against its cost. Such a time was 1931. It is perhaps only a question of emphasis, but one is led to wonder whether the approach in the report of the royal commission gives a true impression of the full meaning of a problem which came not only from the mistakes of man, but also from the basic conditions of Canada and the vicissitudes of the business cycle.

The position of the capital securities of the two railways in the period 1923–1931 shows that both companies had materially added to their fixed charges.[17]

C.N.R. Capital Securities

	Increase, 1923–1931	Total, December 31, 1931
Capital stock	$650	$270,220,963
Funded debt	$471,954,063	$1,276,457,206

These figures do not give the full picture of the increase in the Canadian National Railways debt, for there were also added during the period government loans of $132,468,521 and accrued interest on government loans amounting to $287,663,169. Of the funded debt part was guaranteed by the Dominion or provinces and part was not so guaranteed. The proportions were:

Guaranteed	$1,042,746,777
Unguaranteed	233,710,429

17. *Report of the royal commission to inquire into railways and transportation in Canada, 1931–1932.*

The fixed charges of the Canadian Pacific were also raised during the same period by additions to the debt, due to increased expenditure. The bonded indebtedness remained low as compared with the Canadian National, but the C.P.R. to some extent departed from its traditional policy by floating large issues of bonds.

C.P.R. Capital Securities

	Increase, 1923–1931	Total, December 31, 1931
Capital stock	$131,575,000	$472,256,921
Funded debt	151,824,772	475,374,638

The following tables[18] show the figures for the operating accounts of the two companies over the period 1923–1931.

C.N.R. Operations

Year	Gross earnings from operation	Operating expenses	Net operating revenues
1923	$216,578,175	$204,921,713	$11,656,462
1924	201,224,493	189,460,403	11,764,089
1925	208,218,920	184,373,201	23,845,719
1926	225,547,852	190,173,271	35,374,581
1927*	227,560,927	198,646,705	28,914,221
1928*	260,418,924	217,780,172	42,638,751
1929*	248,222,476	217,223,886	30,998,589
1930*	213,446,581	196,502,057	16,944,523
1931*	171,675,445	171,673,132	2,313

*including Eastern Lines.

C.P.R. Operations

Year	Gross earnings from operation	Operating expenses	Net operating revenues
1923	$192,827,930	$155,040,207	$37,787,722
1924	180,796,044	143,258,643	37,537,400
1925	182,610,791	140,663,058	41,947,733
1926	197,636,215	149,713,398	47,922,817
1927	201,805,486	159,060,224	42,745,262
1928	230,406,354	173,871,972	56,534,381
1929	211,635,660	164,304,606	47,331,054
1930	180,022,386	138,523,657	41,498,729
1931	141,999,359	112,692,927	29,306,432

18. *Steam railway statistics* (Dominion bureau of statistics).

The reports of the Canadian National Railway showed, for 1930, a net income deficit, including interest due to the public, of $61,228,621, and, for 1931, $84,262,718. Whatever might be the explanation of such large deficits, it was clear that the burden on the public was becoming heavy.

Believing that "drastic measures of economy" were "imperative," the commissioners were faced with the necessity of making a most important decision—whether or not to recommend any form of amalgamation. It is probably a reasonable inference that it was just because that decision had to be faced that the commission had been made so large and, geographically at least, so representative. The evidence[19] which the commissioners took gave them a number of opinions which bore directly on the future of the two railways in relation to each other. In Calgary representatives of the United Farmers of Alberta asked for amalgamation under national ownership with a view to lowering the cost of transportation. In Edmonton Premier Brownlee spoke of the "premature development of railway facilities to the far north of the province" by private companies, but expressed himself as satisfied with the joint operation of those northern lines by the Canadian National and Canadian Pacific. He felt strongly that the solution of the railway problem should not be based only on the existing depression, but also on the future of the country. As to amalgamation, he believed that it would be acceptable to the west if it were under public ownership. Representatives of the trade union movement in Alberta demanded that there should be no interference with the principle of public ownership. In Regina the attorney general and the counsel for the Saskatchewan wheat pool both spoke of a strong feeling against amalgamation under private ownership. In Winnipeg the attorney general stated explicitly that "the government of Manitoba is opposed to any form of amalgamation of the railway systems. It is unqualifiedly opposed to any monopoly that is not entirely controlled by the government. In the present circumstances it does not favour a government monopoly of the railways."

In so far, then, as the evidence given indicates western opinion, it was clear that the west was as hostile as ever to a Canadian

19. *Royal commission on railways and transportation: report of proceedings.*

Pacific monopoly and lukewarm about a governmental monopoly. In the east there was a much less clear expression of opinion. The premier of Nova Scotia thought that his province would not fear a monopoly so long as it brought economic advantages. The premier of New Brunswick preferred coöperation to amalgamation, but was evidently more concerned about the port of St. John than either of these alternatives. In Toronto the representative of the Canadian Brotherhood of Railway Employees startled the commissioners by a speech on planned economy, and strongly defended public ownership.

In the intervals of these hearings the commissioners spent long hours on the train in consultation with officers of the two companies, one of whom, S. W. Fairweather, director of the bureau of economics of the Canadian National, sought to show that the savings from amalgamation would not justify a monopoly. How far the commissioners had been affected by the expression of opinion in the west it is, of course, impossible to say, but it was perhaps a new factor to some of them. In Ottawa came the important sessions with the presidents of the two companies. As to the line that Mr. Beatty would take there can have been little question. The Canadian Pacific had never attempted to conceal its alarm at the course of events, either from its own point of view or from that of the country as a whole. Since 1921 it had urged the desirability of some type of amalgamation. The president expressed the view that coöperation, while it would result in saving— estimated at $6,348,000—would not be sufficient. "Under existing conditions in Canada," he told the commissioners, "the only solution which will stand the test of the country's necessities is a consolidation through a lease on a profit-sharing basis of the government railways and the Canadian Pacific." Abandonment of line on a large scale would be possible, to the extent of about 5,000 miles. Particular instances of this were the National Transcontinental between Winnipeg and Nakina, Canadian Northern between Longlac and Ottawa, Canadian Pacific between Glen Tay and Whitby, Woodstock and Windsor, Saskatoon and Unity, Kamloops and Hope. In passenger traffic his officers estimated that 7,500,000 train miles or 16.2 per cent., and in freight traffic, 5,300,000 train miles or 9.2 per cent, could be saved. On the total,

$64,267,000 could be saved on operating expenses. Asked how he would divide the earnings, Beatty answered: "I would take the gross earnings of the combined system, and what is left over I would divide in agreed proportions between the owners of the C.P.R. and the Government of Canada. The agreed proportions would be ascertained by taking, for example, the percentage of each company's earnings to the total over a period of years, net." He stated, in answer to another question, that he was not afraid of the size of the undertaking from an operating point of view. As to the objection against the plan of joint operation that it would result in a monopoly, he argued that the public would be protected by the railway commission or some similar body.

If the Canadian Pacific policy was, in general, known beforehand, there was much uncertainty as to whether Thornton would follow suit or would defend the independent existence of the Canadian National. It has been suggested that he had accepted some form of unification, and only changed his mind at the last moment. Be that as it may, it is certain that he took a clear stand before the commission. Amalgamation, he said, "would be definitely repugnant to the people of the Dominion." Unification under the state would entail some degree of political interference, while under private enterprise it would arouse public apprehension. A further objection would be the removal of competition. Some other solution, then, must be devised. He sketched a plan which would allow for the "development of that form of direction and administration which will, as near as may be, approach that of a prudently and efficiently organized private enterprise, which would necessarily involve the reduction of political interference to a minimum"; and secondly, "the development of an intensive degree of coöperation between the two companies in order that waste in whatever form it is found may be eliminated." The first object, he suggested, would be secured by the appointment of a board of ten directors for the Canadian National, two of whom should be the president and legal vice-president of the company, and the remainder, appointed by the government, to include two Conservatives, two Liberals, two Progressives, one representative of labour, and one representative of the minister of railways and canals.

The practical measures which Thornton suggested for coöperation were pooling of competitive passenger services, elimination of competitive city ticket offices, co-ordination of competitive fast freight services, elimination of dual trackage where possible, consolidation of telegraph and hotel systems, joint use of local facilities wherever possible, and interchange of trackage rights. He contemplated the abandonment of 2,434 miles of track and a total saving of $30,000,000 for both systems. Thornton denied the suggestion made by Ashfield that his plan meant "a complete fusion of the interests of the two railways," but admitted that if freight also were pooled it would mean the end of competition. To enforce coöperation, he suggested the retention of all or part of the royal commission, which would also pass on the annual budget of the Canadian National.

A scheme which was a compromise between those advanced by Beatty and Thornton, and one which revived an older idea, was presented by Gerard Ruel, legal vice-president of the Canadian National. It called for the creation of a single managing company, called the Canadian Railways Company. Five of the ten directors would be nominated by the government and five by the Canadian Pacific. To the company would be entrusted for management all the companies in the Canadian National and all those in the Canadian Pacific which were willing to coöperate. Profits would be divided amongst the owning companies on an agreed basis. It would admittedly put an end to competition, in which Ruel did not believe.

After hearing these and various other opinions on the question of amalgamation, it remained for the commissioners, who, unlike the witnesses had no special interest in the matter, to come to a judicial decision. In their report they declared for the continuance of competition, fearing the power of a monopoly of such magnitude, and distrusting the perpetual lease of one company to the other as equally resulting in monopoly. Seeing, too, a possible growth of population and of railway mileage in the future, they hesitated "to commit . . . future generations, and even the present one, to a policy adopted under the stress of difficult circumstances, which may not be best adapted to a new set of conditions difficult to forecast." As positive aims they set up economy, coöperation, and that the "management of the National Railways should be emancipated from political interference and community pressure."

In pursuit of these aims the commission proposed that the board of directors of the Canadian National should be replaced by three trustees, appointed by the governor in council, of whom the chairman should give the whole of his time to the duties of his office. The trustees would control the annual budget and submit an annual report to parliament. They would also appoint a president as chief operating officer. To provide for coöperation it was recommended that the trustees should meet at regular intervals with an equal number of directors of the Canadian Pacific, and that the united body should discuss "such co-operative measures, plans and arrangements as shall, consistent with the proper handling of traffic, be best adapted to the removal of unnecessary or wasteful services or practices, to the avoidance of unwarranted duplication in services of facilities, and to the joint use and operation of all such properties as may conveniently and without undue detriment to either party, be so used." A statutory duty should lie on the trustees and directors to plan and adopt measures of coöperation, but in case the two failed to agree in the suggested joint committee, the issue was to be settled by a new body, the "arbitral tribunal," consisting of the chief commissioner of the board of railway commissioners and one representative from each of the two railways.

A bill "intended to be a statutory incorporation of the report of the Duff Commission" was introduced into the senate in October 1932 and finally received the royal assent in May 1933. Revised and elaborated by the railway committee of the senate, it was debated at great length both there and in the house of commons. As finally passed, the act (23 & 24 Geo. V, c.33) ended with a statement that "nothing in this Act shall be deemed to authorize the amalgamation of any railway company which is comprised in National Railways with any railway company which is comprised in Pacific Railways nor to authorize the unified management and control of the railway system which forms part of National Railways with the railway system which forms part of Pacific Railways." Such a warning, though regarded by some members as superfluous, well expressed the basic view of the great majority of members of both houses. Here and there, in both houses, were found those who cast longing glances at an amalgamation of some type, but that aspect of the act was never an issue. In the upper house Senator Meighen spoke of the great size of the existing railways and added:

Unite them and you will have a power which, in the hands of competent, shrewd, far-seeing men, could be made an almost insuperable factor in the political life of this Dominion. Some attach to that spectre more sinister and more terrible consequences than do others. That it is undesirable I admit—that it is very undesirable I admit; and I say most emphatically that the great mass of the Canadian people consider it so undesirable that so long as the democracy that reigns in Canada is the democracy of mind that now reigns, there is no possibility of bringing about such a condition of affairs. Those who say that this is so only in regard to political matters—that we are being political when we ought to be businesslike— are really indicting democracy. It is not at all a political party that is being challenged, but democracy itself; and I do not know that democracy is altogether foolish in seeking to guard itself against what conceivably, because of its immensity, might become domination.[20]

The act was divided into three parts. The first empowered the governor in council to replace the existing board of directors of the Canadian National with three trustees, as advocated in the report of the royal commission. The chairman of the trustees was cast for a part rather like Napoleon as first consul: the difference being that in the latter case the part was written for the actor. In the commons the powers and methods of appointment of the trustees and their relation to the government were discussed at some length. Mr. Mackenzie King raised the question as to whether their position would be in accord with the retention of ministerial responsibility. "A ministry," he said, "cannot divest itself of all responsibility. If government ownership and operation means that it cannot be carried on without the ministry divesting itself of all responsibility therefor, then we had better pass a resolution to that effect, and get rid of government ownership altogether."[21]

Part II of the act directed the two railways to endeavour to agree on, and bring into force, measures of coöperation such as

20. *Senate debates*, 1923–1933, p. 297.
21. *House of commons debates*, 1932–1933, p. 2851.

pooling of services and joint trackage and running rights. Part III provided for an arbitral tribunal, consisting of three persons, as sketched by the royal commission. Its powers might be invoked by either company, and were to be very comprehensive. No appeal could be made, except to the supreme court of Canada on a question of jurisdiction. The section dealing with the tribunal was subjected to a good deal of criticism in both houses. It was said by various members to infringe the rights of the Canadian Pacific as a private corporation, and by one member of the commons to be nothing less than amalgamation of operation.

But the fierce lion of coöperation, whose early roars so alarmed the officers of the Canadian Pacific Railway, proved to be a very mild beast when let out of its cage. Little of the act of 1933 was ever put into effect. In December 1933 the directors of the Canadian National were replaced by a board of trustees consisting of C. P. Fullerton (chairman), F. K. Morrow of Toronto, and J. E. Labelle of Montreal, and in the following January they appointed S. J. Hungerford, who had been acting president since the retirement of Sir Henry Thornton, as president. As a move toward coöperation a joint executive committee of the two railways was organized, which in turn appointed a joint technical committee. After investigation, passenger service between Montreal and Toronto, and Ottawa and Toronto was pooled, and some other works, such as switching, car-cleaning and freight shed operations, were undertaken in common. But such coöperation as was actually put into practice was slight indeed as compared with the intentions of the royal commission and of the act. It is significant that the arbitral tribunal was never called into being: significant because it was regarded by both its defenders and its critics as the sanction behind coöperation. Because so small a degree of coöperation was attempted, it is not possible to say whether or not the new policy was capable of being made a success.

Certain it is that the relief which was obtained from 1933 on was negligible. In 1933 the joint annual saving of measures already put into effect was estimated at one million dollars.[22] A detailed list of savings by coöperative measures practised during 1934 showed that this estimate was only slightly below the actual

22. *Canadian Pacific Railway: report of the shareholders' meeting, 1934.*

figure.[23] Of the items in the list, that referring to pooled services between Quebec, Montreal, Ottawa and Toronto accounted for all but a few thousands of dollars. Both companies made efforts, and with some success, to reduce expenditures within their own control. Abandonment of line did not play a major part in this programme, although in 1935 the Canadian National applied to the board of railway commissioners to abandon operation on branch lines with a total of 560 miles. Consent was given in respect to about one-third of the total; a third was refused; and the balance not decided within the year. The various efforts of the companies to make economies, however, whether by coöperative measures or internal changes, enabled them to save themselves from further net losses on operations.[24]

Year	Railway	Gross earnings from operations	Operating expenses	Net operating revenues
1933	C.P.R.	$113,998,657	$89,251,849	$27,746,808
1933	C.N.R.	126,701,228	122,572,229	4,128,998
1934	C.P.R.	125,642,229	97,081,831	28,560,398
1934	C.N.R.	140,824,360	130,296,562	10,527,798

Experience of coöperation, such as it was, led the trustees of the Canadian National to believe that it could be carried further and to express the hope that arbitral tribunals would either be eliminated or little used.[25] On the other hand the president of the Canadian Pacific told his shareholders that

Experience with co-operation strengthens the view that unification alone offers an adequate solution to the Canadian railway problem. No other plan can eliminate the tremendous waste caused by maintaining duplicate services in a country which can no longer afford to pay for the duplication. Unification would also offer a solution to the unfair and dangerous anomaly of a Government-owned enterprise engaging in direct competition with private capital. The solution of the railway problem on fair and sound lines will produce benefits to Canada far in excess of mere operating savings. The Canadian Pacific, in complete coöperation with the Canadian Government—for that is what unification means—can achieve infinitely more for

23. *Canadian National Railways: annual report, 1934.*
24. *Steam railway statistics.*
25. *Canadian National Railways: annual report, 1934.*

the future welfare of Canada than can the two railway systems separately within the present working limits of their statutory authority.[26]

Just what the last sentence means is not quite clear, but for the rest it was the gospel which the C.P.R. had long been preaching—and was preaching with added sincerity, now that the company could no longer pay interest on its capital stock.

Such was the state of the railways in the years of depression, that is, under conditions which touched the railway structure at its weakest point. The Canadian Pacific adopted a perfectly logical policy, and one that could be defended from the point of view of either the company or the country. But logic is never a fixed commodity, and the public as a whole was more ready to face deficits than monopoly. It was hard to startle a people who had already contributed a billion and a quarter dollars in cash, a like amount in guarantees, and an empire in land, so that railways might run throughout the Dominion.

3. THE PRACTICE OF PUBLIC OWNERSHIP

Opinion in Canada has always favoured the construction and operation of railways by private enterprise, and where the Dominion or the provinces have undertaken the responsibility themselves it has been because of the failure of private capital either to undertake or to maintain particular railways. Cases of one or other which have been mentioned are the Intercolonial, Prince Edward Island, Temiskaming and Northern Ontario, Hudson Bay, Pacific Great Eastern and National Transcontinental railways. The dominating principle, therefore, has not been an insistence on private enterprise, but rather a belief that certain lines of railway were essential to the economic and political life of the country. When capitalists could be interested they were given financial assistance by the state, and when they could not be interested direct action was taken by the governments. The establishment of the Canadian National Railways does not run counter to the general rule, but that railway had special characteristics which caused it to be viewed in a somewhat different light

26. *Canadian Pacific Railway: report of the shareholders' meeting, 1935.*

from the other government lines. Besides the federal government railways, it included three great companies (Canadian Northern, Grand Trunk, and Grand Trunk Pacific) which were built in the expectation of profitable operation, and together comprised two transcontinental roads. The Canadian National, then, was bound to be judged on standards similar to those applied to any other transcontinental line, rather than with the tolerance allowed to a pioneer railway undertaken without hope of profit by a government. Hence public ownership was felt to be on trial in a sense that it had not been before.

Two main issues have emerged, both fundamental to a consideration of the success or failure of this great experiment in public ownership. The first of these is the degree of efficiency with which the railway has been managed—interpreting efficiency as meaning a satisfactory relation between expenditure and results. Here a series of difficulties is immediately encountered. By what standard should the Canadian National be judged? The tendency has been to use the Canadian Pacific as that standard, which is very natural since it is the only other important railway in Canada, and happens also to be a private corporation. Obviously, however, such a comparison is very unsatisfactory because of the utterly different character of the railways. The Canadian National inherited, for operation and management, all the Canadian government railways, and to these were added the insolvent private systems. Both groups were grossly over-capitalized, and, when brought together, the units jostled each other in the same territory. The Canadian Pacific, on the other hand, suffered from none of these handicaps.

The royal commission of 1931, while pointing out that such differences affected any comparison between the two railways, conveyed the general impression that the Canadian National had been more extravagant and less efficiently managed than the Canadian Pacific. Their sharpest reproofs are aimed at the Canadian National, while the Canadian Pacific—though manifestly equally extravagant in certain respects—escapes with mild reproof. Probably this attitude on the part of the commissioners may be explained by a sense of responsibility for a public company whose losses were an undoubted burden on the taxpayer. The report, however, does appear to portray a degree of difference in extravagance and efficiency between the two companies which did not, in fact, exist.

Neither the commissioners nor subsequent investigators have been able to find a satisfactory measure to apply to the relative operating efficiency of the companies, though a good deal of light has been thrown on the problem.[27] A comparison of the operating ratios reflects the consistently stronger position of the Canadian Pacific.[28]

Year	C.N.R. %	C.P.R. %
1923	91.8	81.0
1924	92.5	80.5
1925	86.7	77.3
1926	82.5	75.8
1927	84.9	78.5
1928	82.0	75.4
1929	85.6	77.3
1930	91.4	78.4
1931	99.8	80.3

That the ratio of the Canadian National was steadily higher than the Canadian Pacific is due largely to historical causes: the point of interest in the table is that the Canadian National fared worse at the height of the depression than the other company. But the operating ratio is not a satisfactory means of judging the position of a railway. A detailed examination would have to proceed through the various fields of operation. Such an examination has been made by one student of the subject, who arrives at the conclusion that the record of the C.P.R. was markedly better than that of the C.N.R.[29]

Assuming, as the weight of opinion seems to reveal, that the Canadian National had a less creditable record over the nine-year period than the Canadian Pacific, what deductions may be made? There is first the question of the relative density of traffic. Again there is the possibility that the Canadian National lacked an

27. See L. T. Fournier, *Railway nationalization in Canada* (Toronto, 1935); W. T. Jackman, *op. cit.*; J. L. McDougall, "The report of the Duff Commission" (*Canadian journal of economics and political science*, i, 1).

28. *Report of the royal commission to inquire into railways and transportation in Canada*, 1931–1932, p. 50.

29. Fournier, *op. cit.*, chap. viii.

organization comparable to that of the Canadian Pacific, owing, perhaps, to the consistent way in which the latter had maintained an able personnel and directed its work to a steadily increasing task. If such a weakness were to be found the cure would lie in reformed organization and improved personnel: a process familiar to public and private bodies in all periods of history. The alternative deduction is that the Canadian National was weak because it was a public body. This is hinted at in the report of the royal commission.

Running through its administrative practices, however, has been the red thread of extravagance. The disciplinary check upon undue expenditure, inherent in private corporations because of their limited financial resources, has not been in evidence. Requisitions of the management have been endorsed by governments, and successive parliaments have voted money freely, if not lavishly.

Such a problem is of the very essence of public ownership, and as such has been debated from every angle. If it be true that extravagance is a necessary corollary of public ownership, then the whole railway question in Canada must be viewed in that light. Now the experience in connection with the Canadian National is the best test case for Canadian purposes, for, although there have been important experiments in state railways in other countries, it is the Canadian political scene which has to be considered.

The majority report of the royal commission of 1917 vibrates with alarm lest politics should interfere with railways. Both Hanna and Thornton issued grave warnings. The royal commission of 1931 stated as a main consideration that "the management of the National Railways should be emancipated from political interference and community pressure." Indeed, almost every public man and every railway official who has spoken or written on the subject has expressed the same sentiments. The possible dangers are many: the simplest is corruption for the benefit of a party or an official of the railway; another lies in concessions to the railway for the purpose of winning votes; a third is concessions by the railway to a community at the behest of local members of parliament; and a fourth—of a somewhat different character—is governmental extravagance or parsimony intended to aid or hamper a railway for political ends.

The cure for these ills which has been most frequently suggested is to remove the railway from politics. The effect of this would be to approximate the status of a private company, substituting parliament for the shareholders. But the relations between private railway companies and politics have not, in Canada, been idyllic. A number of cases have already been cited in this history in which railways and political parties have gone hand in hand toward their respective goals. That such an unholy alliance is still thought to be possible is evidenced by the fear of the royal commission of 1931 that a monopolistic railway might exercise influence prejudicial to the interests of the Dominion. Less detached observers have painted this picture in more vivid colours. Lobbying and votes on the one hand, and concessions on the other might be written into a *chronique scandaleuse* of Canadian history.[30] Railways and politics have, in fact, never been completely disassociated in Canada, and it is a question whether they will ever be. At best, the hope has been to protect the public railway from the more obvious kinds of political interference, and to leave the government and parliament to protect themselves.

Up to 1933 the control of the Canadian National was in the hands of a board of directors appointed by the government, who also designated its chairman and appointed the president. Such a policy was contrary to that proposed by the royal commission of 1917, whose advice was to utilize a self-perpetuating board of trustees. Inasmuch as the railway was dependent on public money, parliament retained a final control over its budget. In 1924 a select standing committee on railways and shipping owned, operated, or controlled by the government, was first set up, and continued to be appointed in each succeeding session. The committee provided a useful bridge between parliament and the railway officials who appeared before it to give evidence and express their own opinions. The pages of Hansard show that parliament was at least active, if not always wise, in its attention to railway matters. The senate showed more resistance to expenditure than did the house of

30. *See*, e.g., G. Myers, *History of Canadian wealth* (Chicago, 1914).

commons, though such resistance has been sometimes explained
by motives other than those of public interest.

In the report of the royal commission there is advanced the view
that,

the directors' functions have been in practice nothing more than advisory.
It would seem that they generally gave a formal approval to programmes
of expenditures which they appeared to regard as the main concern of the
president and the Government. This left the railway open to political
influence and to public pressure exerted by communities and by associa-
tions of business and labour interests.

Given the consent of the government, the president could exercise
almost unlimited authority, while his financial needs could be met
by the government majorities in parliament. The Canadian
National was guided neither by an active board of directors whose
policies would reflect the limited resources of a company, nor by a
government department which would assume the same responsibility. In effect the chief operating officer of the railway was allowed
almost unlimited funds for objects which he saw to be, from an
operating point of view, desirable. From 1926 to 1930 the Liberal
government, with an adequate majority and in years of plenty,
gave a free hand to Thornton, whose immediate object was to
improve the railway rather than to reduce the fixed charges. In
1929 the business cycle went through another change, and the
Conservative administration which came into office in 1930 was
faced with the very different problem of financing the Canadian
National in time of depression. A policy of retrenchment was
immediately needed, and with the change in policy came a change
in management. Whether Sir Henry Thornton fell because of a
Conservative plot,[31] as the ally of the defeated government, or
as the scapegoat for the extravagance of parliament, it was certain
that in any case a drastic change was almost certain to be made.

In January 1934 three trustees were appointed in place of the
old board of directors. Three months after the appointment of
the trustees, the chairman, the Honourable C. P. Fullerton,
addressed a message to the employees, in which he spoke of an
"agitation" for the amalgamation of the two railways which might

31 As argued in D'Arcy Marsh, *The tragedy of Henry Thornton* (Toronto, 1935).

have "a very serious effect upon the morale of the workers." The first argument for amalgamation, that it would effect large savings, he countered by advocating economy by coöperation. The second argument, he said, was to relieve the management from the evils of political influences. On this he made the comment:

Everyone will admit that political interference can work great harm, and that it is highly desirable that those who are directing any great enterprise should be free to bring to the performance of their task whatever abilities they may have, untrammelled by a consideration of party politics. Let me say once for all that to-day the Canadian National Railways are just as free from having to consider matters from a political angle as is any railway in Canada, and it is the intention of myself and my fellow-trustees that this shall remain so.[32]

An interesting criticism of the machinery for the management of the Canadian National was made by a newspaper, a staunch supporter of the public railway, when the act of 1933 had just been passed.

The chief advantage claimed for the system thus set up, that it will "take the C.N.R. out of politics," must be in one sense illusory. The C.N.R. is a utility owned by the Canadian people, and the trustees, in managing it, will be performing a public or political function. What the bill does is not to remove the C.N.R. from politics but to divest parliament, the organ of public opinion, of its power to direct C.N.R. policy. Whether this was wisely done remains to be seen. The trustees, no doubt, will be beyond the reach of politicians seeking local favours. But they will also be beyond the reach of parliament's will to maintain the C.N.R. as a going concern, and to resist influences hostile to C.N.R. success and growth as a National property.[33]

The system of trustees lasted no longer than the tenure of office of the Conservative government. In 1936 the new minister of railways (C. D. Howe) introduced into the house of commons a bill, the effect of which was to abolish the system of trustees and replace it with a board of directors of seven persons.[34] The trustees, he said, had failed either to improve the position of the company

32. *Canadian National Railways Magazine*, xx, 4.
33. *Winnipeg Free Press*, March 17, 1933.
34. *House of commons debates*, 1936, pp. 2365 et seq.

or to introduce coöperative measures. Furthermore, the board was not representative enough, and "is responsible to no one." It had been the intention of the act under which the trustees were appointed that they should confine themselves to policy, but in practice the chairman had taken over part of the operation.

Under the new arrangement the offices of chairman and president might be held by the same individual, and there were other similarities to the system used before 1933. Howe claimed, however, that his bill did not "change the intent and purpose of the 1933 measure other than to the extent necessary to provide for the substitution of a board of seven directors for the present board of three trustees." He further attempted to disarm criticism by stating that the effect of the bill would not be to return the Canadian National "to the same form of direction that obtained under the late Sir Henry Thornton," the difference being that the new chairman and board would have a greater measure of autonomy.

The minister's speech had been a mixture of criticisms of the personnel of the board of trustees and of the system as such. The way was left open for the opposition to suggest that the whole bill was nothing more than a means of replacing one group of men with another; and they bitterly prophesied that in future the tenure of the board of directors of the Canadian National would be no longer than the life of a government. "I say to the minister", retorted the leader of the opposition, "that he has not made out a case. The only case he has made this afternoon is that in his opinion the chairman has not done his duty and is unfit for his position. . . . What is the sense of saying that they [the directors] are appointed for five years or three or any other term? Why not simply say that they are to remain in office until such time as another government puts someone else in their place?" In spite of this obvious objection to the new measure—whatever may prove to be its merits—the bill passed through parliament, and the Canadian National once more had a board of directors.

The conflicting objects of the supporters of public ownership of railways have not as yet been fully reconciled. There appears to be agreement that the normal operation should be left to men unconnected with politics, and that such executive officers should be free from political interference. But what is meant by "political interference"? Presumably pressure on the railway officers to take action intended to bring advantage to a party or individuals. That, of course, is undesirable. But, if it be recognized that government and parliament must have some control, how are they to exercise it? One can juggle with the word "politics," but the fact is that parliament is a political body, operating by means of a system of organized parties. The risk must be taken one way or the other. If the administration of the railway is insulated from political control, the risk envisaged by the *Free Press* must be faced; if parliament is to retain a supreme function of directing policy, then the dangers of what is loosely called "politics" will be the problem. There seem to be three ways of managing a publicly owned railway: by a government department; by an independent body appointed by the government or parliament; or by a dependent body, appointed by and constantly responsible to the government or parliament. The advantages and disadvantages of each are immediately obvious. Can the advantages of all be combined into one system? A search has earnestly been made for a passage between the Scylla of political control and the Charybdis of an irresponsible executive. If, after the necessary years of experiment, Canadian democracy cannot trust its representatives either to direct, or to appoint those who should direct, a public enterprise, the future of public ownership is doubtful indeed.

CHAPTER XIII

MODERN WATERWAYS

1. ENLARGEMENT OF CANALS

DURING the period after confederation when railways were planned and built, waterways continued to be developed too, as complementary to them in the system of Canadian transportation. Scant attention was given to further development of the waterways during the discussions and negotiations in connection with the federation of the provinces, yet shortly after the Dominion of Canada was born a royal commission was appointed to consider the adequacy of the existing canals and the desirability of constructing certain new ones. It was appointed in 1870 and issued a majority report in 1871.[1] Since the burst of energy in the 'forties little had been done either to deepen existing canals or cut additional ones. The St. Lawrence canals still had a depth of only nine feet, with the Welland a foot better. No steps had been taken toward either the proposed canal across the Isthmus of Chignecto, or that to Georgian Bay via the Ottawa River. The commission had wide terms of reference which covered all these, as well as some minor canals or proposed canals. Their approach to the question is enlightening if it may be taken—as seems reasonable—as not untypical of informed opinion of the day. In a careful examination of the "commercial aspect of the question" the commission found two main uses for canals: for transport to and from the "west," and as a channel of interprovincial trade.

By the "west" they meant not primarily, as in the discussion of railways, the newly-acquired provinces of Manitoba and British Columbia or the North West Territories, but the country bordering on the upper lakes. The "west" was Ontario and such states as Illinois, Michigan and Minnesota, with only a passing thought for the Canadian north-west. This report of 1871 was written in the atmosphere which, for railways, had been dissipated in the 'sixties—an atmosphere in which there flourished

1. *Canada sessional papers*, 1871, No. 54.

dreams of a system of waterways that would bring the trade of half a continent through Canada. The old battle was fought out again on paper.

The commerce of this fertile and progressive country . . . depends on several routes of communication. Nature has intended the St. Lawrence to be the great commercial highway of the West, and if it has not fulfilled its destiny to the extent it should have done, it is because the enterprise of man has endeavoured to divert its trade into other and artificial channels.

The most important of these artificial channels was, of course, the Erie Canal; while the New York railways were gradually draining business from it as well as from the Canadian waterways. The division of traffic may be indicated by the following figures.[2]

Tonnage of Vegetable Food, 1869

Total on New York canals	1,302,613
Total on Welland canal	503,860
Total on New York Central and Erie railways	1,087,809
Charged at Buffalo and Tonawanda by Erie canal	786,436
Cleared at Oswego by canal	267,815
Through Welland canal in transit between U.S. ports	337,530

The obvious way to checkmate the route by Buffalo and the Erie Canal was to encourage the use of the Welland Canal, which, as the commissioners pointed out, had nearly trebled its business in the previous twenty years. Wheat, lumber, copper, and iron from the upper lakes would pass through the Welland Canal in ever-increasing quantities were it not for the fact that the larger boats of this period could not go through. It was stated that three-quarters of the tonnage on the lakes could not use the canal.

The first step, therefore, in the improvement of the Inland Navigation of the Dominion is the enlargement of the Welland Canal, the great link of commercial intercourse, not only with the prosperous Western Country of the United States . . . but with that vast territory belonging to the Dominion, which must ere long be peopled by thousands. . . . On improving the Welland, we take the step pointed out to us by the unerring finger of Progress.

2. *Report of the department of railways and canals,* 1903–1904, pt. v, p. 38.

Descending unwillingly from these dizzy and poetical heights, the commissioners turned to the further problem, which was to divert the traffic, once past the Welland Canal, safely down the St. Lawrence, rather than allow it to break off to New York at Oswego. They found that there had been a steady increase in the amount of flour and wheat going down to Montreal in the previous few years, and they believed that improvement of the St. Lawrence canals would greatly accelerate this increase. The fears of Americans interested in the Erie Canal were quoted as showing the natural advantages of the St. Lawrence route, and the deduction drawn that it only remained for Canadians to exploit that advantage. The commissioners' arguments were largely based on the relative distances, number of locks, and cost of transport, without taking into consideration the advantages of New York over Montreal as a port attracting the shipping of the world. They emphasized in their recommendations the importance of the trunk line to the upper lakes, for which they considered necessary enlargement of the Welland and St. Lawrence canals to twelve feet depth, with locks two hundred and seventy feet long, and the construction of a canal on the Canadian side at Sault Ste. Marie.

The second object to which the commissioners devoted their attention was to facilitate trade between the maritime and central provinces. The goods exchanged would be bulky, such as coal and grains, and therefore demanded cheap and direct water transport. Part of the route—the upper St. Lawrence—would in any case be enlarged sufficiently, and the only new work required would be a short canal across the Isthmus of Chignecto. This was the Baie Verte Canal, an old and natural idea for allowing direct water connection between the Gulf of St. Lawrence and the Bay of Fundy. The commission was satisfied that, if this direct route were opened, a considerable trade in fish, coal, grain, and manufactured goods would develop. In connection, therefore, with communication between the provinces, the commissioners were more concerned with national boundaries than they were in the case of western trade. The St. Lawrence-Baie Verte route was in most ways a companion in purpose to the Intercolonial Railway; though no such parallel existed between the Pacific railway and the western canals.

Besides these two primary routes, the commission considered a number of other canals to which they attached less importance. They advocated deepening the canals on the Ottawa from six to nine feet. The Georgian Bay Canal they regarded as a more remote possibility. They recommended that the Chambly Canal be deepened to nine feet, so that it—together with the Ottawa— might be used for the carriage of lumber to the American market. Finally, they advised that the channel in the St. Lawrence between Montreal and Quebec be deepened to twenty-two feet at low water.

In sum, therefore, the commission had in mind a channel of twelve-foot depth from Lake Superior to Montreal, which they believed was as much as the resources of the country and the needs of lake vessels justified. This route would on the one hand act as a trunk line from the ports of the upper lakes to Montreal and Quebec; and on the other serve interprovincial trade, which would follow through to the Baie Verte Canal and maritime ports. In addition they planned the nine-foot channel across country from Ottawa to Lake Champlain. It remains to be seen how the programme was carried out in succeeding years.

The enlargement of the St. Lawrence canals was undertaken not long after the presentation of the commission's report. The recommendations of the commission were accepted, but before the plan of enlargement had been carried out it was decided to adopt fourteen feet instead of twelve feet as the standard depth. Around the Lachine Rapids a new canal was built to give an immediate depth of twelve, and an ultimate depth of fourteen feet. (The old canal also remained in operation for some years.) The Beauharnois was replaced by the Soulanges Canal, on the north side of the river, although, again, the old canal was retained for the use of a few small boats. The Soulanges was not begun until 1891, and was completed in 1899, with a depth of fifteen feet. Work on the Cornwall Canal was begun in 1876, but the whole was not ready for use until 1900. In this case the old channel was widened, deepened, and straightened, and the new locks put in to allow the regulation depth of fourteen feet and length of two hundred and seventy feet. The three Williamsburg canals (Farran's Point, Rapide Plat, and Galops) formed the last link in the St. Lawrence navigation. The enlargement of these canals to the new standard dimensions was not completed until 1903.

From Prescott through to the Niagara River there was no interruption in navigation, but at the latter point was the old Welland Canal, the enlargement of which had been so much stressed by the commission of 1870. It was decided to deepen the western section of the canal and to install locks of the same size as those adopted for the St. Lawrence. The eastern section, however, from Allanburg to Port Dalhousie, was replaced by a new work following a slightly different course. Fourteen-foot navigation was available by 1887.

For over forty years Canadian shipping depended for an entrance into Lake Superior on the American canal at Sault Ste. Marie, which was in operation from 1855. Although the number of Canadian ships passing through was not large—in 1890 they carried only 3.5 per cent of the total freight—the view was strongly held that the increase of wheat production in the Canadian west necessitated the early construction of a canal on the Canadian side of the straits. The representations of shipowners induced the government to build a lock considerably larger than any other then in Canada, it being 900 feet long and 60 feet wide, with a depth of 18 feet, 3 inches. This canal was opened in 1895.

The proposed Baie Verte Canal was never dug. An alternative scheme for a marine railway across the isthmus was undertaken by a private company subsidized by the government, and a considerable amount of work was actually done. The company, however, got into financial difficulties and the railway was never completed.

On the north and south route the Chambly Canal was left unchanged, but the three canals on the lower Ottawa were enlarged to the dimensions of the old St. Lawrence canals, that is, locks of 200 by 45 feet, with a depth of 9 feet. The extension of the Ottawa system, known as the Georgian Bay Canal, was an attractive scheme. The Ottawa River above the capital, together with Lake Nipissing and the French River, were to be made into a water route to Georgian Bay, and thence to Lake Superior. By this means western grain could be brought to the port of Montreal by the same direct line as that which the North West Company

had used for the carriage of furs. While the roundabout passage
by Lake Erie could be avoided, the old difficulty which the fur-
traders had encountered in the portages on the Ottawa route
would be eliminated by the use of locks. The Georgian Bay route
would be entirely on Canadian territory, whereas the Welland
Canal was available to American vessels which might be *en route*
to Oswego. The Georgian Bay Canal was proposed as an alternative to the Welland, and continued to be advocated even after
the latter had been deepened. Before confederation engineers
appointed by the province of Canada brought in reports in 1858
and in 1860. Again in 1904 a board of engineers was asked to
examine the question, and their report, delivered in 1909, showed
plans for a waterway with a depth of twenty-two feet, twenty-
eight miles of canal excavation, and sixty-six miles of channel-
dredging at a cost of $100,000,000 (later estimated at $125,000,000).
In the spring of 1914 a royal commission (the favourite device
for transportation problems) was appointed, with wide terms of
reference, to consider the matter further. The commission showed
great energy in issuing interim reports containing factual material
concerning the conditions of transportation, existing and potential
traffic, and so on. For some reason, perhaps because the Georgian
Bay Canal had by that time ceased to be an issue, the commission
never made any specific recommendations as to whether the canal
should or should not be built, and the inquiry was suspended.

The Ottawa-Lake Nipissing-French River route was but one,
though probably the most convincing, of the plans put forward
for a short cut from Montreal to the upper lakes, A second proposal was for a waterway from Lake Ontario, at Toronto, to a
point on Georgian Bay. The Huron and Ontario Ship Canal
Company was incorporated to build it, but not a shovel of earth
was ever dug. The commission of 1870 reported that "the cost of
carrying out such a project would be so great as to render it
commercially worthless," and nothing more seems to have been
heard of it. A third proposal, the Trent Valley Canal, when first
advocated, would have been a boon to settlers by providing a
water route from the Kawartha Lakes to Lake Ontario. A modest
start was made in 1833, but the work was then abandoned.
Railways were built to take care of local traffic, while the Canadian

Pacific Railway and the enlarged St. Lawrence canals were designed to carry traffic to and from the west. In 1907 parliament, obsessed by the unfortunate belief that any form of transportation would pay, decided to proceed with the project. Not content with the initial error, the government ensured the uselessness of the canal for through traffic by making some of the locks 134 by 33 feet, with a minimum depth of 6 feet. It followed a circuitous course of 240 miles from Trenton on the Bay of Quinté, through a series of rivers and lakes to Lakes Simcoe and Couchiching, and thence along the Severn River. It never was completed to Georgian Bay, and only vessels of fifteen tons can be carried on the two marine railways which took the place of locks on the lower reaches of the Severn River.

The royal commission found that the Rideau Canal was adequate for the traffic which offered, and no change was made.

2. SHIPS AND CARGOES

Improved by canals, the inland waters of North America give unique opportunities for transport. Marked changes in the character and position of shipping accompanied improvements in canals. Sailing vessels began to disappear before their steam-driven rivals. Passenger traffic by water especially suffered from alternative methods of transport—first the railway and then the motor car— but it did not disappear. St. Lawrence steamers continued to operate from Montreal to Quebec and on to the Saguenay. Above Montreal passenger vessels were operated to Kingston, Toronto, and Hamilton. Further west a combined water and rail route served passengers to the west. After the completion of the Northern Railway to Collingwood (1855) the normal way through Canada to the prairies was over that railway, and by boat to Fort William. With the completion of the Canadian Pacific Railway the Northern ceased to be used, but both the C.P.R. and G.T.R. placed ships on the upper lakes as an alternative route for passengers from the west. On the smaller lakes the vessels which were once essential have disappeared, or, as on the Muskoka Lakes in Ontario, wage an unequal battle with the motor car.

Freight vessels, on the other hand, have been able to maintain and improve their position by virtue of their cheaper transport of bulky articles. The types of vessels have been governed by the size of the locks and the kinds of cargo. As the locks have increased in size, larger vessels have been built. Between 1899 and 1913 the number of Canadian freight and passenger vessels engaged on the Great Lakes, upper St. Lawrence, Ottawa River and Rideau Canal, rose only from 242 to 265, but the tonnage increased from 90,924 to 310,176.[3] Small vessels were found to be less economical, and larger ones were introduced as the canals were enlarged. In 1931 the steel bulk freighters accounted for eighty-five per cent of the total gross tonnage.

The movement toward large freighters was, however, strictly limited. For carriage to Montreal the depth of the St. Lawrence canals (14 feet) was the controlling factor. The vessels used to Montreal were known as "canallers" or "lower lakers," and those through the Sault Ste. Marie and Welland Canals as "upper lakers." While upper and lower lakers were similar in build, the former were most striking in appearance because of their greater length. "The Great Lakes bulk freighter is literally a huge, self-propelling barge with machinery aft, navigating bridge right up forward, and a long, clear parallel almost box-shaped cargo hold between. The machinery portion aft and the forward end are only ship-shaped parts of the hull."[4] The largest vessel in the Canadian service, and on the Great Lakes, the *Lemoyne* (a bulk freighter of a type for carrying grain, coal, or ore), has a length of 633 feet, beam of seventy feet, and 25 hatches. "Package" freighters carrying assorted cargoes are of the same general design as the bulk freighters, but rather smaller, and fitted with booms and winches with which to unload. Oil "tankers" have become common in recent years. The "whaleback," with rounded hull and long, spoon-shaped bow, is disappearing.

The general trend toward large-scale enterprises accompanied the increasing size of ships. A number of companies were organized to operate fleets of various sizes, and these in turn were amalgamated, as in the case of the Canada Steamship Lines, which in 1936 operated 101 vessels ranging from 2,000 to 7,000 tons.

3. *Interim report on the Georgian Bay canal* (*Sessional paper*, No. 19B, 1916).
4. A. C. Hardy, *American ship types* (New York, 1927), p. 201.

The success of Canadian inland shipping has depended primarily on the transport of bulk freight from west to east. The lake carriers have had the advantage of being able to offer low rates for the long distances covered, while the steady improvements in loading mechanism have reduced labour costs and the time spent in harbour. In 1929, for example, the *Lemoyne* loaded her cargo of 555,069 bushels of wheat at the rate of 1,746 bushels a minute. In maintaining their position the lake carriers were obliged to contend with the seasonal character of the business, caused not only by the freezing of the narrow waters, but also by the peak load coming in the short period between the first shipment of the new crop of western wheat and the close of the season of navigation. The latter handicap, however, has been mitigated by vessels being able to transport in the spring the wheat stored in elevators throughout the winter. The depth of water available is affected not only by the standard dimensions of the canals, but also by the level of water in any given season; and "when it is realized that a lake steamer will lose from 35 to 80 tons in carrying capacity, according to size, for each inch of loss of draught of water at minimum load-line, it is not difficult to understand that the water level makes a great difference in the matter of economical operation."[5]

While some departments of lake shipping have suffered from the competition of railways, such loss was more than compensated by the service which the railways rendered in acting as feeders of grain, ores, and coal at ports on the upper lakes. Since both the Great Lakes and the St. Lawrence either form the boundary or run near to it, the ship-owners of the United States and Canada would appear to have an equal chance of gaining from the traffic of two countries. The laws of both countries, however, set limits to the participation of foreign vessels in the coasting trade. The United States forbade Canadian vessels from carrying between two American ports, and for many years Canada had a similar regulation. In the early 'twenties, however, there was a shortage of Canadian tonnage; and to remedy this, and at the same time to tempt American ships down the St. Lawrence, a royal commission

5. W. T. Jackman, *Economic principles of transportation* (Toronto, 1935), p. 760.

of 1923 recommended a change.[6] The Canada Shipping Act was consequently amended in the same year (13 & 14 Geo. v, c.36) giving to the governor in council power to suspend the operation of the act so as to allow foreign ships to trade between two Canadian ports. As the new arrangement did not prove to be successful in its second object, and as there was ample Canadian tonnage, the Canada Shipping Act of 1934 (24 & 25 Geo. V. c.44) restored the position as it had been before 1923.

The Canadian aims were two: to secure as much traffic as possible for Canadian vessels, and to secure as much business as possible for Canadian ports. The following table[7] shows the United States and Canadian bulk freight tonnage on the Great Lakes and canals in 1922, the year before power was given to admit American vessels to trade between Canadian ports.

Description	U.S. gross tonnage	Canadian gross tonnage	U.S. and Can. gross tonnage	Canadian percentage
Steel bulk freighters in ore, coal, grain and stone trades	1,956,189	231,962	2,188,151	10.6
Steel bulk freight barges in ore and coal trades	88,075	3,265	91,340	3.5
Composite bulk freighters in ore, coal and grain trades	6,704	6,765	13,409	50.0
Composite bulk freight barges in grain, pulp and coal trades	673	3,741	4,414	84.7
Wooden bulk freighters in ore, coal and grain trades	43,917	51,299	95,216	54.0
Wooden barges engaged in all trades	34,840	36,253	71,093	51.0
Total freighters and barges	2,130,398	333,225	2,463,623	13.5
Package freighters	100,462	27,968	128,430	21.8
Passenger and freight steamers	69,541	24,853	94,394	26.3
Grand total	2,300,401	386,046	2,686,447	14.4

In the dozen years after 1922 the proportion between United States and Canadian tonnage changed; the former had only increased by about ten per cent in 1935, while the latter doubled

6. *Report of the royal commission on lake grain rates* (*Sessional paper* No. 211, 1923).

7. *Ibid.*, p. 10.

in the same period. The Welland Canal was a strategic point in the route to the sea, since it had to compete with the railways and the Erie Canal from Buffalo. The following table shows the traffic through it.[8]

Year	Canadian vessels		U.S. vessels	
	Number	Tonnage	Number	Tonnage
1900	1,765	575,381	634	437,431
1910	1,852	1,461,499	692	687,018
1920	2,430	2,013,817	694	514,439
1934	3,854	6,216,866	1,296	2,407,577
1935	3,931	6,300,820	1,161	1,896,732

An examination of the figures for 1935 shows that the largest two items in the total tonnage were the down traffic in Canadian vessels from Canadian to Canadian ports, and the down traffic in Canadian vessels from United States to Canadian ports. The opening of the Welland Ship Canal in 1930 attracted more United States vessels, but the advantages of the enlarged canal were to some extent counteracted by the increasing use of the Panama Canal. The traffic on the St. Lawrence canals, as the next table indicates,[9] has been overwhelmingly Canadian as to vessels.

Year	Canadian vessels		U.S. vessels	
	Number	Tonnage	Number	Tonnage
1900	8,737	2,033,206	921	105,151
1910	8,834	2,910,395	1,392	482,144
1920	6,145	3,233,029	813	442,250
1934	9,006	5,602,426	339	238,208
1935	10,009	5,847,341	317	209,798

American tonnage has failed to come to Canadian sea-ports, partly because of the relative disadvantage of those ports as compared with the rival American ones. Neither Montreal nor Quebec is a winter port, while Halifax and St. John are far removed from the points of origin of the principal exports. The rates of ocean shipping are necessarily dictated in part by the ease and safety of navigation, and in part by the prospect of return cargoes; and the lower St. Lawrence, though steadily improved, could never be other than a difficult passage. The position of New York

8. *Canal statistics* (Dominion bureau of statistics).
9. *Ibid.*

as a centre of world commerce continued to make it more attractive to roving freighters seeking to escape a voyage in ballast.

Iron ore has been the basic cargo for the large American bulk freighters, less than five per cent being available for Canadian vessels in 1922.[10] From the time the Canadian west became a wheat-growing area the Canadian bulk freighters found most of their cargoes in wheat from Fort William, though they were also able—as they had been before—to participate in the carriage of American wheat to Canadian ports. In 1922 Canadian vessels carried forty-five million bushels of wheat from Duluth, Chicago, Milwaukee, and Buffalo to Canadian ports.[11] The largest part of their business, however, has consisted in the transport of wheat from the Canadian west. In 1913 eastbound wheat travelled over routes as follows.[12]

Distribution to Interior Ports

	bushels
From Fort William and Port Arthur via Great Lakes	130,181,954
From Duluth via Great Lakes	7,830,740
Total	138,012,694

To Canadian ports (by water)	bushels	American ports (by water)	bushels
Depot Harbor	2,963,915	Chicago	374,967
Port McNicoll	7,774,110	Port Huron	3,992,437
Tiffin	11,639,728	Detroit	15,000
Midland	630,000	Toledo	950,525
Collingwood	337,869	Fairport	5,198,205
Meaford	110,000	Erie	7,628,824
Goderich	6,608,085	Buffalo	54,643,639
Point Edward	386,142		
Port Stanley	340,302		
Port Colborne	20,806,527		
Kingston	1,972,473		
Prescott	80,059		
Montreal	11,559,887		
Total	65,209,097	Total	72,803,597

10. *Report of the royal commission on lake grain rates*, 1923, p. 8.
11. *Ibid.*, p. 11.
12. *Interim report on the Georgian Bay Canal*, 1916, p. 63.

It is apparent that a large number of Canadian ports received some portion of the wheat. Port McNicoll and Tiffin were Canadian Pacific and Grand Trunk ports respectively. Port Colborne, at the western end of the Welland Canal, did the largest business, while only eleven and a half million bushels passed through the St. Lawrence canals to Montreal. Buffalo, on the other hand, took so much Canadian wheat (for rail and water transport to American ports) that the total amount passing through American lake ports was larger than that passing through Canadian. In addition to the wheat passing by all-water route to seaboard (that is, the portion which went to Montreal), and that which went by combined water and rail (that is, all the amounts shown against the other ports, except the small portion that passed through the Erie Canal), 1,030,000 bushels went by an all-rail route over the Canadian Pacific Railway—the only trans-continental line which was complete in 1913. The next table[13] shows the distribution of Canadian wheat to the different ocean ports for export in the same year.

Canadian ports	bushels	U.S. ports	bushels
Montreal	26,834,373	Portland	8,223,463
St. John	7,666,998	Boston	14,334,932
Halifax	554,712	New York	22,616,905
		Philadelphia	12,797,843
		Baltimore	12,690,009
Total	35,056,083	Total	70,663,152

The balance then began to change. In 1933 lake shipments of wheat from Fort William and Port Arthur to Canadian ports amounted to 100,677,537 bushels and to American ports 45,240,497 bushels. Meanwhile other factors had begun to affect the position of Canadian shipping on the Great Lakes. Vancouver first began to export considerable quantities of wheat to Europe, by way of the Panama Canal, in 1921, and sent 31,868,187 bushels to the United Kingdom and 63,130,254 bushels to other countries

13. *Ibid.*

(excluding the United States) in 1928.[14] Prince Rupert and Victoria also entered the picture to a small extent. Possibly significant for the future was the completion of the railway to Churchill, and the beginning of export through Hudson Bay—amounting to 4,049,871 bushels in 1934–1935.[15] Canadian lake boats had secured a larger proportion of the wheat to be carried to ocean ports, but the movement of wheat by rail to the ports of the west and north was a new threat. High prices of wheat, increased acreage, and rising freight rates had led to a great increase in tonnage— from 240,000 to 575,000 tons in the years 1921 to 1931.[16] The demand for tonnage then decreased; freight rates dropped heavily; and the shipping companies ran into difficulties.

Freight rates on the lake grain carriers have fluctuated widely. In 1915 the rate per bushel of wheat from the head of the lakes to Montreal was 4.99 cents. In 1920 it reached a high mark of 11.64 cents and by 1932 was down again to 5.09. Not only in different years, but even as between different parts of the same year, the rates fluctuate. They are not based on standard maxima set by a governmental body, as is the case of railway rates, but on individual contracts. Space in vessels is purchased by individuals, in general before the grain itself is bought, and when the time comes for shipment there may be other cargoes moving at a different rate.[17]

Apart from the relation of existing tonnage to the freight offering, rates on lake vessels are controlled by rival transportation services. The character of the goods carried enables the vessels to compete successfully with Canadian railways for through traffic, but they must maintain their lower rates in order to preserve that position A further source of control lies in the rates on United States routes to the sea. The maintenance of Canadian shipping and of the St. Lawrence route to the sea are twin problems of long standing.

14. On the effects of the Panama Canal on Canadian traffic and rates *see* W. Sandford Evans, "Canadian traffic through the Panama" (*Queen's Quarterly*, xxxvi, 2); H. A. Innis, "Canada and the Panama Canal" (H. A. Innis and A. F. W. Plumptre, *The Canadian economy and its problems* [Toronto, 1934]).

15. *Canal statistics.*

16. F. H. Brown, "Canadian lake shipping" (Innis and Plumptre, *op. cit.*).

17. On the question of rates *see Report of the royal commission on lake grain rates,* 1923.

How can more traffic be attracted to the "natural" route by the St. Lawrence? The answer that has been given by Canadians for over a century is—improve the Great Lakes-St. Lawrence navigation. The depth of the canals was increased first to nine and then to fourteen feet as a means to attain this end. Still another improvement has been advocated in a plan known as the Great Lakes-St. Lawrence seaway.

With the possible exception of the Rideau, the canals of Canada were designed and first built for normal commercial purposes in an age when railways were in their infancy. The St. Lawrence canals were opened as a through route just as the first period of active railway construction was beginning. The completion of the pre-confederation railways—in particular the Great Western and the Grand Trunk—deprived the water routes of a portion of their passenger traffic, and of their freight traffic in certain goods. With the opening of the west the railways aided the canals. They delivered wheat to the freighters at Fort William and Port Arthur, some of which was carried through to the St. Lawrence, some to Buffalo, and some to a number of ports on Lake Huron and Georgian Bay. From these latter ports the railways again picked up the wheat and carried it to tidewater.

Has the expenditure on the improvement of inland navigation—canals, harbours, and lighthouses—been justified? The money spent on canals by provincial and federal governments amounted in 1935 to a total of $339,583,604, including the cost of maintenance and staff. Against this was a total income over the whole period of $31,689,570. The income did not cover carrying charges and depreciation. When tolls were abolished on Canadian canals in 1903, following similar action in European countries and in the United States, the principle was admitted that the returns from governmental expenditure were, apart from the income from rentals for power purposes, to be totally indirect. Such action was different only in degree from that taken with respect to other forms of transportation. In Canada the aid given by government to transportation has been based on the assumption that adequate facilities had to be provided, that the country could not progress without them. Rates on the Intercolonial Railway (which correspond to tolls) were not based on the capital and operating costs of the railway. Assistance given to other railways, amounting to very large figures, was thought to be well spent, whether or not it returned in cash to the government. So it was with canals. Without them, it was believed, the trade of the Canadian, as well as of the American, west would in large part cease to flow through Canada.

3. THE ST. LAWRENCE DEEP WATERWAY

With such considerations in mind, it may seem anomalous that the most ambitious design ever made for the development of the Great Lakes-St. Lawrence navigation should be a joint project of Canada and the United States, more especially when it is realized that the origins of the scheme are as much American as Canadian, and that it is not a plan foisted on a gullible United States by a persuasive Canada. On the other hand, participation of the United States did not affect the fact that, from the Canadian point of view, the St. Lawrence scheme was a possible means of saving the water-borne traffic of the lakes from escaping south before it reached the St. Lawrence. The United States shares the Great Lakes with Canada, and owns the southern shore of the St. Lawrence from its source at Lake Ontario to a point almost opposite Cornwall. From the early years of the existence of the United States there was a desire to make use of the navigation of the Canadian part of the river—that is, from Cornwall to the sea. This right was granted by the Reciprocity Treaty of 1854; and on the abrogation of the treaty, the same right was conceded by the treaty of 1871. Since 1854, too, American vessels have been allowed to use Canadian canals, which, since 1903, have been free of tolls to American and Canadian vessels alike.

For the United States, however, there are two alternative approaches by water to the interior of the continent, by the Mississippi and the Hudson rivers. The former, because of its shallow water, has never been available for vessels of deep draught; and even the artificial connection between the Mississippi and the Great Lakes via the Chicago drainage canal has not threatened serious competition with the St. Lawrence. The Hudson has been a continuous rival. Early in the present century it was decided to

improve the old Erie Canal, long the bugbear of Canadian transportation interests, and by 1918 the new Erie Barge Canal was
opened for traffic after it had been deepened to twelve feet and a
partial change of route made. The canal might also, as before, be
entered from Oswego instead of Buffalo. But, although the barge
canal has carried some grain which might otherwise have moved
through the St. Lawrence, it cannot be regarded as the major
threat to Canada. There have been a number of proposals for deep
waterways through American territory, but none has as yet
received general support. The foremost rivals to the St. Lawrence
route have been the various American railways from Buffalo to
New York.

Such support as the St. Lawrence deepening plan has received
in the United States has been based on a belief that lower transportation costs could be achieved, and—for a time—that existing
facilities were not adequate for the traffic at its peak.[18] Both these
views have been shared by Canadians, with the additional interest
in routing the heavy traffic of the west through the Canadian
section of the St. Lawrence to Montreal. Thus the deepening plan
has been to Americans purely a problem in transportation, and to
Canadians, that, plus a more general economic interest.

The first official move toward a common improvement of the
St. Lawrence came from the United States.[19] In 1913 the senate
unanimously adopted the following resolution, moved by a senator
from Michigan.

Requesting the President to enter into negotiations with Great Britain
with the view to securing an international agreement for the concurrent
or co-operative improvement of navigation in the boundary waters of the
United States and Canada, for the advancement of the commerce of the
two countries.

Some months later the American government suggested that the
International Joint Commission be asked to explore the question,

18. R. S. MacElwee and A. H. Ritter, *Economic aspects of the Great Lakes-St.
Lawrence ship canal* (New York, 1921), chaps. iii and iv.

19. For the history of the deep waterway project *see* G. W. Stephens, *The
St. Lawrence waterway project* (Montreal, 1930); C. P. Wright, *The St. Lawrence
deep waterway* (Toronto, 1935); G. W. Brown, "The deepening of the St. Lawrence"
(*Round Table*, No. 79)

with reference to navigation, power, and fisheries. The outbreak of war put a temporary end to discussion, but shortly after 1918 the pressure of both power and navigation interests brought the matter to a head. Early in 1920 the Canadian and American governments requested the International Joint Commission to examine the possible improvement of the St. Lawrence for navigation and power, and each appointed an engineer to coöperate with the commission in the investigation. In 1921 the two engineers reported to the commission that the development of the river for both purposes was feasible. They advised a channel of twenty-five feet for the present, with structures designed to allow an eventual depth of thirty feet. They reported that nearly all the potential power in the river—some 4,100,000 horsepower—might be developed in connection with the deepening plan, but pointed out that this should not all be developed at once since it could not all be sold in the present or near future. They estimated the cost of a twenty-five-foot channel from Montreal to Lake Ontario, with the development of 1,464,000 horsepower in the international section, at $252,728,200.

After receiving the report of the engineers and conducting public hearings, the Joint Commission recommended that a treaty be entered into between the United States and Canada to carry the plan into effect, and that the new Welland Canal be embodied in the scheme. They recommended that the cost of navigation works be apportioned between the two countries on the basis of benefits received, and that additional construction required for power be divided equally. While accepting the report of the engineers as the basis of work between Montreal and Lake Ontario, they recommended that further investigation be made by an enlarged board of engineers. The proposed board was actually set up in 1924. Shortly before this was done, the government of each country appointed a non-technical advisory committee, that of the United States having Herbert Hoover as chairman, and that of Canada, G. P. Graham (minister of railways and canals), and, after his resignation, W. E. Foster.

Both advisory committees reported in favour of the St. Lawrence scheme and the continuation of negotiations, the American committee reporting in 1926 and the Canadian in 1928. In the meanwhile the joint board of engineers proceeded with a detailed study of the technical aspects of the question, after which it made its report toward the end of 1926. The plans of the board were "prepared in accordance with the recognized principle that the interests of navigation on the St. Lawrence are paramount." They pointed out, however, that the generation of electric power would not conflict with this principle. Their general plan for the improvement of navigation was to flood out the rapids by dams, rather than to make use of side canals as had formerly been the practice. On the placing of dams, the route of the channel, and the depth to be attained the board was not unanimous. All members were agreed that permanent structures should be designed to permit an eventual depth of thirty feet, but for immediate use the majority of the Canadians were in favour of twenty-seven feet (the depth of the new Welland Canal), and the majority of the Americans preferred twenty-five feet. To secure through navigation to Lake Superior it would be necessary to deepen the channels in the Detroit River and the St. Clair River, and possibly to build a new canal at Sault Ste. Marie. The Welland Canal, the remaining link, was already provided for. No single figure can be given as the estimate of cost, since the amounts varied in relation to the various modifications proposed; but for a twenty-five-foot channel between Lake Ontario and Montreal, with the development of five million horse-power, the joint board put the cost at from $620,000,000 to $650,000,000.[20]

From the time of the various reports which have been mentioned the St. Lawrence project moved steadily toward the point at which it could be submitted to the legislatures of the two countries. In July 1932 the treaty embodying the agreement which had been reached by the governments was signed at Washington. Its specific concern was with the international section of the St. Lawrence, where a twenty-seven-foot channel was to be established, the cost to be divided between the two countries, Canada receiving credit for $128,000,000 of the expenditure on the Welland Canal. The remainder of the works necessary to complete twenty-seven-foot navigation from Montreal to the upper lakes were to be undertaken

20. *Report of the joint board of engineers on the St. Lawrence waterway project* (Ottawa, 1927).

by the two governments independently. The treaty also provided for the development of electrical power.

In March 1934 the treaty was rejected by the senate of the United States, in spite of its acceptance being urged by the president. Although a few comic interludes, such as the suggestion that the British government was really seeking a naval base on Lake Michigan, may have pleased the more ignorant constituents, the real opposition to the treaty came from the rival power and transportation interests of certain sections and groups. In any case the senate had exercised its constitutional right, and the treaty was—for some years at least—a dead letter. There was no question, in spite of early suggestions to that effect, that Canada would continue the deep waterway scheme single-handed. All that remained of the seaway route was the Welland Ship Canal, which was opened for some traffic in 1930, and for the largest upper lake vessels in 1932. The dimensions of the locks of the new canal were 859 feet in length, 80 feet in width, and 30 feet in depth. For the time being the depth between locks was only 25 feet, but this was sufficient for the largest upper lakers. The new canal followed in part the route of the old one, but some changes were made. The Lake Ontario entrance was moved from Port Dalhousie to Port Weller, and at other points the course was changed with a view to obtaining a straighter line. The general position, then, was that navigation through Canadian waters to the sea was controlled by the Sault lock (18.2 feet), the Welland Ship Canal (25 feet), and the St. Lawrence canals (14 feet). By making use of the American locks at the Sault (24.5 feet) the largest lake freighters could be navigated between Lake Superior and Lake Ontario, but the St. Lawrence remained closed to upper lakers from the west or large seagoing vessels from the east.

Leaving aside the development of power[21] (which must, however, be taken into consideration in estimating the final cost of the work), it appears that the scheme was one to obliterate the rapids and low water as hindrances to navigation, and to provide an inland waterway from the Gulf of St. Lawrence to the head of Lake Superior—a waterway such as did not, and could not exist in any

21. For a detailed examination of the treaty and the economic aspects of the waterway *see* Wright, *op. cit.*, pp. 281 et seq.

other part of the world. On the merits of this grand design experts have always disagreed, both as to its economic value, and its probable use by large vessels. The second point may be disposed of first. There is general agreement that the present type of upper lakers could not be used on the ocean, inasmuch as their design makes them unsuitable for anything but inland navigation. There is even doubt whether they could be economically and safely worked through the St. Lawrence canals. Similarly it seems clear that ocean vessels working on a fixed schedule ("liners") would not proceed above Montreal; and uncertain whether tramp steamers would use the canals in any large numbers.

The economic value of the deep waterway plan depends on more complicated considerations. In general there must be taken into account on the one hand the total cost, including new construction, deepening, improved harbours, and compensating works—such as for flooded lands; and on the other hand the returns in electrical power, lower freight rates, and added transportation facilities. The advantages of the waterway must also be considered from two points of view: as benefiting the communities of the middle west of the United States and Canada, and as directing a larger amount of traffic through Canadian channels.

The whole economic question hinges on whether such added facilities are required, and whether they would result in freight rates sufficiently lower to justify the cost to the country. Canada has already three outlets to the sea: on the Atlantic, on the Pacific, and on Hudson Bay. The enthusiasm for the deep waterway plan was born in an age when the economic trend was actively upward: is the waterway required for the traffic of the present or immediate future? Clearly the only valid argument in favour of the waterway is that it would bring a net advantage to the people of Canada; that is to say, result in cheaper transportation without an equal loss to the existing facilities.

Many estimates have been made as to the probable saving in cost of transportation. Probably the most optimistic was that of two American writers who argued that,

The saving on grain will amount to from 8 to 10 cents a bushel, and this saving will affect not only the grain which actually moves for export, but practically all that produced within the area tributary to the Great Lakes.

This saving will amount annually to approximately the entire cost of the improvement required to admit ocean vessels into the Lakes.[22]

A more cautious advocate of the waterway scheme has estimated the probable saving at 3.7 cents a bushel.[23]

Whatever the fate of the deepening scheme, water transport continues, and will continue, to play a vital part in Canadian life. No railway, no road, has destroyed its value. And the men who have since the days of the *voyageurs* of New France carried the country's goods, will still follow their lawful occasions.

22. MacElwee and Ritter, *op. cit.*, p. 290.

23. L. R. Thomson, "The St. Lawrence problem" (*Engineering Journal*, April, 1929).

CHAPTER XIV

TRANSPORTATION BY ELECTRICITY AND GASOLINE

1. ELECTRIC RAILWAYS

JUST as the discovery of the force of steam led gradually to its application as motive power on both land and water, so the discovery of the similar qualities of electricity suggested a new, and possibly more satisfactory, form of energy. It was one, however, which could be utilized only under certain conditions. Experiments were made with electrically-driven boats, but it was found that even the smaller ones could not be satisfactorily operated by storage batteries. Only slightly more success was obtained with electric automobiles. Electricity is most efficiently supplied in a continuous flow, and its indirect provision, by means of batteries, is expensive and inadequate for such purposes. The use of electricity in transportation, therefore, was confined to railways operating under conditions where electric power could be supplied through overhead wires or a third rail.

The essential feature of electric traction is the removal of power generation from the train to a stationary power unit, and this fact is responsible for most of its economies and advantages. This same fact also gives rise to the great drawback of electrification, since a large amount of capital has to be expended in providing the overhead or third-rail equipment, together with the necessary feeders, transmission cables, and sub-stations. This capital once expended is definitely tied to the route and cannot be moved if the scheme does not prove a financial success.[1]

The first need of electric railways is, obviously, an adequate supply of power, which may be obtained either from natural water power, or by artificial generation. The most favourable conditions for electric railways are where water power is plentiful and coal scarce, as in Switzerland where thirty-two per cent of the railway mileage had been electrified by 1930. Austria, also mountainous and without coal, has followed the same course.

1. K. G. Fenelon, *Railway economics* (London, 1932), p. 176.

Electric locomotives can be run in either direction without turning; require less labour; can be kept in use more continuously than steam locomotives; have better acceleration and more reserve power; and, not only have greater braking capacity, but can regenerate power through braking. On the other hand, electric railways have not proved profitable over great distances or where traffic is light; for under such conditions the overhead charges are relatively too high. The steam locomotive is in itself a travelling power unit involving a relatively low capital outlay; but the electric locomotive depends on elaborate equipment for power production, which is only economical when in full use. Electric railways are particularly suitable for passenger traffic in well-populated areas. By the elimination of smoke and noise, by ease in starting and stopping, and the small space which it occupies, the electric engine can be used in and near cities. The steam locomotive, on the other hand, is not only an unwelcome visitor to city streets, but cannot be operated economically. It requires a larger train unit and is both clumsy and expensive in starting and stopping.

It will be apparent that the electric railway has had a limited use in Canada. Electric power could not be economically used for long distances in either passenger or freight business, even in those parts of the country where water power existed in large quantities, for the traffic was not sufficient to justify the capital outlay. On the other hand, electric railways were admirably suited for suburban transport. As villages grew to towns and towns to cities, horse-drawn omnibuses appeared on the streets, but were hampered by bad roads. In 1861 the first street railway was opened in Toronto with every sign of enthusiasm, but while rails were used to advantage, the motive power supplied by horses was inadequate, particularly as the city grew in size. Electric railways in Canada date from 1887 when a line was opened at St. Catharines, Ontario. Three years later a second company began operations in Vancouver, and in the next few years the street railways of Ottawa, Montreal, Toronto, and other eastern cities were electrified.

Electric railways were also extended beyond the cities to their suburban areas, or for short runs between cities or towns where the steam railway service was inadequate. Tracks were laid expressly for the purpose, rather than by the electrification of existing railways as has been widely done in England. These "radials" were built in all provinces, and the mileage increased from 256 (including street railways) in 1893 to the maximum figure of 1,737 in 1925. The most far-reaching plan for radials was that put forward by the Hydro-Electric Power Commission of Ontario to operate some 325 miles for rapid transport. Of this total about 150 miles were already in operation, though requiring to be improved for fast trains. There were to be the following lines: from Toronto, through Hamilton, to St. Catharines; from Toronto east to Bowmanville; from Toronto to Guelph; from Hamilton to Kitchener and Guelph; and from St. Catharines to Niagara. The commission had the support of a number of municipalities and believed that there was a great future for electric railways. A new government in Ontario, however, was sceptical of the merits of the plan, and, since financial support from the provincial government was needed, appointed a royal commission to investigate. In 1921 this commission, under the chairmanship of Mr. Justice Sutherland, issued a majority report[2] which was wholly unfavourable to the project. It was argued that "the financial condition of electric railways in Ontario and the United States in and prior to 1920, has been so precarious and unsatisfactory, and the outlook for improvement so dubious and discouraging, that the proposed system of electric railways should not, in our judgment, be entered upon unless the evidence of competent operating experts justifies the conclusion that they will be self-supporting." In the opinion of the commissioners all the evidence indicated that they would not be self-supporting. The commissioners also considered the relation of electric railways to other forms of transport, and came to the conclusion that there would be an uneconomic competition. The business of the Canadian National, they felt, might well be affected by new electric lines, and the Canadian National must be given consideration. Moreover the province had just undertaken a plan for the construction of highways at great cost, and the commissioners believed that the effect of this additional provision for transportation should be observed before the province also committed itself to expenditure on electric railways, which might prove to compete with its roads. The scheme as a whole was dropped; and, while some new lines

2. *Reports of commission to inquire into hydro-electric railways* (Toronto, 1921).

were built, no such sweeping programme for electric railways was ever again brought forward. After 1925 a steady decline in mileage was evident to 1,293 in 1934.

Electric railways, whether in town or country, were dependent on a sufficient supply of electricity at a cost low enough to justify operation. Most of the early street railways used electricity made by steam, but in the 'nineties, at the time when more ambitious lines were being built, hydro-electric power was introduced as an alternative. There was plenty of water power to be developed, and as the machinery was improved power could be transmitted over considerable distances; for example, the power developed at Niagara Falls was used in the cities of western Ontario.

Especially outside the towns, electric railways were designed in a period when the roads were in general so bad as to make travel by them difficult, and when there was an absence of effective motive power on the roads. Even when the motor car was introduced, it was at first too expensive and too primitive for general use, and the state of the roads forbade easy travel by that means. In the early years of the twentieth century the electric railway was regarded in many communities as the most hopeful means of travel for short runs, such as would connect the towns between Toronto and Hamilton with those cities. The bulk of the business of electric railways was in the carriage of passengers. In 1933 the total number of passenger cars owned by all the electric railways was 3,773, while their freight cars numbered only 300. In the same year they carried 585,385,094 passengers as against 1,547,202 tons of freight. The character of the traffic of the electric railways was notably different from that of the steam railways. The former catered to the short haul and the latter to the long; the former used, for the most part, single-car trains, while on the latter the size of trains was constantly increased. Neither of the large steam railway companies had made considerable use of electricity.

Electric and steam railways have both met a loss of traffic from the competition of motor vehicles. Both the urban and suburban electric railways have suffered, but the latter have been particularly vulnerable. Within large cities the street railways have still an important rôle to play, which has been reduced by motor cars but not in most cases by buses, whereas outside the cities lines have felt the full force of the competition from both motor cars and buses. The companies have recognized the effectiveness of competition by themselves operating buses. In many cases the tracks of the radials have been pulled up, and from 1926 to 1934 thirteen interurban and ten urban electric railways ceased operations.

The situation which the radials had been designed to meet— a situation in which there were few good roads and no means of rapid transit by road—had disappeared. For freight and passenger traffic the public turns to that mode of transport which offers the most attractive combination of convenience and economy. The railway was hampered by the inelasticity of its route in that field where its rival was most effective, in the short haul. From its eclipse of many years the road had found a new weapon with which to belabour its old enemy the rail. The internal combustion engine had once again rearranged the balance in methods of transportation.

2. ROADS AND MOTOR VEHICLES

The construction and maintenance of roads was, in the 'nineties, still entirely under the direction of the provinces, with the actual work delegated to the local authorities. Perhaps because of the emphasis laid on railways, little progress had been made in the improvement of roads. In Ontario the sorry condition of the roads led in 1894 to the organization of the Ontario Good Roads Association, which began a campaign, in the newspapers and through public meetings, to interest the public in the need for improvement. At the request of the association, the provincial government appointed a provincial road instructor, whose first report bore out the need for reform. He wrote that roads in many municipalities were worse than they had been ten years before, and that neglect and evasion of statute labour were more general than ever.[3] A report issued two years later continued to paint a gloomy picture, and one that was probably true of all provinces.

It is doubtful if there is a mile of true macadam road in Ontario outside a few towns or cities. There are miles of roads which are covered with dirty gravel or rough, broken stone, and are popularly supposed to be

3. *Report of the provincial instructor in road-making, Ontario, 1896.*

macadamized. To-day the majority are little better than trails. From the middle of October until the end of December, and from the first of March to the end of May, a period of five months, by far the greatest part of the mileage of the province is mud, ruts and pitch-holes. There are at least two months when the roads are practically impassable.[4]

Up to the beginning of the new century there was little change in administration. Roads were built and maintained either by the townships or by toll companies. Statute labour was still the rule, although some of the townships began to abolish it at about this time. The cost of construction, over and above the statute labour, was met by provincial grants. The provincial governments, however, now began to take more responsibility. The first important step was the Highway Improvement Act passed by the legislature of Ontario in 1901, which provided for the sum of one million dollars a year (later increased to two million) as government subsidy toward improvement of roads in the organized counties, to be granted as one-third of the cost of such works. The novel part of the act was that grants would be made only on roads built according to government standards. It was hoped that the weaknesses of the old system, in which there had been evident a lack of expert knowledge, might be avoided.

The federal government first undertook the building of roads in pioneer areas, such as the Dawson road between Port Arthur and Fort Garry. After the gold discoveries in 1896 the Dominion government undertook a programme of road-building in the Yukon Territory, and by 1913 there were some five hundred miles of good waggon roads radiating from Dawson and Whitehorse, together with main roads such as that between those two towns, a distance of 330 miles.

Towards the end of the nineteenth century a vehicle was being developed that could move under its own power, and which would be to roads what the steam locomotive was to rails. The motor car, driven by an internal combustion engine and using gasoline as fuel, came as the result of years of experiment in England and France, and began to be effective in the 'nineties. At this time it was first introduced into Canada, but it was some years before it became a common mode of transport. In 1907, a little more than

4. Quoted in E. C. Guillet, *Early life in Upper Canada* (Toronto, 1933), p. 544.

ten years after the introduction of the first motor car, the total number registered was only 2,130. Compared with the modern car, they were expensive, clumsy, and undependable. The existing roads were unsuited to mechanical vehicles and made driving uncomfortable and hazardous. The first relief to owners came from the manufacturers of cars rather than from road-builders. Continuous attention to the mechanical side led to steady improvement both in safety and dependability. The first low priced cars in North America were put on the market by Henry Ford, and the number of owners increased rapidly. By 1912 there were over fifty thousand motor vehicles registered in Canada.

Early motor cars were for the carriage of passengers rather than freight, but motor trucks began to be common in the years immediately before the war. The privately owned passenger car is the successor to the horse and carriage of the previous period, and has the advantage that it can be used to suit the owner's convenience, and can be driven when and where he may choose, provided that adequate roads are available. It has, however, characteristics that the horse and carriage cannot have—speed and endurance. A car may (and frequently did) break down, but it does not become exhausted. Thus the old system of travel by stages could be replaced by an uninterrupted journey, limited by the endurance of the driver and the state of the roads.

With the increasing use of the automobile there came an additional and powerful argument for better roads, and the provinces were compelled to take a more active part. As the result of the findings of a commission appointed in 1913 a highway department was established in Ontario, with a minister and deputy-minister. Further provision was made for subsidies of twenty per cent of the cost of county roads and forty per cent of trunk roads, the government retaining in both cases the right of approval of the plans. An act of 1917 empowered the government to take over any highway, and to assume sole responsibility for construction and maintenance. By virtue of this arrangement the modern arterial roads began to come into existence. Much the same process was followed in the other provinces. In Quebec the provincial government made grants for county roads and began to take over toll roads from the various companies which held them. The roads branch of the department of agriculture was made into a separate department and a deputy minister put in charge. In each province the steps were the same: grants to local authorities, partial control of construction, and provincial highways.

The Dominion government, too, increased its participation by degrees in road building. In 1911 the Conservative party adopted as part of its platform federal aid to municipal authorities for the construction of roads, and, when returned to power, introduced a bill to that effect. It also allowed for construction of highways by the Dominion government, but the bill failed to pass the senate, and eight years elapsed before the project was revived. The Canada Highways Act of 1919 authorized the expenditure of $20,000,000 on the construction and improvement of highways over a period of five years. A minimum grant of $80,000 was to be made annually to each province, and the remainder to be allotted in proportion to population. At the same time a separate highways branch was established in the department of railways and canals. Finally the federal government entered directly into road construction in 1931 by undertaking the Trans-Canada Highway as a step to alleviate unemployment and to allow travel by road from coast to coast on Canadian soil. The constitutional position of the Dominion in regard to highways involves some nice problems, but it seems unlikely that federal expenditure on roads will be resisted by the provinces.

Before 1914 almost no hard-surfaced highways were to be found in Canada, and motor traffic was severely handicapped. It was no uncommon experience for motorists, as late as 1915, to be stuck in mud holes on the principal highways of Ontario. Motoring was still a series of adventures in which the driver pitted his skill and his luck against mechanical imperfections and the hazards of the road. As the number of motor cars and trucks increased (there were nearly 200,000 in 1917) serious attention began to be given to the roads, and during the war the first highways adequate for motor vehicles, such as the Toronto-Hamilton highway, were begun. The change consisted not so much in cutting new roads as in improving old ones, by straightening, widening, re-surfacing, and lowering the grades. Provincial and federal authorities studied various types of roads and made use of the experiments conducted in other countries. The resulting roads, of course, differed greatly in character, according to the purposes for which they were intended. Only those receiving the heaviest traffic were required to be of cement or other hard surfaces, while in many parts of Canada gravel or earth was the rule. The result over a period of years has been to produce a number of main highways that can be used by motor vehicles at all times of the year, together with many roads that are still difficult in the spring. There remain a number of country roads of unimproved dirt, some of which are impassable when the frost is coming out of the ground. There are still many sections in the northern parts of the central and western provinces that are without good roads, but these are for the most part sparsely, if at all, settled. Recently attention has been given to colonization and tourist routes that cut into the forests of northern Ontario. The Trans-Canada Highway, when completed, will pass through some territory in which there are few inhabitants and little local traffic. The partly completed road through the Rockies is an engineering feat comparable to the railways through those mountains, and will necessarily depend largely on tourist traffic.

The growth of roads in modern Canada lacks some of the romance of the earlier period, when the typical problem was to cut a road through virgin forest; yet the importance attached to good roads, especially in the years since the war, indicates a similar value to the community. The following table[5] shows the character

Province	Unimproved miles	Improved earth miles	Gravel miles	Water-bound macadam miles	Bitum. macadam miles	Bitum. concrete miles	Cement concrete miles	Total miles
Prince Edward Island	1,789	1,651	195	—	—	12	4	3,651
Nova Scotia	7,081	3,722	3,903	30	10	37	—	14,783
New Brunswick	2,567	2,228	6,791	—	13	15	—	11,614
Quebec	—	18,394	14,394	1,396	186	637	142	35,149
Ontario	3,331	18,217	42,112	188	2,312	803	1,687	68,675
Manitoba	28,502	1,307	4,377	—	—	177	26	34,389
Saskatchewan	56,696	96,573	2,363	—	—	68	—	155,700
Alberta	40,109	20,190	2,455	—	80	—	—	62,834
British Columbia	2,906	10,364	8,358	41	613	72	47	22,474

5. *The Highway and motor vehicle in Canada, 1934* (Dominion bureau of statistics). In the case of Ontario twenty-five, and of British Columbia seventy-three, miles of unclassified roads are included in the totals for those provinces.

of roads in the various provinces at the end of 1934. For the whole Dominion the total mileage of roads was: provincial roads, 87,496; other roads, 321,773; grand total, 409,269.

Nova Scotia and New Brunswick have, until very recently, pinned their faith to gravel. Saskatchewan, with much the greatest mileage, has only a small proportion of gravel and few hard-surfaced roads. Of the central provinces, Ontario shows nearly twice the mileage of Quebec, with a fair proportion of macadam and cement surfaces. The different types of roads in use depended on the extent, wealth, population, density of traffic, physical conditions, and financial policy of each province.

The city dweller has an exaggerated idea of the extent to which the horse has been replaced by the motor vehicle: a mistake which may readily be rectified by a visit to a typical country district, especially in the winter when rows of sleighs' will be seen in any village or small town. In some districts, oxen are still in general use for heavy hauling. Nevertheless, the test of a modern road, and especially of any main highway, is its suitability for motor vehicles. The motor car has long since ceased to be regarded as a luxury, or the rich man's perquisite; while its less flashy brothers, the motor truck and the motor bus, play a vital part in transportation. Motor vehicles of all kinds have increased in numbers at a startling rate in recent years. By 1934 the registrations for Canada were as follows: passenger cars (including taxicabs), 952,427; commercial cars, buses, and trucks, 166,799; motorcycles, 10,306—a total of 1,129,532.

The most obvious effect of the combination of motor vehicles and improved roads is to reduce distances and to alleviate the remoteness of even the most sparsely-settled areas. The railway had gone far toward performing this service, but there was a limit to what the railway could accomplish. On the one hand, the towns, villages, and farms have been brought into touch with the cities, and are thus enabled to buy and sell in a larger market. Such products as fruit, vegetables and dairy products may readily be carried in trucks or even passenger cars, and sold with or without the aid of a middleman. At the same time the farmer or villager has a wider choice as a buyer, and in many instances may have goods delivered at his door. The rural delivery of mail and newspapers has also been accelerated by the use of motors. On the other side of the picture is the further destruction of the independent life of villages and small towns, already reduced by the coming of railways. The old self-sufficiency, the local trades, and even the consciousness of local pride and corporate existence have to some extent disappeared.

The principal uses of motor vehicles may be divided into those of the truck, omnibus, and passenger car. The truck may be operated by the company whose business it does, or it may be a common carrier, or a contract carrier. Trucks are commonly used for the delivery of almost all classes of goods in cities and in the areas immediately surrounding them, and many manufacturers and large-scale retailers use them both in the delivery of their products and acquisition of materials. A use of trucks that illustrates their peculiar value is in the moving of household furniture, where the necessity of crating and the inevitable delay attendant on its transport by rail are avoided. The milk supply for the large cities is for the most part carried by truck, a method which allows for the collection of cans at the gate of each farm and their delivery to the dairy with the least possible delay. The produce of market gardens is usually carried to urban centres by truck; livestock are transported to market in trucks designed and licensed for that purpose; and in many cases grain is carried to the elevators by truck, a fact which is significant to the farmer in the saving of time at a busy season. In 1924 the highways branch of the department of railways and canals conducted an interesting investigation into the haulage of farm crops by waggon or truck over rural roads. By means of a questionnaire, it was ascertained that 7.2 per cent of the produce of the farmers who replied was carried by motor truck. At that time only 12,500 trucks were owned by farmers. Transport either by waggon or truck was appreciably cheaper on improved roads. The comparatively small number of trucks used by farmers was in part due to the poor condition of the average market roads, especially in western Canada. By 1931, for 728,623 farms listed there were 48,402 motor trucks, or about one truck for every fifteen farms. At the same time about one-fifth of the farms of Canada were located on unimproved earth roads, while a very small portion were on macadam, asphalt, or concrete highways.[6]

The motor bus has developed rapidly following the construction of first-class highways. It has been of great convenience in suburban and interurban runs particularly. While buses are operated over considerable distances, the bulk of their work is in trips not exceeding one hundred miles. To some extent the motor bus has taken over the traffic formerly carried by electric railways, and to a much lesser extent that carried by steam railways. Like the truck, it can be driven wherever adequate roads are to be found; but, because it necessarily carries a large number of passengers at once, it can hardly offer the door to door service which makes transport by truck so popular. Of a total of 2,255 buses registered in 1929 less than one-half operated outside the limits of cities. Figures prepared for the same year, 1929, show that buses obtained only 1.7 per cent of the total passenger miles.

In contrast, passenger cars were responsible for 78.5 per cent of passenger miles. Private cars rather than buses have brought a revolutionary change in passenger traffic. Nine hundred and fifty thousand passenger cars registered in 1934 stand against one thousand, seven hundred buses of the same year. Besides its obvious use as the private transportation service of countless families, the car is widely employed by persons travelling on business. A commercial traveller can cover more territory in a given time with the aid of a motor car than he can by train, except where his stopping points are far apart; and with a modern car, good high-ways, and a radio as companion, he can roll up a heavy mileage without too much discomfort. Cars, too, may reduce the isolation under which farmers have traditionally lived in Canada.

Tourist traffic has existed since the early days of Canadian history, and all methods of transportation have profited by it, but the characteristic modern tourist traffic is that by motor car. For Canada there are two main sources of motor tourists: from within the country, and from the United States. It is not possible even to guess at the numbers in the first of these classes, for no records are or could be kept. It can only be said that observation

6. *Bulletin*, No. 7, 1925 (Highways branch, department of railways and canals).

shows a large number of Canadian cars on tour during the summer, for periods varying from one day to several weeks. Because of immigration regulations, fairly accurate statistics are available for foreign cars, which in effect means cars from the United States. In 1928, when the tourist traffic had reached important dimensions, the number of foreign cars entering Canada was 3,645,455—fifteen times greater than the figure for ten years earlier. By 1930 the total had increased to 5,409,458. Of these cars 4,110,100 entered on twenty-four-hour permits, 1,297,030 on sixty-day permits, and 2,328 on permits good for six months. Of those entered on the shortest permits, probably the majority went no great distance from the border and cannot be considered as serious users of Canadian roads. But even the 1,300,000 cars admitted for the longer periods, carrying as they did, an average of 3.5 persons per car, represented a migration of important dimensions.[7] For 1934, when the number of cars entering had decreased to 2,373,648, the total expenditure by American tourists is officially estimated at $86,259,000. Tourist traffic has, in fact, become a major industry of Canada. The attraction of touring by motor, whether by Canadians or visitors, depends on a number of factors. Scenery, summer resorts, and sport may be said to form one group, and in all of these Canada is well supplied. A second requirement is in hotels and their more recent counterparts—camps, cabins, and lodging houses. The provision of accommodation has required rapid development, but apparently the supply has kept pace with the demand, for the main highways are studded with all these forms of hospitality. Finally the coming of tourists depends to a large extent on the existence of adequate roads. This has meant the improvement of existing highways and the construction of new ones.

Improvement of highways involves heavy expenditures. Much of this may be balanced against the income from visiting tourists, for although they may enter the country without charge, the money spent indirectly helps to support the roads. No complete figures are available, except in recent years, for the income and

7. *The Highway and motor vehicle in Canada;* also, "The tourist traffic" (*Round Table,* No. 76).

expenditure on roads in Canada, but reference may be made to current figures. Income is derived from licenses for cars and drivers, mileage tax on motor trucks and buses, and gasoline tax, and in each instance is controlled and receivable by the province. For the year 1934 the revenue from all sources and in all provinces was $50,622,683. The whole problem of costs has been actively raised in recent years not so much from the point of view of whether improvement of roads was justified by the returns, as from that of the competition between road and rail traffic. No amount of energy in gathering statistics will make possible a mathematical comparison between road and rail costs. The railways, built in modern times, have a known cost. Capital outlay, maintenance, equipment, and operating expenses are exactly known. A detailed record is kept of all the traffic which moves over them, and there is no possibility of persons using their lines without permission. In none of these instances are corresponding data available for roads. Except in the case of completely new highways the capital cost has been built up over such a long period, and in such a variety of ways (including, for example, statute labour) that it is manifestly impossible to attempt even a guess at their cost. No complete record is or can be kept of the persons who use the roads. Pedestrians, troops, horse-drawn vehicles, agricultural machines, and cattle may at any time take advantage of roads for their various purposes, but no system could be evolved which would relate these uses to the upkeep or capital cost of the road.

Any correlation which may be attempted, therefore, between the cost of roads and the use of them by motor vehicles can be only an approximate one, and will derive its real significance from two considerations: that motor vehicles both require better roads and are the chief agent in their deterioration; and that commercial motor vehicles should be prevented from unfair competition with railways. The conference on rail and road transport organized by the English ministry of transport reached the conclusion that the criterion of allocation of cost should be a combination of ton-mileage and petrol consumption.[8] The royal commission on transportation in Canada, making its report within a few months of that of the

8. *Report of the conference on rail and road transport* (1932).

English conference, recognized the importance of motor vehicles as a form of transport and urged that steps should be taken to investigate the question further.[9] The situation in Canada, however, is complicated by the control of the provinces over roads and taxation of vehicles, and there has not yet existed any pressure sufficient to induce the provincial governments to attempt a joint solution.

Besides making a higher payment for use of the roads, it has been urged that buses and trucks should be subjected—as railways are—to control of rates and working conditions, and these latter suggestions appear to be just and wise. Viewing the question broadly, however, it seems necessary to think of road transport in terms of its social and national value. It is not sufficient to adopt the negative attitude that the country's investment in the railways must, above all things, be protected. As was suggested in reference to canals, emphasis on different forms of transport changes from time to time, and it is neither wise nor possible to attempt to stop the hands of the clock. It is not in the public interest that the economic operation of the railways should be rendered impossible by the subsidization of road transport: on the other hand it must be recognized that road transport has a special service to render which the railways cannot provide. Commercial motor vehicles should be carefully regulated so as to ensure safety and to avoid unlimited competition in rates (which may lead to dangerous operation). An attempt should be made to charge them with the lion's share of the interest charges and maintenance of the roads. If it should then become clear that railways could not compete in rates with buses and trucks quite a different problem would have to be faced. It would then become necessary to decide how far it was socially desirable to maintain the railways by means of rate fixing. But there is no reason to believe that such a question will arise. The problem for the immediate future is to adjust the railways and motor vehicles into their respective spheres, and to produce complementary services which will result in the maximum of convenience and economy for the public.

9. *Report of the royal commission to inquire into railways and transportation in Canada, 1931–1932.*

3. Air Transport

The gasoline (or, later, oil) engine made possible a revolutionary change in air transport, just as, a few years earlier, it had done in road transport. The necessity of motive power and the selection of the gasoline engine apply equally to heavier-than-air and lighter-than-air machines. Before 1914 aviation was in a purely experimental stage, and while some of the tests of the effectiveness of early machines took place on Canadian territory, the latest mode of travel was then only of potential consequence for transportation. It was the pressure of the needs of war that changed the aeroplane from a *rara avis* to a recognized and tried machine. When the war came to an end in 1918 Canada found herself possessed of a large number of military aeroplanes, pilots, and technicians. It was only natural that this new sword should be beaten into a ploughshare, that the aeroplane should be fitted into the scheme of civil transportation.

From its very character it was inevitable that the aeroplane should, in Canada, be the complement rather than the competitor of roads, railways, and ships. Manifestly it could not take the place of the passenger motor car, do the unromantic work of the truck, or carry heavy freight in place of ship or railway train. Its special value was to carry passengers and light goods at high speed; and to carry passengers and goods to areas where no other means of transportation existed. It is conceivable that at some future date the aeroplane may compete with railways or road transport, but so far it has not been a serious consideration in Canada. It is possible, too, that other types of work could be done by lighter-than-air machines, although these have not yet been used for either military or civil purposes in Canada.

Natural conditions in Canada are peculiarly suited to the aeroplane as an additional mode of transportation. With a large area and scattered population the distances to be covered are necessarily great. An obvious rôle for the aeroplane, therefore, is to provide a more rapid means of transport than trains or motor cars. The transcontinental railways afford adequate facilities for all normal purposes, but in Canada, as in other countries, there is a small proportion of passenger, mail, and express traffic which requires greater speed, even at the higher rates which air travel involves. In addition, the aeroplane is needed for those northern areas to which neither railways nor roads have been built. In comparison with the width of its territory, the population of Canada is spread along a narrow belt. North of that belt lies a lonely land, still only partly mapped, whose mineral resources have only begun to be exploited. For journeys of hundreds of miles the aeroplane has offered the only alternative to travel by canoe and dog team. Even where single lines of railway have been run far to the north, there remain districts on each side which have not, and for a long time cannot have, the network of branch lines and roads that serve the people further south. Air transport, therefore, whether of passengers or freight, has served more as a feeder than a competitor to railways.

In 1919 an act (9-10 Geo. V, c.11) was passed providing for an air board of five to seven members, appointed by the governor in council for three years and eligible for reappointment. One member was to be a representative of the department of militia and defence (re-named department of national defence), and one of the department of naval service. It was given wide powers to supervise all matters connected with aeronautics and was to study the development of aeronautics, conduct or coöperate in researches, control licenses, government air stations, and so on. Under the terms of the act, an order in council was passed at the end of the year providing a detailed set of rules for civil aviation. After 1923 the powers and duties of the air board were exercised by the minister of national defence. In 1927 four administrative divisions were created in the department of national defence to deal with different aspects of aviation. One of these was concerned only with military operations; the second, under the director of civil government air operations, administered governmental but non-military aviation; the third, under the controller of civil aviation, was responsible for the control of commercial and private flying, the location and equipment of airways, and construction of airship bases; while the fourth division, that of aeronautical engineering, was intended to give advice on technical questions to both military and civil branches. After the first establishment of a federal organization to supervise aviation, the question was raised as to whether this matter came properly under federal jurisdiction. The point was argued in the Canadian courts and carried to the privy council in 1932, where it was held that the Dominion had exclusive jurisdiction.

The first civil use to which aeroplanes were put in Canada was for transport in the northern areas. The machines built during the war were unsuited to inter-city traffic either for passengers or goods; on the other hand, the flying boats and seaplanes designed for military purposes were well adapted both to the conditions and needs of aviation in the north country. Again, there was as yet no public demand for inter-city service, but a real need for air transport in the north. Valuable work has been accomplished by aeroplanes in exploration, photography, and forest patrol, superseding the canoe. To illustrate the use of aeroplanes in fire-fighting one story may be borrowed from a recent monograph.

A pilot of the Ontario Air Service detects a fire. He at once heads for the nearest forest ranger station. Thirty-five minutes after sighting the fire, he sees a canoe on a small lake. He immediately alights and tells the canoeist, who happens to be the Chief Ranger, about the fire. Continuing his journey, two hours later he is back at the fire with the Deputy Ranger and his equipment. That day and the next and the next—for 10 consecutive days—he makes in all 35 flights before the fire is out and the men are back at their posts. In all the fire burned 3,200 acres and demanded the services of 27 men and 12½ tons of fire-fighting and camping equipment and food, and not a single piece of transport except the D.H. Moth was employed.[10]

The use of aeroplanes for forest patrols has been extended throughout Canada by the provincial governments. The aeroplane has rendered an unique service in the location of mines, and—what is more important in relation to transportation—the conveyance of passengers, supplies, and minerals to and from those mines. The Eldorado radium mine at Great Bear Lake is some 800 miles (by air) from railhead, a distance which can be covered by aeroplane in one to one and one-half days as opposed to two or three weeks by water.[11] In 1932, thirty-two planes were used at

10. A. E. W. Salt, *Imperial air routes* (London, 1930), p. 197.

11. W. R. Finlayson, *Aviation and its place in Canada's transportation system* (M.A. thesis, Toronto, 1933), p. 84.

Bear Lake. Sioux Lookout in northern Ontario became such an important air base that in 1930 it is said to have handled as much passenger and freight traffic as any American airport.[12] From this base the Red Lake mining area was served by air from 1927.

Doctors, nurses, police, clergy, surveyors, traders, and trappers have all been carried by air in the north country for distances which by any other means would take weeks or months. The Hudson's Bay Company has made use of air transport both for packs of furs and its officers. For a land of many lakes the seaplane was particularly useful, for, by using water as a landing place, the necessity for artificial flying fields was obviated. In winter use has been made of aeroplanes equipped with skis.

During the first decade after the war, a remarkable development of air services had taken place in Europe, and Europe's example was being followed in the United States. With the aid of governmental subsidies, companies had been established and maintained regular routes between the leading centres; and air transport—for passengers, mail, and express—was taken for granted as an alternative to that by road or rail. The experience that could thus be drawn upon, together with the probability that American airways would tap Canadian traffic, led the government to begin the encouragement of Canadian lines. Air mail services were inaugurated about Christmas 1927 and were rapidly extended. By the end of 1929 a new route between Fort McMurray, Alberta and Aklavik, near the mouth of the Mackenzie River, was opened. The distance was 1,676 miles, and mail was thus carried three hundred miles within the Arctic Circle. In 1931 the following routes were regularly operated:

All Year:—Montreal-Toronto-Detroit, Montreal-Albany, Sioux Lookout-Red Lake, Toronto-Buffalo, Winnipeg, Edmonton, Fort McMurray-Aklavik, Peace River-North Vermilion, Amos-Chibougamau, Amos-Sisco, Montreal-Moncton-St. John, Winnipeg-Pembina.

Summer:—Rimouski-Montreal, Montreal-Ottawa, Lac du Bonnet-Bisset-Wadhope, Montreal-Quebec.

Winter:—Leamington-Pelee Island, Quebec-Seven Islands, Seven

12. Salt, *op. cit.*, p. 196.

Islands-Anticosti Island, Moncton-Magdalen Islands, Moncton-Charlottetown.[13]

A service was also operated, under special arrangement, between Whitehorse and Dawson, Yukon Territory. The other routes listed above were flown by commercial firms under contract from the post office. The total route-mileage was 5,038 miles. If these routes are followed on a map it will be seen that they cover an enormous area, include every province and the territories, and run from the southern boundary to the far north, and from the Atlantic to the Rocky mountains. They fulfilled the dual purpose of effecting faster mail delivery between points already served by railways and of carrying the mail far beyond the range of railways.

Mail service was, however, but one of the many objects for which regular air routes were designed. There remained the whole field of carriage of passengers and express. For all these purposes there was needed, in addition to machines and pilots, an elaborate equipment on the ground. In providing this equipment the federal government aided commercial aviation. The terminal airports are either at cities or at the end of the route. Between these, which have been partly built by municipalities and commercial interests, there have to be emergency aerodromes at intervals of twenty-five miles, lights as guides for night flying, radio direction beams for darkness and bad weather, radio communication between the airports and the aeroplanes, and meteorological service.

Along these airways, as they were developed, an increasing number of commercial companies began to operate as passenger and freight traffic proved to be available. In 1930 came a merger between Western Canada Airways and a number of companies in eastern Canada, the new organization being known as Canadian Airways Limited. The president of the company was J. A. Richardson of Winnipeg, and it was significant that the presidents of both the Canadian National and Canadian Pacific became vice-presidents of Canadian Airways.

The records[14] of Canadian Airways show a great variety of activities. Freight of all kinds has been carried, from gold to live

13. *Report of the department of national defence, 1932*, p. 69.
14. Canada Airways Limited: *The Bulletin*.

oxen. Their aeroplanes are flown on regular or special services from the Atlantic to the Pacific, from the Arctic to the American border. Into Labrador, on both sides of Hudson Bay, through the Yukon, and over the mountains of British Columbia, mail, passengers and freight are carried. The time-table of the company reads like that of a railway, except that an examination of the names of the stations shows many places far beyond the reach of railways. Could the most enterprising of the Nor'Westers be brought back to life, it would be interesting to show them that 'planes leave once a week from Fort McMurray for Fort Resolution, and once a month for Fort Norman (on the Mackenzie River). The fathers of confederation might be intrigued to see that a daily service takes passengers from Moncton to Charlottetown in an hour at a cost of $9.00, and express for the same distance for four cents per pound.

The operations of Canadian Airways Limited and Quebec Airways Limited may be seen in a table published in the company's periodical.[15]

Year	Hours	Miles	Express Lbs.	Mail Lbs.	Passengers
1931	19,143	1,832,794	764,449	459,458	8,047
1932	13,775	1,294,207	1,870,136	299,066	8,963
1933	12,744	1,165,434	2,522,233	328,618	16,942
1934	16,993	1,591,765	5,766,691	472,308	16,594
1935	17,869	1,674,018	5,275,745	817,678	14,542
1936	21,789	2,068,673	7,749,926	955,214	20,948

The growth of civil aviation in Canada in general may be readily seen in a table.[16]

Item	1925	1930	1934	1935
Firms manufacturing aircraft	2	7	6	10
Firms chiefly operating aircraft	8	100	125	123
Aircraft hours flown	4,091	92,993	75,871	88,451
Total aircraft mileage	255,826	7,547,420	6,497,637	7,522,102
Number of passengers and crew	4,897	124,875	105,306	177,472
Freight and express carried (lbs.)	592,220	1,759,259	14,441,179	26,439,224
Mail carried (lbs.)	1,080	474,199	625,040	1,126,084
Air harbours	34	77	101	96
Aircraft (all types)	39	527	368	380
Licensed personnel	91	780	997	—

15. *The Bulletin*, vii, 2.
16. *Canada Year Book*, 1931, 698; *Canada Year Book*, 1936, p. 698

In all the items listed above there is a marked increase between 1925 and 1930, that is, in the period in which commercial aviation was actively encouraged by the Dominion government, and in which general prosperity allowed expenditure on aircraft and air travel by both public and private bodies. On the other hand, a decrease will be observed in some items between 1930 and 1934. In 1935, when more prosperous times returned, the business done by the commercial firms once more increased.

The slackened pace halted the achievement of a trans-Canada airway, the darling project of those most interested in Canadian aviation. There are striking parallels between the first trans-Canada airway and the first trans-Canada railway. Two of the purposes of the latter were to provide transcontinental transportation of the most modern type on Canadian soil, and so prevent the American systems from tapping Canadian traffic; and to form an "all-red" route from Europe to the far east. Both these motives have been strong in the attempt to construct a trans-Canada airway. Though later than Europe, the United States was earlier than Canada in creating through airways. Since the American air routes touched Canada at a number of points, mail, passengers, and express could —in the absence of a Canadian transcontinental line—be shipped over the American system. A letter from Toronto to Vancouver, for example, could, by the arrangement between the American and Canadian postal authorities, be sent by American air mail. While such facilities were an immediate advantage to Canadians, the continuance of a dependent position might well prevent the construction of a Canadian airway in the future.

The enthusiasts for a Pacific railway linked with it their plans for lines of steamships on the Atlantic and Pacific oceans, to form one complete system of transport. The advocates of a transcontinental airway also envisaged such a through route. Their plan, however, in some ways made a stronger appeal to the imagination; for, not only would the time taken be only a fraction of that by rail and steamship, but one mode of transport could be used throughout.

The appeal for a trans-Canada airway rested on two grounds: the desirability of having an airway on Canadian soil that would retain through air traffic in Canada and serve intermediate points;

and the desirability of making Canada a link in an east-west air-way. On the first point little need be said. If it is safe to use other means of transportation as a test, then it will be evident that trunk lines are essential to the prosperity of any transportation system. If Canadian airways should prove to be no more than branches of an American trunk line, they would have a dependent and uncertain existence, besides losing the profit that accrues from through traffic. The argument in favour of a trans-Canada airway as part of a route between Europe and Asia hinges not only on the desirability of an all-British route (with its potential military advantages) but also on the ground that the northern passage is the shortest.

The construction of the trans-Canada airway also bears a resemblance to the history of the Pacific railway. Owing to financial stringency it was thought to be unwise to embark on a through route at once, and in the meanwhile the intention was to fill in the gaps not covered by available Canadian and American services. The prairie section was attacked first, partly for this reason, and partly because flying conditions were favourable and aerodromes could easily be built. By the spring of 1930 construction in the section was far enough advanced to allow a regular air service from Winnipeg to Calgary and Edmonton. The two sections which had proved most difficult for the transcontinental railway—around Lake Superior and across the mountains of British Columbia—were left for the future, and in the meantime the American airway from Detroit to Pembina was used. In the summer of 1933 construction was recommenced as a measure to reduce unemployment, and by 1934 some 6,000 men were at work in British Columbia, Ontario, Quebec, and the Maritime Provinces.

In November 1935 a meeting was held at Ottawa between representatives of the United Kingdom, Canada, the Irish Free State and Newfoundland to consider the establishment of a trans-Atlantic air service. Arrangements were there made which were intended to lead to trial flights in 1936, to be followed by mail and passenger services on a minimum schedule of two flights a week in each direction. In December a further meeting was held at Washington, after which the following statement was released to the press by the assistant secretary of state.

As a result of the conferences which have been in progress since Thursday, December 5, between representatives of the United Kingdom, the Irish Free State, Canada and the United States, understandings have been reached which it is confidently hoped will bring about the early establishment of trans-Atlantic air transport services connecting these several countries. These understandings are based upon the principle of full reciprocity between the countries interested. They do not operate to exclude similar arrangements between the United States and other countries.

The Department of Commerce has given its approval to the establishment of trans-Atlantic airways by way of Canada, Newfoundland, and the Irish Free State to England, and by way of Bermuda to England, and from Bermuda to Puerto Rico, the latter route to be extended by mutual consent. The Atlantic Sea Board ports in contemplation as termini are New York City; Baltimore, Maryland; Cape Charles or Norfolk, Virginia, and Charleston, South Carolina, any one of which may be designated as ports of entry but no final determination with reference to places has yet been made.

It is recognized that the northern route is much shorter than the southern route and therefore will have the advantage of more economical operation, but this fact does not preclude the possibility of considerable use being made of the southern route. It is expected that experimental flights will be begun early in the summer of 1936 and it is hoped that scheduled services will begin by the summer of 1937. When the full regular service is inaugurated, it is provided that there will be four round trips per week.

The matter of the carriage of mails is necessarily postponed for future consideration.

Further negotiations brought the project within sight of realization in the summer of 1937. The Canadian parliament, in 1937, passed the Trans-Canada Air Lines Act by which a corporation was created known as the Trans-Canada Air Lines, and which was to operate an air service across Canada as part of the route from Europe to the far east. Such a route would make a reality, under new methods, of the dreams of a century ago: a new chapter in the never-ending story of the development of transportation.

BIBLIOGRAPHICAL NOTE

Manuscript sources. There is a wealth of material on the history of transportation in the Public Archives of Canada. The state papers of Nova Scotia (series A), of New France (series C11 A), and of Canada after 1763 (series Q) form the basis of study. There are also a number of other collections of importance, such as the papers of Lord Durham, Joseph Howe, Sir John Macdonald, Sandford Fleming, and Alexander Mackenzie. The Baring papers are also of value.

The Archives of the Hudson's Bay Company are indispensable for the history of transportation in the west over a long period. Some of the most important series for this subject are: the minutes of the committee, correspondence with His Majesty's government, correspondence between London and Rupert's Land, letter books, journals of posts, and the reports of Sir George Simpson.

Government publications. There are an immense number of such publications. The statutes of the provinces and the Dominion, the debates of the Dominion parliament, and the journals of the provincial legislatures are all helpful. The sessional papers form a mine of information, particularly in the reports of the department of railways and canals and the various royal commissions.

The Dominion bureau of statistics issues periodically material on steam railways, electric railways, canals, and highways.

Other contemporary material. Newspapers, of which a large number have been preserved, give both factual material and opinion. Various companies connected with transportation have issued publications. The pamphlet material is considerable, the largest collection being in the Canadian Archives. .

Reference Works. Detailed bibliographies will be found in the *Review of historical publications relating to Canada* (1897–1918), the *Canadian historical review* (1920–), *Contributions to Canadian economics* (1928–34), and the *Canadian journal of economics and political science* (1935–).

The *Canada Year Book*, published by the Dominion bureau of statistics, is a most valuable reference book. For the dates of origin, mileage, and subsequent status of Canadian railways consult M. L. Bladen, "Construction of railways in Canada" (*Contributions to Canadian economics*, v and vii). *Poor's Manual of railroads* also contains useful factual information about Canadian as well as American railways, and has a number of maps. A standard authority which should be used, particularly on recent or contemporary conditions, is W. T. Jackman, *Economic principles of transportation* (Toronto, 1935). *Canada and its provinces*, edited by A. Shortt and A. G. Doughty and published in 1914, has a number of sections on different aspects of transportation. In particular, Volume X will be found helpful.

INDEX

Abbott, J. C., and negotiations for the Canadian Pacific Railway, 242, 243, 249–250; and the "Pacific scandal," 248; and foreign influence on the C.P.R., 273

Acworth, W. H., member of royal commission of 1916, 347; report of commission, 347–350, 358–359

Albany, Fort, established, 19; fur trade at, 21, 48

Alberta Great Waterways Railway, route of, 382; further history of, 382

Allan, Sir Hugh, and negotiations for the Canadian Pacific Railway, 241–250; and the "Pacific scandal," 246–250; connection with Northern Pacific group, 267

American Fur Company, founded, 44

Angus, R. B., member of the committee of the Canadian Pacific Railway, 266; and St. Paul, Minneapolis and Manitoba Railway, 267; and foreign influence on the C.P.R., 273

Ashfield, Baron, member of the royal commission of 1931, 396; comments at, 402

Ashmun, George, acts for S. G. Ward, 181–182

Assiniboia, see Red River Settlement

Astor, J. J., and the fur trade, 35; competition with Canadian firms, 44–47; approached by Hudson's Bay Company, 58

Astoria, Fort, 46–47

Atlantic and North West Railway, route of, 289; leased by Canadian Pacific Railway, 289, 296

Aviation, government control of, 454–455; used in Canada, 453–454, 455–459; trans-Canada airway, 459–461

Baie Verte Canal, proposed, 418, 419; not built, 420

Balises, used on roads in New France, 103

Baring Brothers, and financial problems of the Grand Trunk Railway, 180–184; and communications with the Pacific, 231–234

Baring, Thomas, director of the Grand Trunk Railway, 169; and communications with the Pacific, 231–234

Bateau, used in New France 8–10; used after 1760, 28, 51, 64; description of, 66–67; use of, 68, 134, 219

Beatty, Sir Edward, appointed president of Canadian Pacific Railway, 379; and competition with Canadian National Railways, 379; on freight rates, 394; suggests inquiry into railway question, 396; evidence before royal commission, 400–401; on coöperation of railways, 406–407

Bertron, Griscom and Company, consider furnishing capital to Canadian Northern Railway, 357

Beauharnois Canal, construction of, 83–84; continued use of, 419

Biggar, W. H., on Grand Trunk plans for western expansion, 323–324

Blair, A. G., resigns from cabinet on railway policy, 324; views on railway policy, 324–325

Blake, Edward, and "Pacific scandal," 247; and construction of Canadian Pacific Railway, 254, 255, 256; criticizes contract with Canadian Pacific Railway, 269; opposed to purchase of Great Western and Grand Trunk, 285; railway policy of, 319–320

Boats, introduced by the French, 2, 8; in Acadia, 1–2; in the fur trade after 1760, 28, 31–32, 43, 50–51; used by the Hudson's Bay Company, 217–220; see also Bateau, Durham boat, Kentucky boat, Sailboat, Schenectady boat, Steamships, Team boat, York boat

Borden, Sir Robert L., on railway policy of 1903, 326, 328–329

Bouchette, Joseph, description of roads in Nova Scotia, 126; in New Brunswick, 126–127; in Lower Canada, 133

Brantford, Norfolk and Port Burwell Railway, absorbed by Great Western, 289

Brassey, see Peto, Brassey, Jackson, and Betts

Bridges, in New France, 102, 104; administration of, 108–118; toll bridges, 113, 114; of corduroy, 119, 123; of plank, 123; in New Brunswick, 127; Victoria Bridge, 170–171; Quebec Bridge, 333

Brockville and Ottawa Railway, built, 171; extended, 288; bought by Canadian Pacific Railway, 294

INDEX

INDEX 475

Team boat, used as ferry, 72

Toll roads, in Lower Canada, 113; in Upper Canada, 115; conditions of, 121–122; taken over by government of Quebec, 444

Toronto, Grey and Bruce Railway, built, 288; gauge, 172; acquired by Canadian Pacific, 295

Toronto and Nipissing Railway, gauge on, 172

Travois, description of, 101

Trent Valley Canal, object of, 89; construction of, 421–422

Tupper, Sir Charles, refuses to act as commissioner for Intercolonial, 208; minister of railways and canals, 263; favours private ownership, 263; and negotiations for Pacific railway, 264–265; defends C.P.R. contract in parliament, 268; supports loans to C.P.R., 279

Turnpike roads, see Toll roads

Tye, W. F., suggests that all Canadian railways be operated by a single corporation, 372

Tyler, Sir Henry, interviewed concerning Pacific railway, 264–265; president of Grand Trunk, 293; retires, 330

Van Horne, Sir William C., previous career of, 268; general manager of Canadian Pacific, 268; and Lake Superior section, 272; and construction, 274, 276, 277; and Short Line, 295; on competition with Grand Trunk, 300; and Manitoba railways, 307; president of C.P.R., 310; competition with Hill, 310–311; compared with Thornton, 379

Waddington, Alfred, petitions for charter for Pacific railway, 240, 241

Walkem, G. A., and discussions of Pacific railway, 255

Ward, S. G., agent for Baring Brothers and Glyn, Mills and Company, 180–184

Watkin, Sir Edward, supervises Grand Trunk, 182–184; president of G.T.R., 185; favours confederation, 193–194, 203; negotiations with Hudson's Bay Company, 230–234; resigns as president of G.T.R., 234, 291

Webster, J. C., member of royal commission of 1931, 396

Welland Canal, construction of, 85–87; causes reduced tolls on Erie Canal, 92; related to projected railways, 150; traffic on, 417, 426; shipping on, 70; enlargement of, 420, 435; in relation to St. Lawrence waterway project, 433, 434

Welland Railway, built, 171

Wellington, Grey and Bruce Railway, built, 287; absorbed by Great Western, 287, 289

Wheat, export of, 65, 93–94, 94–95, 97, 395; transport of, 151, 186, 200, 306, 315–317, 319, 323, 326, 328, 333, 417, 418, 427–429, 436

White, Thomas, minister of the interior, on disallowance of railway charters, 308

White, Sir Thomas, minister of finance, on condition of railways in 1916, 346–347; on nationalization of Grand Trunk Pacific, 361–362; member of board of arbitration on Grand Trunk, 364; report of board, 367, 368–369

Williamsburg Canals, construction of, 84; enlargement of, 419–420

Wilson, Sir Charles Rivers, president of Grand Trunk Railway, 330

Winnipeg and Southern Railway, chartered by Manitoba, 307

Winnipeg South-Eastern Railway, chartered by Manitoba, 305

Wisconsin Central Railway, leased to Minneapolis, St. Paul and Sault Ste. Marie Railway, 343

X Y Company, origin of, 35; and portage at Sault Ste. Marie, 38; establishment at Kaministiquia River, 39

Yellowhead Pass, used by Milton and Cheadle, 223; by Fleming, 224; difficulty of railway construction in, 234; Canadian Pacific plans to use, 258, 259, 260, 272; abandoned by C.P.R., 275; used by Grand Trunk Pacific, 325, 335

Yonge Street, on Toronto portage, 41; begun by Simcoe, 134–135; condition of, 136–137; stage coaches on, 141–142

York boat, description of, 219

York Factory, and French competition, 22; and competition with Montreal firms, 48; main port for Hudson's Bay Company, 59, 219; winter road to Norway House, 221